TERRORISM
AN
INTRODUCTION

TERRORISM

AN
INTRODUCTION

Jonathan R. White

Grand Valley State University

Wadsworth Publishing Company
Belmont, California
A Division of Wadsworth, Inc.

Printed in the United States of America

10 9 8 7 6 5 4

Library of Congress Cataloging in Publication Data
White, Jonathan Randall.
 Terrorism : an introduction : a review of domestic and international terrorism for police, military, and security forces / Jonathan R. White.
  p. cm.
 Includes bibliographical references and index.
 ISBN 0-534-13920-5
 1. Terrorism.   I. Title.
HV6431.W48   1990
363.3'2 — dc20

90-37132
CIP

Sponsoring Editor: *Cynthia C. Stormer*
Marketing Representative: *Thor McMillan*
Editorial Assistant: *Cathleen Sue Collins*
Production Editor: *Linda Loba*
Manuscript Editor: *Pamela Evans*
Permissions Editor: *Carline Haga*
Interior and Cover Design: *Lisa Berman*
Art Coordinator: *Cloyce J. Wall*
Interior Illustration: *Cloyce J. Wall*
Typesetting: *Kachina Typesetting*
Cover Printing: *Phoenix Color Corporation*
Printing and Binding: *Maple-Vail Book Manufacturing Group*

To Marcia, Katie Jo, and Charlie White

*Do not return evil for evil or reviling for reviling;
but on the contrary bless, for to this you have been called,
that you may obtain a blessing.   (I Peter 3:9)*

PREFACE

A few years ago I was watching an Air Force officer, who happened to be one of my students, conduct a counterterrorist rescue exercise. After critiquing the assault team, he and I began to discuss the available counterterrorist literature. He had a complaint, and he voiced it vehemently. The literature was too theoretical and too opinionated, he said. He wanted something basic, something his troops could use to understand the scope of terrorism.

Unfortunately, those teaching courses on terrorism and counterterrorism hear variations on this theme each term. We often find that the literature on terrorism fails to help us convey background information to students. Much of it is designed for detailed political analysis or, more frequently, gets lost in ideology. This is not helpful to law enforcement or military personnel searching for introductory information. Students in security-related courses need background information upon which to develop logical responses to potential threats.

I wrote this book to try to supply fundamental information from a security perspective. I hope to provide a practical summary of the historical and social causes of some of the major forms of terrorism. The text is designed for students, and also some practitioners who may face security problems posed by criminal and political terrorism. With the request of my Air Force friend in mind, I try to provide an "intelligence briefing" for those with little or no background in the field.

The book is intended for introductory courses in terrorism and related security problems. In-service law enforcement, military, and security personnel may also find its information helpful. The text incorporates material that I have used in college classrooms and in police and military training classes over the past few years. It is supplemented by a number of maps, as well as cultural and regional information for readers unfamiliar with details of world geography and demographics.

I also attempt to introduce the major controversial issues in terrorism and to summarize some of the major terrorist campaigns. Several chapters address problems related to domestic law enforcement. Each chapter topic ends with a short annotated bibliography designed either to assist students in their research or to guide their further reading.

In brief, the text summarizes the information needed to understand terrorism. It offers no grand theory; nor is it polemic. Rather, it offers its readers background information and tools they will need to study the issues and the controversies further. Its purpose is to explain various scholars' positions on issues of controversy and to illustrate the cultural, historical, and tactical factors of major terrorist conflicts.

Philosophy

The book focuses on small-group violence, which in this context means small in comparison to nations. Therefore, "small groups" can range from a few criminals to a large ethnic political organization numbering in the thousands. The topic of the book, then, is subnational groups engaging in terrorist violence. Even when they are sponsored by states, the violence of these groups represents something less than war. Most frequently it is a form of criminal activity.

Repression is also examined in this book, but not the official repression of totalitarian governments. While it is true that such repression has been the major manifestation of terrorism throughout history, governments ruling by terror do not fall into the category of small-group, subnational violence. Extrajuridical activities of police and military units, however, do fit the category quite neatly. Therefore, repressive terrorism is discussed here in terms of death squads.

Finally, the book is written from a criminal justice perspective. How-to books exist for SWAT teams and bomb disposal units, but officers who respond to a possible terrorist incident generally have no idea of the issues behind what they are facing. They need a "why" book. The same can be said for most military and civilian security forces. The purpose here is to provide criminal justice students—and people in related fields—with information not readily available in undergraduate classrooms or in security literature.

Content

The book is divided into three parts. The first summarizes the organizational dynamics of terrorist groups and explains the different rationales for terrorism in the West, the Middle East, and Latin America. Part II analyzes several major terrorist campaigns of recent decades. Part III discusses some of the major controversial issues in terrorism and counterterrorism.

The book focuses on geographical areas to demonstrate different kinds of terrorism. Models of revolution and repression are discussed in the chapters on Latin America. Small revolutionary groups are presented in chapters on the United States and Western Europe. Ideological terrorism is discussed in terms of the American extremist right, while nationalist terrorism is summarized by examining Northern Ireland and the Basque region of Spain. International terrorism is presented within the framework of Middle Eastern violence.

Learning Aids

The text contains a number of features intended to help students understand the complex nature of terrorism. These aids are designed to help readers organize information without oversimplifying it. These features include the following:

1. Annotated bibliographies at the end of each chapter
2. Maps located throughout the text
3. Objectives at the beginning of each chapter
4. Subheadings based on chapter objectives
5. Boxes summarizing text material
6. Chapter summaries that highlight major points

An additional learning aid is the entirety of chapter 2, which contains a synopsis of the major terrorist and extremist organizations and the locations of their activities. It is designed not only as background information, but as a reference section. By referring back to chapter 2 as they proceed, students will avoid confusion when bombarded with the names of terrorist organizations.

Acknowledgments

Terrorism is a complicated subject that crosses disciplines as freely as it does jurisdictional boundaries. Trying to summarize information for those concerned with security was an arduous task, which many people lightened by supplying tapes, files, background information, training, and interviews. I am grateful to a great many people for their willingness to share information.

While no part of this work is endorsed by any local, state, or federal governmental agency, I am grateful to members of the law enforcement and military communities who readily provided information. I am deeply indebted to the United States Marshal for Western Michigan, John Kendall. I also appreciate the efforts of Howard Safir, Deputy Director of the U.S. Marshals Service, especially for the in-depth briefing he facilitated. Much of the material in this book came from unclassified reports of the Federal Bureau of Investigation. I would like to thank the Detroit and Grand Rapids FBI offices for gladly answering my many requests for information. A special thank-you goes to Special Agent Patrick Corcoran of the FBI.

Several local law enforcement agencies were also willing to help: I am grateful to all the police officers who shared their ideas and expressed encouragement while I was writing the book. In particular I must thank the SWAT Unit of the Los Angeles Police Department and the Training Division of the Detroit Police Department for allowing me to attend special training sessions. I also appreciate the help of the West Michigan Tactical Officers Association.

Congressman Paul Henry's able research staff always responded cheerfully to seemingly endless requests for information. The same can be said of Senator Carl Levin's staff. All their efforts are appreciated.

Several people in the academic community offered direct assistance and critical review. I am grateful for the help of Dr. Howard Stein, Director of the Grand Valley State University Research and Development Center. Guidance, reaction, criticism, and much-needed direction came from my extremely valued and respected criminal justice colleagues. I especially thank Dr. Kenneth Christian of Michigan State University, Dr. Rick Lovell of the University of Wisconsin, and Dr. Richard Holden of Central Missouri State University.

I would also like to thank the reviewers of my manuscript, for their helpful comments and suggestions: Dr. Harold Becker, California State University-Long Beach; Dr. Ken Christian, Michigan State University; Dr. Richard Holden, Central Missouri State University; Dr. Rick Lovell, University of Wisconsin-Milwaukee; Dr. Jeffrey Ian Ross, University of Colorado-Boulder; and Dr. Mahendra Singh, Grambling State University, Grambling, Louisiana.

Two other groups should be mentioned. Thanks go to the Brooks/Cole staff: Thor MacMillan, Claire Verduin, and my editor Cindy Stormer. I am grateful to my "editor-in-chief" Marcia White (and her assistants Katie White and Charlie White).

A NOTE TO STUDENTS

This text is designed to give you essential background information about terrorism; to absorb it efficiently, you'll need to keep several things in mind as you read. First, the book is divided into three parts. The first focuses on terrorist group dynamics and regional styles. Part II focuses on specific groups and campaigns, and Part III discusses controversial issues in terrorism. Each chapter has objectives at the beginning and a summary at the end. If you want to read more, a short annotated bibliography concludes each chapter.

Second, you'll need to know quite a bit about world geography in order to follow the discussion. Several chapters have maps of regions or specific countries. I suggest flagging those pages for ready reference when you are reading about an area with which you are unfamiliar.

Third, when you study terrorism you are bombarded with the names and acronyms of dozens of terrorist groups. Chapter 2, a reference chapter, contains a synopsis of many of the major terrorist groups. Making frequent use of the chapter as you go along will help you to assimilate them.

Finally, I have tried to be objective about this topic, but its very nature produces deep-seated feelings. My biases and assumptions are summarized in the following points:

1. Terrorism is a tactical phenomenon that fluctuates according to geographical and cultural variables. It cannot be strictly defined because it is intangible; typologies do not account for all forms of terrorism.
2. Terrorism is sometimes a tool for revolutionaries and nationalists, but is most frequently used by governments to maintain state power.
3. Terrorism can be used as a tactic in guerrilla campaigns, but most guerrillas are not terrorists.
4. Ideological terrorism is not the exclusive property of the revolutionary left.
5. The use of terrorism to repress populations is not exclusive to the reactionary right.
6. Some forms of criminality cannot and should not be distinguished from terrorism.
7. Some forms of terrorism cannot and should not be distinguished from warfare.

8. Terrorism is not necessarily revolution, and revolution is not necessarily terrorism.
9. The theory and rhetoric of revolution are even further removed from terrorism than revolutionary acts.
10. The Soviet Union is willing to support some forms of terrorism.
11. The United States is willing to support some forms of terrorism.
12. Just about everybody else is willing to support some forms of terrorism.
13. In order to understand assumptions 10, 11, and 12, we must realize that terrorism comes in a variety of forms.
14. Terrorism is difficult to study objectively, because it evokes deep-seated political emotions.
15. Terrorism is essentially a minor threat unless it is allowed to escalate.
16. The American political, military, and criminal justice systems need to develop an understanding of terrorism.
17. Specific terrorists can be defeated with logical policies and tactics, but incidents of terrorism will continue. No policy or tactic will completely eliminate terrorism.

You should keep these biases in mind as you read the text. Use them, along with the opinions of other scholars and the theoretical controversies cited, as a backboard against which to volley your own inferences.

Jonathan R. White

CONTENTS

THE
STRUCTURE
AND
DEVELOPMENT
OF
TERRORISM

DEFINITIONS, TYPOLOGIES, AND TACTICS

The meaning of the term *terrorism* is rarely agreed upon, although analysts have produced a variety of definitions for it and developed several classification systems, or typologies, to describe it. In this chapter you'll review many of these definitions and typologies and learn the weaknesses of and problems associated with each. A tactical typology is presented at the end of the chapter that describes terrorism from a security perspective. You should learn to critically evaluate all of the perspectives, including the tactical typology, because no single view of terrorism answers all of the problems posed in the heated controversies surrounding the subject.

After reading this chapter, you should be able to do the following.

1. Explain the problems inherent in defining terrorism
2. List and summarize some common definitions of terrorism
3. Define terrorism as a tactical process
4. Explain the strengths and weaknesses of various typologies of terrorism
5. Summarize the typologies of Wilkinson, Bell, and Crozier
6. List and define the five basic tactical forms of terrorism
7. Describe the common tactics used in terrorism and the reasons those tactics appear to be complex
8. Describe the relationship between the size of terrorist groups and the role of force multipliers

THE PROBLEM OF DEFINING TERRORISM

The term *terrorism* is rather difficult to define within political circles. It brings out strong emotions, which result in confusion. Many social scientists have developed working definitions of terrorism that suit their particular research models. Philosophers and historians are willing to offer broader but often contradictory definitions. Some police officials believe that terrorism should be defined as a military problem, while many military people see it as a problem for criminal justice. A few lawyers have argued for a legal definition of terrorism, and, indeed, prosecutors frequently counter-act terrorists using criminal codes. Writers often pick and choose from among the definitions offered by noted authorities, simply to reinforce their own political views. Anyone who undertakes the study of terrorism soon finds there are almost as many definitions of the subject as there are opinions on it.

Terrorism is also difficult to define because it has a pejorative connotation. A person is politically and socially degraded when labeled a terrorist, and the same thing happens when an organization is called a terrorist group. Routine crimes assume greater social importance when they are described as being the result of terrorism, and political movements can be hampered when their followers are believed to be terrorists.

Conversely, governments increase their power when they can label their opponents as terrorists, because their citizens seem willing to accept more governmental abuses of power when a "counterterrorist campaign" is in progress. Illegal arrest, torture, and sometimes murder are acceptable methods of dealing with terrorists, in the public mind. The results of labeling, therefore, are not only controversial but deadly. This makes the task of definition all the more difficult.

When viewed across a broad political spectrum, the situation is further complicated by those who wish to intertwine terror and terrorism. The object of military force is to strike terror into the heart of the enemy, and systematic terror has been a basic weapon in conflicts throughout history. Therefore some argue that all military force is terrorism, and that there is no difference between an armed gunman and a soldier. Many members of the antinuclear movement have extended this argument by maintaining that seeking peace through nuclear deterrence is terrorism. Others use the same logic when claiming that street gangs and criminals "terrorize" neighborhoods. These are all examples of efforts to make definitions of terrorism applicable to any form of violence.

It may in fact be proper to describe all of these situations as terrorism, but that may well create a dilemma similar to that of defining obscenity. One Supreme Court justice solved that problem by stating that he did not know how to define obscenity, but that he knew what it was when he saw it. Terrorism seems to present a similar paradox. We cannot agree on a single definition, but we all think we know what it is when we see it.

As the preceding discussion indicates, there are logical reasons for this difficulty in definition. First, definitions of terrorism have changed over time, and a "new" form of terrorism emerged after World War II. Second, the term is pejorative, and labeling is a political act with serious consequences. Third, terrorism is often popularly "defined" by bureaucrats and journalists who have no wish to account for the intricacies of the topic. Finally, there are a variety of excellent yet conflicting historical, sociological, and philosophical definitions of terrorism. These factors make it difficult to know precisely what the term means and how it should be applied.

Some Common Definitions

Despite the problems of defining terrorism, several people have developed their own approaches. A rather simple definition has frequently been used by security personnel. Their approach has been voiced in different publications by Brian Jenkins, Director of Political Science Research for the Rand Corporation, and by Walter Laqueur, Professor of History at Georgetown University. They have defined terrorism separately but arrived at remarkably similar conclusions.

Speaking to a gathering of police, private security, and military personnel in Detroit, Brian Jenkins offered a definition he has frequently used in Rand publications and public forums. Jenkins (1984) called terrorism the use or threatened use of force designed to bring about a political change. In a definition closely related to Jenkins's, Laqueur (1987, 72) said terrorism constituted the illegitimate use of force to achieve a political objective when innocent people are targeted. He added that attempts to move beyond a simple definition are fruitless because the term is so controversial. Volumes can be written on the definition of terrorism, Laqueur wrote, but they will not add one iota to our understanding of the topic.

Both Jenkins and Laqueur foresaw problems with these simple definitions, however. Simple definitions do not limit the topic, and there is no meaningful way to apply a simple definition to specific acts of terrorism. Simple definitions also leave academicians and social scientists frustrated. In short, simplicity does not solve the problem of defining the problem.

Laqueur implied that it is necessary to live with these problems and weaknesses in his definition, because terrorism can mean different things to different people. From a security perspective, Laqueur's conclusion makes sense: terrorism is a form of political or criminal violence using tactics designed to change behavior through fear. This simple approach does not solve the problem of definition, but it allows security personnel to move beyond the endless debates.

A second approach to the problem is to focus on legal definitions, a method that has been very popular among governments. For example, the Federal Republic of Germany has combated terrorism through the legal process. Terrorism is the use of criminal acts for political purposes or in such a manner as to create political disorder, so West Germans have defined the crime of terrorism by law, and specific actions can be taken against terrorists who violate that law (Grosscup 1987, 215–240). The United States Congress has attempted a similar approach in its foreign policy by enacting legislation to protect diplomats and by allowing U.S. agents to arrest people engaging in terrorism on foreign soil (U.S. Senate 1985).

The problem with legal definitions of terrorism is that they account for neither the social nor the political nature of terrorism. Violence is the result of complex social factors that range beyond narrow legal limitations and foreign policy restrictions. Political violence often occurs during the struggle for legitimacy. This implies that someone or some group must have the *power* to label opponents. Groups can be labeled as terrorists whenever their opponents have the authority to make the label stick. Thus, legal definitions do not account for all the problems associated with terrorism.

Some social scientists have opted for a third method of defining terrorism. Martha Crenshaw (1983) was urging this method when she wrote that it is necessary to make a distinction between normative definitions of terrorism and analytical ones. Normative definitions are moralistic and emotional, she wrote, but analytical definitions seek to identify the problem for study.

In Crenshaw's view the act, the target, and the possibility of political success are

DEFINITIONS OF TERRORISM

Type	Definition
• Simple	• Violence or threatened violence intended to produce fear and change
• Legal	• Criminal violence violating legal codes and punishable by the state
• Analytical	• Specific political and social factors behind individual terrorist attacks
• State-sponsored	• Terrorist groups used by small states and the Communist Bloc to attack Western interests
• State	• Power of the government used to terrorize its people into submission

factors that should be analyzed before using the term *terrorism*. Crenshaw also suggested that revolutionary violence should not be confused with terrorism. For example, freedom fighters who attack the forces of repressive governments are not always terrorists. To Crenshaw, then, terrorism means socially and politically unacceptable violence aimed at an innocent symbolic target to achieve a psychological effect.

The practical problem with Crenshaw's approach is that almost all terrorists claim to be freedom fighters. For example, Irish Republican Army (IRA) terrorists frequently murder members of the security forces in Northern Ireland while claiming to be freedom fighters. But Crenshaw has provided a telling litmus test to answer such claims: IRA murders are still symbolic. The IRA is an extremist group opposing any cooperative solution to violence in Northern Ireland. Their murders are designed to produce fear. Therefore, members of the IRA are terrorists, not freedom fighters. Such analytical distinctions have helped make Crenshaw a leading authority on terrorism.

A fourth approach to defining terrorism rejects academic rigor to focus instead on daily problems. Those who define terrorism as a state-sponsored activity follow this path. In the Reagan administration, for example, it became extremely popular to cast terrorism in nationalistic terms. Terrorism was defined as intentional enemy policies designed to attack the United States by means of terror.

Neil Livingstone was one of those who presented this idea to the Reagan administration (Livingstone and Arnold 1986, 1–10). Terrorism, he argued, is World War III strategic warfare on the cheap. In the 1980s, Livingstone wrote, terrorism came to be defined as small powers and Soviet client states using the tactics of terror against American interests. Terrorism is nothing less than a state-sponsored, low-level military activity.

Benjamin Netanyahu, Israeli Ambassador to the United Nations, expanded Livingstone's definition. Netanyahu (1987, 5–15) said that terrorism is a political crime against society. It is also a state of war in which every citizen and nation is threatened with murder and mayhem. The rise of state-sponsored terrorism, according to Netanyahu, is not merely an attack on America but an attack on civilization. The West has been called upon to defend civilization against this incursion.

While the state-sponsored definition is popular in some political circles, there are two problems with it. James Adams (1986) has demonstrated that large terrorist groups are not sponsored by states, while Michael Stohl (1988, 1–28) has sounded another caveat. States may heavily back terrorism, Stohl argued, but the low-level warfare described by Livingstone and Netanyahu is insignificant. Governments use terrorism to maintain political power, not to obtain it: true state terrorism involves the political repression of governmental opponents.

Stohl's view brings us to a sixth definitional type. Professor Edward Herman described "real" terrorism as the network of repressive Latin American governments supported to a large extent by the United States government. In his book *The Real Terror Network* Herman claimed that the United States has improperly supported a number of Central and South American governments in an effort to restrict communism. Many of the governments supported have relied on repressive arrests, murder, and torture to maintain power. The United States has trained Latin American police and military officers, financially supported repressive governments, and shared intelligence information with them (Herman 1983, 84–127). These policies have resulted in misery for far more people than has any other form of state-sponsored terror, according to Herman.

Herman is quite correct, but the definitional problem is further confused by his approach. As Walter Laqueur (1987, 6) said, such acts are certainly terrorism, and one would be foolish to deny that state repression has caused less suffering and misery than has modern terrorism. Yet, Laqueur argued, governmental repression is a long-term political problem, separate from modern terrorism. To include it in the discussion muddies the waters and does little to add to our understanding of terrorism.

The problems associated with defining terrorism have not been solved by these many efforts: each definition has its weaknesses and limitations, but each is also perfectly acceptable. Herman's view of state repression is just as valid as Jenkins's simplicity. The academic rigor of Crenshaw does not detract from the pragmatism of Livingstone. All of these definitions are viable.

Herein lies the problem. As we review the definitions, two facts become clear: there is no standard definition of terror, and each approach to terrorism seems to be based on political biases. There is, as H. A. A. Cooper (1978) so aptly argued, a problem in defining the problem. Alex Schmid (1983, 70–111) approached the problem of definition by focusing on the analysts who provide the definitions. In scholarship's most rigorous examination of the problem, Schmid analyzed the definitions of one hundred scholars and experts in the field. He considered a variety of violent behaviors, including political terrorism, crime, and assassination. He looked for areas of agreement, hoping to glean from them a comprehensive definition of terrorism.

There is no true or correct definition, Schmid concluded, because terrorism is an abstract concept with no real essence. A single definition cannot possibly account for all of the potential uses of the term. Still there are a number of elements common to the leading definitions, and most definitions have two major characteristics: someone is terrorized, and the act's meaning is derived from its targets and victims.

SCHMID'S ANALYSIS OF TERRORISM DEFINITIONS

After analyzing over one hundred definitions, Alex Schmid concluded the following.

- Terrorism is an abstract concept with no essence.
- A single definition cannot account for all possible uses of the term.
- Many different definitions share common elements.
- The meaning of terrorism derives from the victim or the target.

Source: Alex Schmid, *Political Terrorism* (New Brunswick, CT: Transaction, 1983)

Schmid also offered a conglomerate definition of terrorism. His empirical analysis found twenty-two elements common to most definitions, and he developed a definition containing thirteen of those elements. Schmid saw terrorism as a method of combat in which the victims serve as a symbolic target. Violent actors are able to produce a chronic state of fear by using violence outside the realms of normative behavior. This produces an audience beyond the immediate victim and results in a change of public attitudes and actions.

Some scholars believe Schmid has solved the definitional dilemma by combining definitions. Others think that he has refined the undefinable. While analysts wrestle with the problem, most end up doing one of three things. Some follow the lead of Thomas Thorton (1964, 73) and define terrorism in agitational terms. Others follow the example of Schmid and develop their own definitions or use those of others. Finally, some people ignore the problem. They talk about terrorism and assume everybody knows what they mean.

TYPOLOGIES OF TERRORISM

Definitions do very little to illustrate the scope and nature of terrorism. They are important tools of social science research, but, like definitions of crime, they do not adequately introduce the complexity of the subject. Models, classification systems, and typologies, on the other hand, offer another alternative. Some analysts have chosen to approach terrorism through typologies rather than definitions.

The United States Defense Intelligence Agency (DIA) has accepted this postulation. According to the DIA, it is not especially necessary to define terrorist activity, but it is essential to identify the type of terrorism being confronted. Terrorism presents itself in different guises, and it is a fallacy to lump different types into a single definition. For example, the terrorism of a criminal or revolutionary gang is different from guerrilla or state-sponsored activities. The DIA believes that predictive patterns for activity can be developed when sources and types are combined in behavioral models (Nelson 1986).

Other policy makers and scholars have taken a similar approach. They maintain that it is more important to talk about the types of terrorism than to offer a single definition that supposedly encompasses all of the forms. In order to do so, it is necessary to clarify that terrorism is a tactical process. This means that terrorism is not a specific activity, but rather that it comprises a variety of violent activities. Tactically, it is designed to influence the behavior of a target audience through the use of violence.

Typologies have several advantages over definitions. First, the broad scope of the problem can be presented. It is a variety of activities, not a singly defined action. Terrorism ranges from individual acts of crazed criminality to sophisticated operations enjoying support from highly organized political systems. Second, the scope of the problem identified by typologies also allows the level of the problem to be introduced. Terrorism can be a local, national, or international occurrence. Third, when the level of the problem is classified, the level of response can be determined. In other words, typologies can play an important role in deciding policies. Finally, typologies can be used to increase understanding. As the many definitions of terrorism indicate, few people agree on definitions. The types of terror are a different matter; many people agree that terrorism can range from restaurant bombings to concentration camps. By focusing on types of violence and the social meaning of tactics, typologies avoid the heated political debates on the meaning of terrorism.

Typologies are not a panacea, however, and they do not solve all of the definitional dilemmas. First, the process of terrorism is in a constant state of change. Models, taxonomies, and typologies only describe patterns among events. They are generalizations that describe extremely unstable environments. While typologies may increase our understanding of terrorism, each terrorist incident must be understood in its specific social, historical, and political circumstances.

Second, after a model or typology is developed, some people try to fit particular forms of terrorism into it: they alter what they see so that it will blend with their typology. This has been especially true regarding Latin America. Many students, researchers, and diplomats try to fit Latin American violence into urban and rural models of revolution. Of course, changing events to fit a pattern can completely distort reality; when this happens, researchers only see what they want to see.

Typologies may also hide details, because they are so flexible. They produce patterns, not specifics. It is important to remember that when a terrorist campaign does not fit a particular taxonomy, it is time to redesign the model, not the events of the campaign. Many times, however, this is easier said than done.

Finally, typologies do not eliminate the pejorative connotations of the term. At some point in any classification system someone will be labeled as a terrorist and some act will be deemed terrorism. Rational political actors do not want this label and will either resist it or attempt to turn it to their advantage. Authority figures, on the other hand, can consolidate power whenever their opponents are socially accepted as terrorists. Typologies do little, if anything, to eliminate the controversy surrounding terrorism.

Peter Fleming, Michael Stohl, and Alex Schmid (1988, 153–195) have criticized the use of typologies to describe terrorism because they reflect the biases of the researchers and also tend to compare variables that should not be compared across incidents. To be usable, typologies must account for a group's political motivation, origins, scope of actions, and the focus of its attention. Although dozens of terrorist typologies have appeared over the last two decades, none has attempted to provide this in-depth political analysis.

STRENGTHS AND WEAKNESSES OF TYPOLOGIES

Strengths
- Identifies type of problem.
- Level of problem is introduced.
- Level of response can be determined.
- Increases understanding of event or campaign.

Weaknesses
- Terrorism constantly changes.
- Reflects biases of model makers.
- Does not eliminate pejorative nature of definition.
- Inadequately describes details.

Typologies do not solve the definitional problems of terrorism, and they do not provide a method for examining deep-seated political and social issues. Yet they can be useful in the more limited role of tactically identifying a security problem. Some noted authorities have approached terrorism in this manner.

Wilkinson's Typology of Political Terrorism

In one of his early works, noted British terrorism expert Paul Wilkinson (1974) outlined the structure of modern terrorism by means of a political typology. Several analysts (e.g., Wardlaw 1982, 3–13 and Poland 1988, 11–13) have incorporated Wilkinson's approach in their own work. Wilkinson suggested that terrorism is dynamic and should be situationally defined. Rather than elaborating a definition applicable to all types of terrorism in all types of situations, Wilkinson hit upon the idea of classifying terrorism by type of action.

Wilkinson's *Political Terrorism* focused primarily on nationalistic and revolutionary terrorism, but his classification system moved beyond broad, relatively meaningless definitions of terror. Three types of terrorism emerged from his analysis: (1) criminal, (2) political, and (3) state sponsored. In later years Wilkinson added that it is also necessary to distinguish between external and internal terrorism. He concluded that typologies can be employed to enhance our understanding of the forms of terrorism.

Terrorism manifests itself in two different manners: criminal and political. Wilkinson pointed out that criminal terrorism is the least controversial and is thus more easily approached. Some criminal terrorists seek individual psychological gratification, while others may engage in it for profit. For the most part, according to Wilkinson, this separates criminal terrorists from their political counterparts. Criminal terrorism is a problem distinct from political violence.

Political terrorism, on the other hand, is a controversial subject that deserves in-depth treatment. In order to encapsulate political terrorism, Wilkinson pointed to its various forms. The most common form is the use of internal state power to frighten its citizens into obedience. States have also recently begun to sponsor external acts of subnational violence. Wilkinson (1986, 37–55) approached state-sponsored terrorism as a tactic used in international conflict. States unable to attack other states directly have turned to terrorism as a weapon.

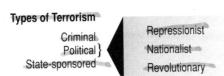

Figure 1-1   Wilkinson's typology of terrorism
Source: Paul Wilkinson, *Political Terrorism,* New York: Wiley, 1974

Wilkinson also identified two other forms of political terrorism and described them in terms of random illegitimate violence. Nationalistic terrorism is conducted to gain political independence from a colonial power or to change the ethnic composition of an existing government without changing its ideological structure. Revolutionary terrorism is conducted to change the political ideology of a social or political unit. Both nationalistic and revolutionary terrorism can stand independently or can be sponsored by a state.

Bell's Typology of Terrorism

About the same time as Wilkinson published his first work, J. Bowyer Bell (1975, 10–18) described six basic types of terrorism: psychotic, criminal, vigilante, endemic, authorized, and revolutionary. Bell spent a significant amount of time examining the final type of terror, revolutionary terrorism.

In general, revolutionary terrorism aims to destroy power. Arguing that most people are referring to revolutionary activities when defining terrorism, Bell wrote that the many forms of revolutionary activities tend to obscure the issue. If you can describe the form of revolutionary violence, he claimed, you can begin to understand the nature of terrorism. This is true, even though the forms of terrorism are not distinct and tend to overlap.

Accordingly, Bell described several forms of revolutionary terror. First, *organizational terror* is designed to maintain discipline within the terrorist group, to frighten members into obedience and punish those who fail to obey. Punishment is not only

---

BELL'S TYPOLOGY OF TERROR

Type	Purpose
• Psychotic	• Psychological gratification
• Criminal	• Profit
• Vigilante	• Retaliation
• Endemic	• Internal struggle
• Authorized	• State repression
• Revolutionary	• Behavioral change through fear

Source: J. Bowyer Bell, *Transnational Terror,* (Washington D.C: American Enterprise Institute for Public Policy, 1975)

BELL'S FORMS OF REVOLUTIONARY TERROR

Form	Purpose
• Organizational	• To maintain discipline in terrorist group
• Allegiance	• To win public support
• Functional	• To accomplish goals and missions of group
• Provocative	• To incite governments to repression
• Manipulative	• To obtain demands through dramatic confrontation
• Symbolic	• To strike at targets for psychological impact

Source: J. Bowyer Bell, A Time of Terror (New York: Basic Books, 1978)

real; it is also ritualistic and symbolic. The punishment is designed to communicate the necessity of obedience.

Second, *allegiance terror* is a form of organizational terror designed to create mass support for a revolutionary cause. Whereas organizational terror is aimed at internal discipline, allegiance terror is designed to coerce the public into support for the terrorist cause. Allegiance terror is applied outside the group. Support can be gained through outright coercion or through efforts to create a show of sympathy. Either way, the public is intimidated. Allegiance terror attempts to shift public loyalty from the government to the terrorists.

Functional terror, according to Bell, refers to the actions terrorist groups take against targets to gain a strategic advantage. Functional terror is designed to accomplish the expressed purposes of the group. Targets are identified, their political purposes announced to the general public, and assaults launched. At times targets may be highly discriminatory; at others, anyone or anything may be the object of assault. Functional terror is designed to intimidate the public at large and to create the impression that the government cannot effectively respond to the threat at hand.

Fourth, *provocative terror* is meant to incite the government. It may develop unexpectedly or it may be the result of calculated planning. Regardless, Bell argued that provocative terror manifests itself when security forces are pushed beyond the limits of their patience and strike back blindly at the opposition. Politically, the security forces are then viewed as overreacting, and their desire for vengeance backfires. Terrorists may believe that such actions reveal the true nature of the state.

Fifth, *manipulative terror* involves the use of hostages or assets to obtain organizational demands. According to Bell, this is the terrorism of negotiation. Demands are made in a public forum, with the lives of hostages at stake. The goal is to force the government into some form of surrender, thus manipulating it into the hands of the terrorists. It frequently becomes a media event.

Bell called the final form of revolutionary violence *symbolic terror*. This goes beyond organizational and functional terror in selecting a victim who epitomizes the enemy. Assassinations are prime examples, as well as targets having no strategic significance. Bell argued that such acts may improve revolutionary morale, but their prime purpose is symbolic action: they attack the essence of the state.

Crozier's Group Classification System

Another method of classifying terrorism was developed by Brian Crozier, the former director of the United Kingdom's Institute for the Study of Conflict. In testimony before the United States Senate, Crozier (1975, 198–199) argued that terrorism could be viewed on a continuum ranging from right-wing neofascist groups to left-wing revolutionary organizations (see Figure 1-2). Not bothering with parsimonious definitions, Crozier asserted that the explication of group activity served to define the topic. In Crozier's typology terrorism is identified by the type of group engaged in the violence.

Crozier began by classifying six types of terrorist groups in Western Europe. First come minority nationalist groups composed of ethnic factions who wish to replace the current political power with representatives from their own ethnic group. Crozier pointed to nationalist terrorism in Ireland and Spain as examples. In later testimony Crozier applied this category to groups outside of Western Europe, focusing on interethnic rivalries in Latin America.

Second are Marxist revolutionary groups who, according to Crozier, have strong ties to the Soviet Union and are linked through a common Marxist ideology. The goal of these groups is to obtain control of the economic modes of production and shift the economic system from capitalism to socialism. Crozier believed there was a direct link between some minority nationalist groups and Marxist revolutionary groups. While Moscow's direct control over all of these groups is open to speculation, the existence of Marxist revolutionary groups cannot be denied.

Anarchist groups, the third type in Crozier's typology, are composed of revolutionaries who seek to destroy social order in the hope that less governmental structure will result in more individual freedom. Crozier included revolutionary groups in West Germany and Great Britain in this category. A fourth type of terrorist organization, pathological groups or individuals, behaves in a pattern similar to that of anarchist groups, but its activities are mainly criminal. Crozier believed its motivation is personal or psychological gain. He did not include terrorism for profit in this category.

Crozier's fifth category included neofascist and right-wing groups. Although his analysis of Western Europe was somewhat dated, it was certainly predictive. Right-wing extremism was a major concern in the 1980s and has grown significantly in the United States. Lacking the intellectual cohesion of Marxist revolutionaries, the right has found occasion to unite under the banners of race and religion in recent years.

Ideological mercenaries compose Crozier's final category. Again prevalent in Western Europe, the concept has expanded to worldwide proportions. Crozier pointed to the Japanese Red Army as a prime example. Members of this revolutionary organization were responsible for a murderous attack on passengers at Israel's Lod Airport in 1972. Crozier could have included several Middle Eastern groups in this category, along with more conservative mercenaries who offer their services to help stabilize African governments.

By focusing on the type of group rather than on the level and type of activity, Crozier was able to avoid developing a dichotomy between criminal and political terrorism. Violent activity regardless of its purpose remains a problem for any political authority. Any form of terrorism demands a political response. The appropriate level of

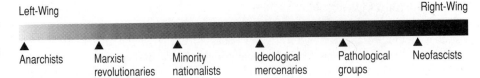

Figure 1-2 Crozier's classification of terrorist groups in Western Europe
Source: U.S. Senate Hearings Before the Subcommittee to Investigate the Administration of the Internal Security Act (Washington D.C.: U.S. Senate, 1975)

response varies with each particular situation, but governments must still respond. For example, a robber who takes hostages because he has observed the police arrive must be approached differently than ideological revolutionaries holding hostages for political purposes. Crozier's typology allows for the classification of both types of incidents while recognizing that government authority will be exercised in a different manner in each case.

The typologies of Wilkinson, Bell, and Crozier are only a few of a host of other classification systems. Fleming, Stohl, and Schmid (1988, 153–195) criticized such systems when they argued that typologies provided no basis for a political and social understanding of terrorism. Yet for those faced with security problems, the typologies of Wilkinson, Bell, and Crozier offer a limited but useful tactical approach to terrorism. By examining the tactical forms of terrorism, typologies of terrorism can be refined. If we keep its limitations in mind, a tactical analysis of terrorist groups might provide further understanding.

THE FORMS OF TERRORISM

For those facing security challenges, the tactics of terrorism become extremely important. Definitions do not address tactical concerns, but typologies can. Wilkinson's, Bell's, and Crozier's ideas can be combined to form concepts applicable for security.

There are five basic tactical forms of terrorism. The first is *criminal terrorism.* As defined by Wilkinson it involves the use of terror for profit or psychological gain. Wilkinson strictly distinguished criminal from political terrorism, and he believed that criminal activities did not merit the same type of attention as revolutionary and nationalistic violence. Bell, on the other hand, classified criminal terrorism as a low-level form of political terror.

Bell and Ted Robert Gurr (1979, 329–347) applied this theory to terrorism in the United States. Domestic terrorism, Bell and Gurr argued, is primarily a criminal activity because American terrorists have lacked political sophistication and the support of terrorists in other parts of the world. They turn to criminal activity because it is the only option available to them: Americans will not support a large-scale terrorist campaign politically. Domestic terrorism thus appears as a criminal activity, while counterterrorism is generally a law enforcement matter.

A second tactical form of terrorism is *ideological terrorism:* the use of terrorism to change the ideological framework of political power. As defined by Wilkinson and

◀ Primarily police concerns   Primarily military concerns ▶

▲   ▲   ▲   ▲   ▲
Criminal   Ideological   Nationalistic   State-sponsored   Guerrilla

Figure 1-3 Five tactical forms of terrorism

Crozier, it employs terrorism only for ideological change, and if ethnic or nationalistic goals guide the terrorists, they are relegated to a secondary role.

Bell implied that ideological terrorism involves revolution, but Ted Robert Gurr (1988) suggested that the relationship between terrorism and revolution is confused. Terrorism can not only be used to effect revolutionary change but can also be used to achieve a variety of political goals. Gurr believed that it is a mistake to associate ideological terrorism solely with revolution.

Some terrorist groups, for example, wage ideological campaigns to maintain governments in power while their actions are officially condemned by the authorities. Death squads fall into this category. Even though their actions might appear to be guided by a repressive state, death squads are really the counterpart of revolutionary terrorists. Both groups are motivated by ideology, and we will need to discuss both of them in order to understand ideological terrorism.

The third tactical form of terrorism was identified by Wilkinson as *nationalistic terrorism*, or terrorism that supports the interests of an ethnic or nationalistic group irrespective of its political ideology. The definition of nationalistic terrorism is fairly simple and much less controversial than is ideological terrorism, but other aspects of nationalistic terrorism must be presented.

As a tactical form, nationalistic violence should not be confused with ideological terrorism, but it frequently is. This happens because nationalistic terrorists often espouse revolutionary and ideological slogans in an effort to please one of the superpowers. Superpower support translates into weapons and war materials. The West tends to supply "our" terrorists, while the East tends to supply "theirs." Any group willing to keep supply lines open obviously needs to talk about an eventual goal of "democracy" or "Marxist socialism."

The first three tactical forms of terrorism are primarily a police problem or, in their worst stages, a problem for police forces augmented by military power. In the case of death squads, uncontrolled police and military forces are the problem. Yet two other forms of terrorism clearly move beyond the realm of criminal and low-level violent political activities. It has become popular to refer to these forms of violence as terrorism, but they may be better conceived as a form of warfare. Indeed, the American military has adopted the term *low-intensity conflict* to describe these activities.

As mentioned in the section on definition, during the Reagan administration it became popular to describe low-level assaults against American diplomatic and military installations as terrorism. This form of violence is called *state-sponsored terrorism* and can be defined as the use or the threat of violence in international relations outside the scope of normal diplomatic protocol. This form of terrorism is typified by such actions as the 1979 takeover of the American embassy in Tehran and by the bombings of U.S. military personnel and diplomatic missions in the Middle East. Nations that support such actions are called "terrorist states."

Guerrilla terrorism is the final tactical form of terrorism and is closely linked to state-sponsored terrorism. It uses terrorism as one technique in a larger campaign of guerrilla warfare. Terrorism is not the primary tactic of a guerrilla force; it is a commando-type tactic, used sparingly to destroy a government's base of support. The indiscriminate use of terrorism in a guerrilla campaign has been disavowed in many theories of guerrilla war. Guerrillas need public support, and terrorizing a population hardly achieves popularity.

By using a tactical typology, then, we can discern five basic forms of terrorism: criminal, ideological, nationalistic, state-sponsored, and guerrilla. In some forms terrorism is a police concern, while in others it falls primarily into the lap of the military. Many times both groups must work together to confront the threat. Despite the scholarly shortcomings of typologies, those people charged with security need to grasp the tactical manifestations of terrorism. It is far more beneficial to discuss five tactical forms of terrorism than to engage in the endless debate on definitions.

THE TACTICS OF TERRORISM

The tactical forms of terrorism are complicated, but its tactics are not. According to Brian Jenkins (1984) there are six basic tactics of terrorism: bombing, arson, hijacking, ambush, kidnapping, and hostage taking. In a later publication, Jenkins (1985, 13) claimed that 95 percent of all terrorist activities fall into these categories.

Jenkins stated that the tactics are straightforward and simple, but that the context of the action makes them appear complex. This means that the *social meaning* of terrorism can be complicated even when the *process* is not. Three terrorist murders can be used to illustrate Jenkins's point.

In the early 1970s less than a dozen left-wing radicals banned together under Donald Defreeze to form the Symbionese Liberation Army (SLA). Prior to the SLA's most publicized action, the kidnapping of Patricia Hearst, the group had murdered the superintendent of the Oakland Public School System. The murder was dramatic. The superintendent was killed with cyanide-laced bullets, a message condemning racism tied to his body. The manner of the murder was significant: killing a public figure in a grotesque manner was symbolic, and the basic crime of murder was thus masked by political rhetoric.

On August 27, 1979 Lord Louis Mountbatten was at sea off the coast of Ireland with family members and a young family friend. Shortly after his boat had cleared the harbor a bomb went off, destroying the boat and killing Mountbatten. Afterward, a British Army patrol was struck by another bomb while responding to the incident, and another set of names added to the long list of the dead in Northern Ireland. Even though the bombings were part of a long-term struggle, the tactics were no different than the type employed by the SLA. Symbolically significant people were murdered in a ritualistic act.

While barhopping outside of a Philippines Air Force base in October 1987, three off-duty United States servicemen were attacked and killed by members of the communist New People's Army (NPA). The murders occurred as a result of a new NPA policy designed to attack American economic and military targets in the Philip-

THE TACTICS OF TERRORISM

- Bombing
- Arson
- Hijacking
- Ambush
- Kidnapping
- Hostage taking

Source: Brian Jenkins, "The Who, What, When, Where, How, and Why of Terrorism" (Detroit Police Department Conference, 1984)

pines. The NPA was unveiling specialized urban hit squads to murder off-duty or unprotected American military personnel. Hence, the crime of murder became secondary to the political drama of killing American military personnel.

In Jenkins's view, two tactics were used in the preceding examples: ambush and bombing. The tactics themselves were simple, but the political context of the crimes made the tactics seem complex. The murders in all three examples were designed to convey social and political messages, and the symbolic context of the homicides made the tactics appear to be something more than the simple process of murder. The terrorist process is simple; its meaning is not.

Christine Ketcham and Harvey McGeorge (1986, 25–33) cited a second factor that makes terrorist tactics seem to be something more than simple crimes. They argued that because technology has enhanced the capabilities of terrorist weapons and made them increasingly sophisticated, the potential destructive power of these new weapons complicates the phenomenon of terrorism.

To illustrate their point, Ketcham and McGeorge divided terrorist weapons into several categories. These ranged from the simplest forms of weapons, such as nails used to puncture tires, to devices of mass destruction, such as nuclear weapons. They noted that technology has improved the striking power in each category. Terrorists can be more effective because their weapons are more effective, Ketcham and McGeorge said. The effectiveness of terrorism adds a new dimension to terrorist acts.

The tactics of terrorism are very similar to the tactics of war. Their basic principles are fairly straightforward and do not change over time. The process by which the principles are applied, however, makes war and terrorism seem complex, and the complexity is exacerbated when the technology of weapons is improved. The tactics are relatively constant and easily learned, but the social meanings attached to the actions complicate the issues.

Force Multipliers and Tactics

If the tactics of terrorism are made complex by the social meanings attributed to the actions of terrorists, groups of terrorists further confuse the issue by trying to portray an image of omnipotence. That is, terrorist groups try to make the public believe that they are something more than they are, that terrorism can strike anywhere and that terrorists are in control of everyday life. Adding symbolic meanings to tactics helps to accomplish this objective, but there is a more significant factor. The success of terrorism generally depends on the size of the terrorist group.

A loose general rule can be applied to the amount of terrorism and the size of a group: usually, the amount and effectiveness of terrorism correlate directly with the size of the group. Large groups account for large amounts of terrorism, and smaller groups account for less. The general rule therefore, is large terrorist groups are more effective than small ones.

For example, the Irish Republican Army (IRA) has carried out a campaign of terrorism in Northern Ireland for decades. The IRA could not have continued had it not been for its size. It is physically large enough to continue terrorizing its victims even when security forces neutralize entire cells. In addition, the IRA enjoys a clandestine network of supporters and manages a large organized crime syndicate. The size and resources of the IRA make it a deadly adversary. It is a large group capable of a high level of activity.

Small groups are aware of the general correlation between group size and strength, so they have a political incentive to act beyond their capacity. Yet small groups frequently lack the ability to expand their operations. They don't have the resources to behave like a large group, and they can't mount a full campaign of terrorism. This creates a problem for small terrorist groups. If they cannot convince political authorities that they are a powerful threat, they can be ignored. They are forced, therefore, to seek alternatives.

Brian Jenkins (1985) believed that terrorists turn to "force multipliers" to give the illusion of increased strength. In military lexicon, force multipliers increase the striking potential of a unit without increasing its personnel. For example, an infantry battalion can multiply its striking power by supplying its personnel with hand-held rocket launchers. Jenkins maintained that small terrorist groups routinely seek force multipliers.

Research conducted by the author suggests that terrorists use three techniques to increase their striking power (White 1986a). First, the mass media are manipulated to expand the aura of the group. Second, transnational support networks give small groups logistical support and mobility. Third, technology allows terrorists to increase the striking power of their weapons. Obviously, weapons of mass destruction can become the ultimate force multiplier.

As they do in military settings, force multipliers raise the level of activity for any terrorist group regardless of its size. It becomes self-serving to employ force multipliers as terrorist groups try to create an illusion of strength. Increased striking power makes the public believe in the possibility of increased violence. Force multipliers have therefore become an important tactical weapon in the terrorist arsenal.

SUMMARY OF CHAPTER ONE

The purpose of this chapter was to introduce a general framework within which to examine terrorism. Many people have attempted to define terrorism, but almost everybody has encountered problems in doing so. Definitions of terrorism tend to reflect political biases; also, *terrorism* is a highly emotional and pejorative term. No definition, moreover, has been able to embrace all the forms of terrorism.

When terrorism is viewed as a tactical process, it is possible to approach the topic for discussion and analysis. One of the most common ways to do this has been through the use of typologies. Typologies help to provide a conceptual basis, if they are limited to generalizations. Typologies of terrorism do not provide details, however.

Three of the earliest typologies were developed by Paul Wilkinson, J. Bowyer Bell, and Brian Crozier. Wilkinson's classification system was closely linked to Bell's. Both scholars used the actions of terrorists to classify types of terrorism. Crozier's system, on the other hand, was based on group type. The three typologies complement one another and have served as the basis for further classification in recent years.

As a tactical process, terrorism exists in criminal, ideological, nationalistic, state-sponsored, and guerrilla-sponsored forms. All terrorists tend to use simple tactics, but the simplicity is confused by the social meanings attributed to terrorist actions. Tactics are enhanced and the situation made more complex through the use of force multipliers.

IF YOU WANT TO READ FURTHER . . .

There are volumes of new works covering our present understanding of modern terrorism. Most of them are of questionable rigor, and many are laced with political values and opinions. Paul Wilkinson's *Political Terrorism* and *Terrorism and the Liberal State* are proving to be classics. Many classify Wilkinson as a conservative, but he has provided one of the strongest overall introductions to terrorism.

Walter Laqueur's *The Age of Terrorism* is outstanding but somewhat difficult to read. It is highly detailed and assumes a solid background in history. Laqueur is also frequently described as a conservative, although even his critics have proclaimed the excellence of his work. Martha Crenshaw has edited a good selection of readings titled *Terrorism, Legitimacy, and Power,* which complements Wilkinson and Laqueur.

Richard Rubenstein's *Alchemists of Revolution* is very strong and gives a contrasting view. Its section on the origins of modern terrorism is second to none. *The Financing of Terror,* by James Adams, is also excellent and extremely readable. It asks us to reconceive modern terrorism by examining its support networks. *The Explosion of Terrorism* by Beau Grosscup is a liberal polemic but provides a good summary of events.

There are several excellent, readable introductions to terrorism. Among the best is Grant Wardlaw's *Political Terrorism.* Wardlaw provides an excellent introduction to the major issues of terrorism, and he discusses the policy problems that face Western democracies. James Poland's *Understanding Terrorism* is also quite good. *Introduction to Political Terrorism,* by Leonard Weinberg and Paul Davis, is another solid work along with *International Terrorism* by Donna Schlagheck.

Several collections of readings are informative. Yonah Alexander has edited a number of fairly good books on a wide array of topics. In my opinion, the best on the market is Michael Stohl's *The Politics of Terrorism.* Stohl presents a variety of opinions, featuring some outstanding analysts and articles. If you are interested in comparing various views, it is productive to contrast Stohl's readings with the works of Laqueur and Wilkinson. Henry Han's *Terrorism, Political Violence, and World Order* is more difficult to read, but it contains some outstanding articles.

Extreme right-wing and left-wing views are prevalent on the market and on library shelves. You should read such books with caution. Right-wing books tend to maintain that terrorism is an international communist conspiracy, while left-wing books claim that eliminating injustice will eliminate terrorism. Neither of these simplistic ideological positions begins to approach the complexity of terrorist violence.

AN ATLAS OF EXTREMISM
AND TERRORISM

This chapter provides background information on some of the more prominent terrorist and extremist groups in the United States, Latin America, Western Europe, and the Middle East—it should give you a chance to become familiar with these groups before encountering them in later detailed discussions. You will find that any study of terrorism eventually requires a working knowledge of a myriad of groups and locations. When you become familiar with the contents of this chapter, you will be better prepared to discuss and understand the types of terrorist groups operating throughout the world.

After reading this chapter, you should be able to do the following.

1. List and identify the major terrorist and extremist organizations
2. Summarize the political philosophy and activities of each major group
3. Correlate terrorist groups with geographical regions
4. Use this chapter as a reference tool for identifying terrorist groups

HOW TO USE THIS CHAPTER

As you review this chapter, you will read a synopsis of many of the major terrorist and extremist groups around the world. There are hundreds of terrorist groups in the world, and sometimes the same group will use a variety of different names. Tracking groups can be extremely confusing. Even after you finish this chapter, you'll probably want to return to it when you encounter some of the less familiar groups.

You will also find that it's necessary to become familiar with geography to study terrorism. Our topic involves both domestic and international locations and cannot be meaningfully discussed without geographical reference points. For example, it is superfluous to discuss connections between revolutionaries and drug traffickers in Colombia unless you have a mental picture of Colombia and its geographical proximity to drug-smuggling operations. Accordingly, a variety of simple maps throughout the chapter will show you where the major terrorist groups are operating and their positions relative to one another.

▶ EXTREMISM AND TERRORISM IN THE UNITED STATES

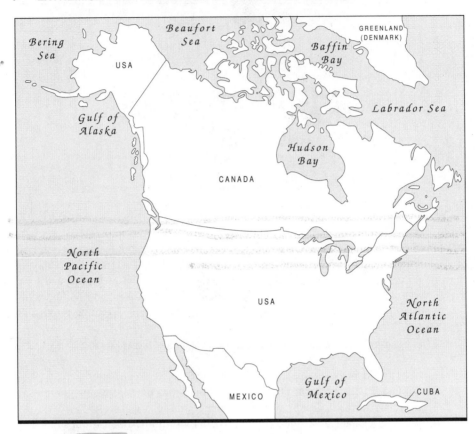

Aryan Nations
Black Liberation Army
Christian Patriots Defense League
The Covenant, the Sword, and the Arm of the Lord (CSA)
Jewish Defense League
Ku Klux Klan
Macheteros
Move
Neo-Nazis
New World Liberation Front
Omega 7
The Order
Posse Comitatus
Puerto Rican Armed Forces of the Revolution (FALN)
Skinheads
Symbionese Liberation Army
United Freedom Front
Weather Underground

GROUP: **Aryan Nations**
AREA OF ACTIVITY: Northwestern United States; headquartered in Hayden Lake, Idaho
PHILOSOPHY: Right-wing extremism, white supremacy
SYNOPSIS: Aryan Nations is a right-wing extremist group that has become the focal
point of many organizations on the right. While it is not a terrorist group, groups
employing violence have reflected the philosophy of Aryan Nations. Its leader and
founder, Richard Butler, vehemently denies all links to groups advocating violence or the overthrow of the United States government. Aryan Nations maintains
a doctrine of white supremacy, including a belief that all races should be separated. The group believes that the current American government is controlled by
Jews (the Zionist Occupation Government, or ZOG), and that power should be
returned to white Christian Americans.

Aryan Nations grew out of the Christian Identity movement in California and
came to Idaho under Richard Butler's direction. It has become the major clearing
house for right-wing literature and the focal point for unification among right-wing
groups. Christian Identity is preached through the Church of Jesus Christ, Christian. Butler is officially the pastor of the church.

Beginning in the early 1980s, Aryan Nations began holding an annual Aryan
National Congress. White supremacists and Christian Identity believers regularly
assemble at the congress. Speakers have included Robert Miles of the Mountain
Church of Jesus Christ, Louis Beam of the Ku Klux Klan, and William Pierce,
author of *The Turner Diaries,* a right-wing fantasy novel. Aryan Nations also runs
a computer network linking several right-wing American groups.

The group claims a following numbering in the hundreds of thousands, but its
total number of sympathizers and allies is probably less than 5,000. Of these, only
a few dozen support violence. Butler has taken pains to disassociate himself and
Aryan Nations from militant activity. In 1988 he was charged with conspiracy to
overthrow the United States government, but was found not guilty along with
several codefendants. The jury believed that the literature and tenants of the Aryan
Nations was rhetorical and did not constitute an incitement to violence.

GROUP: **Black Liberation Army**
AREA OF ACTIVITY: Northeastern United States; New York area
PHILOSOPHY: Militant racial egalitarianism, left-wing revolution
SYNOPSIS: The Black Liberation Army became active in the late 1960s and was most
noted for its attacks on police officers in New York City. After a series of
robberies and murders, most BLA members were in jail by the mid-1970s. The
BLA surfaced again in 1979 and made headlines by raiding a prison to free one of
its members who was serving a sentence for murdering a New Jersey state trooper.

In 1981 members of the BLA participated in an armed robbery planned and
conducted by members of the Weather Underground. During the following investigation, most members of the BLA were captured or killed by a joint law
enforcement task force.

GROUP: **Christian Patriots Defense League**
AREA OF ACTIVITY: Midwest; southern Illinois and Missouri

PHILOSOPHY: Christian conservatism, white supremacy
SYNOPSIS: The Christian Patriots Defense League is best classified as an extremist organization rather than one that participates in violent activity. It has been known for its rhetorical support of white supremacy, survivalism, and Christian Identity. The group has also been linked to other right-wing extremist organizations, and it has been a cosponsor of "Freedom Festivals," in which right-wing groups congregate to share religious and military training. The CPDL is apparently well financed. It maintains conservative Christian religious connections and its rhetoric is extremely violent.

GROUP: **The Covenant, The Sword, and the Arm of the Lord (CSA)**
AREA OF ACTIVITY: Southern Missouri, northern Arkansas
PHILOSOPHY: Christian Identity, white supremacy
SYNOPSIS: The CSA was a right-wing extremist group located around the Missouri-Arkansas border south of Springfield, Missouri. The group lived in communal fashion under military discipline on its farm, Zarapath-Horeb.

Heavily armed, the CSA drew the attention of law enforcement officials due to its militant rhetoric and its military training. Zarapath-Horeb contained a number of illegal weapons, and members of the CSA were suspects in several crimes, including the murders of law enforcement officials. The farm was raided and the organization disbanded in the mid-1980s after the murder of an Arkansas state trooper and an armed attack on a Missouri court house. In the spring of 1988 two members of the CSA testified against other right-wing extremists and entered the government's witness protection program.

GROUP: **Jewish Defense League**
AREA OF ACTIVITY: Based in New York City
PHILOSOPHY: Militant Zionism, anti–Soviet Union stance
SYNOPSIS: The JDL was formed in New York City for the avowed purpose of preventing violence against Jews; its slogan "Never again!" is a response to the Nazi holocaust. The JDL believes that only militant action can protect Jews against anti-Semitism, and they attack all forms of discrimination against Jews with the utmost vigor.

Operating primarily in New York City, the JDL has organized an extremely vocal campaign against governments endorsing anti-Semitic policies. Its primary targets are the Soviet Union, the Palestinian Liberation Organization (PLO), and Arab states supporting the PLO. In terms of terrorism, the JDL is most frequently associated with bombings. Targets have included diplomatic missions, Soviet businesses in the United States, and American businesses that maintain friendly relations with JDL enemies.

GROUP: **Ku Klux Klan**
AREA OF ACTIVITY: Several groups across the United States
PHILOSOPHY: White supremacy, some groups having recently moved toward survivalism and Christian Identity
SYNOPSIS: Although it is one of the oldest terrorist groups in the world, it is no longer

possible to speak of a single Ku Klux Klan. There are several Klans that operate on a fairly autonomous basis, including four major divisions. Klan activity ranges from the maintenance of traditional hate groups to openly terrorist activities.

The Klan has passed through three distinct historical phases. The original Klan was formed and disbanded after the American Civil War. It experienced a resurgence in the 1920s, and its activities climaxed during the Great Depression. The third historical period began after World War II, and Klan activity steadily increased until the Civil Rights movement of the 1960s. During this period the Klan came into open confrontation with federal authorities and fragmented into several splinter groups.

In the 1980s various Klan organizations became associated with neo-Nazi movements as well as other right-wing organizations. An effort to ideologically unite the Klan has been mounted in Hayden Lake, Idaho, under the leadership of Louis Beam and Richard Butler. The myriad of Klans tend to congregate under the United Klans of America.

Although many members do not go beyond rhetoric and cross burnings, some have been responsible for acts of terrorism. The Klan has been America's longest lasting extremist group. Its message of hate and racial supremacy has been rejuvenated by other right-wing movements of the 1980s.

The major Klan groups in the United States are as follows:

The Invisible Empire
The Knights of the Ku Klux Klan
United Klans of America
The National Knights of the Ku Klux Klan

GROUP: **Macheteros**
AREA OF ACTIVITY: Puerto Rico and New England
PHILOSOPHY: Puerto Rican nationalism, Marxism-Leninism
SYNOPSIS: The Macheteros were formed in the late 1970s in a complex, highly centralized structure. Some leaders of the group are believed to have been trained by the Cuban secret police. The group is well funded, and some of its members enjoy salaries and medical benefits. It is probably the best-organized terrorist organization in the United States. The infrastructure is especially strong in New England.

The Macheteros began operations in Puerto Rico in 1978 with the murder of a police officer. They established links with other Puerto Rican nationalist groups, but maintained a distinct identity. Since 1979 they have waged a particularly violent campaign. In Puerto Rico the Macheteros have been responsible for numerous assaults on U.S. military personnel, including a highly organized attack on a Navy bus that wounded nine sailors and killed two others. They also claimed responsibility for destroying eight military aircraft in a 1981 bombing attack. In the United States the Macheteros have been charged with a $7.2 million armored car robbery in Hartford, Connecticut.

The Macheteros represent one of the most effective terrorist groups operating in the United States. They are highly organized, well trained, and their infrastructure has allowed the group to wage a campaign of terrorism. They maintain links with other U.S. left-wing revolutionary groups, but their main strength comes from their own training and organization.

GROUP: **Move**
AREA OF ACTIVITY: Philadelphia
PHILOSOPHY: Rejection of technology, proponent of communal living
SYNOPSIS: Move was a communal group composed of a number of ecological radicals who expressed their politics by rejecting the municipal health code in Philadelphia. Living in a commune in the city, Move came to national attention in the late 1970s when a police officer was killed during a violent confrontation with the group. Attention was drawn to Move again in 1984 when the Philadelphia police attacked the group while serving a warrant. The police literally bombed the building in which Move was located, destroying almost a full city block in the resulting fire. The city and its police force were severely criticized for overreaction.

GROUP: **Neo-Nazis**
AREA OF ACTIVITY: Small groups throughout the United States
PHILOSOPHY: Anti-black, anti-Jewish; goal of creating a fascist state
SYNOPSIS: American Nazis became a fractured lot in the 1970s and 1980s. The old American Nazi Party of George Lincoln Rockwell has given way to a variety of neo-Nazi and fascist movements. With no single leader, these groups range from "national socialists" and "white people's" parties to militant organizations called SS Action Groups. Neo-Nazis have identified with the right-wing movement, but they have not been absorbed by it.

GROUP: **New World Liberation Front**
AREA OF ACTIVITY: West Coast
PHILOSOPHY: Left-wing revolutionary; goal of prison reform
SYNOPSIS: The New World Liberation Front gained attention in the 1970s with a bombing campaign of municipal and corporate offices in California. The group embraced a variety of political and ecological causes, but settled on the goal of prison reform. By the late 1970s the NWLF had completely immersed itself in an alliance with ex-convicts and two prison revolutionary gangs, the Tribal Thumb and the Black Guerrilla Family. The latter groups have gravitated to other left-wing organizations, while the activities of the NWLF have diminished.

The NWLF serves as a good example of a radical group in search of a cause. They were ready to bomb, but they wanted to ennoble their violence with righteousness. They never seemed able to embrace a purpose entirely.

GROUP: **Omega 7**
AREA OF ACTIVITY: New Jersey and New York City
PHILOSOPHY: Anticommunist, anti-Castro
SYNOPSIS: Omega 7 was first identified by New Jersey police in 1975. The group has been classified as a right-wing extremist organization by many law enforcement

agencies, but its extremism should not be confused with that of the white supremacy movement. Omega 7 is at war specifically with Fidel Castro and the Cuban government. Its members want to return Cuba to a military dictatorship free of communists.

Their primary method of operation has been to bomb Cuban offices in America and American offices having friendly relations with Castro. Most of the bombings have taken place in the New York City area. Although the group is small, its structure has frustrated federal authorities. It is a tightly knit network of Cuban exiles and their families that has proven extremely difficult to infiltrate.

GROUP: The Order
AREA OF ACTIVITY: Idaho, Colorado, and northwestern United States
PHILOSOPHY: Right-wing extremism, white supremacy
SYNOPSIS: The Order began as a secret group of violent right-wing extremists in the early 1980s. Lauded by such right-wing groups as the Silent Brotherhood and the *Bruder Schweign,* The Order crossed the border between rhetoric and action in 1983. Although many members have been arrested and sentenced, The Order remains one of the most violent groups in the right-wing movement.

Members of The Order were responsible for several robberies, assaults, bombings, and acts of arson. One of their most publicized acts was the assassination of a radio talk show host in Denver. A member of The Order was killed in a shoot-out with the FBI, while others have been sentenced on a vast array of criminal activities. In 1988 two members were arrested for allegedly planning to assassinate black presidential candidate Jesse Jackson.

Many news articles have attempted to establish a link between The Order and Aryan Nations. Richard Butler, leader of the Aryan Nations, has denied the link and has publicly denounced the violence of The Order.

The group may have taken its name from *The Turner Diaries,* a futuristic novel of right-wing revolution in the United States. Earl Turner, the hero of the book, joined a secret revolutionary organization called The Order. In the book Turner's group was largely responsible for the destruction of the American government. The name may also be a variant on an Italian fascist group known as The Black Order.

According to U.S. Marshals, the group seems to be strongly influenced by Norse mythology, leading some investigators to speculate that right-wing leaders may believe they are immortal. Evidence indicates that members have participated in rituals used in medieval Norse religions. During a ritualistic execution of an informant, for example, the victim was struck in the back of the head with "the hammer of Thor."

It is also notable that several prison inmates have been converted to Christian Identity through a prison ministries program run by right-wing extremists. Many members of The Order came to the terrorist organization in this manner.

GROUP: Posse Comitatus
AREA OF ACTIVITY: Midwest, especially Nebraska, Kansas, and Wisconsin
PHILOSOPHY: White supremacy, Christian Identity, tax protest

SYNOPSIS: Posse Comitatus is a tax protest group that achieved fame for the murder of law enforcement officials in Nebraska and Arkansas. It has also been linked to an assault on a sheriff's office in Kansas, and frequently confronts officials who are repossessing farms.

Combining Christian Identity with the doctrine of white supremacy, Posse Comitatus believes the American government has been taken over by Jews. Members feel America must return to its Anglo-Saxon origins and to the holy purpose of the U.S. Constitution. That purpose, the Posse preaches, is to limit government and protect free white men under God. Tax protesting is a method of fighting the Jews and their government, and the Posse encourages nonpayment of tax. They believe the highest level of government should be at the county level.

Taped prayer services and political meetings indicate that the Posse endorses violence, and, unlike most right-wing extremists, members of the Posse have been known for violent confrontation. Their most celebrated incident was a murderous shoot-out by tax protester Gordon Kahl.

The group is extremely decentralized, and violence cannot be linked to a single hierarchy. Several leaders of local groups claim to be the spokesperson for Posse Comitatus.

GROUP: Puerto Rican Armed Forces of the Revolution (FALN)
AREA OF ACTIVITY: Puerto Rico, New York and northeastern coast, Chicago
PHILOSOPHY: Puerto Rican nationalism
SYNOPSIS: The FALN has proven to be one of the most durable of the Puerto Rican nationalist liberation groups. It gained national attention in 1950 by attempting to assassinate President Harry Truman and made headlines again later in the fifties when it attacked the floor of the United States Congress. In 1981 they were foiled in a plan to kidnap President Ronald Reagan's son in an effort to exchange him for jailed FALN members.

The most effective campaign of the FALN, however, was not these celebrated assaults on federal officials but a series of bombings that have taken place since the 1950s. The bombings have occurred mainly in Puerto Rico and New York, but in the 1980s the FALN expanded its operations to Chicago.

In the early 1980s the FALN formed an alliance with another Puerto Rican revolutionary group, the Macheteros. They have also been ideologically and administratively linked with three other Puerto Rican terrorist groups: (1) the Organization of Volunteers for Puerto Rican Revolution (OVRP), (2) the People's Revolutionary Commandos (CRP), and (3) the Armed Forces of Popular Resistance (FARP). Of these groups the Macheteros are the most organized, while FARP has the most violent record. All the Puerto Rican groups have claimed responsibility for Machetero attacks.

GROUP: Skinheads
AREA OF ACTIVITY: Urban centers, spreading across the United States
PHILOSOPHY: White supremacy, fascism
SYNOPSIS: The Skinheads are a relatively new movement in the United States. Imported from England, their motivation comes from neo-fascism. In the late 1970s, groups of English teenagers began shaving their heads and dressing like punk

rockers. Rejecting the norms of their parents, they embraced fascism and racial superiority.

The movement fit quite well with the white supremacy movement in the United States, and in the early 1980s Skinhead Americans were preaching a message of right-wing revolution. Unlike in England, in America the Skinheads found allies. While right-wing extremists may have been reluctant to embrace its music, they have embraced the Skinheads, which has become an Aryan youth movement.

American Skinhead dogma seems to be going the more traditional route of right-wing extremism. According to a major federal law enforcement agency, the real danger the Skinheads pose lies in the influence the older white supremacists seem to be having on them. Given their youth, Skinheads are more prone to violence than are older members of American extremist groups.

At this point, the Skinheads do not constitute a group with an organized infrastructure. They are potentially violent people, not a terrorist group. To date their violence has been random. Their most noted activity was the beating and crucifixion of a former leader who fell in love with a young black woman.

GROUP: **Symbionese Liberation Army**
AREA OF ACTIVITY: Mainly central and southern California
PHILOSOPHY: Left-wing revolutionary
SYNOPSIS: The SLA was a terrorist group of the 1970s with a small infrastructure and no more than a dozen operatives. Although the group is defunct, it is listed here for two reasons. First, the SLA experience is frequently cited to demonstrate the effect publicity has on terrorism. The SLA was able to maintain a high public profile by exploiting the willingness of the media to sensationalize their activities. Second, the group is frequently mentioned in studies of American terrorism.

The SLA was responsible for murders, bank robberies, and the famed kidnapping of Patricia Hearst. The group was small and had very little organization. Members were able to evade authorities, however, because of the group's size and use of sympathizers. After the Hearst kidnapping, members were gradually arrested. The remaining terrorists were killed in a shoot-out with the Los Angeles Police Department Special Weapons and Tactics Team.

GROUP: **United Freedom Front**
AREA OF ACTIVITY: Northeastern United States, Ohio, and Virginia
PHILOSOPHY: Left-wing revolutionary
SYNOPSIS: The United Freedom Front officially began its actions in 1982, but its members had operated under a variety of other names since 1975. The UFF represents a rebirth of 1960s-style left-wing groups. Originating in Portland, Maine, the group was fairly successful in launching military-type strikes and avoiding capture.

The UFF believed that it could overthrow the United States government with a "Tupamaro-styled" revolution. They believed that small strikes against industrial and government targets would create a revolutionary environment. They launched their campaign in the hope that other left-wing groups would join them.

Members of the UFF became masters of deception, going to great lengths to mislead authorities. The terrorists frequently used new hairstyles, disguises, and changes in body weight to avoid being recognized.

During its most active period, from 1983 to 1985, the UFF concentrated on bombing corporate, government, and military buildings. They were able to infiltrate security in one Navy yard to bomb the officers' club. According to a 1986 federal grand jury indictment, the UFF was responsible for a terrorist campaign. It financed its bombing campaign through a series of bank robberies from 1975 to 1984.

In 1988 the leading members of the group went on trial for the alleged crimes in the 1986 grand jury indictment. The leader of the group has been found guilty of murdering a police officer, and several other members have been charged with varying counts of assault.

Aside from bombing and robbery, the UFF's greatest strength has been its links to other left-wing movements. It has received rhetorical support from such groups as the May 19 Communist Organization and the Weather Underground. It has also been associated with militant correctional revolutionary groups.

GROUP: **Weather Underground**
AREA OF ACTIVITY: Northeastern United States
PHILOSOPHY: Left-wing revolutionary
SYNOPSIS: The Weather Underground is a by-product of the 1960s' radical student movement. Growing out of the Students for a Democratic Society (SDS) and its militant offshoot The Weathermen, the Weather Underground began waging a bombing campaign in the 1970s. After the arrest of most of its members, the group was thought to be defunct.

Despite the official dormant status of the Weather Underground, the group attacked an armored car in 1981 and killed its security guard. They also killed two police officers while making their escape. The purpose of the robbery was to raise funds for a new campaign, but in the following months most members were apprehended by a joint federal, state, and local antiterrorist investigative team.

Although membership in the group is at extremely low levels, activities continued in the eighties. The most recent surfacing has been a renewed bombing campaign waged by an allied group called the Armed Resistance Unit.

Other Terrorist Groups in the United States

Domestic terrorism and extremism is not the exclusive property of indigenous or "homegrown" terrorist groups. Some foreign groups have trained for terrorism on U.S. soil, while other foreign groups have attacked their enemies in the United States. Some groups have operated in America simply as a matter of convenience; these groups include Sikhs from India, Serbo-Croatians fighting for independence in Yugoslavia, Armenians fighting Turks, and various Latin American groups who bring their internal disputes to the United States. In addition, some groups have threatened to bring a campaign of terrorism to the American shore. These external groups are summarized in other sections.

▶ **EXTREMISM IN WESTERN EUROPE**

Angry Brigade
Armed Revolutionary Nuclei (NAR)
Basque Nation and Liberty (ETA)
Communist Combatant Cells (CCC)
Direct Action (AD)
First October Anti-fascist Resistance Group (GRAPO)
Irish National Liberation Army (INLA)
Military Sports Group Hoffman
Official Irish Republican Army
Provisional Irish Republican Army
Red Army Faction (RAF, also known as the Baader-Meinhof Gang)
Red Brigades (BR)
South Moluccan extremists in Holland

Ulster Defense Association
Warriors of Christ the King

GROUP: **Angry Brigade**
AREA OF ACTIVITY: Great Britain
PHILOSOPHY: Militant pro-labor, left-wing revolutionary
SYNOPSIS: Between 1968 and 1971, the Angry Brigade planted a number of bombs in
the London area and was responsible for defacing several government buildings.
In imitation of The Weathermen in the United States, members of the Angry
Brigade began turning to robbery and assault in 1971. In their last stage, they
attempted to imitate the Baader-Meinhof Gang.

The Angry Brigade remains one of the few examples of internal terrorism in
Britain. It sought to bring about a change in government policy and eventually to
usher in an age of socialism by murdering government officials. The group was
decimated by arrests in 1971.

GROUP: **Armed Revolutionary Nuclei (NAR)**
AREA OF ACTIVITY: Italy
PHILOSOPHY: Right-wing revolution, fascism
SYNOPSIS: The NAR was extremely active in Italy between 1977 and 1982. Although
the group became fairly dormant in the later 1980s, police believe its infrastructure
is still intact.

The NAR is an outgrowth of Italy's fascist movement, and it has been Italy's
most active right-wing terrorist group in recent years. Its method of operation is
very similar to that of the Red Brigade, but its support network is not as strong.
Several right-wing groups usually claim credit after an NAR operation.

Members of the group have trained at PLO camps in Lebanon. They also have
links to organized criminals in Italy, but they take pains to distance themselves
from traditional crimes. In addition to bombings and assassinations, the NAR has
been fairly successful in intimidating mainstream political parties.

The expressed goal of the NAR is to produce urban rioting that will lead, they
believe, to a fascist state. They believe that Italian society must have a fascist
structure in order for Italy to emerge as a world power and to stand firm against
communism. Like other Italian right-wing groups, the NAR began with indiscriminate bombings in public places. By 1977, however, most of their operations imitated left-wing activities.

GROUP: **Basque Nation and Liberty (ETA)**
AREA OF ACTIVITY: Northern Spain and southern France
PHILOSOPHY: Basque independence
SYNOPSIS: The ETA has long waged a terrorist campaign for an independent homeland. The Basque region is located near the Pyrenees Mountains on the border
between France and Spain. Inhabitants speak their own language and have their
own culture and customs. The area has been involved in a struggle for independence for several hundred years.

In the 1960s the ETA began a terrorist campaign to intensify the struggle, aiming most of its efforts at Spain. The Spanish government responded in 1968 by declaring a state of emergency in the Basque region and enacting tough anti-terrorist legislation. Several ETA members were arrested, but Spanish Prime Minister Luis Blanco was assassinated in revenge in 1973.

The struggle has continued into the late 1980s despite arrests and Spanish attempts to recognize Basque nationalism. Several secret fascist organizations have emerged in Spain, partly as a response to the ETA.

The ETA has a sophisticated organizational structure with work divided into logistical, political, and military operations. It does not have a great amount of popular backing in the Basque region but has overcome that problem through organization. Socialist in their rhetorical propaganda, members of the ETA are believed to have received training in Algeria, Libya, and the Soviet bloc.

GROUP: **Communist Combatant Cells (CCC)**
AREA OF ACTIVITY: Belgium
PHILOSOPHY: Left-wing revolutionary
SYNOPSIS: The CCC grew out of student revolts in the 1960s. Although their rhetoric has been particularly violent and they have engaged in many acts of terrorism, they have been noticeably ineffective. Their chief accomplishment has been the contin-ued bombing of a NATO fuel line. American businesses have also frequently been targeted. In an effort to increase its striking power, the CCC made an alliance with France's Direct Action in the mid-1980s.

GROUP: **Direct Action (AD)**
AREA OF ACTIVITY: France, with links to groups throughout Western Europe
PHILOSOPHY: Left-wing revolutionary
SYNOPSIS: Direct Action is unique among the powerful left-wing revolutionary groups in Europe. It is a "second-generation" terrorist group and has emerged as a leader. AD does not trace its links to the revolutionary period of the 1960s; rather, it developed in the late 1970s. In the 1980s it came to dominate Western European terrorist groups.

AD grew through several phases. It began as a communist revolutionary group, but soon turned to a more limited anti-American campaign. As a result of its anti-American stance, it attacked Israel and Jewish interests, eventually embracing the cause of the Palestinians. In the last half of the 1980s, AD focused its attention on an anti-NATO campaign.

Although it was isolated and autonomous in its early phases, AD created a new trend in West European terrorism by providing a framework to link left-wing terrorist groups from France, Belgium, West Germany, and Italy. AD enlisted the CCC, RAF, and Red Brigades in its anti-NATO campaign. Originally based in Paris, AD transformed itself into a truly international group.

The effectiveness of AD is debated among experts. Some observers have been alarmed by the unification of terrorist groups; others believe unification to be a sign of weakness. Police authorities believe AD would have no infrastructure were it not for the support it receives from other groups. Although AD is still active and engaging in headline-grabbing events, the level of left-wing violence has dropped in Europe since the unification.

GROUP: **First October Anti-Fascist Resistance Group (GRAPO)**
AREA OF ACTIVITY: Spain
PHILOSOPHY: Anarchism
SYNOPSIS: GRAPO emerged in the mid-1970s as a militant wing of the Spanish
  Communist Party. It is controlled by an executive commission and claims to
  operate throughout Spain. In reality, GRAPO is an urban organization, most of
  whose activities have been limited to Madrid. Although its rhetoric echoes communism, GRAPO is more a product of the deep-seated political divisions that still
  plague Spain. Its primary activities have been assassinations of political opponents. Members model themselves on nineteenth-century European anarchist
  groups.

GROUP: **Irish National Liberation Army (INLA)**
AREA OF ACTIVITY: Northern Ireland
PHILOSOPHY: Irish nationalism (see Official and Provisional IRA)
SYNOPSIS: The INLA was formed by militant members of the Official Irish Republican
  Army in the early 1970s. Disgruntled by the peace overtures the Officials were
  making to the British, militants broke away from the IRA to form the INLA. They
  formed an on-again, off-again alliance with the Provisional IRA, and their sympathies have remained with the Provisionals because they refuse peace with
  Britain.
      The INLA believes that a socialist Ireland can come about only through
  militant proletarian revolution. They are at war not only with the British but with
  the entire capitalist economic system. Unlike the Provisionals, who rhetorically
  apologize for terrorist murders, the INLA has engaged in indiscriminate violence.
  All murder is good in their eyes, because it creates a climate of revolution.
      The INLA has broken with the traditional pattern of Irish republicanism,
  reflecting instead a Marighella-type belief in revolution: violence creates the
  political situation. Their activities have included not only attacks on security
  forces but also bombings and murders of ordinary citizens who have little to do
  with the conflict. Such attacks, they believe, demonstrate the power of revolution.

GROUP: **Military Sports Group Hoffman**
AREA OF ACTIVITY: Federal Republic of Germany
PHILOSOPHY: Neo-Nazi, anti-Jewish, anti-American
SYNOPSIS: Military Sports Group Hoffman was a small group of neo-Nazis founded by
  Karl Heinz Hoffman in the late 1970s. The group was fiercely nationalistic,
  anti-American, and anti-Jewish. Officially a sports league, members of the group
  were organized along military lines and conducted mock military exercises.
      In 1979 sixteen members of the group went to Libya to train in PLO-
  sponsored terrorist training facilities. Upon returning to Germany, they attempted
  to wage a terrorist campaign. German police, however, intervened and eliminated
  the group by 1982. Some experts believe the group was linked to right-wing
  bombings, including a massive bombing during the Munich Oktoberfest. No direct
  evidence or definite proof has linked the Military Sports Group Hoffman to the
  Oktoberfest bombing, but the group is indicative of the potential for right-wing
  terrorism in the Federal Republic of Germany.

GROUP: **Official Irish Republican Army**
AREA OF ACTIVITY: Northern Ireland
PHILOSOPHY: Irish nationalism
SYNOPSIS: The Official Irish Republican Army was born of a 1916 rebellion in Dublin.
James Connolly led an anti-British guerrilla group called the Irish Volunteers in
the rebellion. In addition to having republican sentiments, Connolly was a Marxist
who wished to see Ireland under a socialist form of government. Although
Connolly was executed in a particularly brutal manner by the British, his ideas
lived on and came to dominate the IRA.

Some members of the IRA, however, became disenchanted with the emphasis
on socialism; they favored more direct action against the British and demanded
war. In the early 1960s this group broke away from the IRA and formed a
Provisional wing. The socialists remained in the original IRA, referring to themselves as the Official wing of the organization.

Internal struggle for control of the IRA typified the 1960s until Northern
Ireland was bathed in violence in 1969. When British troops came to quell the
disturbances, the Official IRA made peace with the Provisionals and joined to
fight the British. The Officials then broke ranks in 1972 to sign a separate peace
treaty with the British.

The peace treaty caused dissension within the Official IRA. Many members
believed that they should work for the peaceful evolution of socialism in Ireland,
but more militant ones wanted to continue the terrorist campaign against Britain.
This dissention had three results: The Irish National Liberation Army burst from
the ranks of the Officials to continue the war. Other Officials simply left to join the
Provisionals. Finally, some Officials who had no desire to leave the IRA engaged
in terrorism on their own in the name of the Official IRA.

GROUP: **Provisional Irish Republican Army**
AREA OF ACTIVITY: Northern Ireland
PHILOSOPHY: Irish nationalism
SYNOPSIS: The Provisional Irish Republican Army sees itself as the true heir of Irish
republicanism. Members trace their origins to the turn of the century and the Irish
Republican Brotherhood. During a rebellion in Dublin in 1916, Patrick Pearse, the
leader of the revolt, declared himself commanding general of the Irish Republican
Army. He was executed by the British but was replaced by Michael Collins, who
led the IRA during the Black and Tan War, which resulted in Irish independence.
The Provisionals identify with both Pearse and Collins.

The IRA was united throughout the struggle against Britain, but split in a civil
war that followed independence. Eamon de Valera, a leader of the Republic of
Ireland, virtually destroyed the IRA in that civil war. By the end of the 1930s, IRA
activities were limited to songs in Irish pubs, but the spirit lived on.

The IRA could not accept the division of Ireland into a Republic and a
northern section; a new group of terrorists sprang to life in 1945. After an
unsuccessful terrorist campaign against the North in the 1950s and 1960s, the IRA
sought peace with the British government. Some members, however, refused to
abandon terrorism and formed a Provisional wing to carry on the fight. The fight
became internal and soon involved Provisional attacks on the old Official IRA.

The Provisionals agreed to a temporary truce with the Officials in 1969 in order to fight the British in Ulster. Although the Officials signed a peace treaty with the British in 1972, the Provisionals continued the struggle. In terms of terrorism, the Provisionals have become the Irish Republican Army. They have been responsible for hundreds of murders and since 1985 have waged a campaign to sabotage the Anglo-Irish Peace Accord.

The Provisionals have developed a large organized crime network to support their operations. They have also allied themselves with other republican terrorist organizations, including the militant INLA. The political wing of the Provisional IRA is the *Sinn Fein*. Generally, when the media refer to the Irish Republican Army, they mean the Provisionals.

GROUP: **Red Army Faction (RAF)**
AREA OF ACTIVITY: Federal Republic of Germany
PHILOSOPHY: Left-wing revolutionary
SYNOPSIS: The RAF has become synonymous with Western European terrorism. Among the most resilient terrorist organizations, the group has been "destroyed" several times only to rise from its ashes. The RAF began as a mixture of student radicals and activists at the Free University of Berlin in 1968. Its activities soon turned violent under the direction of Andreas Baader and Ulricke Meinhof. By 1972 the RAF had been dubbed the Baader-Meinhof Gang, which was responsible for a number of terrorist actions in the Federal Republic.

In its early days the RAF financed its operations through bank robberies. Under Baader's influence, members became extremely proficient at the task. Throughout the 1970s the RAF set the standard for left-wing terrorist groups.

The staying power of the RAF was tested after the arrests of many of the leading members, including Baader and Meinhof. The group's support system remained intact after Meinhof's death in 1976 and Baader's suicide in 1977. The infrastructure allowed a new generation of terrorists to begin an assassination and bombing campaign in 1981.

By the mid-1980s, the character of the RAF had changed. The freewheeling days of banditry had given way to an organized anti-NATO campaign. Prime targets were U.S. military personnel stationed in Germany. As group members were arrested, remaining terrorists began to target the families of U.S. soldiers. The RAF was responsible for the attempted assassination of two NATO commanders. Currently, the RAF has joined with France's Direct Action in an anti-NATO campaign.

GROUP: **Red Brigades (BR)**
AREA OF ACTIVITY: Italy
PHILOSOPHY: Left-wing revolutionary
SYNOPSIS: Originating in 1970, the Red Brigades grew from an established left-of-center political party, the Metropolitan Political Collective. Feeling that the only acceptable road to communism was through violent revolution, a small group of self-proclaimed "historical nuclei" met in 1970 to begin a campaign of urban terrorism.

The Red Brigades group began with small-scale violence, but it was able to launch a full-scale campaign of terrorism after 1975. Among its more noted activities were the kidnapping and murder of Italian Prime Minister Aldo Moro and the kidnapping of American General James Dozier.

The Red Brigades were effective in the late 1970s and early 1980s due to their structure and strict discipline. They developed the ability to launch coordinated assaults, drawing on different cells. Prior to 1982 several Italian cities contained a Red Brigades cell capable of taking independent action. The Red Brigades came closer than any other Western European group to achieving a Latin American–style urban terrorist revolt.

In 1982 the fortunes of the Red Brigades began to wane. The Italian police, armed with information from several informants, began a nationwide crackdown. Many of the Red Brigades cells were destroyed, and remaining terrorists fled to France. The surviving cells joined the French Direct Action in 1985. Italian police believe that Red Brigades members are currently rebuilding their infrastructure.

GROUP: **South Moluccan Extremists in Holland**
AREA OF ACTIVITY: The Netherlands
PHILOSOPHY: South Moluccan independence
SYNOPSIS: The historical national homeland of South Molucca is in the Indonesian archipelago. When Indonesia won independence from the Netherlands in 1949, the Indonesians refused to allow the Moluccans national independence. Several thousand Moluccans fled to the Netherlands and pressured the Dutch government to exert its influence over the Indonesians. The Dutch have steadfastly refused, and Indonesia has been allowed to determine its own political destiny. Independence for South Molucca has not been on its agenda.

In the 1970s some members of the South Moluccan community in the Netherlands turned to terrorism to publicize their demands for an independent homeland. South Moluccan terrorism received a lot of press coverage because it involved major hostage incidents. Terrorists were involved in the highjacking of a train, which was successfully stormed by Dutch Marines, and the seizure of the Indonesian Consulate in Amsterdam. They also took over a Dutch school to secure the release of jailed compatriots, and they planned to kidnap the queen in the early 1980s.

The activities of these extremists prompted the Dutch government to form a special counterterrorist unit, which includes some of the most noted hostage negotiation experts in the world. The nationalist cause is popular among the South Moluccans, but the number of militants is extremely small. Most of the terrorists are second-generation exiles.

GROUP: **Ulster Defense Association**
AREA OF ACTIVITY: Northern Ireland
PHILOSOPHY: Anti-republican
SYNOPSIS: The Ulster Defense Association emerged in the 1970s in Northern Ireland as a unionist vigilante organization. Unionists want to remain under the protection of Great Britain and refuse to join the Republic of Ireland to the south. The UDA's primary targets have been members of the Provisional IRA, but they allegedly support a variety of unionist terrorist organizations.

Organized efforts on the part of Irish republicans have historically encountered militant unionist responses. The UDA should be considered in this light. Far from being the new organization that its birthdate suggests, the UDA and its actions are reflective of a unionist tradition. Unionist terrorist organizations have not received the attention devoted to groups like the IRA because they generally steer clear of government authority.

In the early 1970s the UDA adopted a pro-British position. Growing to more than 13,000 members by 1975, the UDA only supported strikes against republicans, supposedly after republican attacks in unionist areas. After 1975 they expanded their support of terrorist operations due to movements against the UDA by security forces and the growth of unionist terrorist organizations. Many unionist terrorist groups endorsed a campaign of terror against the republicans irrespective of republican actions.

The UDA is officially a political organization, and it denies involvement in terrorist activities. Terrorist groups associated with the UDA include the following:

Ulster Volunteer Force
Ulster Freedom Fighters
Red Hand Commandos

GROUP: **Warriors of Christ the King**
AREA OF ACTIVITY: Spain
PHILOSOPHY: fascism
SYNOPSIS: The Warriors of Christ the King are linked to the fascist movement in Spain. They dress in Nazi uniforms and usually operate in the open. They are more of an extremist group than a terrorist organization, but they do endorse violence.

The Warriors of Christ the King have connections with the Spanish National Syndicalist Party, a national fascist group, and they are reportedly linked to fascist terrorist organizations. They first appeared as a religious group that assaulted left-of-center priests. They expanded their goals to include a Spanish fascist state in the 1980s.

Other Terrorist Groups in Europe

Western Europe has many other terrorist groups (there are dozens in Italy alone), but they tend to fall into ideological camps. Most European groups have been responsible for only a small number of terrorist incidents, whereas the major groups have been responsible for entire terrorist campaigns.

The 1980s brought a major shift in European terrorism. Despite the continued activity of nationalist groups and the unification of left-wing terrorists, the majority of European terrorism originated in the Middle East. Europeans were not necessarily the targets of this new wave of terrorism; rather, it started to spill over from squabbles in the Middle East. Europe became a convenient battleground. Some of the groups responsible for this shift are discussed in the next section.

▶ EXTREMISM IN THE MIDDLE EAST

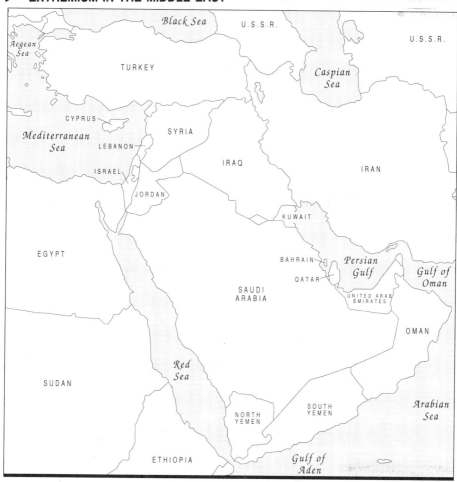

Abu Nidal
Black June
Black September
al-Fatah
Hizbollah
Irgun Zvai Leumi
Islamic Jihad
Japanese Red Army
Palestinian Liberation Organization
Popular Democratic Front for the Liberation of Palestine
Popular Front for the Liberation of Palestine
Popular Front for the Liberation of Palestine—General Command

GROUP: **Abu Nidal**
AREA OF ACTIVITY: Middle East and Western Europe; bases in Iraq, Syria, and Libya

PHILOSOPHY: Purification of Fatah
SYNOPSIS: Abu Nidal is the code name of Sabri al-Banna and is also used as the name
of the terrorist group he leads. Abu Nidal is one of the most secretive and deadly
terrorist groups in the Middle East. It originally began as a splinter group of
al-Fatah. Al-Banna became disillusioned with Fatah's leader, Yasser Arafat,
because he believed Arafat was becoming too moderate.

Al-Banna went to Baghdad, Iraq, in the early 1970s as Arafat's representative, for the purpose of establishing a Fatah branch office. He soon began to
operate independently, however, setting up an organization that rivaled Fatah's.
After the Camp David Peace Accord between Egypt and Israel, al-Banna broke
completely with Arafat and thereafter dedicated himself to a struggle for a united
kingdom of Islam and the destruction of Israel. Assuming the *nom de guerre* of
Abu Nidal, al-Banna included all moderate Arabs on his hit list.

The primary tactic of Abu Nidal has been assassination, although his group
has also sponsored masterful hijackings. The group has ruthlessly targeted anyone
who disagrees with its position. Ironically, the majority of its targets have been
Arab. The group has been responsible for the murders and attempted murders of
officials from Syria, Jordan, Kuwait, and Egypt. Of course, Israelis and their
American allies have also been targeted.

The group's headquarters have shifted between Iraq and Libya, and it has
obtained international support. Abu Nidal's terrorists have trained in Eastern
Europe, China, and North Korea as well as in the Middle East. The Abu Nidal
group has been responsible for a number of highly publicized operations. In 1985
terrorists hijacked an Egyptian airliner and murdered fifty-nine people. Later the
same year, two terrorist units opened fire on passengers waiting in ticket lines at
the Rome and Vienna airports during the Christmas season. In 1986 the group
bombed a Turkish synagogue, killing twenty-one worshippers. Abu Nidal has
become the master of international terrorism. Intelligence sources think he may be
dying of stomach cancer or that he has already expired.

GROUP: Black June
AREA OF ACTIVITY: Middle East and Western Europe (Black June is an operational arm
of the Abu Nidal group; see Abu Nidal)
PHILOSOPHY: Purification of Fatah
SYNOPSIS: Abu Nidal broke away from the PLO's al-Fatah in the mid-1970s and
formed his own terrorist group to purge the PLO leadership. In 1976 Abu Nidal
named the group Black June to protest Syrian expansion into Lebanon. Abu Nidal,
a Palestinian, welcomes no Syrian expansion at the expense of his people.

Black June can be viewed as an extension of Abu Nidal, but it must also be
seen as a reflection of continuing intra-Arab strife. Black June assassins have been
used against the PLO, Fatah, the PFLP, and Syria. Black June favors unification
of all Arab states (Pan Arabism) under a socialist democracy.

GROUP: Black September
AREA OF ACTIVITY: Israel, Lebanon, and Western Europe
PHILOSOPHY: Military wing of Fatah

SYNOPSIS: Yasser Arafat formed Black September after the PLO was expelled from Jordan in 1970. He developed the group as a terrorist strike force for Fatah, and the group took its name from the time of the Jordanian offensive.

Black September was responsible for several attacks in Israel, but became most noted for its seizure of Israeli athletes during the 1972 Munich Olympics. Toward the end of the 1970s, Israeli intelligence believed it had eliminated the group after a clandestine offensive that included the assassination of Black September's leadership.

Despite the Israeli offensive, Black September was restructured and redeployed by 1981. To the surprise of the Israelis, however, its major function was not to attack Israel, but to defend Fatah against attacks from Abu Nidal's Black June. Black September was damaged during the Israeli invasion of Lebanon, but it remained intact. It is currently being deployed against rival Arab targets in the Middle East and Western Europe.

GROUP: **Al-Fatah**
AREA OF ACTIVITY: Middle East, primarily Israel
PHILOSOPHY: Restoration of Palestine
SYNOPSIS: In 1963 Yasser Arafat and other militant Palestinian leaders sought to take control of the PLO. They hoped to turn it from a weak political structure into an organization that could wrest control of Palestine from Israel. Although the PLO remained a confederation of varied interests, Arafat gradually gained control of the organization. With his militant advisors he sought to develop the *fedayeen,* warriors prepared to die for Allah. Fatah became the organization of the *fedayeen*.

Arafat chose the name by arranging the initials of the leaders. Symbolically, Fatah stands for the Movement for the Liberation of Palestine. After the 1967 Arab-Israeli War, Fatah became the primary striking force for the PLO.

By 1971, Fatah's fortunes began to wane. The PLO had been expelled from Jordan in 1970, and Arafat was faced with a number of militant leaders who were not willing to subject themselves to Fatah's dictates. Many of these leaders began to break away to form their own terrorist organizations.

The major break in Fatah came when Abu Nidal left the group to form his own terrorist group and network in the mid-1970s. Abu Nidal believed that Arafat had grown soft in his approach to Israel and that Fatah was no longer fit to house the *fedayeen*. Although it remains one of the principle terrorist arms of the PLO, Fatah's importance had diminished by the late 1980s.

GROUP: **Hizbollah**
AREA OF ACTIVITY: Iran and Lebanon
PHILOSOPHY: Restoration of the kingdom of Islam under Shiite control
SYNOPSIS: Hizbollah is the name of a political party in Iran and of an Iranian-supported militia in Lebanon. Literally translated, it means the Party of God. It was revitalized in 1978 as a method of attacking the Shah of Iran, and it was used to help consolidate the revolution and the Ayatollah Khomeini's power. Since 1982 Khomeini has used Hizbollah to expand the Iranian Revolution into other countries. It is engaged in a holy war with the enemies of Shia Islam.

Directed through Iran, Hizbollah is most noticeable in Lebanon where it acts as a major militia in the civil war and as an umbrella for several terrorist organizations. It also maintains links with Shiite groups throughout the Middle East, including the Iraqui-based Shiite party al-Dawa. Hizbollah probably directs a Lebanese terrorist group, the Islamic Resistance Front, and it controls Islamic Jihad, a larger terrorist organization based in the Bekka Valley of Lebanon.

Hizbollah extremists are most noted for their suicidal bombing attacks. *Entehri* (suicide attacks) have been undertaken by a variety of terrorist organizations operating under Hizbollah's control. The names of two of the groups, Brides of Blood and Volunteers for Martyrdom, are indicative of the philosophy of Hizbollah.

According to Amir Taheri, a journalist who has covered Shiite terrorism, Hizbollah is distinguished by four characteristics.

1. It is an extension of the Iranian Revolution and seeks to bring about a Pan Arabic Islamic Republic.
2. Shiite theology dominates the group.
3. Its members, especially younger ones, accept a cult of martyrdom.
4. Hizbollah's Iranian leadership has shown no willingness to compromise.

On one level Hizbollah can be seen as a clearing house for a variety of Shiite terrorist groups. On another level it should be viewed as an Iranian political movement with Pan Islamic aspirations.

GROUP: **Irgun Zvai Leumi**
AREA OF ACTIVITY: Palestine (from 1945 to 1947)
PHILOSOPHY: Zionist homeland
SYNOPSIS: The Irgun Zvai Leumi was a Jewish terrorist group that fought for the establishment of modern Israel. Evolving from a 1930s group called the Stern Gang, the Irgun was responsible for waging a bombing campaign against the British Army in Palestine and against Arab Palestinians. The purpose of the campaign was twofold. On one hand, the Irgun was attempting to make the British occupation of Palestine too costly. On the other, it hoped to frighten Palestinians away from a Jewish state.

After the United Nations agreed to partition Palestine in 1947, Irgun terrorists began to kill individual Arabs and Arab families who remained in the Jewish sector. Such actions were especially common in Jerusalem. When the state of Israel was established, some members of the Irgun took a leading role in the Israeli government.

GROUP: **Islamic Jihad**
AREA OF ACTIVITY: Lebanon
PHILOSOPHY: Expansion of Iranian Revolution
SYNOPSIS: Islamic Jihad (literally, the Holy War of Islam) appeared as a terrorist group in Lebanon after the 1982 Israeli invasion. Although the group is quite nebulous and is an umbrella group for Shiite extremists, it should be viewed as an extension of the Hizbollah militia. American intelligence agencies believe Islamic Jihad is directly controlled by Iran.

Headquartered in the Bekka Valley, Islamic Jihad's main bastion of strength is Beirut. It has operated at times with Syrian approval; at other times it has opposed the Syrians. Some Muslim groups in Lebanon consider themselves to be at war with Islamic Jihad and have waged direct assaults upon it. Islamic Jihad has been limited to terrorist missions because it does not have the strength of other Lebanese militias.

Islamic Jihad has engaged in four primary activities since 1982: car bombings, ambushes, kidnappings, and suicide bombings. Kidnappings have achieved the greatest amount of publicity and have provided the most frustration for the West, especially for the United States. Islamic Jihad, under the direction of Hizbollah, has claimed responsibility for kidnapping and holding over twenty Western citizens. Unlike most terrorist kidnappers who begin to identify with their victims, members of Islamic Jihad routinely torture victims. They have also executed prisoners for propaganda value.

GROUP: **Japanese Red Army**
AREA OF ACTIVITY: Global
PHILOSOPHY: Anarchist; group has adopted the Palestinian cause
SYNOPSIS: One of the most enigmatic groups operating in the Middle East is the Japanese Red Army. The group has undergone several periods of reorganization, along with several brutal internal purges. Formed in the early 1970s, the Japanese Red Army is loosely based on an amalgamation of Marxism and feudal Japanese religious and warrior customs.

Although the group works toward a worldwide Marxist revolution, it is most noted for international attacks in support of the Palestinians. In 1972 three members of the Japanese Red Army murdered twenty-six Puerto Rican pilgrims in Israel's Lod Airport. In 1977 the Red Army obtained $6 million in ransom for the release of an airliner. In 1988 its members killed two U.S. sailors in Italy and allegedly planned to place a number of bombs in the United States to protest American policies in the Middle East. They operate around the world in the name of the Palestinians and their own mystical cause.

The Japanese Red Army is composed of a small group of militant radicals. It is based in Japan but has an infrastructure in the Middle East and is supported by Middle Eastern terrorist groups. It has embraced the cause of the Palestinians as a statement of international communist revolution.

GROUP: **Palestinian Liberation Organization**
AREA OF ACTIVITY: Middle East, Western Europe; various splinter groups are located throughout the Middle East
PHILOSOPHY: Restoration of Palestine
SYNOPSIS: The Palestinian Liberation Organization was formed in 1964 as a revolutionary movement designed to recapture Palestine from Israel. It is not a single cohesive group; rather, it is a confederation of various Palestinian interest and terrorist groups. Militant members of the PLO are called *fedayeen,* those prepared to sacrifice their lives for Allah.

After the 1967 Arab-Israeli War, the PLO fled to Jordan under the domination of Yasser Arafat and his military organization, al-Fatah (see Fatah). After the failure of conventional Arab armies in 1967, *fedayeen* from Fatah achieved several tactical successes against the Israelis by launching hit-and-run raids from Jordan. The Israelis struck back, often sending aircraft and ground forces into Jordan. The growing political strength of the PLO prompted Jordan's King Hussein to attack the PLO bases in September 1970. The PLO was driven into Lebanon after suffering 7,000 casualties.

Arafat formed Black September as a response to Hussein's offensive, but Fatah began to splinter. Several militant terrorist groups formed in the early 1970s, and many still exist today. When the PLO fled to Lebanon, it found itself becoming the pawn of several Arab states; this was the main cause of Fatah's splintering. Each new splinter group represented the position of a particular Arab state.

The most serious blow to the PLO came in 1982 when Israel invaded Lebanon. Faced with conventional battle, Arafat was forced to retreat north to Beirut, only to be attacked by the Syrians. Arafat's supporters and Fatah were forced to scatter.

Since 1985 Arafat has been attempting to reconcile Fatah with Syria. Reconciliation has been difficult, because Syria has political designs on the Mediterranean coast irrespective of the Palestinian question. The Syrians see themselves in direct competition with Arafat for control of territory in Lebanon and Israel.

In 1987 and 1988 Arafat attempted a new tactic against the Israelis. As Fatah was splintered and his military fortunes were in dire straits, Arafat encouraged Palestinians under Israeli control to begin a campaign of passive civil disobedience. The tactic was a political success because the Israelis overreacted and killed dozens of Palestinian demonstrators, damaging the Israelis in their allies' eyes.

The future of the PLO is in question, and Arafat does not control the majority of terrorist groups. By the end of the eighties, Fatah had temporarily abandoned its terrorist campaign; other PLO groups had not. Militant groups of PLO terrorists include the following:

Arab Liberation Front (pro-Arafat)
al-Fatah (pro Arafat)
Black June (Abu Nidal, anti-Arafat)
Palestine Liberation Front (pro-Syrian)
Popular Democratic Front for the Liberation of Palestine (opposed to all diplomatic settlements with Israel)
Popular Front for the Liberation of Palestine (pro-Syrian)
Popular Front for the Liberation of Palestine—General Command (pro-Syrian)
al-Intifada (pro-Syrian)
Popular Struggle Front (pro-Syrian)
Black September (pro-Arafat)

Most of the PLO groups were formed in the 1970s, with their primary target being Israel. The formation of Black June by Abu Nidal signaled a new era as anti-Arafat groups began an internal terrorist struggle to wrest control from Arafat. In 1983 the Syrians formed the Popular Struggle Front to gain control of the PLO. They also supported a 2,500-member PLO militia, al-Intifada, under the control of Colonel Saed Musa. Arafat formed the Arab Liberation Front and revitalized Black September to protect himself from Abu Nidal and the Syrians.

According to intelligence sources, Abu Nidal is gravely ill or dead, but his organization lives on. Black June is a Palestinian organization at war with Arafat; only the desire to purify Fatah caused Abu Nidal to approach his archenemies, the Syrians. Abu Nidal harbored no love for the Syrians, and Black June's alliance with Syria is based only on mutual hatred of Arafat. The PLO, in short, is a highly splintered organization.

GROUP: Popular Democratic Front for the Liberation of Palestine (PDFLP)
AREA OF ACTIVITY: Lebanon, Israel; headquartered in Syria
PHILOSOPHY: Restoration of Palestine
SYNOPSIS: The PDFLP broke away from another PLO splinter group, the Popular
Front for the Liberation of Palestine, in 1969. Formed by Naif Hawatmeh, a Greek
Orthodox Christian from Jordan, the PDFLP attacked the PFLP in Beirut and
Amman. Direct intervention by Arafat brought fighting to a close, but the struc-
tures of both groups remained intact. Hawatmeh then focused most of his attention
on Israel throughout the 1970s.

Although the PDFLP was not overly active in the 1980s, it remains one of the
more interesting groups in the Middle East. First of all, Hawatmeh is neither
Muslim nor Palestinian. Second, the PDFLP advocates socialism over nationalism, and, despite its terrorist attacks on Israel, advocates equal rights for Palestinian Arabs and Jews. Control of Palestine, the PDLFP maintains, should be
determined by direct elections in a socialist republic. Neither Arabs nor Jews
should be allowed to dominate the region as a homeland.

GROUP: Popular Front for the Liberation of Palestine (PFLP)
AREA OF ACTIVITY: Lebanon, Israel; headquartered in Syria
PHILOSOPHY: Restoration of Palestine
SYNOPSIS: The Popular Front for the Liberation of Palestine was formed in 1967 after
the Arab defeat in the Six-Day War. It was composed of a variety of small groups
united through the efforts of Dr. George Habash and his chief of staff, Dr. Wadi
Hadad. The PFLP swore to reject any settlement in the Middle East that failed to
specify the destruction of Israel and the return of Palestine to Arab Palestinians.
Known as the Rejectionist Front, the position is supported by many Middle
Eastern leaders, including Moamar Khadaffy.

In the 1970s the PFLP developed a reputation for sponsoring the PLO's most
savage attacks against Israel. In 1975 Habash expelled Hadad, reportedly for
Hadad's endorsement of extreme violence, but many intelligence sources believed
this move was designed to give Hadad more autonomy.

The PFLP received three serious blows in the 1980s. The Israeli invasion of
Lebanon forced the organization into a general retreat, and George Habash's
health failed. In addition, Syria began to form rival organizations inside the PLO.

**GROUP: Popular Front for the Liberation of Palestine—General Command
(PFLP—General Command)**
AREA OF ACTIVITY: Lebanon, Israel; headquartered in Syria
PHILOSOPHY: Restoration of Palestine
SYNOPSIS: The Popular Front for the Liberation of Palestine—General Command was
formed in 1959, and it joined the Popular Front for the Liberation of Palestine after

1967's Six-Day War. Disillusioned by the internal fighting inside the PFLP, the General Command broke away in the early 1970s for its own campaign against Israel.

The structure of the General Command remained intact after the 1982 Israeli invasion of Lebanon, and the organization has emerged from the Lebanese civil war as one of the most militant organizations in the Middle East. With a strength of nearly 800, the PFLP—General Command is a staunchly pro-Syrian force.

Other Terrorist Groups in the Middle East

Many other groups are operating in the Middle East. As inhabitants of the area seek to define their political structure and the future of Islam, violence and terrorism will continue. The Palestinian question will plague the area for quite some time, as will the future course of the Iranian Revolution. New terrorist groups are created routinely in this climate of violence. For a more comprehensive view of the Middle East, see Chapter 5.

▶ EXTREMISM IN LATIN AMERICA

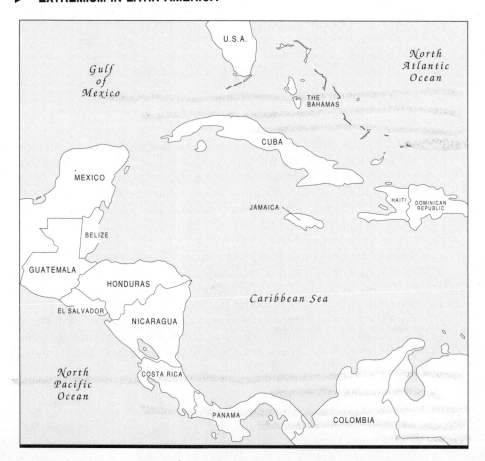

Argentine Anti-Communist Alliance (Triple A)
Farabundo Marti Front for National Liberation (FMLN)
Montoneros
M-19
National Liberation Alliance (ALN)
National Liberation Movement (MLN) (Tupamaros)
Orden
People's Revolutionary Army, Argentina (ERP)
People's Revolutionary Army, El Salvador (ERP)
Shining Path

GROUP: **Argentine Anti-Communist Alliance (Triple A)**
AREA OF ACTIVITY: Argentina (from 1972 to 1981)
PHILOSOPHY: Right-wing death squad
SYNOPSIS: The Triple A was formed secretly by members of Argentina's police and
    military forces. Faced with the collapse of the government and the threat of
    left-wing revolution in the 1970s, the police and military began to illegally "arrest"
    political opponents and murder them. Most of the victims were listed as having
    "disappeared."

Prior to 1975 the Triple A was formalized with a secret infrastructure, and its activities were carried out apart from government functions. After 1975, when Argentina was ruled by a military junta, the Triple A was less clandestine, becoming a semiofficial government organization.

GROUP: Farabundo Martí Front for National Liberation (FMLN)
AREA OF ACTIVITY: El Salvador
PHILOSOPHY: Unification of El Salvador's revolutionary forces
SYNOPSIS: The FMLN was gradually formed in the late 1970s as El Salvadorean leftists began to unite under a common banner. Although right-wing governmental coalitions refer to the FMLN as a terrorist group, it actually represents a coalition of guerrilla forces. There are groups inside the coalition that use terrorism, but the FMLN has rejected it.

The groups that compose the FMLN in El Salvador are the following:

Popular Forces of Liberation (FPL), a communist group formed in 1970
People's Revolutionary Army (ERP), a terrorist group formed in 1971
Front for United Popular Action (FAPU), originally a political party of urban workers who joined the rural guerrillas in 1974
Popular Revolutionary Block (BPR), rural guerrillas formed in 1974
February 28 Popular Leagues (LP-28), guerrillas recruited from San Salvador's slums in 1977
Armed Forces of National Resistance (FARN), a guerrilla group formed in 1974
People's Revolutionary Army of the Armed Forces of National Resistance (ERP-FARN), a splinter group formed by FARN in 1975 to wage urban terrorism

With the exception of the ERP and the ERP-FARN, the revolutionary movement in El Salvador does not routinely employ terrorism. Governmental forces in El Salvador have encouraged North Americans to brand all groups as terrorists and communists in the hope of obtaining more American aid.

GROUP: Montoneros
AREA OF ACTIVITY: Argentina (from 1975 to 1979)
PHILOSOPHY: Left-wing Peronists
SYNOPSIS: The Montoneros were formed by left-wing followers of Argentina's former leader, Juan Perón. In the early 1970s Perón returned from exile to lead the Argentinean government, but failing health forced him to leave office. In a confused political situation, the military seized control of the government. The Montoneros formed in 1975 to protest that military takeover.

The Montoneros employed terrorist tactics in a bid to take over Argentina's labor movement, but most of their violent activity was focused on a rural guerrilla campaign. After failing in the labor arena, urban squads began a campaign of bombing, assassination, and kidnapping. The Montoneros were brutally destroyed by military repression.

GROUP: M-19
AREA OF ACTIVITY: Colombia

PHILOSOPHY: Left-wing revolution

SYNOPSIS: M-19 is a powerful left-wing terrorist group operating in Colombia. The group has been linked to narcotics and its actions have helped coin the term *narcoterrorism*. In the late 1970s, M-19 represented a small group of urban radicals in Colombia. The group formed an alliance with organized criminals there to provide protection for the Colombian drug trade, and its ranks swelled.

Organized crime has no vested interest in terrorism, but it has found the alliance with M-19 profitable. Crime syndicates produce drugs and prepare them for international distribution. M-19 furnishes transportation out of the country and protection against government raids. The criminals pay the terrorists well for their services, and the money is recycled into revolutionary activities.

M-19 has achieved quite a bit of publicity in the United States for two particularly dramatic acts. In one instance, the group attacked the Supreme Court building in Bogota to keep the Colombian government from extraditing a drug dealer to the United States. Fighting was heavy, and mechanized infantry units from the Colombian Army were required to retake the building. Several justices were killed and overall casualties were heavy.

In the second instance, terrorists from M-19 assassinated the attorney general of Colombia in 1988. The prosecutor was known for his diligent efforts to eradicate the drug trade and to attack organized crime. He had announced a series of arrest warrants after a lengthy investigation. In response, M-19 killed him and his bodyguards as he left work for home one evening.

Several terrorist groups have tried to follow the pattern of M-19, but none have achieved the same level of success. M-19 grew from 500 followers in the late 1970s to 20,000 by the mid-1980s. They have become masters of the narcotics trade.

GROUP: **National Liberation Alliance (ALN)**
AREA OF ACTIVITY: Brazil (from 1968 to 1972)
PHILOSOPHY: Left-wing revolution
SYNOPSIS: The National Liberation Alliance was a communist revolutionary group that operated in Brazil from 1968 to 1972. Closely allied with the Popular Vanguard of the Revolution (UPR), the ALN operated almost exclusively within an urban environment. This was in stark contrast to the conventional wisdom of the Cuban Revolution, which suggested that operations be run from a rural setting.

The ALN was not successful in bringing about revolution, and it was virtually destroyed along with other left-wing groups in Brazil during a police crackdown in 1972. Rural guerrilla activities in Brazil did not cease until 1975.

The ALN had importance beyond its short life. Its founder and leader was Carlos Marighella, who was killed in a police ambush in Sao Paulo in 1969. He popularized ideas of urban terrorism far beyond the boundaries of Latin America by means of his two books, which became popular among terrorists: *For the Liberation of Brazil* and *The Minimanual of the Urban Guerrilla*.

GROUP: **National Liberation Movement (MLN) (Tupamaros)**
AREA OF ACTIVITY: Uruguay (from 1963 to 1972)

PHILOSOPHY: Left-wing revolution

SYNOPSIS: The MLN, whose members were better known as the Tupamaros, was formed in 1963 during a period of labor unrest in Uruguay. Operating almost exclusively in the capital city of Montevideo, the Tupamaros came to embody urban terrorism. Their organizational models and methods have been copied by terrorists around the world. No other group in Latin America or Europe has come closer to perfecting the Marighella-type revolution.

   The Tupamaros began by raiding a hunting club and ended by helping to bring down the democratic government of Uruguay. They were destroyed by a repressive government when they reached their zenith in 1972. The full story of the Tupamaros is told in Chapter 8.

   Aside from their revolution in Uruguay, the Tupamaros remain important because they have served as a model for urban revolution. Groups ranging from Italy's Red Brigades to America's right-wing group called The Order have followed the Tupamaros' organizational and operational patterns.

GROUP: **Orden**
AREA OF ACTIVITY: El Salvador
PHILOSOPHY: Death squads, counterrevolution
SYNOPSIS: Orden was formed as a secret society in El Salvador in the early 1950s to counter revolutionary activities. It drew its ranks from the National Guard, the Treasury Police, and right-wing sympathizers. Orden became an official agent of the government in the 1960s but was disbanded by 1979 under pressure from the United States.

   Despite official denial, Orden continues to exist. It has been responsible for many deaths, thousands more than can be laid to left-wing terrorists in El Salvador. Orden's basic tactic is to "arrest" suspected revolutionaries. Victims are then either tortured and killed, or tortured and dropped at police or National Guard stations. Executed victims are frequently disposed of in a large dumping ground outside of San Salvador, and they commonly have EM, a Spanish acronym for Death Squad, carved in their foreheads or chests.

   Of its thousands of murders, Orden's most noted were the assassination of Catholic Archbishop Oscar Romero during the celebration of a mass and the rape-murder of four American churchwomen who worked with El Salvador's poor. Although Orden supports government policies, it officially exists outside the government and membership in it is illegal. Members, however, are rarely prosecuted.

GROUP: **People's Revolutionary Army (ERP), Argentina**
AREA OF ACTIVITY: Argentina (from 1969 to 1980)
PHILOSOPHY: Left-wing revolution
SYNOPSIS: The ERP developed as an offshoot of the Revolutionary Socialist Party in 1969. One of many groups vying for power in the post-Perón era, the ERP carried out a twofold campaign. They conducted a rural campaign, Cuban fashion, but they also maintained urban terrorists who raised money through robberies and kidnappings.

In the 1970s the ERP went to war with the Triple A, assassinating suspected members of right-wing death squads. As Triple A's pressure increased, the ERP began to murder family members of Argentina's police and military personnel. The ERP coordinated most of its activities through the Junta for Coordinating Revolutions (JCR), an organization that nominally linked communist groups throughout South America.

Even though the urban units were devoted exclusively to terrorism, the ERP fought mainly as a rural guerrilla group. They briefly joined forces with the Perónist Montoneros, and after 1972 several of the Tupamaros fleeing Uruguay joined the ERP.

Despite its successful urban campaign, the ERP proved no match for terrorism on the right. In 1976 its primary leaders were arrested, and by 1980 it had been reduced to small urban cells incapable of supporting a campaign. The ERP still exists and enjoys sympathy from left-wing intellectuals and theologians, but it lacks the infrastructure to conduct terrorist activities. It should not be confused with the ERP of El Salvador.

GROUP: **People's Revolutionary Army (ERP), El Salvador**
AREA OF ACTIVITY: El Salvador
PHILOSOPHY: Left-wing revolutionary
SYNOPSIS: The ERP of El Salvador is one of a number of revolutionary groups fighting under the banner of the Farabundo Martí Front for National Liberation (FMLN). It was formed in 1971 and specializes in individual acts of sabotage and terrorism. In 1975 the Armed Forces for National Resistance (FARN) formed a splinter version of the ERP and waged its own campaign of terrorism. Both FARN and the ERP can be considered terrorist groups, although not all revolutionary forces in El Salvador endorse terrorism.

The ERP has been responsible for a number of assassinations of Salvadorean officials, and it is also responsible for the murder of a U.S. Navy SEAL commander and six U.S. Marines in separate instances (see FMLN).

GROUP: **Shining Path**
AREA OF ACTIVITY: Peru
PHILOSOPHY: Left-wing revolutionary
SYNOPSIS: The Shining Path began operating in Peru in the late 1970s. Beginning as a guerrilla group, it had turned to the tactics of terrorism by 1981. Aside from reportage on its terrorist campaign, the group received its most extensive news coverage when it blacked out almost half the nation during a visit from the Pope.

Other Terrorist Groups in Latin America

The problems of terrorism, guerrilla warfare, and violence in Central and South America are discussed in other parts of this book. This section is purposely limited because the definition of terrorism can be extremely broad in Latin America. The groups discussed here are only those operating *outside* of government control. Not all aspects of Latin American terrorism are presented, nor is there any attempt to discuss governmental repression or revolutionary guerrillas. For a more in-depth discussion of these points, see Chapter 4.

There are many groups operating in Latin America. Those presented here were selected because they are prominent and directly related to events or phenomena discussed in the text. They are a far from exhaustive sampling.

While some scholars have attempted to construct models of revolution and repression in Latin America, others have argued that North Americans have failed to understand the political dynamics of the area. This debate makes any discussion of terrorism in Latin America extremely controversial and confusing. As we are focusing on the nature of terrorism in general, our discussions are necessarily limited. When you read about Latin America in this book, keep in mind that terrorism is specifically limited to groups outside of and apart from governmental authority.

SUMMARY OF CHAPTER TWO

This chapter has listed terrorist and extremist groups in selected geographical regions. You should preview this chapter to become familiar with the groups, but it is primarily designed to be a reference tool. As you study terrorism, you will encounter the names of a multitude of organizations. This chapter can be used to refresh your memory.

IF YOU WANT TO READ FURTHER . . .

Peter Janke has produced one of the most definitive anthologies of terrorist groups. Titled *Guerrilla and Terrorist Organizations: A World Directory and Bibliography,* it is one of the best reference works available. Janke arranged his work by country and provided a detailed description of almost every terrorist group in the world. The book is highly organized, well written, and backed by excellent research. Janke's details allow you to walk through some of the most complex political situations with ease, and you need not have an extensive background in terrorism to understand the concepts.

Another excellent reference work is George Rosie's *The Directory of International Terrorism.* This is a fairly unique book, containing summaries of incidents, groups, counterterrorist organizations, and intelligence units. Rosie even lists the names of the major participants in terrorist incidents, including the terrorists, the police, and the victims. It is a handy guide.

Rosie's directory can be complemented by John Thackrah's *Encyclopedia of Terrorism and Political Violence.* Thackrah's book contains detailed descriptions of terrorist groups and the issues surrounding them. Groups are listed alphabetically along with subjects such as narcoterrorism, hostages, and media. Thackrah's approach is a bit less focused than Janke's, but the breadth of his information makes the book helpful and valuable.

One of the better bibliographical guides is *International Terrorism: A Bibliography* by Amos Lakos. Lakos has assembled hundreds upon hundreds of books and articles on every major division of terrorism. He considers each group by geographical location. Bibliographies on groups are complemented by subject headings concerning specific types of terrorism. Lakos has given researchers, students, and the public an indispensable research tool.

PROPAGANDA BY THE DEED:
TERRORIST TRADITIONS IN THE WEST

Western civilization has produced its own brand of terrorism. In the late 1700s when monarchies started giving way to democracies, struggles erupted among groups competing for power. The Industrial Revolution in the 1800s added complexity to the situation. Western terrorism emerged from this context, usually presenting itself as a revolutionary activity. The methods of terrorism were developed by nineteenth-century anarchists, but they were subsequently adopted by nationalistic and ideological movements. Far from being part of a conspiracy or network, Western terrorism grew out of demands for democracy and evolved into a revolutionary ideal. This chapter summarizes the development of terrorist thought in the West.

After reading this chapter, you should be able to do the following.

1. Discuss the controversial role of democracy in the practice of Western terrorism
2. Briefly describe the impact of the Enlightenment and the revolutions of the 1700s on democracy
3. Summarize the role of nineteenth-century anarchists and their influence on revolutionary, nationalistic, and right-wing terrorism
4. Identify the proponents of violent revolutionary change among the nineteenth-century anarchists
5. Trace the spread of revolutionary violence from Europe to America through Johan Most
6. Describe how interpretations of the Russian Revolution and Trotsky's ideas have confused the central issues of Western extremism and terrorism
7. Define "old" and "new" terrorism

THE CONTROVERSIAL RELATIONSHIP OF DEMOCRACY AND TERRORISM

Modern terrorism in the West did not develop in a vacuum; it was a result of changes in political philosophy and governmental policies. More directly, it reflected changes in the general attitude of the population: common people started to believe that governments should be controlled by their citizens. Naturally, some governments did not want to relinquish their control to the citizenry and scoffed at the idea of democracy.

By the mid-1800s strife between the controllers of industry and the industrial workers had added to the ideological debate over democracy. All of these social changes did not create terrorism, but they provided fertile soil in which it could grow.

Terrorism has always been present in Western civilization in the sense that a government's will could be imposed through tactics of terror, but modern terrorist ideology was a product of the 1800s. It developed because several factors came into play to produce an environment allowing terrorism to grow. Without those conditions, terrorism could not have evolved in its patchwork fashion in the West.

Some researchers believe that democracy was one of the most crucial factors in the development of Western terrorism. Without democracy, these analysts have argued, revolutionary terrorism could not have survived. Terrorists need freedom and mobility to operate; democracy gave them the ability to organize and attack. This fact has caused some researchers to focus on problems inherent in democracy.

Other analysts have been highly critical of this line of logic. They have pointed to the rise of anarchist terrorism in czarist Russia as an example of a nondemocratic context. The "philosophy of the bomb," which translates as the use of violence to convey a message, and "propaganda by the deed"—committing terrorist acts to publicize a cause—were tactics first practiced in Russia, critics have maintained, and spread only rhetorically to the Western democracies. In addition, some democracies, such as those in Scandinavia, have experienced almost no terrorism. Hence, not all analysts believe that democracy is closely related to terrorism.

Walter Laqueur (1987, 73) explained the first position well. According to Laqueur, democracy gives terrorists the opportunity to maneuver. In open societies, terrorists are free to organize, select targets, and obtain resources. Under a repressive government individual terrorists can more easily be traced, monitored, controlled, and eliminated. Repression is the worst enemy of terrorism, democracy its best friend. Terrorists need freedom. Laqueur's logic has been accepted by a whole host of researchers who correlate the rise of Western democracies with the rise of terrorism.

Analysts who stress the correlation of democracy to terrorism do not argue for the end of democracy, but rather for more rigid social controls within democractic norms. Paul Wilkinson (1974, 23) argued that practicing democracy does not necessarily imply that terrorism must be tolerated; he believed a democratic state could practice counterterrorism. That is, a state could maintain democratic norms while using its power against terrorists to stop their violent activity. He cited Israel as an example of a democratic state that employs counterterrorism.

This position has spawned a heated debate among specialists in terrorism. Some people have argued that Wilkinson and Laqueur represent a conservative position. Beau Grosscup (1987, 24–28) claimed that this conservative position is used to justify an increase of executive power in democratic governments, and that the relationship between democracy and terrorism is thus exploited to the advantage of executive authorities.

Grosscup stated that terrorism experts often cite "democratic excesses" as the primary reason for the resurgence of terrorism in the 1960s. By this reasoning, terrorists can be seen as a group of spoiled children who cannot discipline themselves. The West is experiencing an explosion of terrorism because society became too tolerant, according to the conservative line of logic. Grosscup stated that conservatives have attempted to popularize this thesis. In their minds, he said, permissiveness spawned terrorism.

Grosscup went on to say that this argument has served to foster an antipermissive ideology, or set of beliefs, which is accompanied by a whole set of incorrect assumptions. Grosscup pointed out that conservatives encourage us to simplify terrorism, to see it as a communist threat rather than the outcome of complex social processes. They also encourage us to ignore the evidence of permissive democratic societies that experience little or no terrorism.

Grosscup analyzed incidents in several areas of the world to demonstrate his thesis, arguing that most terrorism is the result of regional disputes that have little to do with either democracy or superpower confrontations. For example, conservative researchers look at the Middle East and see the ominous hand of the Soviet Union behind most acts of terror. This is absurd, Grosscup said: Middle Eastern terrorism is the product of regional tensions.

Richard Rubenstein (1987, 49–64) agreed with Grosscup's position. Terrorism experts, he wrote, have become no more than spokespersons for counterterrorism and the maintenance of governmental power. They approach their topic with biases and a political agenda of conservatism. Using a Marxist framework for analyzing violence, Rubenstein cautioned that most terrorism experts miss the point. They focus on the form of government instead of looking at the form and patterns of violence.

Michael Stohl (1988, 22–23) was also critical of Laqueur's position, although he didn't endorse critics such as Grosscup and Rubenstein. Stohl said that focusing on the relationship between democracy and terrorism causes us to miss an essential element of the topic. Terrorism is most frequently used to repress political beliefs. In this sense, it has no relation to democracy at all. Terrorism is antidemocratic by nature. In addition, Stohl believed that insurgent terrorism is simply a popular method of struggle—and democracies have no special claim to insurgent terrorists.

Kachig Tololyan (1988) was highly critical of the whole argument. He wrote that analysts like Laqueur and Wilkinson have spoken of a special role for democracy, and that their critics have argued against them. The entire debate misses the point, in Tololyan's analysis. The real issue behind terrorism is not the current structure and response of democratic states, but the conditions that produce terrorism. In other words, terrorism is the result of specific historical and cultural factors. In the West this implies a relationship with the struggle for and rise of democracy, but democracy has little bearing on terrorism in other parts of the world.

No matter which position is correct, Tololyan makes a point we should consider. The rise of modern terrorism in the West is linked to the struggle for freedom in the Western world. In the 1700s and early 1800s most Europeans did not enjoy freedom, and America was still only an experiment. A change in social perceptions and actions, however, revolutionized the system and structure of Western governments. Many forms of violence accompanied the struggle for democracy; terrorism was one of them.

Enlightenment, Revolution, and the Growth of Democracy

The evolution of Western terrorism can be traced by following the growth of democracy. Modern Western democracies have been directly influenced by two phenomena evolving in Western Europe over the past 200 years. The first was a gradual philo-sophical change that took place mainly in the 1700s. The second was a series of violent revolutions, combined with legislative victories, that occurred generally in the 1800s.

In historiography the philosophical change of the eighteenth century is known as the Enlightenment or the Age of Reason. It grew out of a revolution in scientific inquiry in the 1600s and dominated many of the intellectual activities of the 1700s. Democratic principles were at the base of the Enlightenment.

The thinkers of the Enlightenment began to question the logic of European social structures. The scientific discoveries of the 1600s had shaken centuries of belief in the order of creation. Social philosophers of the late 1600s and throughout the 1700s were given the authority and ability to question the social makeup because of that revolution in science.

Just as Isaac Newton had isolated the principles of motion, social philosophers believed they could find the principles governing social actions and organizations. They divided themselves into many competing schools of philosophy, yet together they helped to create an environment in which the old rules of social order no longer held true. From this platform they began to question the authority of kings. As was to be expected, kings and other nobles were not enamored with this.

Almost without exception Enlightenment philosophers from France, England, and the German states called for the establishment of democracies to guarantee freedom and personal rights. Even though they disagreed on the structure and methods of government, Enlightenment thinkers universally gravitated toward democracy.

The enlightened philosophers held several ideas in common. Citizens had rights, the philosophers argued. Governments were to be created to protect those rights and common people were to control the government. Rights were to be guaranteed by a social contract or constitution that spelled out the rights of citizens and limited government power. The flame of democracy began to burn throughout the West, and by 1770 revolution was in the air.

By the late 1700s talk of democracy had moved from intellectual circles to the streets and eventually to the battlefields. In North America the British colonies revolted, demanding the same democratic rights as British citizens. They ended by forming an independent United States of America. It was an enlightened democracy, a product of the 1700s.

The American Revolution was important to Europe, but it was viewed primarily as a "conservative" revolution. The locus of power simply moved from London to Philadelphia, and most American leaders (with notable exceptions, such as Thomas Jefferson) perceived the United States to be a British democracy without Britain. The birth of the United States was a lengthy evolutionary process. The Revolutionary War was seen within the context of traditional European power struggles and its outcome as resembling Britian without a king. Such perceptions of democracy would change in the streets of Paris.

By 1795 France was in the midst of a class revolution. The American Revolution had merely transferred power from the British upper classes to the American upper classes. In France, however, power was transferred *between* classes. Primarily, the middle class wrested power from the nobility and did so in an internal struggle dominated by ideological positions. It was extremely bloody and the first revolution in the modern sense of the word.

If America represented a long-term evolution toward democracy, in 1795 France represented a radical shift in power structures. European governments not only took notice, but the nobles and their upper-class supporters were frightened beyond their wildest dreams. They mobilized their armies to stop the French, and Europe was at war for twenty years.

Ironically, the term *terrorism* appeared during this period. Edmund Burke, a noted British political philosopher of the eighteenth century, used the word to describe the situation in revolutionary Paris. He referred to the violence as the "reign of terror." It is extremely interesting to note that he was referring to neither the revolutionaries nor the violence created by radicals. Burke coined *terrorism* to describe the actions of the new government. The reign of terror involved the slaughter of enemies of the revolution after the government had been seized from the French king.

Today the word evokes different connotations and is most frequently associated with revolution and crime, not with repression. Terrorism is now viewed as clandestine, subversive warfare in the West.

The reason the meaning of terrorism changed in Western minds was essentially due to the nature of European violence in the 1800s. In the short run, the French Revolution did not bring democracy; it brought Napoleon. Under the surface, however, democratic ideas continued to grow. The ideas led to further political struggles and demands for freedom.

The democrats of the early 1800s were not a united lot. Most believed in middle-class democracy and were reluctant to take to the streets, if the legislative process was available. They would fight to seize power, as a series of revolutions in 1848 indicated, but they usually worked for the rational development and transfer of organized political power. The main objective of most middle-class democrats was to obtain a constitution ensuring liberty.

Other democrats were not so limited in their approach to democracy. Looking at the pain caused by the Industrial Revolution and the growing power of capitalists, they argued that democracy should be based not only on freedom but also on social equality. This meant that the class structure and distribution of wealth also had to be reorganized. These were radical ideas compared to the notions of middle-class democracy, but many democrats embraced them.

Democrats working for the redistribution of wealth became known as radical democrats and socialists. They maintained that all institutions should be democratic, including ownership and control of the means of production. All power was to be held in communal form. The concept of socialism was especially popular among some groups of displaced workers.

One of the chief spokespersons for the socialists was Karl Marx. A German writing from London in the 1840s, Marx developed an international following. He claimed that the key to democracy was the ability to control economic power, and he developed an elaborate argument to justify his position. Marx and his colleagues claimed that the capitalist economic system exploited the lower classes for the benefit of others. He called for a change in the system.

The process of democratization was slow, however, and some of the radical democrats began to feel that violent revolution was the only possible course of action. A small number of the radical democrats went underground, choosing subversive violence as a means to challenge authority. They became popularly known as "terrorists," and modern Western terrorism was born.

Marx referred to "revolutionary" change, but he never clarified what he meant by revolution. Further, he did not advocate political bombing and assassination—in fact, on most occasions he publicly condemned it. Socialism was to be a reflection of democracy, not of violence. A massive seizure of power by the general population might be justified, but individual acts of murder were not.

Marx could not deter the radical democrats who wanted to revolt, but violent socialists lacked the political and military power for direct confrontation. In 1848, after revolts in almost every major center of Europe, conservative forces prevailed. Socialists who wanted overt, violent revolution were forced to settle for covert revolution. Though they could not successfully confront armies and police forces in Paris or Berlin, they could plant bombs and set factories aflame. A campaign of subversive revolutionary violence followed. The term *terrorism* was increasingly used to describe this violence.

TERRORISM AND THE ROLE OF THE ANARCHISTS

By the 1850s the militant socialists had separated themselves from mainstream socialists. This group of thinkers referred to their movement as anarchism. The term *anarchy* was not new; it originated several hundred years earlier when Greek philosophers spoke of eliminating governments, but the nineteenth century gave it a new twist: these anarchists were socialists and, initially, attuned to the ideas of Karl Marx.

Pierre Joseph Proudhon (1809 to 1865) was at the source of modern anarchism. His political activities eventually landed him in a French prison, but Proudhon was not a man of violence. He called for the extension of democracy to all classes, to be accomplished through the elimination of property and government. Property was to be commonly held, and families living in extended communes were to replace centralized government.

Proudhon disagreed with Marx and other socialists about the role of government. Most socialists saw a centralized government as a necessary evil. Like the democrats, the socialists believed that government had to exist to protect the individual rights of citizens. Proudhon rejected all such notions, and he subsequently rejected the communists for their belief in government. He believed that all government was an evil whose existence would always conflict with the rights of people to behave as they wished. Small communes thus held the best hope for a free Western civilization.

Proudhon had revolutionary ideals, but his message was similar to Marx's call for revolution in that he believed in peaceful change. Despite many internal contradictions in his writings, Proudhon generally believed that reason and logic would lead to the peaceful dissolution of Western society. Benign anarchy would develop through a natural evolution in human understanding.

Not all of Proudhon's disciples followed his call for this logical evolution; a number of them believed that society had to be violently destroyed. They were called

THE MILITANT ANARCHISTS

- Mikhail Bakunin
- Sergey Nechaev
- Peter Kropotkin
- Elisee Reclus
- Johan Most
- Emma Goldman

anarchist terrorists, and they changed the meaning of terrorism in Western civilization. There were several important terrorists among these anarchists.

Mikhail Bakunin (1814 to 1876) was a Russian revolutionary who fought the czar. He was joined in revolutionary activities by Sergey Nechaev. Later Russian terrorists formed an anarchist organization called the Narodnaya Volya, which operated from 1878 to 1881. The primary spokesperson of the Narodnaya Volya was Nikolai Morozov, and the organization's main tactic was to assassinate Russian government officials. Russian anarchists killed several officials, including Czar Alexander II.

Anarchists did not limit themselves to Russia. Karl Heinzen (1809 to 1880) was a radical German democrat who also embraced anarchy. He came to the United States after the 1848 revolutions failed in Europe. Prince Peter Kropotkin (1842 to 1921) was a displaced Russian who advocated revolution from exile in France. Johan Most was born in Germany in 1846 and emigrated to the United States. He advocated terrorism from a New Jersey–based newspaper, calling for "propaganda by the deed" and the "philosophy of the bomb." Violent action was the best form of propaganda, according to Most. Most was joined by Emma Goldman (1869 to 1940).

Anarchism was an international movement, and leaders from several countries were assassinated by its terrorist followers. This caused some opponents to believe that an international anarchist conspiracy was threatening to topple world order. This was hardly the truth, because anarchists were united only in spirit. Indeed, an international organization of anarchists would have been contradictory, as they were inherently opposed to large organizations. Regardless, fear of such a conspiracy grew, and many people came to believe that anarchists were universally organized.

Ironically, nationalistic trends accompanied anarchist violence in the West. At the same time that anarchists were calling for an end to government, a number of organizations surfaced who demanded a right to self-government. If the 1800s witnessed the growth of anarchism, it also saw the growth of nationalism. Many nationalists under foreign control adopted the tactics of the anarchists to fight foreign powers occupying their lands. Nationalist groups throughout Europe turned to the philosophy of the bomb and followed the pattern set by the anarchists.

Nationalist groups did not view themselves as terrorists. Anarchists, they believed, were fighting for mere ideas, while they were fighting for their countries.

Anarchists were socially isolated, but nationalists could hope for the possibility of greater support. Governments labeled them as terrorists, but nationalists saw themselves rather as unconventional soldiers fighting in a patriotic war. They adopted only the tactics of the anarchists.

The nationalistic Irish Republican Army emerged during this period. Unlike anarchists, who rejected all government, the IRA believed that Ireland was entitled to self-government. They didn't reject the notion of governmental control—they just wanted to nationalize it. Because they lacked power, they adopted the terrorist tactics fostered by the anarchists. In the twentieth century other nationalist groups in Europe followed the example of the IRA.

Even though they held two distinct positions, it is not possible to completely separate nineteenth-century anarchism and nationalism. Grant Wardlaw (1982, 18–24) saw a historical continuum between anarchism and nationalistic terrorism. Richard Rubenstein (1987, 122–125) made this same point after examining contemporary anarchist and nationalist groups. The stages terrorists must go through to employ violence, Rubenstein said, are similar for both types of terrorism. The moral justification for anarchist and nationalist terrorism is essentially the same.

J. Bowyer Bell (1976) gave an excellent example of the links between the anarchistic and nationalistic traditions by pointing to the IRA. Since 1916 the IRA has been inundated with both socialist revolutionaries and nationalists who reject some aspects of socialism. Even though the two sides have frequently been at odds, both are heir to the same tradition. Modern nationalistic terrorism has its roots in anarchism, and both traditions formed the framework of modern European terrorism.

Terrorism in the modern sense, then, originated with late-1800s violent anarchists who carried their campaign from Western Europe to other parts of the world. The most successful actions took place in Russia prior to the 1905 and 1917 revolutions. In America anarchism took the form of labor violence, and American anarchists, usually immigrants from Europe, became linked with organized labor. The American anarchist movement did not gain as much strength as it did in Europe, and it was generally limited to industrial areas. Right-wing extremism was never part of the anarchist movement, but by the mid–twentieth century right-wing groups had begun to imitate the tactics of violent anarchists in America.

Marie Fleming (1982, 8–28) analyzed the relationship of nineteenth-century anarchism to modern terrorism in a different manner. There is no simple link between anarchism and terrorism, she said, and they are not synonymous. For one thing, terrorist violence comes from sources other than the left, so terrorism cannot simply be summarized as a left-wing activity. Modern Western terrorism is related to anarchism, Fleming argued, but not in a superficial way.

The more complex link between terrorism and anarchism is to be found in ideology. Fleming maintained that an ideology of revolution was created by nineteenth-century anarchists and was adopted not only by the left, but by right-wing, nationalist, and criminal terrorist groups. Anarchist ideology was born of the struggle for democracy, but its original goals were replaced by a philosophy of violence. This philosophy expanded to embrace several other political causes, but it originated with violent anarchists of the nineteenth century.

Richard Rubenstein (1987, 98–99) also believed that Western terrorism is linked to its anarchist past. Rubenstein was not willing to extend its impact to nationalist and right-wing groups, however; he limited the link to revolutionary terrorism. He said the anarchists of the nineteenth century had three goals: to inspire others to imitate them, to provoke repression, and to trigger a general uprising. Rubenstein said that these goals are still common among revolutionary terrorists.

The anarchists came to believe that violence was a far more powerful statement than revolutionary rhetoric. "Propaganda by the deed" suggested that more could be accomplished by taking violent action than by working peacefully for social change. Stated simply, subversive violence was a better propaganda measure than a subversive press. This attitude gave rise to the "philosophy of the bomb"—the belief that violence was the only means of social change.

Despite the vehemence of their position, according to Laqueur (1987, 15) nineteenth-century anarchists still relied mainly on the underground press and fiery speeches. Laqueur believed that anarchists frequently spoke of violence but were reluctant to wage a campaign of terror. He argued that anarchists were essentially moral people who wanted to reject the notion of violence. They used terrorism only as a last resort, when they felt the status quo was morally intolerable. Their writings were violent, Laqueur wrote, but for the most part their actions were not.

Early Proponents of Revolution

French Sources

Researcher Marie Fleming believed that mid-nineteenth century France was the first center of terrorism, tracing the movement to two men, Elisee Reclus and Peter Kropotkin. Reclus was a well-known geographer as well as an anarchist active in the socialist movement. He envisioned a universal kinship among anarchists and applauded violence throughout Europe.

Kropotkin was even better known. The son of a Russian nobleman, he emigrated to France and was to become more nationalistic than most French natives. Having studied Italy's wars of unification, Kropotkin believed that violence was the only path to socialism. He adopted the phrase "propaganda by the deed," and Reclus endorsed the call to violence as a form of political communication. Kropotkin wrote that violence was the sole method of social change.

According to Fleming, neither Reclus nor Kropotkin was important because of his deeds. Each one's main contribution to terrorism was his rhetorical call to violence. Reclus and Kropotkin both believed that the capitalist economic system was fundamentally immoral. Kropotkin also believed that any governmental hierarchy that limited individual freedom and actions was similarly wrong, and that when governments linked themselves with the economic system they needed to be destroyed.

Breaking away from mainstream socialists in the 1870s, both Reclus and Kropotkin formulated a doctrine of anarchist revolution, which Kropotkin began to popularize. Their historical importance, Fleming believed, came from Kropotkin's efforts to export the ideals of anarchist revolution. Fleming maintained that communist anarchists such as Reclus and Kropotkin were responsible for making anarchism acceptable among revolutionaries in Spain, Russia, and the United States.

Walter Laqueur (1987, 48–51) agreed with Fleming about the influence of Kropotkin, but took a more limited view of his effectiveness. The French anarchists, Laqueur stated, were extremely vocal and raised alarm in the middle class, but they had little ability to carry through with their threats. They lacked the ability to select and strike a target. Kropotkin, endorsing propaganda by the deed in his rhetoric, would ultimately back away from the unlimited use of violence.

L. John Martin (1985) felt that Kropotkin's effectiveness lay in his understanding of publicity and the role of news coverage. The philosophy of the bomb was self-defeating if people were not aware of the purpose behind the violence. The bombing philosophy was based on the concept that violence could change things. It became a deed of propaganda only if the press picked up on the event. Without news coverage, there was no terrorist bomb. Martin said the anarchists, Kropotkin in particular, understood this. They began to master the art of violent communication.

In "The Spirit of Revolt," Kropotkin (1987, 90–96) provided the philosophical justification for terrorism. He argued that the conditions of human society necessitated revolution. The machinery of government was hardly a democratic institution, Kropotkin said; rather, it represented a force charged with maintaining the existing order. As the existing order was not based on social justice, the government that protected it was immoral.

The only moral response, Kropotkin said, was action—violent action designed to awaken the minds of the masses and breed a spirit of revolt. In Kropotkin's rhetoric, propaganda by the deed created the environment for revolution.

German Sources

Among the anarchists advocating greater violence was a radical German democrat named Karl Heinzen. According to Laqueur (1987, 28), Heinzen was the first modern terrorist. In 1848 a series of revolutions swept through Europe, almost all of them unsuccessfull. Heinzen believed they failed only because revolutionary forces did not have the strength to confront governmental power. In order to muster a viable force, revolutionaries needed a weapon; Heinzen urged them to turn to the bomb.

Heinzen argued that bombs should be planted indiscriminately. This would create a situation of constant disorder. The forces of order, he argued, would not be able to respond to widespread confusion. For Heinzen the bomb was the weapon of revolution. Violence would create anarchy, and anarchy would result in revolution.

Walter Laqueur and Yonah Alexander (1987, 47) felt that Heinzen's short revolutionary tract titled "Murder" was the most important call to revolution in the early history of terrorism. It first appeared in 1849—the year after the European revolutions—and sounded the call for immediate further revolution. Heinzen provided the method for anarchists to take action, and his tract has been cited repeatedly by those wishing to take "direct" action.

Heinzen (1987, 53–64) ironically began "Murder" by claiming that all life was sacred. It violates the laws of humanity, he wrote, to take the life of another. Humans were destined to live without murder, he opined, yet, when governments arose, they used murder to maintain their power. They called it execution or war, but it remained murder.

In this climate the only option for the oppressed masses was to resort to murder. Individual murders or mass bombings were the only methods available to strike back at governments. It is called murder only by governments, Heinzen said; the masses must see it as a legitimate weapon with which to strike at power. Heinzen said that European barbarity (organized government) had allowed no other recourse for the people.

The moral response to murder has always been linked to self-interests, according to Heinzen. Minor murderers, he wrote, were routinely executed while government-backed murderers were freed and rewarded. He concluded that murder has not only been the historical tool of power, but it has remained a political necessity. Heinzen said that the oppressed needed to employ murder in the same manner as states used it to maintain power. Murder used by the masses to overthrow injustice could become a moral force. Heinzen's argument remains popular in terrorist circles.

Heinzen was also realistic in his call to violence. Murder by itself would not serve the purpose, since the barbarians outnumber the democrats. State powers have a decided advantage in organization, training, numbers, and means of destruction. The 1848 revolutions had demonstrated those advantages. The only method of countering governments was to find a new set of tactics. Heinzen said revolutionary forces needed to be able to mount attacks supported by small numbers that could inflict heavy damage.

Even before Reclus and Kropotkin, Heinzen came to see the bomb as the primary tool of revolution. The bomb could give anarchists the tactical edge they needed to attack the state. Others would coin the phrase, but the philosophy of the bomb was obvious to Heinzen's mind. The bomb was the weapon that would allow small numbers to inflict heavy damage.

Russian Sources

Despite Heinzen's call, Western European anarchists continued to remain mostly rhetoricians. In prerevolutionary Russia, however, anarchism took another form, with some of the Russian anarchists becoming violent revolutionaries. Walter Laqueur (1987, 40–41) examined the Russian terrorism of the late 1800s and compared its characteristics to those of modern terrorism

According to Laqueur, the philosophy of anarchist terrorism in Russia was embodied by Mikhail Bakunin and Sergey Nechaev. Their revolutionary thought developed separately, but they met in the 1860s, forming an intellectual union. Both spoke of a revolt against the czar and both endorsed violence as the means to achieve it. Yet even in the nation that would experience a violent anarchist campaign and eventually a communist revolution, Bakunin and Nechaev basically stuck to rhetoric.

The writings of the Russians were powerful. Nechaev (1987, 68–71) laid down the principles of revolution in his "Catechism of the Revolutionary." His spirit has been reflected in writings of the late twentieth century. Rubenstein (1987, 103) compared the "Catechism" with Carlos Marighella's *The Minimanual for the Urban Guerrilla* and found no essential differences.

Bakunin (1987, 65–68) argued that the Russian government had been established through thievery. In "Revolution, Terrorism, Banditry" he argued that the only method of breaking state power was open revolt. Such rhetoric did not endear Nechaev and Bakunin to the czar, but it did make them popular with later revolutionaries.

American Sources

Propaganda by the deed came to the United States in the form of a Western European export. Born in Germany in 1846, Johan Most grew up under the influence of

European anarchists. He emigrated to the United States in 1882 after serving a jail sentence in London for praising the assassination of the Russian czar. America seemed to be right for Most, its relative freedom and exuberance to provide a place where he could flourish. Most believed anarchism could take root in America. He was wrong.

Bernard Johnpoll (1976, 32–34) said that Most was hailed by American socialists on his arrival. Most took up the call for socialist revolution and turned to the ranks of industrial workers for strength. He attempted to capitalize on labor disputes, and found receptive audiences among other immigrants. Yet Most alienated the socialist mainstream. His continual calls for violence did not mesh with the American socialist belief in the ballot box. With the exception of a few immigrants', Most's call to arms generally fell on deaf ears.

Johnpoll claimed that Most was the first American to provide a philosophical rationale for terrorism. The American labor movement was violent, and Most pictured anarchism as an extension of labor unrest. Violence, Most argued, was the only method available for overcoming tyranny. The power of the state was maintained through wealth, and violence could shake the foundations of that wealth. Therefore, Most saw the need for terrorists to employ dynamite sticks against wealthy business owners.

Despite sporadic dynamiting, however, Most fit into the pattern of the European anarchists, tending to limit his activities to rhetoric. He gained his reputation through his revolutionary newspaper, *Freiheit,* which means "freedom" in German. Together with other revolutionaries Most published *Freiheit* in New Jersey, targeting a readership amidst the East Coast's industrial areas. As did Most himself, *Freiheit* took a strong pro-labor stance; it frequently discussed the value of organized violence in labor struggles. *Freiheit* became an incitement to violence.

Laqueur (1987, 53–59) pointed out that *Freiheit* became Most's terrorist weapon. From it he advocated a terrorist bombing campaign designed to bring down American government and industry. He developed plans for a letter bomb, a unique American contribution to the terrorist arsenal. In one of his more ambitious plots he fantasized about bombing corporations from the air. He believed that such an action would allow a few terrorists to attack a large portion of government holdings. But despite his rhetoric, Laqueur argued, Most did very little aside from inciting others to violence. This became the pattern of American anarchism.

Most's sometime companion was Emma Goldman, a Russian who emigrated to the United States in 1885. In 1889 she joined the anarchists in New York and assisted with the publication of *Freiheit*. After a violent strike at the Carnegie Steel Company, where guards had killed several striking workers, Goldman joined in a plot to kill the company president. Although she was not convicted of participation in the attempted murder plot, she was arrested for a variety of minor offenses over the next two decades until she was eventually deported back to Russia.

Goldman did not limit herself to rhetoric—she once bullwhipped Most during a disagreement—but she cannot be viewed as a modern terrorist. Like Most, she was closely linked to the labor movement, and her primary activity was rhetorical. She advocated dramatic social change and saw violence as a tool for achieving it.

When many American anarchists became disillusioned in the late 1890s, Goldman kept the rhetoric while completely rejecting violence. American anarchists in the nineteenth century were modeled after their European counterparts, whose violence usually manifested itself as rhetoric. Terrorism was generally limited to a call to arms.

THE EFFECTS OF ANARCHISM ON TERRORISM

Propaganda by the deed developed in the nineteenth century and was somewhat predictive of modern terrorism. The Kropotkins, Heinzens, and Mosts called for terror and the Bakunins were actually associated with it. Their rhetorical stances moved some people to action. Propaganda by the deed mainly took the form of bombings and assassinations. Both of these tactics worked for small groups and gave frustrated individuals a chance to make a statement.

The technology of dynamite was a major innovation for terrorists. With increased explosive power and the ability to ignite the explosion in a variety of manners, dynamite became the terrorists' main tool. Bombings were accompanied by newspaper coverage and public panic. Dynamite helped shape propaganda by the deed into the philosophy of the bomb.

Two other aspects of Western terrorism also began to emerge in the 1800s. Right-wing extremism featuring racial bigotry emerged in Europe and the United States. Right-wing groups tended to operate in the open, engaging in public harangues and demonstrations. In their early stages they did not behave like the anarchists. Groups like the Ku Klux Klan and anti-Jewish organizations in Central Europe were secretive, yet they relied on public demonstrations and overt intimidation to achieve their goals. After World War II, they would shift their tactics and mimic the more clandestine behavior of the left wing.

Nationalistic terrorists were much quicker to capitalize on the anarchist position. Influenced by anarchist rhetoric, nationalistic groups formed to seek independence through bombing, assassination, and clandestine assault. Their most noted activities began in Ireland and Southern Europe, and their violence has spilled over into the present day. Nationalistic terrorists adopted the rhetoric of anarchist revolution, but more importantly, they developed anarchist tactics.

In an ideological sense, terrorism in the West evolved from the anarchistic rhetoric of the late 1800s. As Fleming and Laqueur argued, most of the rhetoric was characterized by attempts to philosophically justify violence. Few anarchists were terrorists, and those who were generally selected their targets with great care. The nature of terrorism has changed with modern technology, but the philosophy of twentieth-century terrorism was formed by nineteenth-century anarchists. Their rhetoric provided a springboard to violence.

The Problem of the Russian Revolution

The Russian Revolution of 1917 has had a tremendous impact on the rest of the twentieth century; to cite one example, it has inspired many in the West to blame communism for every possible social ill. Because it was founded on an ideology that conflicted with Western mores, the Revolution engendered fear in the West. That fear in turn has confused many modern-day issues, one of which is terrorism.

After World War I many people in the West believed that anarchist terrorism was behind the 1917 overthrow of the czar. The campaign of the Russian anarchists in the late 1800s, and the willingness of European and American anarchists to identify with them, seemed to make that clear. Few in the West understood the popular nature of the revolution, and most people began to fear the spread of revolution through terrorism.

Fear of a terrorist campaign on the part of the Soviets was ungrounded. As Richard Rubenstein suggested in a section of his book titled "The Noncauses of Terrorism," the Russian Revolution has no part in the terrorist tradition of the West. The Soviets used terror, but in a different manner.

Helmut Andics (1969, 41–50) noted that Vladimir Lenin accepted terrorism as a weapon in armed struggle and that his deputy, Leon Trotsky, gave ideological form to the concept. Trotsky saw terrorism as the key to controlling the revolution. He used it to intimidate enemies and to control the populations under revolutionary jurisdiction. Fear and intimidation could achieve results. Like many other revolutionaries, Trotsky called on terror to consolidate the revolution.

Though both Lenin and Trotsky used state terror to maintain domestic power, in foreign relations Trotsky chose a different route. He saw terrorism—specifically the threat of revolution—as a way of intimidating enemy powers and acting against them. The threat would not be strong enough unless his Western enemies believed violent revolution was possible, so Trotsky increased his rhetoric and subversive action. He saw that terrorism could be used as a tactic by which minor powers could threaten major ones.

Lenin's successor, Joseph Stalin, perceived that Russia could employ small espionage units against the West to relieve international pressure, since the West seemed to fear internal subversion. In 1936 the People's Commissariat of Internal Affairs (NKVD) began actively to export subversion. The NKVD became the forerunner of the Bureau of State Security, the KGB.

If the NKVD had not murdered so many Russians, it would have been a tremendous historical joke. The NKVD was incapable of toppling a Western government or even attacking one. It became a political police force and was primarily used to murder Communists. Under Stalin's mandate, the NKVD's primary foreign mission was to ensure that Russian dissidents would not return to the Soviet Union. They commissioned special squads to hunt down and kill disgruntled Communists who had fled to the West. Ironically, one of their first victims was Leon Trotsky, who was murdered by NKVD assassins in Mexico City. This was completely misinterpreted in the West, and the actions of the NKVD were used as further evidence of Soviet involvement in terrorism. For many Westerners the terms *terrorism, communism,* and *bolshevism* became interchangeable.

This problem is discussed in a later chapter. For now, you simply need to realize that the birth of the Soviet Union and Trotsky's Red Army were not part of the heritage of terrorism. When the Soviets began to use terrorism for internal political control, they could no more mastermind an international terrorist conspiracy than could the anarchists. The Soviets only preached world revolution to disconcert their enemies.

The face of terrorism changed after 1945, prompting some analysts to dichotomize the Western experience of terrorism. We therefore need to clarify the differences between modern terrorism and its historical antecedents before leaving this discussion.

OLD AND NEW TERRORISM

The Western tradition of terrorism is not new, as we have seen. Modern revolutionary terrorism evolved from anarchist violence of the late 1800s. Confusion about this point has resulted from misreadings of the Russian Revolution. Terror from the right, meanwhile, was hardly noticed, even though after World War I fascist gangs emerged in Europe and took over the governments of Spain, Italy, and Germany. Like the Soviets, fascists ruled by terror, but they were not terrorists in the modern sense. Contemporary terrorism was to emerge only in the 1960s.

James Fraser and Ian Fulton (1984, D1) maintained that a distinction should be drawn between terrorism prior to World War II and modern-day terrorism. He referred to these phases as "old terrorism" and "new terrorism." According to Fraser, old terrorism was tied to the anarchist ideology. It was based on the radical philosophy of the bomb and, other than eliciting fear from established governments, was not very effective. New terrorism is quite a bit different, he felt, not in its philosophy but in its effectiveness.

Fraser identified several factors that distinguish "new" terrorism from "old." The first is the news media. Terrorism reaches more people than it did in the past. This factor is closely related to a second, communications. News of terrorist incidents would not spread quickly were it not for instantaneous global communication links. Third, terrorist weapons are increasingly sophisticated and deadly. Old terrorism was linked to dynamite, but new terrorism employs a vast array of technological weapons. Finally, modern terrorists have increased their striking power through mobile command, support, and communications networks. New terrorists also enjoy increased mobility overall. All of these factors have changed terrorism, according to Fraser.

Walter Laqueur (1987, 91) noted another difference, which can be summarized as improved targeting. Laqueur argued that modern terrorists are more ruthless than their historical counterparts were, using experiences in Russia to support his contention. Not only did Laqueur believe that their terrorism was mainly rhetorical, he pointed out that Russian anarchists were extremely selective about their targets. He cited one case in which an anarchist refused to toss a bomb at a Russian official because he was afraid he would injure innocent bystanders.

Laqueur noted that this sensitivity is hardly typical of modern-day terrorists. Modern terrorism, he said, has been typified by indiscriminate violence and the intentional targeting of the civilian population. Modern terrorists strike at governments by killing their citizens: they strike airliners, buses, and other targets containing innocent noncombatants with no vested interest in the outcome of a political struggle. Modern terrorists engage in the sensationalized murder of innocents.

Richard Rubenstein (1987, 103) wholeheartedly objected to such attempts to dichotomize violence into new and old phases. He claimed that there is no evidence that terrorists have become more violent, believing instead that conventional opinions are incorrect. Rubenstein believed that terrorism today is the same as it was yesterday, and that there is little or no difference between old and new.

But setting aside the old-versus-new debate, it is clear that terrorism in the Western experience follows a certain tradition: in the West terrorists are motivated by ideology or nationalism. This became clear after World War II. Terrorism was rejuvenated in the 1960s as a tool used by zealots across the political spectrum. Nationalist and revolutionary groups began to view themselves as protagonists in a struggle against Western authorities. According to David Rapoport (1988), the Viet Nam War, the anticolonial movement, and the general questioning of social order seemed to provide cohesive links among terrorist groups.

In the final analysis, the West believed that it faced a new form of terrorism in the violence that erupted in the 1960s. Rubenstein correctly noted that it was linked to a revolutionary tradition, but technologically it was something more than nineteenth-century anarchism. In the 1960s terrorism was supported by better communications and technology. This was new. In addition, revolutionary terrorism appeared in Third World countries taking the form of colonial revolts. The ideology of terrorism may have remained constant, but the process hasn't.

SUMMARY OF CHAPTER THREE

In the Western tradition modern terrorism is a reflection of the growth of both democracy and anarchist violence. Terrorism could not have grown without democracy, and it originated with radical democrats. Left-wing nationalists were the first group to understand and exploit the significance of anarchist violence, but it also spread to the right. This form of terrorism reemerged in the 1960s and now ranges across the political spectrum.

Modern terrorist groups in Europe and the United States have emerged from the West's radical past. They lack mass appeal and tend to fragment as they expand. The two sources of radical terrorism are political ideology and nationalism. The growth of Western terrorism can be confusing to track, because it took place at a time when Latin American and Middle Eastern forms of terrorism were gaining worldwide attention. The philosophy of the bomb and propaganda by the deed, however, are typical of a specifically Western experience with terrorism.

As with any complex social problem, there have been attempts to simplify critical issues in terrorism. One of the most misinformed attempts to summarize terrorism has been to confuse its origins with the Russian Revolution. The Soviets ran their state by terror, but they did not develep an ideology of revolutionary terrorism.

The role of democracy is hotly debated among terrorism authorities. One group maintains that democracy helps terrorism flourish. Another argues that democracy should not be changed in response to terrorist violence and that individual freedom has little to do with terrorism. Regardless of the debate, terrorism in the West has definitely developed in a democratic framework.

IF YOU WANT TO READ FURTHER . . .

Most recent works on terrorism have focused on its development in the West. Many of the readings listed in Chapter 1 have sections on the history of terrorism in the West. For a good summation of the debate regarding the role of democracy, see Chapter 2 of Beau Grosscup's *The Explosion of Terrorism*. It's also helpful to compare Rubenstein's *Alchemists of Revolution* with Laqueur's *The Age of Terrorism*. None of these books resolves the debate, but they all alert you to the issues.

The history of anarchism and nineteenth-century terrorism is well documented. Three works will give you an excellent background. David Miller's *Anarchism* offers a theoretical background of the movement. James Joll's *The Anarchists* provides an excellent synopsis, while George Woodcock's *Anarchism* is one of the definitive histories of the movement. *The Social and Political Thought of Michael Bakunin,* by Richard Saltman, takes you into the mind of a nineteenth-century terrorist. Zeev Ivianski and Kachig Tololyan have two excellent historical articles on David Rapoport's *Inside Terrorist Organizations.* If you're interested in reading original works by terrorists, pick up *The Terrorism Reader,* edited by Walter Laqueur and Yonah Alexander. It contains a variety of excellent selections, and the commentary of Laqueur and Alexander adds depth. The work covers some of the contemporary issues in terrorism and reflects an appreciation of the historical elements. It provides solid background reading for many forms of terrorism, including the traditions that have emerged in the West.

The debate on "new" versus "old" terrorism reflects a difference of perception. Most scholarly analysts have ignored the issue or refused to acknowledge a difference. Others, Laqueur for example, talk about differences in modern terrorism. Military and police personnel generally refer to "new" terrorism because their roles in responding to terrorism have changed. Keep this in mind when reading works like Jonathan Harris's *The New Terrorism.*

REVOLUTION IN THE REVOLUTION:
TERRORIST TRADITIONS IN LATIN AMERICA

South and Central America present an intriguing twist in the logic of modern terrorism. Latin America has had a tradition of revolution and repression apart from terrorism, but since 1963 terrorism has been a part of many revolutions. This has been complicated by the repressive nature of some Latin American governments. In addition, contemporary urban terrorism in Western Europe and the United States has been strongly influenced by Latin American thought and action. All of these factors combine into a pattern unique to Latin American terrorism.

After reading this chapter, you should be able to do the following.

1. List the factors necessary to understand the political background of terrorism in Latin America
2. Explain the relationship between colonialism and revolution
3. Summarize the Guevara and Marighella styles of revolution
4. Describe several scholars' analyses of Latin American violence
5. Relate revolution in Latin America to the U.S. fear of communism
6. Describe the role of death squads in counterrevolutions

POLITICAL FACTORS IN LATIN AMERICAN VIOLENCE

To many North American minds, Latin America has come to epitomize violence, revolution, and repression. Stereotypes are not always accurate, but it is true that Latin America has experienced a great deal of political violence, including terrorism. Failure to account for the factors that have led to Latin American violence can result in a complete misunderstanding of the role played by terrorism in the region. Latin American terrorism must be judged within the context of its own traditions, so before we launch into a general discussion of terrorism, we need to briefly review some of the factors involved in revolution and repression in Latin America.

Latin America has not been noted for political stability over the past two centuries. When the Spanish and the Portuguese were removed from the region, they left neither governments nor institutions that could meet the needs of such a diversity of populations. They did leave a class structure in their wake, which relegated the majority of people to poverty and fostered competition for resources in the middle and upper classes. As a result of this competition the twentieth century has witnessed continued class struggles.

Journalist A. J. Langguth (1978) said one of the primary problems the United States faces in relating to conditions in Latin America is that southern problems are viewed through northern spectacles. The United States has been willing to export its particular form of government even though its policy makers exhibit little concern for the cultural, historical, and geographical uniqueness of Latin America. Langguth remarked that American eyes are perpetually turned toward Europe, leaving Latin America to take care of itself.

Despite Langguth's contentions about a European orientation, the United States has certainly been willing to intervene in Latin American affairs, and some scholars have suggested that it perpetually views Latin America with a colonial mindset. The problem is that the United States intervenes strictly on its own terms, and recent U.S. fears of communism have exacerbated its interference in Latin America. This has been especially true since the Cuban Revolution. Since Castro took over the Cuban government, Americans generally have dichotomized violence in Latin America as being either procommunist or anticommunist. This is an overly simplistic analysis of a complex set of problems.

Many scholars argue that Latin America must be evaluated within its own cultures and traditions. Hugh Thomas (1977, 707), an authority on the Cuban Revolution, said the United States has not come to grips with the problems that spawn Latin American violence. He cited the Cuban Revolution as a prime example. Walter LeFeber (1983) devoted an entire book to the argument that Latin American revolutions represent much more than a simple struggle to spread communism. Both internal and external issues fuel the violence, and the unequal distribution of wealth and power makes revolutions inevitable, according to LeFeber.

Ernest Duff and John McCamant (1976) cited four major indigenous problems associated with Latin American violence: (1) poverty, (2) the plurality of cultures, (3) neocolonialism, and (4) the unstable political climate of many countries. Poverty is the overriding factor. In almost every country only a handful of people control the wealth; the remaining population is locked into poverty. Most movements for social justice can ultimately be traced to the unequal distribution of wealth. Of all the elements endemic to Latin American politics, poverty is the most critical.

The problem of poverty interacts with the problem of cultural plurality. Duff and McCamant wrote that although it would seem logical to expect a single culture to have emerged from Latin America given its Iberian heritage, that is not the case. Actually, Latin America represents diverse patterns of culture (including a variety of indigenous Indian groups) with a complicated weave of political structures. Violence has become the factor common to all those cultures, and poverty is one of the chief causes of violence because it promotes instability. This leaves Latin America with a political heritage of violence and repression.

Unlike the United States and Canada, Latin America is closely tied to its colonial past. The class structure of colonial times has remained intact and Western investments in Latin America are frequently viewed as a form of neocolonialism. Revolutionaries in Latin America frequently draw on older anticolonial sources for their rhetoric. In

INDIGENOUS PROBLEMS LEADING TO LATIN AMERICAN VIOLENCE

- Poverty
- Plurality of cultures
- Neocolonialism
- Unstable political climates

Source: Ernest Duff and John McCamant, *Violence and Repression in Latin America* (New York: Free Press, 1976)

this sense, Latin American violence is linked to anticolonial struggles throughout the world. It is proper to approach Latin American violence and terrorism as part of a non-Western tradition. In many ways it is more typical of revolt in the Third World.

Latin American politics take place in an unstable environment. The simple fact is that no matter what type of government comes to power, few remain for long. This is complicated because of Latin America's powerful northern neighbor. Most non-democratic governments in the southern hemisphere offend the United States, exacerbating deeply entrenched anti-American feelings among Latin Americans. This is further complicated by the willingness of many North Americans to lump Latin Americans together irrespective of their diverse political traditions. It is much simpler to dichotomize them as communists and anticommunists than to study their reality.

Terrorism in Latin America remains a most pejorative term. Anyone who is out of power but employing violence to obtain power is likely to be labeled a terrorist. By the same token, those fighting to gain power have an incentive to call themselves "freedom fighters." Governments who can label their opponents as communist terrorists can hope for aid from the United States. Communist governments, on the other hand, frequently claim that violent opposition is backed by the CIA. The flinging of pejorative terms helps to justify the use of governmental repressive violence, while repression helps to justify revolution. This becomes one of the reasons for cyclical violence.

In reality, only a small amount of violence in Latin America is terrorism as defined in this book. More common is violence linked to guerrilla movements. Guerrillas usually work toward conventional confrontation with established forces rather than via terrorism. And by far the greatest amount of violence in Latin America comes from governmental repression. Whether from the left, right, or center, repression has been and remains the main source of Latin American violence even though many people believe the source to be revolution.

A full discussion of revolution and repression is beyond our purpose. It should be understood, however, that Latin American terrorism is frequently described simplistically in revolutionary terms, and that it operates in a variety of cultures dominated by poverty and instability. As Michael Radu (1987) suggested, Latin American terrorism has generated its own unique justifications and operations. Radu is among the many analysts who have argued that Latin American terrorism is distinct from other forms around the world.

CONTINUING COLONIAL REVOLUTION: FANON AND DEBRAY

The rise of modern terrorism has often been associated with developments during the past two or three decades. Some authorities, noting this, frequently link Latin American terrorism with the Third World revolutionary literature that has emerged since World War II. Journalists Christopher Dobson and Ronald Payne (1982b, 19) represent this trend. Rather than examining individual backgrounds or historical developments, they looked for a broad explanation for the recent style of terrorism. They found their answer in Third World anticolonial revolutions, blaming the rise of modern terrorism on revolutionary thought. Specifically, they cited Regis Debray and Frantz Fanon as the forerunners of terrorist revolution. Their perspective should be considered here because it directly relates to the situation in Latin America.

In one sense Dobson and Payne were absolutely correct. Revolutionary thinkers *are* linked to terrorism. During the fifties Frantz Fanon, a psychiatrist from Martinique, called for violent revolution and terrorism to oust colonial powers from the Third World. Among his most ardent disciples has been Abu Nidal, of PLO fame. Regis Debray, who joined the French government in the early 1980s as a political advisor, helped to popularize the idea of guerrilla revolution in Latin America in the 1960s. Debray became the unofficial spokesperson for the Cuban Revolution. Both theorists can be linked to modern terrorism.

Fannon and Debray were not from Latin America, but they became important in the region by endorsing revolution. Their views became a part of terrorist theory in Latin America, not because they created modern international terrorism, as Dobson and Payne suggested, but because they sought to intellectually justify the spirit of anticolonial revolution. As such, modern terrorism became a means of Latin American political expression.

When Latin American terrorism is employed in revolutions, it is often related to anticolonial violence and sentiment. One of the most influential and militant proponents of anticolonial violence in the post–World War II era was Frantz Fanon. Born on Martinique in 1925, Fanon studied medicine in France and became a psychiatrist. In the 1950s, when the Algerian revolt broke out, Fanon was sent to Algiers to work in a mental hospital. His experiences there caused him to side with the rebels.

Fanon believed that the pressures caused by exploitive imperialism were the primary causes for mental illness in Algeria. He produced his two most famous works, *The Wretched of the Earth* and *A Dying Colonialism,* as a result of his Algerian experiences. He died of cancer in 1961, unable to play a leading role in revolutions, but his thought was strongly imprinted on Africa, Asia, and Latin America.

Fanon provided a persuasive indictment of colonialism and a justification for terrorism in *The Wretched of the Earth*. He believed that Western powers had dehumanized non-Western people by destroying their cultures. Ethnic values had been rendered immaterial and were supplanted by Western values. To accomplish this, the West created a native middle class that embraced Western values and turned its back on the general population. Native culture was forgotten by the middle class, and native intellectualism became based on Western traditions. The masses ended up suffering a perpetual identity crisis: in order to succeed, they were forced to deny their heritage.

Although Fanon was addressing an African audience under direct colonial rule, his ideas became popular among lower economic classes in many cultures. Fanon wrote that his ideas might well be applicable to people living in a postcolonial environment or to oppressed minorities, and the concept of dehumanizing exploitation gained popularity across the world.

Fanon wrote a prescription for colonial revolution. He believed that revolts would begin with nationalist concepts, but that they had to spread througout the Third World. The exploited in Africa, Asia, and Latin America needed to join forces to reject colonialism. They should speak, Fanon maintained, with one voice and one purpose. They were to be united against a common enemy, the West.

To be sure, Fanon was no Ghandi. His only argument was for violent revolt, including guerrilla warfare and acts of terrorism. He claimed that decolonization was destined to be a violent process because it involved replacing one group of powerful people with another group. No group would willingly surrender power; therefore, Fanon stated, revolt could be called national liberation or restoration of statehood, but it was inherently a violent process. That notion caught the attention of the West as well as the Third World.

Revolt was violent, Fanon wrote, because colonization was violent and the lower classes could not be ruled without violence. In this context, only violence could challenge violence. Challenges to power could not be conducted in the form of abstract rationalism, he argued; they had to be pragmatic, and violence was the only pragmatic action. Political action and peaceful efforts toward change were useless. Only when oppressed people recognized that they must become violent would they be assured of victory.

Fanon saw the tools of revolution as guerrilla warfare and individual acts of terrorism. Guerrilla war was the initial method of revolt, because Third World revolutionaries could not mount a direct conventional campaign at the beginning of their struggle. The guerrilla movement was to be based in rural areas, but it should spread to the cities. Terrorism was to be limited to specific acts in support of the guerrilla campaign.

Fanon argued that terrorism should not be used against the native population in general; like Mao Tse-tung, he believed it would alienate supporters. Instead, he proposed two targets for terrorism: white settlers and the native middle class. Both would already be allied with the colonial power, so terrorism would not alienate them. On the contrary, it would terrorize them into submission. Individual murders, bombings, and mutilations would force the white settlers to leave the country and frighten the native middle class away from their colonial masters. Brutality would be the example. It would bring on government repression, but this would only cause more natives to flock to the guerrilla banner.

When revolts developed in the Third World, Fanon believed that the nature of the colonial revolutions was completely misunderstood. He said the international system of capitalism complicated revolts. Since the colonial nation was tied to the foreign capitalist structure, capitalism was automatically threatened during any revolt; therefore, nationals almost always found themselves fighting not a single power, but a whole economic system. Revolts took on new meaning.

Capitalist countries were generally well armed, Fanon argued, while revolutionary nationalists were not. The nationals were thus forced to turn to socialist countries for arms and support. Capitalist countries saw this as a challenge, socialist countries as an opportunity. The nationalist aspects of the revolt were frequently hidden, Fanon concluded, because the struggle took on overtones of East-West confrontation. He noted that Western economic aid usually came only when the West was trying to enlist a nation as an ally against communism.

Popular throughout the Third World, Fanon's ideas flourished in Latin America where, although direct rule by colonial powers had ceased in most Latin American countries by the 1960s, the class structures and economic systems were analogous to those in colonies. The successful example of the Cuban Revolution served further to fan the revolutionary flames. Fanon's concepts became standard dogma in Latin American left-wing intellectual circles. There remained only a need for some group to put the ideas into practice; Regis Debray became one of the people who would do so.

Regis Debray can be linked even more closely than Fanon to Latin American revolution. Whereas Fanon wrote from an African base, Debray carried out his writing and activity in Latin America. He became a leading spokesperson for left-wing revolution and helped popularize the ideas of Ernesto "Che" Guevara.

In *Revolution in the Revolution?* Debray summarized his concept of Latin American politics. The region had one dominating issue, Debray wrote. That issue was poverty. It threaded through the entire fabric of Latin American life and entwined divergent cultures and peoples in a common knot of misery. Poverty was responsible for the imbalance in the class structure, as the wealthy could not be maintained without the poverty of the masses. Debray saw only one recourse: the class structure had to be changed and wealth redistributed. Since the wealthy would never give up their power, revolution was the only method of change.

Debray's prime target was the United States. While it did not maintain a direct colonial empire, as did the countries of Fanon's focus, it did hold sway over Latin America. The United States dominated Latin America through economic imperialism. Behind every power in the south stood the United States. Debray held the United States responsible for maintaining the inequitable class structure, and he held the common Marxist belief that North American wealth caused Latin American poverty. It was quite logical, therefore, to target the United States.

Like Fanon, Debray continually talked of revolution. He saw little need for terrorism, however, and he minimized the role of urban centers in a revolt. Debray believed that revolution was essentially an affair for poor peasants and that it could only begin in a rural setting with regional guerrilla forces. Terrorism had no payoff. At best it was neutral, and at worst it alienated peasants needed for guerrilla support. For a revolution to work, Debray wrote, it must begin with guerrillas fighting for justice and end with a united conventional force. Terrorism would not accomplish this objective.

The writings of Fanon and Debray bring us to a crucial point in our understanding of terrorism in Latin America. Fanon viewed terrorism as a potential revolutionary tool, yet it was rejected by Debray. This struggle over the role of terrorism in revolution has not been resolved. Comparing two revolutionary processes in Latin America will further illustrate this conflict. In the final analysis, Debray and Fanon were theoreticians. Others took action.

Yet an adequate approach to revolutionary violence must delve deeper. Michael

Stohl (1988, 1–20) said that terrorism is not simply a Third World problem and that it cannot always be linked to revolutionary thought. Stohl's point merits consideration, particularly in Latin America where fighting is generally over the distribution of resources. Even though Dobson and Payne claim that the Fanons and the Debrays are behind the new outburst of terrorism, they only represent one form of terrorist violence: revolution. There are other forms of terrorism in Latin America.

MODERN REVOLUTIONARY MODELS: GUEVARA AND MARIGHELLA

Ernesto "Che" Guevara was born in Argentina in 1928. After earning a medical degree at the University of Buenos Aires, he turned his attention from medicine to the plight of the poor. He believed that poverty and repression were problems that transcended nationalism and that revolution was the only means of challenging authority. He served the government of Guatemala in 1954 after a communist revolution, but fled to Mexico City when the communist regime was overthrown. In Mexico City he met a Cuban Revolutionary leader named Fidel Castro; like Castro, he gravitated toward Marxism.

Guevara immediately impressed Castro, and the two worked together to oust the Cuban military dictator Fulgencio Batista. Castro began his campaign in Cuba by secretly meeting with partisans. After organizing a command and support structure, the partisans expanded to form regional guerrilla forces. As Castro's strength grew, he moved to more conventional methods of warfare and triumphantly entered Havana in 1959. Throughout the campaign Guevara had been at Castro's side.

Guevara's role merits our consideration for three reasons. First, he completed a tract on the Cuban Revolution that provides a model for Latin American revolt. It cannot be called a "how-to" model, but it can be deemed a "how-we-did-it" guide. Second, Guevara's experience illustrates the difference between guerrilla activity and terrorism. Finally, Guevara must be discussed because he was the most popular Latin American revolutionary leader of the left. His stature grew after his death and, even though he had disowned urban terrorism, his opponents frequently associated his ideas with it.

Translated copies of Guevara's *Guerrilla Warfare* appeared in the United States as early as 1961, but the book didn't enjoy mass distribution until toward the end of the decade. It could have been more aptly titled "Here's How We Did It," because it was a detailed examination of his view of the revolution: it describes both Guevara's evolution to Marxism and the revolutionary process in Cuba. It details the structure and strategy of Castro's forces and the guiding philosophy of the Cuban guerrilla war. Guevara also outlined the revolutionaries' methods of operations and principles of engagement. With the advantages of hindsight, it makes a stirring description of how victory was achieved.

Anthony Burton (1976, 70) said that Guevara did not provide a model for revolution, but that such a model could be extrapolated from *Guerrilla Warfare*. Burton argued that guerrilla revolutions based on the Cuban experience are typified by three progressive phases, each one designed to complement the previous ones. The goal of the strategy is to develop a conventional fighting force, or at least a force that renders the conventional opponent impotent.

According to Burton, the first phase of the process is highly clandestine. It begins with the formation of a guerrilla *foco,* a small group of indigenous rebels and professional revolutionaries who will build the revolution. The purpose of the *foco* is twofold. It assesses the weaknesses of the government, developing plans for an eventual offensive, and it becomes the center of revolutionary operations, acting as a kind of general staff. The basic purpose of the *foco* is to expand and form a base of operations. Secrecy is of paramount imporance. If police or other government forces discover or infiltrate the *foco* in the first stage, the revolution will be destroyed before it gets off the ground.

The second phase of the revolution begins when members of the *foco* move from the centralized command structure to farming regions. Rural areas become bases for regional guerrilla units. The job of regional unit commanders is to recruit, equip, and train a guerrilla force. Potential guerrillas are armed and acclimated to survival and fighting. They graduate to small training exercises such as blowing up a radio tower or ambushing a police car. As the units begin to operate, the veil of secrecy is raised and the guerrillas are exposed. The government becomes aware that it is under organized attack. Burton said this is the most critical phase for the guerrillas.

It is critical because it leads to the third phase of the revolution, the formation of guerrilla battalions, or columns. The job of each column is to wrest control of a rural area from the government. As each region is secured, columns join each other in ever-increasing strength. When guerrilla strength overreaches the conventional striking power of the government's armed forces, the guerrillas begin an open offensive to take the seat of government. In reality, these were the three phases of the Cuban Revolution.

There is a limited role for terrorism in Guevara's guerrilla framework. Although Guevara's focus was on the countryside and rural guerrilla columns, he saw the need for small urban terrorist groups to wage a campaign of support. These actions, however, were to be extremely selective; their purpose was to keep government forces off balance, to terrorize them in their "safe" areas, never letting them relax. The main purpose of terrorism was to strike at the government's logistical network; the secondary purpose was to demoralize the government. Terrorism was a commando-type tactic.

Even though the Guevara model of revolution may not be applicable to all guerrilla wars, Burton's analysis was extremely important. By using the model, Burton differentiated between guerrilla war and terrorism while still leaving a role for terrorism in guerrilla revolts. Paul Wilkinson (1974, 79) demonstrated why this was important: guerrillas cannot resort to terrorism because it alienates the population they are trying to seduce.

By briefly returning to the positions of Frantz Fanon and Regis Debray, we can see the logic of Guevara's position for Latin America. Fanon endorsed acts of terrrorism against foreigners and their native middle-class representatives even though it would alienate those groups from the revolution. He could risk alienating them, since they would never join the revolution anyway.

For Fanon, terrrorism was a message. It warned government sympathizers and supporters to beware. Support of the government could mean torture or death. When the government reacted to terrorism with general repression of the native population, the revolutionary ranks would swell.

Guevara completely avoided this position and so did Debray when he popularized

Guevara's method of revolution. Terror was to be just one tactic, used selectively while an army was being assembled in a rational process. Debray and Guevara might well have agreed with Fanon's lust for revenge against authority, but they felt that terror was generally counterproductive. Murder, assassination, and other forms of terrorism could be justified, but only in terms of the peoples' will. For Guevara and Debray the revolution had to be well under way before any limited form of terrorism was utilized. Even then, it was a disruptive tactic, not a method of communication.

Guevara's position was not shared by all Latin American revolutionaries. After the rural-based revolution in Cuba, many people believed that the violent overthrow of governments would begin in the countryside. By the end of the 1960s, however, a new school of thought would emerge.

Beginning in Brazil, some revolutionaries came to believe that the city would be the focus of Latin American revolution and that it was not necessary to build a guerrilla army. The revolutionary could create a context for a spontaneous general uprising through the use of terrorism. Almost directly reflecting Fanon, these revolutionaries believed that terrorism could communicate with the people and infuse them with the spirit of revolt. The foremost proponent of this idea in Latin America was Carlos Marighella.

Marighella was a Brazilian legislator, a leader of the nationalist communist party, and eventually a fiery revolutionary terrorist. He was killed by Brazilian police in an ambush in Sao Paulo in 1969. His two major works were *For the Liberation of Brazil* and *The Minimanual of the Urban Guerrilla*. Marighella's works were designed to be practical guides, and they have had more infuence on recent revolutionary terrorism than has any other set of theories.

Marighella wanted to move violence from the countryside to the city, and although his call to terrorism was politically motivated, his model was apolitical. He designed a method for organizing a campaign of urban terror that, for the past twenty years, has been employed by groups ranging across the political spectrum.

Marighella believed that the basis of revolution was violence. Violence need not be structured, and efforts among groups need not be coordinated. Violence created a situation in which revolution could flourish. Any type of violence was acceptable because it contributed a general feeling of panic and frustration among the ruling classes and their protectors. Marighella's most original concept was that all violence could be urban based and controlled by a small group of "urban guerrillas." This concept of revolution spread from Brazil throughout the world.

Robert Moss (1972, 70–72) provided an excellent synopsis of Marighella's writings in a four-stage model. Urban terrorism was to begin with two distinct phases, one designed to bring about actual violence and the other to give that violence meaning. The violent portion of the revolution was to be a confederate campaign employing armed revolutionary cells to carry out the most deplorable acts of violence. Targets were to have symbolic significance, and while violence was designed to be frightening, its logic should remain clear with regard to the overall revolution. That is, those who supported the revolution need not fear terrorist violence.

The terror campaign was to be accompanied by a psychological offensive to provide peripheral support for terrorists. Not only would the psychological offensive join students and workers in low-level challenges to governmental authority, it would be used to create a network of safe houses, logistical stores, and medical units. In essence, the supporting activities would carry out standard military support functions.

A campaign of revolutionary terrorism in an urban setting could be used to destabilize government power. A psychological assault would convince the government and the people that the status quo no longer held. They would come to feel that the terrorists were in control. When this situation developed, Marighella believed, the government would be forced to show its true colors. With its authority challenged and the economic stability of the elite eroded, the government would be forced to declare some form of martial law. This would not be a defeat for terrorism, but rather exactly what the terrorists and their supporters wanted. Governmental repression was the goal of terrorism at this stage.

While this might appear to be contradictory at first glance, there was a method to Marighella's madness. Marighella believed that the general public supported government policies because they did not realize the repressive nature of the state. The terrorist campaign would force the government to reveal its claws, thereby alienating the public. With no place to turn, the public would turn to the terrorists, and the terrorists would be waiting with open arms.

As the ranks of the urban guerrillas grew with the rush of public support, Marighella believed, the revolutionaries would gradually abandon their terrorist campaign. Their efforts would focus more and more on the construction of a general urban army, an army that could seize key government control points on cue. When the urban army had reached sufficient strength, all its forces would be launched in a general strike. Government communication and control mechanisms would be destroyed, and the general public would rush through the streets to proclaim and legitimize the new government.

Marighella's theory was that terrorism would create a massive social movement and lead to a new social order. While Guevara's prescription was highly organized and methodical, Marighella relied on the shock effects of immediate violence. Any size of group would serve to assist the revolution, and actions did not need to be coordinated. Any form of violence that contributed to disorder was acceptable.

There was and is only one flaw in Marighella's model: it does not work. When urban terrorists have provoked governmental repression, popular support has endorsed those restrictions on their freedom. In Uruguay, where the Tupamaros followed Marighella's plan to the letter, governmental repression was welcomed by the people in 1972. In West Germany more restrictive measures against terrorists were the result of popular pressure, not of governmental repression. Even in Northern Ireland the Emergency Powers Act, which gives the Irish authorities expanded police power, enjoys a limited support among Protestants and Catholics alike. To date, Marighella-style terrorism has rallied people to the forces of order, not of revolution.

Revolutionary terrorism in Latin America tends to alienate people, especially the middle class. Peter Waldmann (1986, 275–276) saw this as exploding one of the great myths of revolution and urban terrorism. In order for revolution to work in Latin America, Waldmann said, it must appeal to this middle class. By no stretch of historical evidence has Marighella's model had such appeal. The middle class is more readily accepting of the rationalism and selective violence of Guevara.

To simplify, Guevara may have written the "how we did it " book of revolutions, while Marighella seemed to have outlined "how we tried to do it." Even though Marighella's model has not worked, a brief review of his *Minimanual* is worth our attention because he presented the "new," modern version of revolutionary terrorism in it. As an examination of the *Minimanual* will indicate, Marighella had far more use for terrorism than did Guevara.

Marighella wrote that the purpose of the urban guerrilla is to shoot. Any form of urban violence is desirable because a violent atmosphere creates the political environment needed for success. Terrorism could be utilized to create that environment, and terrorism could be employed with minimal organization. Therefore, terrorism was to be the primary strategy of the urban guerrilla.

Marighella outlined the basic structure needed for an urban terrorist group in the *Minimanual*. The main operational group of a terrorist organization should be the firing group. Composed of four to five terrorists each, several firing groups were needed to construct a terrorist organization. They could join together as needed to concentrate their power, but their small size ensured both mobility and secrecy. For Marighella, the firing group was the basic weapon of the urban guerrilla.

When groups joined together for operations, Marighella referred to the expanded organizations as firing teams. Firing teams were tactical formations not unlike brigades in modern military structures. They were to be formed for specific operations and disbanded when the operation was terminated. Firing teams were to be used only for major operations for which the strength of one firing group would not suffice.

The terrorist campaign was to be controlled by a strategic command group working in conjunction with a centralized group of planners. The major function of strategic command was not to wage revolution, but rather to maintain the logistical and communications networks necessary to run a terrorist campaign. In essence, the strategic command was to run logistics and take responsibility for internal discipline.

The supportive role assigned to command reflected Marighella's unwavering belief in the power of the firing group. The strategic control group did not exercise military command because it did not have to. If the firing groups did their jobs, they would creat chaos. This was more important than coordinated command and control. The function of the strategic command was to allow the firing group to operate. Political chaos would create the revolution.

Marighella had a tremendous influence on modern terrorism. Inside Latin America, his ideas became the source of inspiration for abandoning the long-term, rural approach of Guevara and instead immediately taking revolution to the streets. He formed two terrorist organizations in Brazil, and the Tupamaros of Uruguay were modeled directly on his concepts. Outside of Latin America, Western European revolutionary groups patterned themselves along *Minimanual* guidelines. In the United States, left-wing terrorists followed Marighella's example and were in turn mimicked by the right in the 1980s. Marighella might not be a household word, but his methods of terrorism are universally familiar. He represents the point at which Latin American and Western methods of terrorism merge.

If there is a relationship between terrorism and anarchism in the West, there is a stronger relationship between terrorism and revolution in Latin America. Yet, as previously mentioned, terrorism cannot simply be summed up as a revolutionary activity. Terrorism is more frequently used as a form of repression than as a means to revolution. Although the repressionists and revolutionaries emerge from the same bag, those who repress revolutionaries have their own brand of terror. We need to shift from standard revolutionary rhetoric back to our original discussion of Latin American politics to understand this point.

SCHOLARLY THEORIES OF LATIN AMERICAN VIOLENCE AND TERRORISM

Several theories have been offered to explain Latin American violence. It would take far too long to summarize them here, but a few of the more prominent views can be presented. It is necessary to do this to explode the common misconception that Latin American terrorism is always linked to revolutionary activities. Many conservatives have incentives to practice terrorism in Latin America. A brief review of the theories of Latin American violence will help to explain why.

According to Ernest Duff and John McCamant (1976, 1–7), Latin America has typically four kinds of governments: (1) constitutionally elected governments, (2) traditional dictatorships, (3) dictatorships that have come to power through emergency measures, and (4) totalitarian states. Within this typology, they argued, the central task of political science is to explain the violence that has dominated all four forms of government. Duff and McCamant concluded that Latin American violence is the result of perpetual political instability.

The research of Duff and McCamant focused on the broad problems of violence and repression in Latin America. Terrorism was only one aspect of the problem, a reflection of the continual threat of violence there. Almost all political violence, including terrorism, is the result of specific conditions inside a country, according to Duff and McCamant.

For a nation to be at peace, they found, it had to have a stable economy, established social institutions, and governmental policies that promote the welfare of its citizens. After an extensive quantitative analysis, they concluded that socially cohesive governments experienced less political violence than did governments with little cohesion. The major problem is that Latin American politics do not work toward cohesion, but rather toward instability.

We can infer from Duff and McCamant that terrorism must somehow be related to social stability and cohesion, since it is a form of political violence. Neither Marighella- nor Guevara-type activities develop in countries in which conditions are not ripe for violence. Duff and McCamant also linked instability with repression; as we've noted, terrorism is also a tool of counterrevolutionaries (Chomsky and Herman 1977; Herman 1983).

Ernst Halperin (1976) was not convinced that the myriad of struggles in Latin America reflected global competition between East and West. On the contrary, they represented intense, local competition for very limited financial resources. He outlined this thesis in a brief but crucial work, *Terrorism in Latin America.*

Halperin said that the rationale for Latin American revolutions can be found by examining the experiences of recent regimes. Historically, the conquest of a state has

Figure 4-1 Halperin's model of Latin American revolution
Source: Ernst Halperin, *Terrorism in Latin America* (Newbury Park, CA: Sage, 1976)

provided power and prestige for the new rulers. After taking power in a Latin American government, new rulers are free to reward their followers and to create a variety of positions for their educated supporters.

Halperin maintained that this fight for resources is the basic pattern of Latin American revolutions, and that it evolved from nineteenth-century class relations. Modern revolutions are swathed in the rhetoric of Marx and liberation theology, but the real issue in Latin America is the competition for limited resources. Halperin believed both communists and capitalists failed to understand this.

To explicate and support his thesis, Halperin looked at class relations and the special role of education. Latin America maintains a two-tiered class system composed of the upper classes and the commoners. With the exception of Argentines, Halperin said, members of the urban and rural working classes have almost no political power. Governments can afford to ignore them because they have little political influence.

Given their ability to neglect the lower classes, the governments of Latin America cater to the upper classes, Halperin wrote. The upper class and the educated middle class keep Latin American governments in power. Therefore, almost all governmental policies are aimed at mollifying the upper classes. This is accomplished primarily by providing economic opportunities for them.

Halperin believed that the upper classes, especially the middle class, turn to education in order to maintain their position. In Latin America education is widely regarded as the passport to the upper class, and it gives the upper classes the skills they need to function. This gives education special power. Halperin said that the power of education is increased in Latin America because most educated people are channeled into a government-controlled economy. Problems develop when the economy cannot expand rapidly enough to absorb the influx of college graduates. This results in upper-class unemployment, which is a frequent scenario because economic resources are severely limited in Latin America. When a new government takes power, it has trouble maintaining its position if the upper classes are threatened. Latin American governments therefore cannot afford unemployment in the upper classes.

The problem of unemployment is complicated by the political power of students. Halperin stated that the role of students in Latin American revolutions is hotly disputed and frequently misunderstood. Universities with radical reputations, he noted, usually have little real involvement in radical affairs. Student power only becomes important when it is mobilized at a critical point in a political crisis. Student support can become a decisive advantage in a revolution when it is employed at the proper time. The problem for many governments, Halperin said, is that students frequently have the economic motivation to join revolutions.

In Halperin's analysis, student activism is based upon careerism. Students who are not traditionally part of the ruling class and its allies must use their university period to foster the proper social connections. This produces a system of intense personal loyalty and individual identification with particular groups. Group success translates to individual success. When a group obtains prestige and power, it can reward its members.

Halperin said that various Latin American student groups almost always express their concern for justice and freedom, but these ideals are never attained because the true goal of student activism is to achieve power for the group and, subsequently, personal power and prestige. It isn't that the students wish to ignore justice issues. They can't attain these ideals, no matter how hard they try, because of the overriding poverty. There simply is not enough money to support a class revolution whether it's for democracy, Marxism, or liberation theology. Economic issues dictate the structure and function of student activism.

Halperin advanced a theory of Latin American revolution within this context. The pressure for economic rewards among the upper classes never ceases, and it forms the root of political violence in Latin America. It creates a basis for terrorism and guerrilla war. Armed struggle in Latin America is primarily reflective of a struggle among segments of the upper classes for a limited amount of resources.

Terrorism, Halperin added, represents a special form of violence. Terrorism is an upper-class form of violence in Latin America, and people with an unusual tendency toward violence end up in terrorist groups. They are almost always students who have no social connections but who nonetheless aspire to success. Revolutionary terrorists attempt to identify with the working class through ideology, but ideology is always secondary. This is why Latin American terrorist groups generally lack working-class support.

It is popular to cite theories of revolution and economic development as the causes of Latin American terrorism, but Halperin maintained those theories usually develop only after the violence has started. Both Marxist and capitalist models of revolution have proven too simplistic and limited to explain Latin American terrorism, Halperin argued. The model of upper-class competition remains constant in both communist and capitalist regimes.

Halperin also took an unconventional stance on Latin American poverty. It is popular, he said, to cite North American prosperity as the source of Latin American poverty. Called the "Vampire Complex," this theory asserts that the North is wealthy due to the sacrifice and exploitation of the South. Halperin admitted that it is not popular to criticize this theory, but he did so.

He concluded that proponents of the Vampire Complex ignore basic economic relationships, and that they fail to acknowledge that export economies have been extremely profitable for the people of Latin America. The peoples' poverty and anti-American sentiments are used as rhetorical weapons in the upper-class struggle, disseminated by revolutionaries because they're popular.

If Halperin's conclusions are correct, they lend weight to the Duff-McCamant argument regarding the relationship between social stability and revolution. More importantly, his argument runs contrary to many assumptions underpinning U.S.

foreign policy. Far from reflecting a struggle between Russia and the United States, Latin American violence represents an internal struggle. East-West rhetoric is flung in the fight, but it's still an internal fight for limited resources.

Another extremely important conclusion can be drawn by expanding Halperin's thesis. Struggles for resources are never ending; even when revolutionaries are successful, the struggle for resources continues. Once a group achieves power, it must struggle to keep it. A group can do so by establishing a government that expands the economy. If it cannot offer economic growth, however, it must repress its opponents. There are not enough resources to allow everyone to share them, so repression is a logical step. It is another—and frequently overlooked—source of Latin American terrorism.

George Lopez (1988) also examined the role of terrorism in Latin America and concluded that the problem was somewhat unique. Terrorism has played a major role in the region since World War II, and this has changed the nature of Latin American violence. Lopez believed there are three types of modern terrorism in Latin America. *Insurgent terrorism* is a short-term strike against a government, with little planning toward a strategic outcome. *Revolutionary terrorism* is incidental to other violence during an existing revolution. *Nongovernmental terrorism* develops outside of government authority and is primarily manifested in vigilante murders and threats.

Lopez believed there are several reasons for insurgent terrorism. The deterioration of economic conditions and the perpetual up-and-down swing of most national economies breeds instability and competition for resources. There are also powerful ideological forces within this economic context: revolutionaries, counterrevolutionaries, and religious actors. A violent tradition of revolution and repression combines in Latin America with social intolerance for dissident opinion. These conditions are generally similar to those identified by Halperin, and they help to produce a continual cycle of violence.

Repressionist terror complements insurgent terror, according to Lopez. There is no single explanation for repressive terror, but several factors join to produce a climate conducive to repression. Lopez cited what he called Bureaucratic-Authoritarian structures that have risen to replace personal dictatorships; their military leaders rely on repression to maintain power. These structures also must protect their economic interests and work against those seeking economic redistribution. A shared ideology among Bureaucratic-Authoritarian leaders has convinced governments that repression works. Again, these findings are generally congruent with Halperin's thesis.

Two of Lopez's ideas have been amplified by other analysts. Gordon McCormick stated that the role of ideology is extremely important in understanding Latin American terrorism. He cited the Shining Path of Peru as an example. The Shining Path is one of the deadliest insurgent groups in Latin America, having killed almost 10,000 people since 1980. It is a secret communist society based on mysticism and Maoist revolutionary thought. Ideologically, Shining Path is based on fierce group loyalty and the acceptance of violence. Terrorism is deemed to be the "shining path" to victory.

Yet, as Lopez said, ideology and group loyalty dominate the other side as well. In a study of American support of repressionist governments, Noam Chomsky and Edward Herman (1977) focused on the use of terrorism by ruling elites in military dictatorships. Terrorism on the part of a government stops revolution. Dictators know this and so does the U.S. State Department, according to Chomsky and Herman. They claim that the United States has looked the other way in order to continue supporting a "safe" repressive government.

The United States has acknowledged the problems of repression, but has placed far greater diplomatic emphasis on guerrilla wars and revolutionary terrorism. The 1984 *Report of the President's National Bipartisan Commission on Central America* illustrates this position. Chaired by former Secretary of State Henry Kissinger, the Commission Report addressed security concerns. It focused primarily on El Salvador and Nicaragua. Repression was viewed as a major political problem, but not as a form of terrorism.

The Commission concluded that Central America is in a state of crisis. Terrorism, guerrilla wars, and violence have been fostered by Soviet-Cuban expansionism, and Nicaragua has been used as a puppet to accomplish Eastern objectives. The Commission feared that Nicaraguan-type revolutions would spread. It condemned political repression but viewed the major problem as communist expansionism.

According to the Commission, a climate of communist revolution and terrorism has been fueled by economic deterioration and political repression. It condemned all forms of political repression in Latin America and called for massive U.S. economic and military aid for the region. The only way to end repression, the Commission said, was to encourage democracy and bolster regional security.

The Commission probably would have agreed with Duff and McCamant about the effects of political stability on violence, but it did not note the upper-class struggle of Halperin's thesis. It reported two factors to explain the Central American violence of the 1980s. First, Central America's export economies have been in trouble for twenty years. This has caused massive discontent, which is linked to the second factor, the spread of communism.

The Commission implied that terrorism resulted from guerrilla-type activities. Its report dwelled in detail on the activities of guerrillas in El Salvador and Guatemala, and portrayed the struggles there as comparable to the Viet Nam War. Terrorism is a sideshow in these guerrilla wars, which reflect a larger struggle between the Soviet Union and the United States.

The Bipartisan Commision did not spend a great deal of time on the problems caused by repression, which they felt could be handled by democratic reforms once the communist threat was eliminated. It also failed to address the role that U.S. police and security forces have played in repressionist systems. Others have, however. Edward Herman (1983) questioned the assumption that communist expansion is behind Central America's woes. He said the United States has supported a network of terror in its desire to block communism, and he expressed concern over U.S. support of repressive governments in Latin America based solely on their fervent anticommunist positions. The United States overlooks torture, murder, and repression on the part of these governments in the name of anticommunism; its fear of Soviet expansion and Cuban adventurism has caused it to ignore the largest terrorist network in the world. Repressionist governments supported by the United States have killed thousands more people than have the relatively few revolutionary terrorists. Herman believed that U.S. policy in Latin America is guided by anticommunist hysteria.

Herman believed that this policy has had three primary results. First, repressive police states are given a climate in which they can form and function. Second, power is maintained through torture and execution; if the United States complains, that power continues to be maintained via "illegal" death squads. Finally, the problems of Latin America are falsely simplified and dichotomized in terms of a superpower confrontation. Herman therefore believed U.S. policies in Latin America to be fundamentally immoral.

Herman's book focuses on state terrorism, and his thesis is beyond our scope. We are focusing on illegal groups who engage in terrorism outside of governmental authority. Still, many of Herman's ideas apply to our topic. The motivation for repression and counterrevolutionary terrorism are the same for governments and private groups. Counterrevolutionary and revolutionary groups are involved in the same fight for limited resources. Herman indicated that there are illegal repressionist groups operating in Latin America, in addition to government repression. These illegal groups will be the source of our inquiry, as they are terrorist groups in every sense of the word.

The Bipartisan Commission on Central America and Edward Herman stood worlds apart in their political orientation, and while they both acknowledged the role of poverty, neither took into account Halperin's point regarding a bitter upper-class struggle for limited resources. The Commission viewed repression as the result of instability, while Herman believed it to be supported by U.S. anticommunist hysteria and Halperin implied it reflected an ongoing struggle. Regardless of the merits of each position, one thing is clear. Repression is a problem that should be considered a form of Latin American terrorism. Herman's analysis and the mention of extralegal repressionist groups open the door to our inquiry.

DEATH SQUADS AND COUNTERREVOLUTIONARIES

While a body of theoretical literature addresses revolutionary terrorism, very little has been written on the death squad. No Frantz Fanon has justified it and no Carlos Marighella has outlined it. In Latin America, however, death squads do have a theoretical base: they are all antirevolutionary. Members of death squads study Guevara and Marighella and arrive at the solution of terrorizing opposition into submission.

In the Western tradition, fascist-type groups outside of governmental authority generally follow the pattern of the left wing. Both groups seek revolutions, but fascists seek a right-wing revolution. For example, the left-wing Weather Underground and Red Army Faction are tactically very similar to the right-wing Order and Military Sports Group Hoffman. This pattern does not hold true in Latin America. Death squads represent a new twist, as they practice terrorism strictly for counterrevolutionary purposes. They are fighting to maintain power, not to overthrow it.

Death squads come into being in Latin America when people who have a vested interest in power feel their position is being threatened and that the government is doing very little about it. First appearing in Brazil in the 1960s, death squads were formed from the ranks of urban police agencies. They spread to include members of the military forces and became commonplace in many Latin American countries.

The purpose of a death squad is to eliminate opposition when the law and the government are unwilling or unable to do so. The pattern developed in Brazil was simply to kidnap and shoot an opponent. Unfortunately, this practice was soon refined; counterrevolutionary terrorists came to realize that torture and an atmosphere of constant fear have effects similar to murder. Violence became symbolic.

Torture is a very effective means of sending a message to any opponent. It is worse than murder, because the people who receive the message know that the victims suffer. Potential victims know what is in store for them if they are taken by the death squads. Long-term torture sends a clear message and has become a favored medium of death-squad communication.

The tactics of death squads vary. They range from semiofficial raids on governmental opponents to secret murders. In a common scenario, uniformed members of a death squad will "arrest" a victim. Careful not to maintain any records, the arresting officers frighten lucky victims and torture and murder the unlucky ones. In other cases, people simply disappear. For example, in the late 1970s when Argentine death squads reigned supreme, thousands of people "disappeared."

While death squads have been associated primarily with right-wing activities, they are used across the political spectrum. For example, after the 1979 Sandinista revolution in Nicaragua, unofficial groups began to crack down on the press and potential opposition parties. People who opposed the Communists began to disappear (U.S. Department of State, 1986). Death squads provide equal opportunities to all who wish to employ their tactics.

The death squad represents a third form of Latin American terrorism, and it cannot be understood apart from the patterns of Latin American violence. If Halperin is correct, the revolutionary and the counterrevolutionary spring from the same well. Death squads exist outside of government authority and therefore differ from state terrorism, which is a legal and rational diplomatic problem. Death squads, however, pose the same problems as do other terrorist groups.

SUMMARY OF CHAPTER FOUR

Latin America has often been characterized by violence, revolution, and repression. Political fluctuations make it difficult to understand terrorism in Latin America, and its colonial past and poverty serve to obscure many issues. Latin American terrorism takes place within cycles of revolution and repression and has its own unique flavor.

Anticolonial literature and rhetoric has had a tremendous effect on Latin American violence. Since the 1960s, the works of Fanon and Debray have underpinned certain revolutionary movements in the region. Terrorism therefore developed in Latin America from an anticolonial perspective.

Three models of Latin American terrorism have emerged in recent years. Terrorism as a tactic in a guerrilla war is described in the writings of Guevara. Marighella detailed the use of terrorism as an urban strategy. The most deadly form of terrorism in the region, however, is practiced by death squads. Death-squad terrorism has been frequently ignored by terrorist experts, but its prevalence is apparent when patterns of Latin American violence are examined.

IF YOU WANT TO READ FURTHER . . .

There are several good books on Latin America, although most reflect the authors' political biases. One of the best places to begin is with general political overviews. Walter LeFeber's excellent work titled *Inevitable Revolutions* strikes a balance between liberal and conservative positions and provides solid background. Robert Leiken's *Soviet Strategy in Latin America* gives the background on superpower confrontations in the area.

If you're looking for revolutionary theory, both Fanon and Debray are musts. Debray deals directly with Latin America in *Revolution in the Revolution?*, while Fanon provides a theoretical overview of Third World revolutions in *The Wretched of the Earth*. Death-squad terrorists have no popular theoretical statement, but A. J. Langguth's *Hidden Terrors* covers their perspective well.

Revolutionary writings can also be used to understand the practice of terrorism. Guevara's work on guerrilla war, *Guerrilla Warfare*, has been translated for mass market paperback distribution in America, and copies are still available. Marighella's *Minimanual* has been published by underground presses, and sections of it appear in several scholarly works on terrorism. Several U.S. government agencies have complete translations. You can check Jay Mallin, *Terror and Urban Guerrillas*, for a partial text and excellent commentary.

Edward Herman's critical analysis of U.S. policy in Latin America, *The Real Terror Network*, is readable and should be read. This should be complemented by Ernest Duff's and James McCamant's *Violence and Repression in Latin America*. The book is becoming a classic study of Latin American violence. Ernst Halperin's book is often overlooked, but it is outstanding. The report of the investigative committee chaired by former Secretary of State Henry Kissinger is also good. It has many objective sections and condemns repression as a method of dealing with guerrilla war and terrorism.

NATIONALISM AND HOLY WARS:
TERRORIST TRADITIONS IN THE MIDDLE EAST

Latin American terrorism may seem confusing, but it cannot compare to the complexities of terrorism in the Middle East. Turmoil in the Middle East results from conflicts between old and new—the Middle Ages and the twentieth century—and from not only cultural and value conflicts, but also deeply felt religious conflicts. It is a geographical region of immense economic importance as well as one where superpower interests collide. Since World War II it has been the scene of a series of conventional wars; it has also become closely associated with the growth of modern terrorism.

It is difficult to provide a thorough background to the Middle East in an introductory chapter; a basic orientation only is possible. After you read this chapter, you should be able to do the following.

1. Describe the three primary sources of terrorism in the Middle East
2. Explain the symbiotic relationship of the different types of Middle Eastern terrorism
3. Summarize the history of each source of terrorism
4. Describe the significance of intra-Arab rivalries and of the 1967 Arab-Israeli War with regard to terrorism
5. Offer an explanation for the intense hatred of the United States by some people in the Middle East
6. Explain the exportation of Middle Eastern terrorism to Western Europe
7. Explain the potential danger for superpower confrontation as a result of terrorism
8. Explain the effectiveness and popularity of terrorism as a military tactic

THREE SOURCES OF TERRORISM IN THE MIDDLE EAST

In order to understand terrorism in the Middle East, it is necessary to appreciate certain aspects of the region's history. In the late 1800s the Ottoman Empire, the "sick man of Europe" in Bismarck's words, was falling apart. Various nationalistic, tribal, and familial groups were fighting for power as Turkish influence over their domains

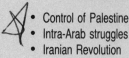

THREE SOURCES OF MIDDLE EASTERN TERRORISM

- Control of Palestine
- Intra-Arab struggles
- Iranian Revolution

dwindled. European nations with imperialist ambitions also fought for power as they sensed the weakness of the Ottoman Turks. Farther to the east, in Iran, Great Britain and Imperial Russia had already taken control of the old Persian Empire. The Middle East, which comprised a large part of the Ottoman Empire, was literally up for grabs in the late 1800s.

The problems resulting from European imperialism became obvious in World War I. The British encouraged the Arabs to revolt against the Turks, promising their support for Arab unity and independence. Britain had no intention of leaving the Arab countries autonomous, however; they only wanted Arab help in destroying the Turks. The truth was that both Britain and France hoped to carve new imperial colonies from the Middle East when the war ended. Russia and Britain kept Iran divided into spheres of influence, and the British had also secretly promised Jewish Zionists a homeland in ancient Israel. When the war ended in 1918 the region was controlled by the British, French, and Russians, but it was a powder keg. It began to ignite in the latter part of the twentieth century.

The sources of modern Middle Eastern terrorism lie in the political settlements made after World War I. The first source was the fate of Palestine. Would Arabs or Jews control this region, which the British had promised to the Jews? A second source was internal Arab struggles to control newly freed political domains; families, tribes, and eventually nations began to use terrorism as a means of gaining political control. A third postwar potential trouble site was Iran. Although it was relatively quiet after the war, ancient religious traditions there would be fueled in time by anti-imperialist sentiments. Those feelings would explode in violence in 1979.

The Palestinian question, intra-Arab rivalries, and the Iranian Revolution became three separate sources for modern Middle Eastern terrorism, but they were also interrelated. The sources of terrorism in the Middle East are symbiotic; that is, they are independent arenas of violence with a dynamic force of their own yet also related to and dependent on each other.

All forms of Middle Eastern terrorism exhibit certain common traits. Primarily, all Arab groups express a universal hatred of Israel. They are not necessarily pro-Palestinian, but they find the notion of a European-created non-Arab state in their lands offensive. Most Middle Eastern terrorist groups are also anti-imperialist. The intensity of their passion wavers according to the type of group, but terrorism has largely been dominated by anti-Western feelings. Another symbiotic factor is the Pan Arabic or Pan Islamic orientation of terrorist groups. Although they fight for local control, most wish to revive a united kingdom of Islam. Finally, Middle Eastern terrorism is united by kinship bonds. In terrorism, as in Middle Eastern politics in general, familial links are often more important than national identification.

When the Israelis practice terrorism, they usually claim their activities are conventional military actions. There have been times, however, when the Israelis have used the same tactics that the PLO used in the 1960s and 1970s. It is perhaps more accurate to argue that all Middle Eastern violence, Arabic and non-Arabic, is locked into symbiosis. To approach this problem, we need to examine the first postwar problem giving rise to terrorism, the birth of modern Israel.

Terrorism and the Palestinian Question

Modern Israel is the creation of a European Zionist movement begun in the late 1800s. The goal of Zionism was to create a national Jewish state in the area of the ancient kingdom of Israel. European Zionists looked to Palestine as their traditional homeland. Although it was officially under Arab control and inhabited by Bedouin tribes, Zionists were emigrating to Palestine in large numbers by the beginning of the twentieth century, hoping to reestablish a Jewish homeland there.

Yonah Alexander (1976, 211–257) argued that the early Zionist settlers hoped for peace, and there was every reason to think this would be possible. Both the Jews and the Arabs were Semitic people, and both identified with Palestine. Furthermore, the Zionists originally appeared to have no desire to displace the Palestinians; they wanted to coexist with them. Some had a hidden agenda, however. According to Alexander, the most ardent Zionists envisioned a state under Jewish rule, while the Palestinians had assumed that Arabs would remain in control of Arab land.

Alexander also pointed to another factor that became a source of Arab discontent. The Zionist movement took place at the same time the Ottoman Empire was breaking up. This encouraged several Arab groups to espouse nationalism for lands formerly dominated by the Turks. The Palestinians believed themselves to be part of Syria, and since the Turks had objected to Jewish settlement, the Palestinians were willing to consider Jewish immigration as an expression of Syrian nationalism. It was a fatal mistake, Alexander argued, for the Zionists held no such belief: the Jews had no intention of becoming part of Syria.

The question of Jewish immigration was immensely complicated by World War I. The Allied powers were actively fighting in the Middle East against the Ottoman Turks, who had joined the Central Powers. The Allies encouraged Arab nationalism and revolt in order to divert the Turks. At the same time they encouraged Jewish ambitions. They followed this policy while maintaining their own imperialist designs on the Middle East. As the war spread to the Middle East, the area became an immense power vacuum wherein various interests fought for control.

The British were the first to exploit the situation, with a set of contradictory foreign policy arrangements. In 1915 and 1917 the British formalized arrangements with both the Arabs and the Jews. On October 24, 1915 the British made an unclear promise to the Arabs. In return for a general Arab revolt against the Turks, the British agreed to support the creation of a united, independent Arab state at the close of the war. They refused to be specific about the boundaries because they did not know what the French would claim (Becker 1984, 9).

The British promised

the Arabs: a united Arab kingdom for an Arab revolt against the Turks.

the Jews: a Jewish homeland for Jewish support of the war.

the Europeans: Russian and French spheres of influence in the Middle East for participating in the war.

Figure 5-1 Britain's contradictory promises in World War I

The British believed this to be sound foreign policy. They had promised nothing, due to the nebulous nature of their understanding with the Arabs. The Arabs, on the other hand, felt they had been promised a new realm for the kingdom of Islam. Although the British had gained an ally at little expense, the circumstances were ripe for resentments.

While the British were courting the Arabs with meaningless promises, they also played to Jewish interests by promising British support for a national Jewish homeland in Palestine. Again, the British viewed this as good diplomacy. It would create Jewish support for the war, especially in America, and it would bring the Zionists into the war against the Turks. Western Zionist economic assistance might help to keep the French and Russians out of the area at the close of the war.

There was an added incentive: the Palestinian Jews had offered to raise troops to back the British cause, and this promised another force to fight the Turks. On November 2, 1917 the British government issued the Balfour Declaration, promising their support for a Jewish national homeland in Palestine.

These British diplomatic moves proved to be good wartime politics. Arabs fought, believing that they had been promised independence. Jews fought, believing that they were to receive an independent homeland. The French were reluctant to move into the area, because the British had promised the Arabs and Jews independence. The Russians were excluded from everything save their traditional hold on northern Iran (Becker 1984, 9–14). The policy worked well, at least until the war ended.

At the end of the war the British created a series of Arab kingdoms dominated by strong, traditional family groups. Far from representing a united kingdom of Islam, the kingdoms were challenged internally by rival families and externally by other kingdoms. Each family and each kingdom seemed to wish to unite Islam under its own banner. Three major states emerged from this scenario: Syria, Iraq, and Saudi Arabia. After World War II these powers would be joined by another independent state, Egypt. All the new nations dreamed of a Pan Arab kingdom, but none was willing to let another run it.

The Arabs also could not counter the continuing British influence. Neither a Pan Arabic kingdom nor a Jewish national state could develop under the watchful eyes of the British. In 1922 Great Britain received permission from the League of Nations to create the Protectorate of Transjordan. This gave them control of Palestine and placed them in the center of Middle Eastern affairs. It left neither Arab nor Jew satisfied; the Arabs believed they had received a false promise, while the Jews avidly demanded their right to a homeland.

While the British established the Protectorate, in Palestine feelings of nationalism and anger were at the boil. Both Jews and Arabs resented the British, but neither side was willing to submit to the other if the British could be expelled. Sporadic violence began in the 1920s and spilled into open revolt prior to World War II.

The Arab revolt in Palestine began in 1936 and lasted until 1939. It was primarily aimed at the British, yet the brewing hatred and distrust between the Arab and Jewish communities also came to the surface. Both Jews and Arabs fought the British, but they fought each other at the same time.

According to Alexander, the Arab revolt took the form of rioting. As anti-British riots grew, Arabs increasingly included in their targets individual Jews or Jewish businesses. Some Arab Palestinians demanded that the British stop Jewish immigration. The Jews began striking back. With a secret organization called the Stern Gang, militant Jews attacked both British and Arabs. This violence was the immediate predecessor of modern terrorism in Palestine and Israel. It was overshadowed by the events of the early 1940s but resurfaced after the war. Both Jews and Arabs firmly believed that the only possible solution to the problems in Palestine was to expel the British and eliminate political participation by one another.

In late 1945 and 1946 thousands of Jews displaced by the Nazi holocaust flocked to Palestine. Palestinian Arabs, seeing the danger presented by this massive influx of Jews, began to arm themselves. They had little assistance. The British empire was collapsing, and other Arabs were too concerned with their own political objectives to care about the Palestinians. Officially, the British had banned Jewish immigration, but there was little to do about it. Jews continued to arrive, demanding an independent state.

In 1947 the situation was beyond British control. Exhausted by World War II, the British sought a United Nations solution to their quandary in Palestine. The UN suggested that one part of Palestine be given to the Arabs and another to the Jews. The Zionists were elated; the Arabs were not. Caught in the middle, the British came to favor the UN solution. They had reason to support it. The Jews were in revolt.

Modern terrorism resurfaced in Palestine just before the UN partition. A Jewish terrorist organization called the Irgun Zvai Leumi launched a series of attacks against British soldiers and Arab Palestinians. The purpose of the attacks was twofold. The Irgun believed that individual bombings and murders of British soldiers would make the occupation of Palestine too costly. Second, the Irgun was concerned about the presence of Arabs in newly claimed Jewish areas. Threats, beatings, and bombings were used to frighten the Arabs away.

In 1947 the United Nations recognized the partition of Palestine and the modern nation-state of Israel. The Arabs attacked the new Jewish state immediately, and the Irgun's terrorism fell by the wayside. Both Arabs and Jews shifted to conventional warfare and would fight that way until 1967.

From 1947 to 1967 the Middle East was dominated by a series of short conventional wars. Arab states failed to achieve unity, often seeming as willing to oppose each other as they were to oppose Israel. Rhetorically, all the Arab states maintained an anti-Israeli stance, but Jordan and Saudi Arabia began to pull closer to the West. They were enthusiastically led by the Shah of Iran.

In the meantime the Israeli armed forces grew. Highly mobile and combining combat units, the Israeli Defense Force became capable of launching swift, deadly strikes at the Arabs. In 1967 the Israelis demonstrated their superiority over all their

Arab neighbors. Although the combined Arab armies were equipped with excellent Soviet arms and outnumbered the Israeli forces, in six days Israel doubled its territory and soundly defeated its opponents. Clearly, the Arabs needed a new tactic. They found an alternative in the person of a Palestinian leader, Yasser Arafat.

It is difficult to obtain an objective picture of Arafat in the West. He is viewed as a bloodthirsty terrorist by many, especially those whose sympathies are with Israel. On the other hand, he is perceived as a revolutionary hero and spokesperson of the Palestinians by many people on the left. The real Arafat probably can be discerned somewhere between the two views; in any case, he emerged as the leader of the Palestinians after the 1967 Six-Day War. He brought militancy and terrorism to the Palestinian cause in the form of a group called al-Fatah.

Fatah was created in the Gaza Strip in the early 1960s. Arafat believed its purpose should be armed conflict with Israel. He felt the rights of the Palestinian people were at stake and could only be regained through force of arms. When Arafat emerged as a major force in the Palestinian Liberation Organization (PLO), he brought the Fatah philosophy with him. The PLO should encourage hit-and-run strikes against Israel, he argued. Actually, Fatah was capable of doing little else. It was hardly a military power, or for that matter much of a political force. The massive Arab losses in the conventional Six-Day War changed that situation.

At the end of that war the Arabs were in full retreat; Egypt had lost the Sinai and Gaza, Syria had lost most of its tank force in a major armored vehicle battle, and Jordan had lost the West Bank of the Jordan River and—worst of all—Jerusalem. The Israeli blitzkrieg had been complete. The Arabs sued for peace because they were no longer able to fight.

Fatah, however, continued striking. With its *fedayeen*—holy warriors ready to die for God—Fatah launched the only attack it was capable of mounting. As Arafat had urged, Fatah began to launch hit-and-run strikes across the Israeli border. Since it was hardly strong enough to take on organized Israeli forces, Fatah chose farms, settlements, and other civilian targets.

Walter Laqueur (1987, 216) said Fatah was limited to three tactics: (1) sending small ambush teams from the Jordanian border, (2) planting bombs, and (3) shelling Israeli settlements from Jordan. Arafat called this guerrilla war; the Israelis called it terrorism.

Their initial successes caused the status of the PLO to rise throughout the Arab world, and Arafat's fortunes rose along with them. With all the conventional Arab armies in disarray, only the PLO had the courage and the will to strike. They were outnumbered and outgunned, and they didn't even have a country. They had only the *fedayeen*. Their action was indirect, but the Arabs liked it. Furthermore, the invincible Israeli Defense Force seemed to be incapable of combatting the PLO's clandestine tactics.

Edward Weisband and Damir Roguly (1976, 261–262) said Fatah did not emerge as a significant fighting force until 1968, when it was forced to conventionally defend one of its base camps. Tired of raids from Jordanian-based PLO camps, the Israelis launched a mechanized assault on the village of Karamah on March 21, 1968. Weisband and Roguly said that both sides distorted the facts, but the battle had an impact in the Arab world.

Jillian Becker's (1984, 62–64) account of the raid on Karamah is extremely pro-Israeli, yet it reflects the impact the raid had on the Arabs. According to Becker, the Israelis dropped leaflets two hours prior to the raid, telling Jordanians in the area to leave. The Jordanians dispatched a military force to resist the violation of their territory, and al-Fatah dug in at Karamah. The Israeli attack was ferocious, supported by armor and helicopter gunships. After heavy fighting, Karamah held firm.

To the Arab mind it was a victory for the PLO, more specifically for Fatah and Arafat. Becker claimed this was ironic, because the Jordanian army stopped the Israeli armor and Arafat had already fled the scene. Yet, as Weisband and Roguly pointed out, Karamah became a PLO legend and Yasser Arafat a bona fide hero.

After Karamah the PLO began a terrorist campaign in earnest against Israel. Terrorism became the only viable military tactic open to the PLO, and a whole set of other terrorist groups began to grow within the organization. Like Fatah, they were not strong enough to strike the Israeli Defense Force directly, and they could not rely on stands like Karamah's forever.

Terrorism represented the only method for a small group of relatively weak people to launch an offensive against a superior force. By attacking civilians, hijacking airliners, and planning assassinations, terrorist groups within the PLO could attack the Israeli military indirectly. This tactic was not ensconced in a tradition of philosophy as in the West, nor was it based on political models of revolution and repression as in Latin America. Terrorism was adopted by the PLO for the same reason Irgun had used it two decades earlier: it was the only tactical option available. Terrorism was a military convenience.

In the meantime, Arafat became aware that terrorist targets were receiving considerable worldwide media attention. Under his tutelage, the PLO campaign became increasingly dramatic and public. Savage attacks received media attention. Hijackings and hostage-taking incidents brought extended press coverage. It appeared that the Palestinians were one in their struggle against Israel, and Arafat was willing to use the attraction of press coverage to bring attention to the plight of the Palestinian people. Terrorism thus became an expression of political unity for Arafat.

For others in the PLO it was not. Despite Arafat's attempt to coalesce the movement, various terrorist groups in the PLO started to go their own way as early as 1970. Walter Laqueur said when the history of the PLO is written, it will be a chronology of continuous splits among splinter groups. Becker, albeit in a most biased account, simply said that the PLO has already declined due to factionalism and Israeli counterstrikes. Regardless, the PLO splintered.

Why would a group lose the power it gained after the Six-Day War when no other power was willing to strike the Israelis? Why would a group that so desperately needed unity splinter? The answers are found in the symbiotic relation of the sources of Middle Eastern terrorism. The Palestinian question is important, and hatred of Israel is surely one of the ties that binds the Islamic world, but the Palestinians also play a role in a broader struggle for control of the Arab world. This is the focus of the next section.

Terrorism and the Intra-Arab Power Struggles

Although the modern struggle for control of the kingdom of Islam dates from the breakup of the Ottoman Empire, we may join the sequence by continuing our examination of the PLO. After Karamah the PLO launched a full-blown terrorist campaign against Israel, and its popularity soared in the Arab world. As its prestige and power grew, the PLO came to represent something more than an anti-Israel terrorist group to leaders in Syria and Iraq.

Arab leaders in Syria and Iraq had long been rivals of Jordan's King Hussein. They began to view the PLO as a potential instrument with which to achieve their foreign policy objectives and as an ally against Jordan. The popularity of the PLO allowed it to act with more and more autonomy, and it joined with Syrian-and Iraqi-sponsored opposition parties in Jordan. This did not please the king of Jordan.

King Hussein of Jordan viewed the increasing strength of the PLO in his land with growing concern. He had entered the war against Israel with some reluctance and preferred to take a moderate stance in the Pan Arabic struggle. Jordan, closely identified with British culture and friendly with the West, did not endorse the radicalism of Syria and other militant Arab states. King Hussein was especially wary of Syrian and Iraqi expansionist dreams and was more concerned with the protection of Jordan than with a united Arabic kingdom.

As the PLO grew, it identified more closely with militant Arab states, giving them a potential base in Jordan. In 1970 King Hussein told the displaced PLO forces in Jordan to cease their activities against Israel. He was not trying to protect Israel but trying to eliminate rival influences in Jordan.

The PLO was on an all-time high and not about to quit. Radical elements in Iraq and Syria encouraged Arafat to defy Hussein's order. Members of the Ba'ath party, a Pan Arabic socialist movement with branches in Syria and Iraq, saw the PLO as a tool that could be used against the Israelis. More importantly, however, they came to view the organization as a weapon to help the cause of revolution and socialism among the Arabs. Arafat defied Hussein's order and stepped up operations against Israel with the support of Syria and Iraq.

Arafat continued training in Jordanian PLO camps and invited revolutionaries throughout the Middle East to participate. His exiled Palestinian government took no orders from its Jordanian host. Raids against Israel were conducted by a variety of PLO and foreign terrorist groups, and Arafat's reputation as a revolutionary hero spread beyond the Middle East. This became too much for King Hussein. In September 1970 Hussein attacked the PLO.

Arafat and the PLO were taken completely by surprise. The PLO terrorist offensive against Israel had worked because the terrorists operated in base camps that, although subject to Israeli attack, were relatively immune from annihilation. This was not the case when King Hussein's Jordanian army struck; the PLO had nowhere to run. As Jordanian regulars bombarded PLO camps and launched an all-out assault, Arafat had no alternative. Too weak to stand and fight, he fled to southern Lebanon. It was his only option.

The expulsion of the PLO from Jordan in 1970 marked a turning point in Middle Eastern terrorism. The campaign against Israel continued as a Fatah group called Black September made ready for an attack on the 1972 Olympic Games in Munich, but the Arabs had realized the potential of the PLO's tactics for other conflicts. As various terrorist groups split off from Arafat's control, a host of Arab states offered support and assistance. Ironically, their prime target was not Israel, and they were not overly interested in the Palestinian cause. The splintering PLO groups were to be used as terrorist agents against rival Arab states.

Iraq became a factor in the spread of internal Arab terrorism. Supported by a socialist party, leaders in Iraq envisioned a Pan Arabic state under socialist control. Of course, Israel had to be eliminated, but conservative Arab states were just as threatening. In addition, Syria posed a serious challenge to Iraqi leadership in the Arabic world.

In the early 1970s, a Fatah recruiter came to Iraq to open a training center in Baghdad. The Iraqis began instead to recruit him and suggested that he use his terrorists not only against Israel and its Western supporters, but also in the wider struggle for Pan Arabism. His name was Sabri al-Banna, better known in the West by the name Abu Nidal (Melman 1986, 69–75).

Syria became an even stronger presence. With designs on Lebanon and eventually Israel, Syria's territorial dreams, born after World War I, had not faded away. Syria followed a twofold policy with respect to terrorism. First, it actively encouraged the breakup of PLO terrorist organizations and promoted a situation of general anarchy in Lebanon. Second, it recruited radical splinter groups from the PLO and prepared them for a variety of missions. While Israel was always deemed to be the main enemy in the Middle East, the Syrians attacked Arab targets as well. Terrorism would be used against Iraqi and Lebanese forces opposing Syrian influence. Most notably, anti-Syrian elements in the PLO would be subject to attack.

Libya entered the fracas in 1969 when Colonel Moamar Khadaffy began to finance the PLO. Khadaffy had territorial interests, including the elimination of Egypt as a rival power in North Africa, and he supported the concept of a Pan Arabic socialist state with Libya having supreme control. Although Libya enjoyed a fairly substantial income from its oil production, Khadaffy faced a problem similar to that of Syria and Iraq. His conventional military forces could not support his dreams. Terrorism, on the other hand, seemed an interesting alternative. In 1974 Khadaffy introduced his own faction in the PLO and established base camps for terrorist training (Reese 1986).

Although an international campaign of terrorism was being waged by a myriad of tiny terrorist groups in the 1970s, Israel and the West were not the only targets. The Arab states were fighting each other for their own national interests, and terrorism was one of the weapons in their arsenals. Lebanon serves as an example of conflict in this arena. Several groups began to fight each other in the Lebanese civil war, and most were willing to employ terrorism in an effort to obtain their objectives.

In Lebanon the mainstream PLO under Arafat became a fairly autonomous and potent force in the south. Further to the north, nationalistic Lebanese Christian and Islamic militias opposed each other as well as the Palestinians and foreign interests. Syria backed its own militia in the hope of increasing its influence in Lebanon, while Iran joined the fighting after the Islamic revolution of 1979. This complex situation was complicated even further by the 1982 Israeli invasion of Lebanon.

Every Lebanese group, with the exception of the Christian militia, has fought the Israelis, but the groups have spent most of their time fighting each other. Terrorism has been used frequently and remains a popular tactic. While it has been used by factions combatting Israel and its Western supporters, it has also been used against other Arabs. Small terrorist groups were absorbed by competing militias and states by the mid-1980s.

Neil Livingstone, a terrorism expert who frequently worked as a consultant to the Reagan administration, suggested that the pattern in Lebanon reflected an important change in Middle Eastern terrorism (Livingstone and Arnold 1986, 11–23). According to Livingstone, the nature of terrorism began to change in the 1970s. Small terrorist groups fighting for ideological causes were absorbed into nation-states. Nations offered sanctuary and supplies for the terrorists, who in return were expected to do the nation's bidding.

The situation in Lebanon typifies Arab states using terrorism as a military tactic against both Israel and each other. Livingstone said the process started with arms transfers to the PLO in Lebanon and culminated in direct sponsorship and control of terrorist groups by revolutionary Iran. This shift in terrorism has resulted in a change in the nature of war.

This factor has not been readily accepted in other Western approaches to terrorism. Rather than seeing terrorism as a weapon in internal struggles, some analysts believe Middle Eastern states simply use it to attack Israel and the West. In January 1986 a group of Western and Israeli authorities on terrorism met in Tel Aviv to discuss state-sponsored terrorism (International Security Council, 1986). Most of the participants were government officials, experts on military affairs, or representatives from the media. After a general meeting, in which terrorism was universally condemned, the main group broke into smaller panels to define a strategy against state-sponsored terrorism.

The working groups of the International Security Council concluded that all terrorism—that is, every form of terrorism in the world—existed thanks to state sponsors. State-sponsored terrorist groups were targeting Israel and the West in a campaign of terror. They were all united, and were supported by Iran, Syria, Cuba, North Korea, and Libya. The Council made no mention of terrorism in intra-Arab struggles. To their minds, terrorism was a tactic used only against the West.

Critics of groups like the International Security Council have maintained that they ignore the evidence. In their zeal to explain attacks against the West, they have failed to see how terrorism has been incorporated as a military policy in the manner suggested by Livingstone. Israeli and Western targets have been hit, but terrorism is used most frequently in Arab-versus-Arab struggles.

After the Six-Day War, only the PLO dared strike out at Israel. Even though Hussein expelled the PLO from Jordan in 1970, various PLO factions continued to make headlines and drew attention to the Palestinian cause. Some Arab leaders wondered, If it worked against Israel and the United States, will it not work against our Arab rivals? The answer appeared to be a resounding Yes! This was especially true for states like Libya, which had no method of attacking a major power, and for nations like Syria, which wished to disguise its actions.

In many ways the question of the Palestinian struggle has been pushed aside. Terrorism began anew in 1967 when the conventional forces of combined Arab armies were soundly defeated by Israeli forces. Some Arab leaders, envious of the success of the PLO, took advantage of Palestinian factionalism and incorporated terrorism as part of the national posture. Far from being used exclusively against the West, terrorism is used as a tool to help settle issues that remained unclear after World War I.

Shia Islam and Revolutionary Terrorism

In the 1980s Americans found it convenient to speak of Iranian terrorism. After all, the Iranians had violated international law in the early stages of their revolution by taking the American embassy in Tehran. They were alleged to be behind several bombings in Lebanon as well as attacks on other American interests in the Middle East. They had mined the Persian Gulf and were responsible for the deaths of U.S. servicemen. Finally, intelligence sources reported that the Iranians were allied with other terrorist states, and that they supported a shadowy group known as Islamic Jihad. The media attributed this rise in terrorism to the rise of Islamic fundamentalism in Iran.

In some ways this popular conception is correct, but in others it completely misses the mark. The 1979 revolution in Iran represented the flames from friction that started in the early 1800s and was exacerbated by European imperialism. Far from being a rebirth of fundamentalism, it is far more indicative of a sectarian split in Islam.

At first glance, Iran seems to fit in the category of an intra-Arab struggle. It uses terrorism against the West, but the tactic is also used against its Islamic neighbors. It even waged a long, costly conventional war against Iraq. Certainly Iran's willingness to sponsor terrorism fits Livingstone's description of the change in warfare. Yet the issue runs deeper.

Iranians are not Arabs, and they practice a version of Islam somewhat distinct from orthodox practices. In addition, they have been willing to export revolutionary ideals through terrorism, not for the sake of increasing Iran's grandeur, but for liberating Islam in a holy war. Iran is at ideological war with the world, and its recent actions make it a third source of terrorism in the Middle East.

In order to understand the Iranian Revolution and terrorism, we need to focus on four major factors. First, it is necessary to consider the development and practice of Islam. Second, the recent imperial past of Iran should be reviewed; it will help to explain the Iranian hatred of both the West and the Soviet Union. Third, Iran's use of terrorism must be considered—specifically, why is it attractive and how is it used? Finally, the first three factors must be drawn together into the ideology that supports terrorism. The last two factors can be brought into focus rapidly once the first two are understood.

Islam is at the heart of the Iranian Revolution. Mohammed, the founder of the religion, is said to have received a series of revelations from God through an angel around 600 A.D. Mystified by his encounter with the angel and unable to write, Mohammed returned to his family after each encounter and related the angel's accounts of God's purposes on earth in a series of poems and verses. Dutiful family members recorded these revelations, and they were incorporated into a holy book called the Koran. Mohammed, elated by his angelic encounters with the Almighty, spread a message of universalism and monotheism.

While Mohammed's message was essentially based on love, discipline, and submission to God's will, merchants in his hometown of Mecca were incensed by his religious pronouncements. Their reasons were economic: Mecca was a trade center, where various cultures crossed paths and many deities flourished in an atmosphere of polytheism. There was a profit to be made in statues, charms, and relics. Mohammed's talk of one deity and a universal power uniting humankind was bad for business. The merchants took the only logical step they could see. They tried to kill Mohammed and chased him from Mecca.

The Prophet's utterances did not stop, however. Outside of Mecca he gained a large following. In a few years he returned to Mecca not only with a message of love and submission, but with a sword. He declared a holy war, a *jihad,* on all nonbelievers.

Mecca became a holy city and the kingdom of Islam spread. Mohammed was vener-
ated and worshipped as the final prophet of God.

When he died in 632, Mohammed left no one to watch over the new religion.
Several followers joined to select a caliph, an earthly leader to replace the Prophet, but
as in the case of Western Christianity, religion gave way to politics. Within forty years
after the Prophet's death, various caliphs had managed to assassinate their way to
power, and Islam had divided into two primary groups. The Sunnis were orthodox
followers who accepted the reign of temporal leaders. The Shias, on the other hand,
believed their leaders to be descended from Mohammed; as such, they were divinely
inspired and infallible.

Toward the end of the 600s a group of Shias lead by the Imam (religious leader)
Hussein ibn-Ali marched on the Sunnis in what Hussein hoped would be a gesture of
reconciliation. Hussein was warned in a dream that no reconciliation would take place,
and that he and his followers would be destroyed in a battle with the Sunnis.
Dismissing all but seventy-two of his most faithful followers, Hussein went to meet the
Sunnis near the village of Karbala. They were massacred by 10,000 soldiers.

Since that time the Shiites have attracted the poor and the hopeless. Karbala stands
as the example of supreme willingness to submit to the will of God with the understanding that rewards will come after death. Karbala was the rallying cry of the
Shiites for centuries as the religion moved to the eastern geographical realm of Islam.
By the twentieth century Shiites accounted for about 10 percent of all the Islamic
peoples, but they constituted a majority in Iran. The message of Karbala and the
martyrdom of Hussein became the rallying cries of the Iranian Revolution.

Dilip Hiro (1987, 103–135) made an important point about the relationship of
Shiaism to fundamentalism in Iran. While many Western observers believe that the
fanaticism of the revolution was due to a resurgence of fundamentalism, in reality it
gained its intensity from the repressed lower classes of Iran emerging to practice their
traditional religion. According to Hiro, Shiaism became the official religion of Iran
around 1500, but Shiites were always oppressed, first by the dominant Sunni masters
of the Ottoman Empire, then by the Westerners who controlled Iran through much of
the past two centuries. In an important way, religion is an expression of nationalism in
Iran. A brief examination of Iran's colonial past explains why.

Imperialism had come to Iran in the 1800s. According to Ramy Nima (1983,
3–27), after 1850 the British began to view Iran as the northern gate to India. They
were also very concerned about possible Russian expansion. For their part, the
Russians saw a potential opportunity to gain a warm-water port and further their
empire. They moved into northern Iran and prepared to move south. The British
countered by occupying southern Iran. Both countries used the occupation for their
own economic and military interests.

Oil production had a tremendous impact on the way the British used Iran,
according to Nima. In 1909 the British established the Anglo-Persian Oil Company and
started taking oil profits out of Iran. Although direct economic imperialism has ended
in Iran, Iranians still view Western oil companies as an extension of the old British
arrangement. They believe the Shah stayed in power by allowing Western corporations
to exploit Iranian oil.

To some extent this attitude reflects the history of Iran. Nima said the British became very concerned about Iran in the 1920s after the communist revolution in Russia, believing Iran might well be the next country the Communists would target. No longer in direct control of the south, the British searched for a leader to stem the potential Soviet threat, a leader whose Iranian nationalism would make him a Russian enemy. They did not believe such a man would be difficult to find, since working-class Iranians hated the Russians as much as they hated the British. The British found their hero in one Reza Shah Pahlavi. In 1926, with British support, he became Shah of Iran.

Reza Shah was under no illusions about his dependency on British power. In order for Iran to gain full independence, he needed to develop an economic base that would support the country and to consolidate his strength among the ethnic populations in Iran. Dilip Hiro (1987, 22–30) said he chose two methods for doing so. First, he encouraged Western investment—primarily British and American—in the oil and banking industries. Second, he courted various power groups inside Iran, including the Shia fundamentalists. At first these policies were successful, but they created long-term problems.

Hiro pointed out that Reza Shah had to modernize Iran in order to create the economic base that would free his country from the West. He introduced massive educational and industrial reforms and embarked on a full-scale program of Westernization. This brought him into conflict with the Shiite holy leaders, who had a strong influence over the Iranian lower classes. Modernization threatened their traditional hold on the educational system as well as their power base. The Shiites, however, did not bring about the fall of Reza Shah; World War II did.

Both Hiro and Nima explained Reza Shah's long-term failure as due to his foreign policy. Much of it was simply out of his control as the world prepared to go to war. In the 1930s, Reza Shah had befriended Hitler. He saw German relations as a way to balance British influence. He had guessed that Iran would profit from having a powerful British rival as an ally. His plan backfired. When World War II erupted, the British and Russians believed that Reza Shah's friendship with the Nazis could result in German troops in Iran and Iranian oil in Germany. In 1941 the British overran southern Iran while the Russians reentered the north.

Reza Shah was finished. He fled the country, leaving his son, Mohammad Reza Pahlavi, nominally in charge of the country. Mohammad Pahlavi became the modern Shah of Iran, but his ascent was traumatic. An Allied puppet in the beginning, the Shah had to fight for the same goals his father had failed to achieve. When he was on the verge of achieving power in the early 1950s, he found himself displaced by democratic and leftist forces. Like his father, the Shah fled the country.

In August 1953 Pahlavi returned to an office that had been denied him during Iran's brief fling with democracy. The Iranians had attempted to create a constitutional assembly, but the British believed they were moving too far to the left and that they would be swept into a communist revolution. Using the fear of communism as a drawing card, the British convinced the American Central Intelligence Agency that the only hope for stability in Iran was to replace the deposed Shah. The CIA acted and the Shah returned. America looked on the Shah as a friend, never realizing that the Iranians viewed America's actions as part of a long tradition of imperialism.

Hiro (1987, 30–100) provided a detailed account of the Shah's attempt to build his base and of his eventual failure. As the Shah looked out on the streets of Tehran in

August 1953, he formulated a plan to stay in power. Like his father, he believed that only modernization would lead to Iranian autonomy. Yet he also feared his own people. He created a secret military police force, SAVAK, to locate and destroy his enemies. SAVAK was aggressive, to say the least.

The Shah used a fairly effective strategy to employ SAVAK. Rather than taking on all his enemies at once, he became selective. He allied with one group to attack another. SAVAK's enthusiasm for the torture and murder of political opponents complemented the policy. After 1953, the Shah found it convenient to ally with the Shiite holy men, who welcomed the Shah's support and turned a blind eye to SAVAK's activities.

By the 1960s the Shah's tenuous relationship with the fundamentalist clergy began to waver, according to Hiro. The Shah no longer needed their support, and the Western reforms of Iranian society were popular with the middle class, who profited from modernization. The Shiite clergy, however, felt the increasing power of the state as Shia influences and traditions were questioned or banned. From their seminary in the holy city of Qom, the clergy began to organize against the Shah, but it was too late. The Shah no longer needed the fundamentalists.

As the clergy organized demonstrations among theology students in Qom and marches of the faithful in Tehran, the Shah unleashed his forces. SAVAK infiltrated Shiite opposition groups in Tehran, and the army attacked Qom. There were thousands of arrests and demonstrators were ruthlessly beaten or, in some cases, shot in the streets. By 1963 many potential opponents were murdered, and the Shah had many others in custody. One of his prisoners was the Hojatalislam Ruhollah Khomeini. In a gesture of mercy the Shah ordered Khomeini deported to Iraq instead of executing him. That proved to be a mistake.

Nima (1983, 41–77) described Khomeini's rise to power among the fundamental Shiites. The Shah and his father had been very successful in limiting the power of the clergy due to the popularity of their reforms. The Shiite clergy began to make an impact on Iranian politics in the 1960s by wisely sidestepping the reforms and attacking the Shah where he was most vulnerable. Khomeini had spoken several times about the Shah's love affair with America. This raised the ire of common Iranians, to whom America seemed no different than their former Russian and British colonial masters.

Although Khomeini was arrested and deported in 1963, his influence actually increased. He was promoted to the rank of ayatollah and ran a campaign against the Shah from Iraq. Under his leadership the mosque came to be perceived as the only opposition to the Shah and the hated SAVAK. Nima said that Khomeini headed a network of 180,000 Islamic revolutionaries in addition to 90,000 mullas (low-ranking clergy), 5,000 hojatalislams (middle-ranking clergy), and 50 ayatollahs (leaders). The Shiite clergymen were able to paint the Shah in satanic terms due to his relations with the United States; they called for a holy revolution and the restoration of Islam.

In his description of the revolution in Iran, Hiro (1987, 66–96) saw the Shah's fall from power as a sequence of events beginning with Western criticism of the Shah's repressive policies. One of the most important factors was the election of Jimmy Carter as president of the United States. Carter pressured the Shah to end SAVAK's human rights abuses. Fearful of a loss of American aid, the Shah ordered SAVAK to ease off the opposition. Khomeini, who viewed Carter as a manifestation of satanic power, felt no gratitude toward the United States. He increased his revolutionary activities from Iraq.

The Shah pressured Saddam Hussein, the president of Iraq, to remove Khomeini. According to Hiro, this was one of the greatest ironies of the revolution. Khomeini was forced to flee Iraq in fear of his life and received asylum in Paris. Ironically, he was better able to control the revolution from Europe because Paris had a modern phone system from which he could directly dial Tehran.

In 1977 Khomeini's revolutionary headquarters in Paris maintained an open phone line to Tehran. Khomeini sent hundreds of revolutionary sermons to a multiple tape machine in Tehran, and his words were duplicated and delivered throughout the Iranian countryside. Khomeini's power increased dramatically.

Khomeini returned to Tehran in 1978. There was little the Shah could do. Although he had unleashed SAVAK and had ordered his troops to fire on street demonstrators, the public had risen against him. Several groups were vying for power, but Khomeini seemed to be on top. In February 1979 the Shah fled from Iran.

Khomeini, riding victoriously through the streets of Tehran, was still faced with problems. It was necessary to eliminate all opposition if the Islamic revolution was to succeed. The starting point was to attack all things Western. In his first victorious addresses, Khomeini pulled no punches. It was time, he said, to launch a holy war against the West and the traitors to Islam.

The Iranian Revolution of 1979 caused another form of terrorism to spread from the Middle East. Khomeini, filled with hatred for Saddam Hussein after being driven from Iraq, was content to wage a conventional war with his neighbor. Such direct tactics would not work against a superpower, however. The United States, and the Soviet Union if it dared to intervene, would be subjected to a lower-level form of warfare. Since the superpowers could fight and win out in the open, the Ayatollah Khomeini chose to fight in the shadows.

Khomeini used a mixture of repressive tactics and political strategies to consolidate his power in Iran, and he is best understood within the Shiite tradition of Islam. Even after his death in 1989, Khomeini's call to Karbala and his message of martyrdom remain. The contemporary Iranian political experience can be approached from this context. It is also possible to approach terrorism from this perspective, as it is a tactic in Iran's holy war.

Robin Wright (1986) made this point in her examination of Shiite Islam titled *Sacred Rage*. According to Wright, the Ayatollah Khomeini was guided by the message of Karbala. Along with the Shiite clergy of Iran, he believed the Iranian Revolution was the first step in purifying the world. Israel must be eliminated and returned to Islamic rule. The West had become the handmaiden of the Jews, but worse yet, the West was and remains the source of imperialism. Its influence is satanic and must be destroyed. Holy warriors are called to battle. Wright said Iran exports terrorism in this vein with revolutionary zeal.

Wright stated that Lebanon serves as an excellent example of how the Shiite clergy hope to export the revolution. Torn by civil war, Lebanon is a vast network of militant interest groups fighting for political control of geographical regions. Lebanese nationalists are represented, but many foreign powers also fight for control. Hizbollah and its terrorist unit, Islamic Jihad, are one such power, under the control of the Iranians.

Wright correctly noted that Lebanon only represents the starting point of Iranian dreams. A major goal is to correct Islam. To do this the Iranians must overthrow the governments of other Middle Eastern states. Certainly Iraq was the major target, given the Persian Gulf War, but Kuwait, Saudi Arabia, and the other Gulf states are next on the list.

While the holy war embraces much more than terrorism, the use of terrorist tactics has become a part of the exportation of the revolution. Amir Taheri (1987) offered an explanation of this process in *Holy Terror*. Taheri claimed that the Islamic Revolution does not represent the major shift in Islam that many people seem to think. Far from being a new revolutionary philosophy or a purification movement within Islam, the Iranian Revolution is almost a historical accident. In the midst of struggles for freedom, a group of medieval Islamic clergy assumed control of the government. Their agenda is based on Karbala, but this is not necessarily the will of the Iranian people. Ergo, under Khomeini's leadership, the Shiite clergy have silenced the opposition.

Taheri was skeptical of referring to Khomeini's exported violence as Islamic terrorism. He pointed out that there has been no attempt, for example, to portray the activities of the Irish Republican Army as Christian terrorism. Confusion arises in the Islamic world because the Shiite clergy dominating Iran have subjugated everything to the name of religion. Such "Islamic terrorism," in Taheri's analysis, is characterized by a willingness to reject all contemporary ideologies save Shiaism and Karbala.

Westerners did not understand this and thought Khomeini to be a spiritual person. According to Taheri, Western Christian leaders believed they could approach Khomeini on religious grounds. But Khomeini had no time for "cross worshippers." He was locked in a battle with Satan, and the devil could present himself in various ways: as an American corporation, a military force, a communist, or a Christian clergyman. In all forms Satan must be destroyed.

Taheri maintained that this attitude has kept Iran from forming tactical alliances with potential friends. He cited Nicaragua as an example. Members of the Sandinista government courted Khomeini for possible assistance in dealing with the United States. Nicaraguan officials believed they and Iran were fighting a common enemy. Khomeini would not send assistance, however, because the Nicaraguans were infidels. They worshipped Christ and the cross. The Sandinistas were not alone in their disappointment. When Khomeini first came to power, some members of the U.S. foreign service believed he would be an ally because he hated the Russians. Obviously, no such alliance has been formed.

Taheri described the Iranian government's perceptions of the world. The theological leaders of Iran believe themselves to be God's City of Faith on earth. The City of Faith must be in conflict with the City of War, or Satan's representatives on earth. As representatives of the City of Faith, it would be immoral to enter into any arrangements with the City of War, no matter how attractive or politically expedient such an alliance might be. Shias are at war with the devil. No follower of God can ally with Satan.

The call to battle is the call to martyrdom, according to Taheri. One can serve God in conventional war such as the fight against Iraq, or one can answer the call to terrorism. The type of battle is completely immaterial, the purpose of battle all-important. When waging war against the supreme form of evil, nothing pleases God more than sacrifice. Terrorism is not terrorism when practiced in response to Khomeini's call to battle; it is an extension of the holy war. In the final analysis, terrorism is justified for the Shiite martyrs.

The final chapter on the Iranian Revolution has yet to be written, but for our purposes we can place the late Khomeini, his clerics, and his followers within the context of Middle Eastern terrorism. Khomeini's struggle is a war for control of the kingdom of Islam, and it differs from the intra-Arab struggle for a united Arab state. Khomeini's Shiites have rejected all ideas save their own, and they view Arab socialism or worldly political ambitions as belonging to the City of War. Those who accept the godliness of the Iranian Revolution will use any power to export revolution. Terrorism is not terrorism to the true followers of God. It is holy war against the infidel.

INTERNATIONAL ASPECTS OF MIDDLE EASTERN TERRORISM

Even though terrorism emanates from three sources in the Middle East, the early 1970s brought a change to the practice of terrorism. Middle Eastern terror grew beyond its regional boundaries. It spread to Western Europe, and some analysts have suggested it will spread further. Indeed, the current prime minister of Iran has called for a worldwide terrorist war against the West.

Phillip Windsor (1986, 26–36) offered an interesting analysis of the international dimensions of Middle Eastern terrorism. He maintained that even though the objectives of Middle Eastern terrorism are located within internal struggles, it has emerged as a global problem. Violence has been routinely carried across borders. While the disputes take place in nationalistic or regional terms, the targets assume an international dimension. Windsor said the sources of Middle Eastern terrorism have become hidden in this process. He urged the West to attempt to recognize and solve Middle Eastern internal problems rather than to assume that the West is under attack.

Dennis Pluchinsky (1986, 5–26) agreed. He approached international terrorism from the standpoint of national security in Western Europe. A major problem with Middle Eastern terrorism, according to Pluchinsky, is that it has "spilled over" into Western Europe. Western European security forces, normally concerned with their own indigenous terrorism, have been forced to confront a new, unique problem.

Pluchinsky offered a fivefold analysis of the attractiveness of Western Europe to Middle Eastern terrorist groups. First, Western Europe has large Arab communities that can supply logistical bases and infrastructures. Second, Western Europe is close to the source of conflict. Third, there are a large number of attractive, easy targets in Europe. Fourth, news coverage in Europe gives any action immediate worldwide attention. Finally, the relative freedom of democracies offers an alternative battleground for intra-Arab struggles. It is easier to fight in Europe than in an authoritarian state.

Pluchinsky presented an informative empirical analysis of Middle Eastern targets in Europe. From 1980 to 1985 there were a total of 233 Middle Eastern terrorist attacks

FACTORS MAKING EUROPE
AN ATTRACTIVE ARENA FOR MIDDLE EASTERN TERRORISM

- Europe has large Arab communities.
- Europe is close to the source of conflict.
- Europe has a large number of easy targets.
- European news coverage gives international attention.
- European democracies provide easy access for terrorist groups.

Source: Dennis Pluchinsky, ("Middle Eastern Terrorist Activity in Western Europe" *Conflict Quarterly* 3: 5–26)

in Western Europe. Of those, 62 percent of the targets were Arabs or Palestinians; Israelis only accounted for 17 percent of the targets followed by Europeans at 16 percent and Americans at 5 percent. If Western Europe has become the battleground, the West is not the primary target.

Pluchinsky concluded his analysis much in the same manner as did Phillip Windsor. Both pointed to the American air raid on Libya on April 15, 1986 as an essentially misguided response to the international spread of Middle Eastern terrorism. The purpose of the raid was to punish Libya for supporting international terrorism.

Although the strike was originally planned to be made by submarine-launched cruise missiles, the Reagan administration opted to use aircraft after the submarine scheduled to launch the assault experienced problems. Naval forces struck Benghazi from the United States Sixth Fleet, while the American Air Force flew from Britain to bomb Tripoli. Two American flyers were killed as several logistical and training bases were destroyed. Moamar Khadaffy was targeted by a laser-guided bomb, but he escaped uninjured.

Pluchinsky said that the short-term effect of the American raid was to reduce Libyan-sponsored terrorism. It was a message warning Khadaffy not to carry his disputes too far into the NATO alliance. In the long run, however, Pluchinsky said Middle Eastern terrorism is much more complicated than the Libyan factor. The air raid could not and did not address the deeper issues.

Phillip Windsor agreed with Pluchinsky. He pointed to long-term political solutions as a means of limiting terrorism. The air raid was indicative of another problem, and it merely caused Khadaffy to decrease his public profile. Libya still sponsors terrorism; it has simply taken a new form. The air raid did not solve the underlying problems of Middle Eastern terrorism.

Walter Laqueur offered a sobering reflection on the Middle East and terrorism in general. Laqueur (1987, 9) said terrorism at this time is not too important; that is, it is very unlikely to change major political and economic structures. The international danger, however, is that terrorism can escalate. A single act of terrorism could lead to military actions, which in turn could lead to general war. It's a sobering thought amidst a confused, violent atmosphere.

SUMMARY OF CHAPTER FIVE

Middle Eastern terrorism is a complex affair. It represents the most extensive forms of modern terrorism, and it has not limited its arena to the Middle East. Unlike terrorism in Latin America, terrorism in the Middle East seems to have no model. It is not linked to a particular type of war. Also, Middle Eastern terrorism differs from the terrorist tradition in the West. While both are rooted in history, both emanate from extremely different sources.

There are three sources of terrorism in the Middle East. The first source is the Palestinian question. The second is the intra-Arab struggles for power. The Palestinians play a role in this type of violence, but they are not the primary actors. The third source of Middle Eastern terrorism is the exportation of the Iranian Revolution. In many ways this represents state-sponsored terrorism.

Although Middle Eastern terrorism originates from these three distinct sources, they are united in a symbiosis. All forms of terrorism in the region feed on the other forms of violence and certain commonalities link them. The foremost unifying factor is hatred of Israel and its allies, of whom the United States is considered to be the greatest.

Middle Eastern terrorism has grown to international dimensions. Intra-Arab conflicts have spilled across borders, and some groups have recruited terrorists from other countries. Radical groups have tended to embrace the Palestinian cause. Europe has become a primary battleground for Middle Eastern terrorists, with fellow Arabs the main targets. One of the major dangers of this international terrorism is its potential for escalation into general war.

IF YOU WANT TO READ FURTHER . . .

The Middle East provides subjects for some of the most fascinating and informative books written about modern terrorism, as well as some of the most biased accounts you can imagine. *O Jerusalem* by Larry Collins and Dominique Lapierre is written in the form of a novel and is extremely readable. Although it is somewhat dated and its material is not presented in a scholarly manner, it is an excellent starting point, especially if you have no background on the Palestinian question. Jillian Becker's *The PLO* contains a lot of information, but it is extremely biased. If you ignore the editorial comments, the book provides an adequate summary.

Other books deal with the Palestinian question on a much more scholarly level. Among the best is Helene Cobban's *The Palestine Liberation Organization*. Unlike Becker, Cobban paints an objective picture of the PLO. She also does an outstanding job of describing the factions and internal squabbles of the PLO. Some analysts believe Cobban's work to be the definitive treatise on the subject. Aryeh Yodfat's and Yuval Aron-Ohanna's *PLO Strategy and Tactics* is not nearly as objective, but it is informative.

Other works are more sympathetic to the Muslim view. *The Road to Ramadan* by Mohammed Heikel is worth reading. Of even more interest is a book by the PLO intelligence chief, Abu Iyad. *My Home, My Land* is a history of the Palestinian struggle from the Palestinian viewpoint. In addition it contains an apology for PLO actions, including an explanation of terrorism. Thurston Clarke's *By Blood and Fire* gives an account of the Irgun.

Three more recent books deserve mention. Robin Wright's *Sacred Rage* is outstanding. It is well written and provides an excellent explanation of the sources of tension in the Middle East. *Iran Under the Ayatollahs* by Dilip Hiro is similarly outstanding, though not quite as easy to read as Wright's book. Hiro gives a comprehensive summary of the Iranian Revolution as well as the religious background. *Holy Terror* by Amir Taheri gives the logic behind the ideological justification of terrorism.

If you are searching for quick, informative summaries, Walter Laqueur has a good section on the PLO in *The Age of Terrorism*. Phillip Windsor has one of the better critiques of Middle Eastern conflict in Lawrence Freedman, et al., *Terrorism and International Order*. Well-noted experts such as Paul Wilkinson, Martha Crenshaw, and J. Bowyer Bell have good commentaries on the Middle East in most of their major works.

One man's terrorist is another man's freedom fighter

CHAPTER 6

JUSTIFYING ILLEGITIMATE VIOLENCE

In this chapter we'll shift from the historical and cultural factors we examined in the past three chapters to focus on the criminological aspects of terrorism. Every warrior for every cause must ultimately be able to justify the use of violence; terrorists are no different. They are motivated in much the same manner as any person, and they behave according to common social and psychological patterns. Experienced hostage negotiators are keenly aware of the human needs and fears of even the most hardened terrorists. In the end, terrorists must be able to justify their actions, at least to their own satisfaction. The purpose of this chapter is to examine some of the justifications terrorists use.

After reading this chapter, you should be able to do the following.

1. Discuss the relationship of group reinforcement to justifying acts of terrorism
2. Summarize Cooper's "doctrine of necessity"
3. Name Hacker's three types of terrorists and briefly describe each
4. Describe Rubenstein's sociological approach to the causes for and justification of terrorism
5. Summarize three political payoffs that justify terrorism
6. Discuss the roles of youth, religion, and ideology in characterizing and justifying terrorism
7. Describe the means-to-an-end argument and its relation to terrorism

GROUP REINFORCEMENT AND THE JUSTIFICATION OF TERRORISM

Every person who uses force must seek to justify it. As the amount of force increases, the need to justify it becomes greater. Deadly force demands the greatest amount of justification. When a person threatens to kill or kills another person, he or she must feel it was right to do so. Executioners cannot cross-examine themselves if they want to be good at their job.

When a person engages in violent activity on behalf of the state, the government unveils its most sacred symbols and rituals to reward the person. The warrior needs such rewards. Terrorists have the same need for social approval, but they rarely obtain it because their actions are not sanctioned by the governments they attack, and they are routinely condemned by the population at large. Even when citizens approve of the terrorists' cause, they are reluctant to embrace and endorse the methods of terrorism. Terrorists must therefore look outside of normative social channels to gain approval for their acts.

The terrorist group becomes the primary source of social reality for individual terrorists; they provide social recognition and reinforcement for one another. Like soldiers, who undergo a similar bonding process during basic training, potential terrorists join groups for varied reasons: they may be sympathetic to the cause, or they may simply be social misfits. No matter; the terrorist group reshapes identities and provides a ticket to social acceptance.

For social acceptance to work, however, the terrorist group must be isolated from mainstream society. Terrorist individuals cannot find recognition within current social norms, even when large populations support their cause. Richard Cloward's and Lloyd Ohlin's (1960) study of American urban youth gangs provides an analogy. The gang is a self-referential group in a world gone awry. By rejecting the norms of the urban environment, the gang is free to create its own norms. Members evaluate their leadership and their actions on the basis of gang norms. In order to be effective, terrorist groups must operate in the same manner. By this method they seek to justify their actions.

Even state-sponsored terrorists must go through this isolation process. Israel's experience with Arab suicide bombers has shown that terrorists must be isolated prior to beginning a mission, only interacting with others directly involved in the mission. During this period the terrorist is constantly indoctrinated in the importance of the mission and reminded that the goal is more important than human life. Suicidal terrorists are often identified and housed together so that they can continue reinforcing each other.

Paul Wilkinson (1974, 23-25) said that terrorist groups reinforce individual loyalty through the process of justification. They may argue that terrorism is a just revenge for social evils or that it is a lesser evil than the exercise of government power. Terrorism is also often justified as being the only course of action available. Regardless of the argument used, Wilkinson demonstrated, the terrorist group must develop its own parameters of ethical normalcy and go through a process of moral justification.

Jerrold Post (1987) compared the process of justification with the group reinforcement dynamics inside terrorist organizations. Post's research was designed to measure the effects of retaliation on terrorist groups. Some politicians have argued that terrorists can be stopped only when they know they will be repaid harshly for every act of violence. This is a politically popular deterrence argument, similar to the criminological school insistence that swift and sure punishment deters crime. Post was not convinced that such an argument was applicable to modern terrorism.

Post said that there is no single terrorist personality, but that terrorists do follow similar behavioral patterns. The most important pattern has to do with group and individual acceptance. Terrorist groups are very much like criminal groups in having been rejected by mainstream society. The group becomes the only source of social reward, because of its members' isolation. Post said this pattern holds true across cultures.

The individuals who are attracted to terrorist groups are as much outcasts as the organizations they seek to join. According to Post, terrorists are usually people who have been rejected by mainstream society and who fall in with like-minded individuals. This not only explains the group character of terrorist organizations, but it also demonstrates the reason that terrorist groups remain isolated. Individual members only find rewards within the group, so the desire to remain isolated is reinforced. Post said this results in an us-against-them mentality.

The constant reinforcement of antisocial behavior in terrorist groups produces conforming behavior inside the organizations, with the exception of strong leaders who may splinter the group. When mainstream society is rejected, the individual's only hope of social acceptance lies in the group that rewards behavior. If the group rewards antisocial behavior, the fanatic is further motivated to attack the norm. According to Post, the rejection of external authority results in the acceptance of internal authority, because behavior must be reinforced somewhere.

This set of dynamics is applicable to any group rejecting social norms. For example, a young religious person who joins a fundamentalist denomination might well experience the same set of dynamics. The person will be encouraged to reject the norm and turn to the new way of life within the denomination. The initiate can spurn outside behavioral reinforcement and norms because the group provides its own set of incentives. Religious conversion in this sense is psychologically similar to accepting the values of any deviant group.

Yet religious and deviant group conversion does not necessarily lead to terrorism; in fact, it almost never does. Post said the key point for conversion in terrorist organizations is when the group shifts from rhetoric to action. Once the group engages in criminal activity a distinct split with society occurs. The crimes required by terrorism become the final gestures of social rebellion. Crime both reinforces the group dynamics and increases the risk of leaving the group. In Post's analysis, criminal activity marks the true beginning of a terrorist group.

THE "DOCTRINE OF NECESSITY" JUSTIFICATION

H. A. A. Cooper (1977b, 8–18) described the process terrorists must undergo to justify their actions. Cooper believed that terrorists are like most people in society. They have dreams and aspirations similar to those who receive socially acceptable rewards for their behavior, but terrorists have a problem. They cannot accept the world as it is, and while many people would join them in the rejection of current norms, terrorists also reject the possibility of peaceful means for social change. This is why they become terrorists.

Cooper argued that terrorists may abhor violence, almost to the point of rejecting it completely. Most do not relish the thought of indiscriminate violence and murder. Still, Cooper said, terrorists are driven by their utter hatred of the social status quo. The first step in becoming a terrorist, according to Cooper, is the violent rejection of normative society.

While terrorists may not enjoy violence or wish to adopt terrorist methods, they are forced toward violence. Cooper said they cross the line into terrorism when they come to believe that continuance of the status quo is worse than the violence implicit in acts of terrorism. He referred to this decision point as the acceptance of the "doctrine of necessity."

According to Cooper's analysis, terrorists must feel that they are *forced* to turn to violence. Violence becomes necessary because there is no other alternative for correcting the injustices of contemporary society. This attitude engenders an ideology or doctrine of violence. Once potential terrorists accept the doctrine, they are free to engage in terrorism. A group can reinforce their decision, and a campaign of terrorism can be undertaken. A doctrine of necessary violence justifies acts of terrorism, and once it is accepted, refraining from violence becomes immoral.

HACKER'S CRIMINALS, CRAZIES, AND CRUSADERS

Frederick J. Hacker (1976), a physician who developed expertise in terrorism and hostage negotiation, found that terrorists sought reinforcement based on their orientation to life. He referred to three types of terrorists: criminals, crazies, and crusaders. The categories are not mutually exclusive; any terrorist group could contain a variety of these personality types. Critics have maintained that Hacker's approach is too simplistic. American police hostage negotiators, on the other hand, frequently use Hacker's typology as they initiate negotiations with hostage takers. Even if it is simplistic, Hacker's approach should be explored.

Street criminals composed the first segment of Hacker's typology. Although almost all terrorists use criminal means, Hacker argued that there are few truly criminal terrorists. Criminals who terrorize society do so frequently for monetary gain or to seek some sort of vengeance. Organized criminals frequently terrorize entire groups of citizens for economic gain, but this does not involve disruptive acts of political terrorism. Organized crime cannot be classified as terrorism, because criminals have a vested interest in the status quo. Criminals rarely turn to terrorism, because there is little economic payoff. For most street criminals, terrorism is generally a spur-of-the-moment idea involving hostage taking.

Crazies, Hacker's term for mentally unstable violent people, are motivated by a variety of factors, but they are seeking some sort of psychological reward through terrorism. They are not political terrorists, although they may be used by political organizations. They are motivated by the thrill of violence or the feeling of power they get while engaging in violence. That feeling justifies their actions. Mass murderers and serial killers fit into this category. Charles Manson's murders in California would be an excellent example of this type of terrorism.

According to Hacker, crusaders make up the bulk of political terrorists. Hacker describes the category as people who are using terrorism to change society. They are most likely to believe in Cooper's doctrine of necessity: violence is accepted and justified in the name of the cause. Crusaders feel that they must be violent in order for society to change for the better.

Hacker's classification system may indeed be too simplistic to approach the problem of justification, but it has helped in localized hostage negotiations by American law enforcement. Famed former New York City police negotiator Frank Bolz used

Hacker's approach before beginning negotiations. In a police training session, Bolz (1984) said the first step in successfully negotiating for the lives of hostages is to determine the motivation of the hostage takers. Hacker's method of classifying terrorists is useful in doing so, according to Bolz.

THE SOCIAL CONDITIONS JUSTIFICATION

There is an emerging opinion that behavioral approaches such as Post's and Cooper's do not fully explain terrorism. Behind this relatively new attitude is the belief that behavioral theories of terrorism are politically biased, that they are used to deny the legitimacy of certain causes. If a proponent of a cause can be labeled a terrorist, the cause itself comes into question.

Richard Rubenstein (1987, 49–64) agreed that terrorists must ultimately justify their acts, but he was reluctant to view them as a group of psychological misfits. If this were the case, he wrote, psychoanalysis would become the logical method for approaching terrorism. He argued instead that social and economic conditions cause terrorism and are used to justify acts of violence.

Rubenstein believed that two explanations for terrorism become popular among Americans. The first is the conservative belief that terrorism is ultimately part of a communist plot. The other theory, more acceptable in liberal circles, is that a permissive society has created the conditions for terrorism. According to both theories, the actual enemy is not the deranged terrorist, but rather the anti-western, anti-democratic governments supporting him. Psychological theories help security forces respond to individual situations, according to this doctrine, and attacks on sponsoring states can solve the broader problem of group activities.

Rubenstein rejected both lines of logic on several counts. Social conditions, such as poverty and hopelessness, are one of the main causes of terrorism. These have been ignored, Rubenstein argued, because they are difficult to approach. Rubenstein illustrated his point with the examination of a 1983 bombing incident in Beirut, Lebanon.

On October 23, 1983 a stakebed truck laden with explosives was driven into U.S. Marine headquarters in Beirut. At the wheel was a suicidal terrorist. Moving at more than 35 miles per hour, the truck smashed through the security perimeter and detonated inside the Marine building. The explosion killed 241 military personnel and wounded over 100 more. Within a few days, U.S. ground forces were withdrawn (U.S. Department of Defense, 1983).

Retired U.S. Navy Admiral Robert Long chaired the commission that investigated the incident; Rubenstein took exception to the commission's conclusions. According to the Long Commission Report, the disaster in Beirut was an act of state-sponsored terrorism, and the tragedy showed that it was necessary to retrain American military forces in counterterrorism. Rubenstein believed it would be more appropriate for the United States to look into the sources that cause terrorism. He implied that retraining the military and identifying the states that support terrorism would do little to alleviate the problem.

According to Rubenstein, the source of the bombing in Lebanon was a disgruntled, disenfranchised Shiite community surrounding the Marine barracks. Its members viewed the Israelis as invaders, and when U.S. troops arrived, they perceived the Marines as Israeli allies. Terrorist attacks had been plentiful in the area because the Shiites had an extremely powerful political base. Terrorism was the only weapon in their arsenal. Given the presence of an enemy, they felt justified in using it. Rubenstein believed a more comprehensive analysis of the social situation in Lebanon would have revealed this point.

Rubenstein was probably wrong to insist that a military commission should avoid a tactical analysis and focus instead on the nebulous social causes of violence. But, on a policy level, he made a critical point. There are different forms of terrorism in the world. Emotional rhetoric that brands all forms of undeclared warfare as terrorism ignores some fundamental problems. There is no such thing as a stock terrorist personality, Rubenstein said. There are, however, social factors that produce acts of terrorism, and this is especially true when terrorism is employed as an extension of military policy.

In a more comprehensive sense, Rubenstein's position leads to the conclusion that we must differentiate among the forms of terrorism. It is necessary to isolate the types of terrorism, and then to identify the social conditions that produce them. Terrorist actions are ultimately justified by social circumstances. Rather than calling every low-level action terrorism, a more effective policy is to search for the social causes and justifications of terrorism.

THE POLITICAL PAYOFFS JUSTIFICATION

The payoffs for political terrorism are so real that they serve in themselves as justification for violence. Since the Second World War terrorism has been used to obtain three primary benefits: (1) to gain attention for causes that threaten to pass unnoticed, (2) to express political impotence and frustration, and (3) to carry out low-level warfare on behalf of client states who cannot afford direct combat.

The PLO used terrorism to bring world attention to their cause. As a method of transnational communication, violence has been successful for the PLO. Although it turned to public demonstration tactics in 1988, the PLO originally claimed fame through terrorism. Traditionally, displaced minority groups have earned little world media attention, but the PLO was able to use terrorism to trigger international concern about the plight of the Palestinians. Terrorism can be justified when it communicates such a need to the rest of the world.

Ted Robert Gurr (Stohl, 1988, 43–45) has argued that terrorism can also be justified as a means of expressing frustration with a political system. Violence, according to Gurr, can be a symbolic means of overcoming political impotence. Actions do not necessarily have to be successful; simply taking action itself produces a feeling of success and potency. Participation in violent activity is a method of dealing with frustration.

In the 1980s terrorism has also been justified as a form of low-level, low-cost warfare. Larry Cable (1986) argued that nations have explored this option when they are unable to use military force. Terrorism is used by governments in two manners, according to Cable. First, it provides an option for a weak power that lacks the ability to strike openly at a superior power. Second, a state may use terrorism when it wishes

THE POLITICAL PAYOFFS OF TERRORISM

- Gaining attention
- Expressing frustration
- Engaging in low-level war at minimal cost

to avoid direct confrontation and deny its involvement in any ensuing conflict. As Cable pointed out, the two motivations are not mutually exclusive.

YOUTH, RELIGION, AND IDEOLOGY IN THE TERRORIST MAKEUP

Almost all analysts agree that there is no single terrorist personality. Most also believe that no single characteristic of a terrorist personality can be isolated and defined, with the exception of youth. For the most part, young terrorists also seem to be the most fanatical. They are convinced of the utter righteousness of their causes, and they will sacrifice anything to achieve their aims. They have seen The Truth, and they are willing to kill and die for it.

Jerrold Post (1987) made note of this trait in examining the behavior of individual terrorists. According to Post, terrorists are true believers in every sense of the word, and they tend to congregate only with other true believers. This fanaticism gives groups internal power and allows them to take fanatical actions.

The extremist atmosphere of terrorist groups, Post said, produces absolutist rhetoric. There is no room for compromise, and every aspect of life is painted in shades of black or white. The world is divided into two camps, and the process of labeling enemies draws terrorists closer to their fellow true believers. The group expresses its absolutism in idealistic terms and comes to accept it. Post said this is the crucial point in understanding how far terrorist groups will go with violence and destruction. They may detest violence, but they firmly believe they are justified in using terrorism to change a world that threatens them.

Young people are particularly susceptible to extremist beliefs. Except for a few career terrorists, many tend to outgrow their activities. Those who remain often join the command or infrastructures, where they do not need to be mesmerized by the cause in order to support it. The terrorists who actually throw the grenade into the shopping center or execute the hostage on television must unquestionably believe in the cause. Perhaps this accounts for the abundance of young people in terrorist movements. They provide a ready source of true believers.

A propensity to strong belief alone, however, will not suffice; a specific cause is needed. That is, the fanatic must believe in something—something that ideology and religion can supply. A political ideology or a set of religious beliefs readily becomes the source of truth for—and the basis for violent action by—young fanatics, be they a small group of revolutionary terrorists or the operatives of a nation-state. Such principles can be used to transform the true believer into a terrorist and justify the acts of terrorism at the same time.

Religious belief is a ready-made source of terrorism because it can sanctify the terrorist. When a person becomes a true believer, and when the religious doctrine sanctions the use of violence, terrorism is deified. This means that the act of terrorism itself is made sacred and holy. Religious terrorists are no longer working for mere mortals; they're on a mission from God.

Contemporary Iran is an excellent example of a country with a mission. Revolutionary ideology and religion there combine to create an environment conducive to fanatical true believers. Supporters of the late Ayatolah Khomeini seek to export the ideal Shiite republic to the Islamic world. No one is allowed to question the decisions of the ruling clerics, because they supposedly receive their instructions directly from God. Terrorism and martyrdom have become acceptable paths of behavior.

Mark Juergensmeyer (1988) described the condition that must be present to use religion as a terrorist ideology. Believers must identify with a deity and believe that they are participating in a struggle to change history. They must also believe in cosmic consequences; that is, the outcome of the struggle will lead to a new relationship between Good and Evil. When they feel that the struggle has reached the critical stage, violence may be endorsed and terrorism may result. According to Juergensmeyer the proper combination of these beliefs can produce a fanatical terrorist.

Religion embodies a sacred ideology. When performing acts in the name of the deity, a religious person feels justified and righteous. This is true whether the cause is love or war, and it is not limited to socially illegitimate forms of violence. Governments frequently call upon citizens to "praise the Lord and pass the ammunition." True-believer terrorists have done little more than mimic mainstream social patterns. They use the established social paths of religion and ideology to justify their actions.

THE MEANS-TO-AN-END JUSTIFICATION

The debate between process and outcome in political action is ancient and buttressed by reams of philosophical expression. It is closely associated with ideological questions, and can be used to justify terrorism. The dilemma, stated simply, goes something like this: Is it acceptable to use evil to obtain good? If so, to what extent may evil be used? The answer depends on the ideological position of the people asking the question and the value they place on the resulting good. It is essentially an economic equation. Some evil is generally tolerated to obtain a greater good.

This is perhaps the most prevalent justification of modern terrorist violence. It is useful to the fanatic and serves to limit the terrorist's guilt. Atrocious actions are necessary because the final outcome will remake the world as it was intended to be. Terrorists become soldiers on a crusade, guerrillas in a struggle for world liberation. In the new age, violence, murder, and death will be things of the past. Today, however, violence is necessary because the new age must be ushered in. In the world of terrorism, the promise of things to come justifies the crimes of today.

An excellent example of means-to-an-end logic in action is the Red Brigades in Italy. The Red Brigades were not overly active in the late 1980s for a variety of reasons, one of which was the internal dissension that has plagued the group since its origins. The command structure is not well defined, and members have hotly debated the methods they should use to create a revolution. This has resulted in splintering inside the group (Hewitt 1984).

The Movimentalists are a faction in the Red Brigades that attempts to minimize violence. A revolution is necessary, in the Movimentalists' minds, because communism can only be achieved through violent revolution. Yet the violence of revolution is appalling and must therefore be minimized.

In their effort to limit violence the Movimentalists make a distinction between "innocent" and "legitimate" targets. Innocent targets include bystanders or people not associated with the Italian or Western European governments; legitimate targets include any official functionaries or industrialists. In planning operations, the Movimentalists will not condone the attack or injury of innocent targets. In some cases they even minimize violence against their "legitimate" enemies. Blatant violence is not the purpose of terrorism, in their world view.

The position of the Movimentalist has a pragmatic aspect as well. By minimizing violence and directing it away from the population at large, they hope to win the sympathy of the Italian people. The other reason behind their actions is that they simply do not feel justified in taking innocent lives. Death and destruction are ideally reserved for their enemies: they do kill government officials and police officers and feel morally justified.

The Militarists are another wing of the Red Brigades who scoff at the moralism of the Movimentalists. The Militarists see little distinction between the murder of a government official and the murder of a citizen who supports the government. Both represent the enemy and both are legitimate targets. All forms of violent activity serve the revolution.

The Militarists believe themselves to be the vanguard of the Italian communist revolution. As such they have been blessed with a special understanding of the new age to come and the procedures necessary to usher society into it. History will excuse their excesses because violence is the only proper method of formulating revolution. They alone understand this, and they alone must find the courage to act. Violence and violence alone will bring about the new age. The Militarists see themselves as the brokers of terrorist violence.

Both factions use the means-to-an-end argument. The Movimentalists justify their actions by the final outcome, but they believe only the guilty should pay. The Militarists, believing that only violence will bring change, have adopted the doctrine of violence. The Movimentalists seem to find violence more distasteful than the Militarists, but both sides justify terrorism in terms of the final outcome.

Once again, terrorists using the means-to-an-end argument are no different than many citizens in the mainstream society. Terrorists may be true-beliver extremists, but they justify their actions in much the same manner as the rest of us do. There is no magic formula to this logic; it's just another method of justifying action. It works as well in everyday life as it does in alleviating terrorist guilt.

SUMMARY OF CHAPTER SIX

Every person who engages in violent activity must ultimately be able to justify that violence. This is applicable to police officers and soldiers as well as terrorists. Terrorists face a special problem, however, because their violence is usually illegitimate—that is, not condoned by established social institutions.

A variety of theories has been proposed to explain the process of justification. Some focus on the individual, others on the group. Post's and Cooper's positions offer behavioral explanations of the process of justification. Rubenstein's work typifies the growing concern with the social causes of terrorism. Neither position has provided a comprehensive explanation, and each reflects a particular political bias.

There are several political payoffs to engaging in terrorism: it attracts attention to "lost" causes, expresses frustration, and enables low-cost, low-level military campaigns to be carried out. All three benefits are used to justify terrorism. They are complemented by ideological and religious justifications. The logic of terrorism seems to be particularly attractive to young extremists, who accept the righteousness of a cause without reservation.

One of the oldest methods of justifying violence is to argue that the end justifies the means. This argument also been used to justify terrorism. Terrorists frequently believe that a new age is coming that will replace the suffering of the current world. If violence is necessary to usher in the new age, then its employment is justified.

IF YOU WANT TO READ FURTHER . . .

To understand how terrorists justify their actions, you must study both terrorists and terrorist groups. No one has developed a prototype of a terrorist personality; still, many have tried. Frederick Hacker's *Crusaders, Criminals, and Crazies* is dated and somewhat simplistic. It has advantages, however. It is directly applicable to many hostage situations faced by U.S. police. Complement it with Frank Bolz's and E. Hershey's *Hostage Cop*.

Most attempts to explain justification end up by stereotyping revolutionary terrorists. An example is Charles A. Russell's and Bowman H. Miller's "Profile of a Terrorist" in *Contemporary Terrorism*, edited by John Elliot and Leslie Gibson. After studying a variety of terrorist actions over twenty years, Russell and Miller assembled a portrait of the "typical" terrorist. Included in their portrait is an explanation of why terrorists believe in causes so fanatically. Most analysts agree with Walter Laqueur, however, that such portraits are too generalized to be useful.

David Rapoport suggests studying the works of terrorists to learn more about their behavior. Members of such groups as the IRA, the PLO, and several guerrilla organizations have written apologies or memoirs. Rapoport conducts an analysis of these terrorist works in an essay published in *Inside Terrorist Organizations,* noting that Ted Robert Gurr disagrees with this type of approach.

The type of justification a group uses tends to vary with the cause. Study the history of a particular group or campaign, looking for the ways in which both the terrorists and the counterterrorists seek some method of rationalizing their actions. For an in-depth understanding, research the social and political background to a terrorist campaign. Justifications for the violence will begin to emerge from several vantage points.

Martha Crenshaw has been awarded a grant from the Ford Foundation to develop a theory of terrorism. Undoubtedly her study will be an important contribution to the literature of terrorism, and perhaps she will be able to explain the many factors that seem to justify terrorist violence. Such an accomplishment would be a mighty task as the motivation to engage in terrorism is as abstract as the motivation for any other individual and group behavior. When her study is completed, it should be read.

THE STRUCTURE AND DYNAMICS
OF TERRORIST GROUPS

With the exception of the psychopathic killers, terrorists are participants in a group activity. Terrorist groups are socially organized, managed, and maintained. Successful groups must be structured according to the same organizational principles as any other group promising to provide a service. Labor must be divided in particular ways, and each subunit in a terrorist organization must complete its assigned specialty in order to complement the work of other units. Even though its goals are more difficult to accomplish because the work must be completed with extreme secrecy, a terrorist group must be organized and managed for success. This chapter will discuss that organization.

After reading this chapter, you should be able to do the following.

1. Describe the relationship between group size and the effectiveness of terrorist operations
2. Discuss the roles that public opinion and political popularity play in generating support for terrorist actions
3. Describe the basic organizational patterns common to terrorist groups
4. Outline the management problems facing terrorist groups
5. Summarize Adam's thesis on the importance of financing terrorist groups

THE RELATION OF GROUP SIZE TO EFFECTIVENESS

In 1970 a small group of radicals joined together in San Francisco to form the New World Liberation Front (NWLF). According to John Wolf (1981, 63–64), the NWLF was responsible for thirty bombings over the course of the next seven years. The NWLF claimed to be a "moral" revolutionary group, and it attacked only "legitimate" targets symbolizing corporate capitalism. Utility companies were a favorite, especially given the rising cost of fuel in the 1970s. The NWLF also bombed two sheriff's vehicles in the San Francisco area. They were at war with the establishment.

As the NWLF attempted to expand its operations in the 1970s, its leadership may have come to see the irony of its campaign. Even though the NWLF had hoped to be the vanguard of a revolutionary movement, few were willing to join the revolution. In an attempt to compensate, the NWLF "expanded" its operations by forming a number of revolutionary brigades. In reality, the brigades represented nothing more than the same few radicals operating under a variety of new names. (U.S. Marshals Service 1988).

In frustration, the NWLF turned to its final ploy to obtain support. Linking up with another small band of militants, the group joined the prison reform movement and allied itself with a group of militant ex-convicts called The Tribal Thumb. This sealed the fate of the NWLF; whatever chance it had had to obtain even the slightest political support was lost through the alliance. Its association with violent felons cemented public opinion against the group. The NWLF was denounced and alienated. Aside from improving corporate security and law enforcement investigative techniques, the NWLF was a dismal failure.

The experience of the NWLF is one of hundreds of examples of the structure and failure of many modern terrorist groups. In order to make a major impact, a terrorist group must have the resources to launch and maintain a campaign of terrorism. Technological weapons and industrial sabotage are starting points, but they do not provide the basis for extended operations. Groups have to be large—at least larger than a few social misfits armed with bombs. In order to become large, the group has to generate popular political appeal. Their cause must be acceptable to a large segment of the public.

Most terrorist groups do not have this appeal. They are organized like the NWLF, developing ornate organizational schemes and grandiose plots but lacking the ability to carry out a meaningful campaign. Small groups generally sponsor small amounts of violence. Individual acts may gain the public's attention through media exposure, but they lack the ability to maintain steady pressure on their opponents.

Ted Robert Gurr (Stohl, 1988, 23–50) conducted an empirical analysis of terrorist groups operating in the 1960s in an attempt to identify some of their operational characteristics. His work remains an important study of their organizational structure. In the 1970s many people assumed that terrorism was the result of revolutionary activities, just as many today have assumed that it is state sponsored. Gurr's data called such simplistic conclusions into question.

Gurr's analysis produced some fairly interesting conclusions. First, most actions involve only a few terrorists who generate more noise than injury. Second, while it is popularly believed that political revolutionaries dominate terrorist groups, the majority of successful groups embrace other doctrines, such as nationalism. Third, in most instances only large groups achieve results by mounting campaigns of terrorism; small groups cannot do so. Gurr concluded that there were other, diverse causes for terrorist violence and that many remained to be identified. No matter what the cause, however, most terrorist campaigns end within eighteen months of the initial outburst of violence.

Terrorism occurs in either isolated events or campaigns, but the campaign promises the greatest opportunity for success. Gurr concluded that many terrorist activities fall by the wayside because they lack a supportive structure, which is necessary to challenge authority. Political revolutionary and radical groups tend to lack the popular appeal needed to gain support for their activities. This is why, Gurr concluded, successful terrorism is generally based on a popular political cause.

An additional policy implication may be drawn from Gurr's study: if his conclusions are correct, they imply that most terrorist organizations are only a law enforcement problem. Terrorism is waged to gain political ends, but the scope of most terrorist activities is too restricted to pose a serious threat to the state. The level of most terrorist activity would seem to dictate a police response. Small groups are not able to substantially alter the political environment. As in the case of the NWLF, standard investigative procedures can be used to stop small terrorist movements.

Vittorfranco Pisano (1987, 24–31) illustrated this concept with an analysis of terrorism in contemporary Italy. Pisano pointed to the tremendous number of terrorist actions in Italy, along with the relatively large number of groups responsible for the attacks. The reason for the plethora of groups, according to Pisano, is that most terrorist organizations are not capable of mounting a long-term campaign against the government. They can strike only a few times before their resources run dry or they are captured.

Large Italian terrorist groups take advantage of this situation, using many different names in an attempt to confuse authorities. But as only a handful of groups can launch a campaign, Italian terrorism has generally remained a police matter. Pisano cited national cooperation among police as a necessary new element in countering terrorism, but it still remained a police affair.

As terrorist groups become larger, however, the level of response to the problem must be raised. Christopher Hewitt (1984) considered this issue when he began a study of the effectiveness of counterterrorist policies. Hewitt reflected Gurr's position by stating that small groups do not have the resources to damage an opponent over an extended length of time: they cannot launch a campaign. He believed that terrorist campaigns were more important than isolated acts of terrorism, and terrorist campaigns demand expanded political responses.

Terrorist campaigns, Hewitt argued, became important after the Second World War for two primary reasons. First, the campaigns of large terrorist organizations accounted for the majority of terrorism around the world. Small, isolated terrorist organizations have failed to match their larger counterparts. Second, large terrorist organizations have prompted governments to employ macropolicies. Large terrorist organizations can actually bring about a change in government political response because they represent a problem far beyond the means of local law enforcement. Large groups therefore represent political threats.

This introduces an interesting paradox. Despite the relationship between size and success, most terrorist groups are small. Their size limits their potential for success, while their extremism prevents them from establishing a large following. Therefore, small groups frequently do everything in their power to act like a larger group, and they project the illusion of enjoying public support. They have to. In a terrorist campaign, having the support of the public wins the ball game.

PUBLIC SUPPORT IN RELATION TO GROUP SIZE

Terrorist groups can be eliminated without public support. Gurr demonstrated that most actions last from one day to a few weeks and that the majority of groups have fewer than fifty members. To compensate for their relative weakness, small groups must turn to other alternatives to increase public support for their cause. They choose a variety of methods.

Though violence is a statement of propaganda by the deed, the older method of propaganda by the word is still alive and well in the ranks of terrorists and extremists. The case of the NWLF can be used to illustrate this. Although the group was extremely small and socially isolated, the NWLF attempted to build a following by a series of underground publications. It published and circulated several tracts outlining its philosophy and calling for revolution. Members of the NWLF frequently gave instructions in bomb making and assassination in their literature, and they almost always called on readers to murder corporate, government, and police officials. By widely circulating this literature, they hoped to convince the public that the NWLF was something more than a few radicals. They wanted to convince potential supporters that they were the vanguard of a popular social movement.

Right-wing extremists in the United States have also used propaganda as a method to convince their followers that they are strong enough to launch a revolutionary campaign. Based in areas like Hayden Lake, Idaho, extremists publish a variety of newsletters, pamphlets, and political booklets designed to defend their cause. Aryan Nations of Hayden Lake even claims to link a computer network of thousands. There is a purpose beyond proselytizing for the cause, however: the circulation of propaganda gives an illusion of strength.

Yet extremists rarely attract a political base—except among other extremists. People in general do not readily flock to small terrorist organizations. Large groups like the Basque Nation and Liberty and the Irish Republican Army have gained support because their causes are so popular among their reference groups. Their methods may be extreme, but their political appeal has a broader base. Many small groups recognize this and attempt to follow the examples of the larger groups. By rhetorically abandoning their extremist positions and taking on a more popular political cause, small groups hope to broaden their appeal.

Extremists try to hide the most radical positions in nationalistic and religious messages. Murder and theft are disguised as patriotic acts. For example, in an anonymous tract titled "Wann alle Bruder Schweigen," a romanticized account of The Order, the writer claimed the terrorists to be nothing more than American patriots fighting for their Constitutional rights. Posse Comitatus reflected the same sentiments in "The Last Letter of Gordon Kahl," the story of a man who shot it out with police officers instead of paying taxes (Sapp 1986). The Red Army Faction makes similar claims from the other side of the political spectrum.

Despite attempts to expand and develop a broader political following, most terrorist groups fail miserably when they try to increase their size. Walter Laqueur (1987, 9) said this is because they are composed of fanatics. Such people do well to convert even other fanatics, and they have virtually no appeal in mainstream society. Terrorist groups remain small because they cannot see beyond their immediate agendas.

BASIC ORGANIZATIONAL STRUCTURES OF TERRORIST GROUPS

James Fraser, a counterterrorist specialist in the United States Army, discussed the organization of terrorist groups by analyzing two factors, the structure of the organization and its support. According to Fraser (Fraser and Fulton 1984, 7–9), terrorist

	Command
	Active cadre
	Active supporters
	Passive supporters

Figure 7-1   The Structure of terrorist groups

Source: James Fraser and Ian Fulton, "Terrorism Counteraction" (Fort Leavenworth, KS: U.S. Army Command [FC-100-37], 1984)

groups are necessarily designed to hide their operations from security forces, so analysis is difficult. Still, certain organizational principles are endemic to all terrorist groups. Organizations employ variations of command and control structures, but they are frequently organized along the same pattern no matter what causes they endorse.

The typical organization is arranged in a pyramid. It takes many more people to support terrorist operations than to carry them out; therefore, the majority of people who work in terrorist organizations serve to keep terrorists in the field. The most common job in terrorist groups is support, not combat.

According to Fraser, the hierarchical structure of terrorist groups is divided into four levels. The smallest group is at the top and is responsible for command. As in military circles, leadership makes policy and plans while providing general direction. Other researchers have often pointed out that the command structure is not as effective as in legitimate organizations because of the demand for secrecy. The command structure in a terrorist organization is not free to openly communicate with its membership; therefore, it cannot exercise day-to-day operational control.

The second level in Fraser's hierarchy contains the active cadre. Albeit *cadre* is a military term, these are the same people commonly known as "terrorists." The active cadre is responsible for carrying out the mission of the terrorist organization. Depending on the size of the organization, each terrorist in the cadre may have one or more specialties. Other terrorists support each specialty, but the active cadre is the striking arm of the terrorist group. It is important to realize that, after the command structure, the cadre of active terrorists is the smallest organization in most terrorist structures.

Under the active cadre is the next largest, and by far the most important, level of a terrorist organization. Active supporters are critical to terrorist campaigns. Any group can carry off a bombing or kidnapping, but to maintain a campaign of bombings and kidnappings takes support. Active supporters keep the terrorists in the field. They maintain communication channels, provide safe houses, gather intelligence, and ensure that all other logistical needs are met. This is the largest internal group in the organization.

The last and largest category is the organization's passive supporters. This group is extremely difficult to identify and characterize, because they do not readily join a terrorist group. Many times they are used without their knowledge; they simply represent a favorable element of the political climate. When a terrorist group can muster political support, it will have a relatively large number of passive supporters. When its cause alienates the mainstream, passive support dwindles. Passive support complements active support.

Most terrorist groups number fewer than fifty people and are incapable of mounting a long-term campaign. Under a command element that generally consists of a few people, the group is divided according to specific tasks. Intelligence sections are responsible for assessing targets and planning operations. Support sections provide the means necessary to carry out the assault, while the tactical units are responsible for the actual terrorist action.

Larger groups are guided by the same organizational principles, but they have major subunits capable of carrying out extensive operations. In particularly large groups, subunits have the ability to act autonomously. Large groups have the tactical units and the support sections to conduct terrorist campaigns.

Anthony Burton (1976, 70–72) complemented Fraser's analysis by describing the basic structure of subunits. Terrorist organizations have two primary types of subunits: the cell and the column. The cell is the most basic type. Composed of four to six people, the cell usually has a specialty; it may be a tactical unit or an intelligence section. In some organizations the duties of tactical cells vary with the assignment. Other cells are designed to support the operations.

Groups of cells form to create columns. Columns are semiautonomous conglomerations of cells with a variety of specialties and a single command structure. As combat units, columns have questionable effectiveness. They are too cumbersome to be used in major operations, and the secrecy demanded by terrorism prevents effective intercolumn cooperation. Their primary function is combat support, because elements in a column can be arranged to support the tactical operations of cells.

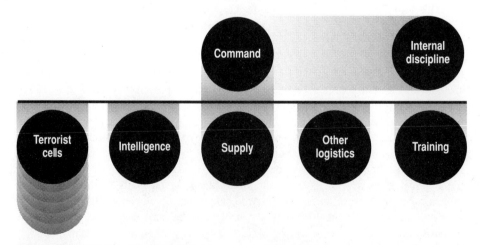

Figure 7-2   Terrorist group organization

Source: James Fraser and Ian Fulton, "Terrorism Counteraction" (Fort Leavenworth, KS: U.S. Army Command [FC-100-37], 1984)

PROBLEMS OF TERRORIST MANAGEMENT

- Communicating within an infrastructure of secrecy
- Coordinating activities despite decentralization
- Maintaining internal discipline
- Avoiding fragmented ideologies
- Maintaining logistics
- Training
- Financing

MANAGEMENT PROCESSES AND PROBLEMS

Outlining and diagraming terrorist structures is fairly simple, but the dynamic aspects of the organization—the actions produced through the interaction of groups and individuals—can be unpredictable and difficult to control. Structure, however, cannot be separated from the organizational dynamics. Terrorist leaders face operational problems and seek to solve them with managerial strategies, as many executives do. There are certain problems endemic to any terrorist organization.

The first problem is the need for secrecy. It dominates the operational aspects of terrorism and leads to a variety of problems not encountered in open organizations. Ironically, while secrecy is the greatest strength of the terrorist organization, it also reveals its greatest weakness. As an old joke goes, sometimes a terrorist group's work is so secret that even the members don't know what they're doing. Terrorism demands secrecy and secrecy prevents effective communication.

Since the necessity for secrecy is so great, each cell and each column is usually allowed a relatively high degree of autonomy. Terrorism is a decentralized affair, and the larger the group, the greater the degree of decentralization. This is not the most desirable kind of organization, but it is an operational necessity. A centralized structure is easily infiltrated and destroyed by security forces. One well-placed informant can destroy an entire organization. Decentralization offers relative security: very few people know many other members of the organization. It's great protection, but it's difficult to manage.

The organization of the Provisional Irish Republican Army can be used to illustrate the problem. The IRA is organized like most large terrorist groups. It is governed by a Supreme Council whose members are drawn from IRA battalion or column commanders. Column commanders are responsible for a number of cells, which in the IRA are frequently called by military names such as platoons, squadrons, and companies. The command of the IRA, however, has problems that emanate from secrecy and decentralization.

On paper the organizational chart looks extremely logical. In practice, that logic is modified by the need for each unit to be protected from discovery. This means that members of various cells and columns usually have no idea who the other members of the IRA are and what they are doing. They get their orders from one man, and that person supposedly represents the Supreme Council. This paves the way for potential splintering, or at the least, misunderstandings. It is easy to see why the IRA is difficult to manage.

To prevent factionalism and excessive autonomy, terrorist commanders turn to internal discipline for control. In essence, what the commanders continually threaten to do is to terrorize the terrorist organization. Factionalism and autonomy are controlled through fear of retribution.

Ironically, internal discipline can become a major stumbling block in the terrorist organization. There are two opposing dynamics at work, one pulling for cohesion and cooperation through fear and the other for autonomy through decentralization and secrecy. Sometimes attempts at discipline backfire. For example, when leaders attempt to punish errant members by assassination, they may well find themselves the target of disgruntled followers. As a result, large terrorist organizations frequently find themselves splitting.

Another problem of terrorist management is gaining immediate tactical support for operations. As suggested by Fraser, the most important element of a terrorist campaign is the amount and structure of active supporters. Without active supporters, it is impossible to launch a campaign. While the press has frequently pictured terrorist leaders as secretive plotters controlling hidden armies of true believers, in reality terrorist leadership must exert itself to develop and maintain active support. The majority of time must be given to creating networks of active supporters, not to launching headline-grabbing operations.

Yoseff Bodansky (1986b) illustrated this point in his analysis of state-sponsored terrorism. According to Bodansky, the logistics of mounting a terrorist campaign are massive. In order to maintain political pressure on an established government through the use of terrorism, a vast infrastructure of active supporters must be created.

Bodansky outlined the types of activities that accompany terrorist campaigns. At a minimum, terrorists need three basic operational supports. Intelligence is necessary to plan and carry out an attack. This includes everything from the selection and observation of the target to the forging of documents and travel papers. A direct logistical network must be established to supply terrorists with weapons, and this is complicated by security procedures designed to detect them. Finally, a support network for safe houses, transportation, food sources, and medical supplies has to be arranged. Bodansky concluded that it takes thirty-five to fifty support people to keep a single terrorist in the field.

Training is another need that complicates the business of terrorism. True believers may have the political motivation to engage the enemy, but they frequently lack the practical skills to do so. Terrorists must maintain bases to prepare for such tactical necessities as target practice and bomb making. True believers are easy to find, but trained fanatics are not. Terrorist groups must have both facilities and resources to support training activities.

Managing a terrorist campaign is a complicated matter. It is conducted in secrecy, yet the demands on the terrorist command structure are as great as the demands on the leaders of any organization. To compensate for the difficulty, some large international organizations have routinized their approach to terrorism by developing large bureaucratic organizations to manage their affairs. It is an alternative to allowing a state sponsor to dominate the internal affairs of the group.

Brian Jenkins (1987) considered the problem of this increase in terms of bureaucracy. According to Jenkins, the bureaucratization of terrorist groups brought many complications to terrorism in the 1980s. Some large terrorist organizations unintentionally developed into bureaucratic structures, Jenkins said, in order to meet the rigorous organizational demands of a terrorist campaign. Others established them on purpose. Once the bureaucracies were in place, a new set of problems developed, essentially resulting from a standard bureaucratic problem: once formalized, these structures must produce reasons to justify their existence.

All terrorists face management problems, and the issues involved in launching attacks are not simple. It takes political support, planning, organization, and resources. Every terrorist group, regardless of size, must take these factors into account. Yet the resources must come from somewhere. Some analysts have argued that attempts should be made to uncover the resources behind the organizations. They believe too much time has been spent on examining the organizational structure of terrorist groups, and that not enough energy has been devoted to the support networks behind the structures. James Adams, defense correspondent for the London *Times,* recently raised this argument.

ADAMS'S ANALYSIS OF THE FINANCING OF TERRORISM

James Adams (1986) presented an excellent analysis of terrorist organizations in *The Financing of Terror*. His thesis was that terrorism had changed between the 1960s and the 1980s, and that most Western defense policies had failed to account for the change. Led by the United States, defense policy has been aimed at uncovering state-sponsored terrorism.

This has resulted in a fundamental misunderstanding of the function and nature of terrorism, Adams said. Major terrorist organizations are independent of states, and they have created independent financial support networks to stay in business. The best way to attack terrorism, Adams concluded, was to attack the financial structures that support independent terrorist organizations.

Adams believed that modern terrorism grew from the revolutionary violence in the 1960s. As violence grew, Adams said, the West developed two schools of thought to approach the problem. One school saw increased terrorism as a state-sponsored activity, used to support national military functions. The other school said that terrorism could only be eliminated when the political causes of terrorism, such as injustices, were uncovered and eliminated. Adams believed that both groups had a point, but that they missed a central issue.

Terrorism in the late 1980s became distinct from violence in the 1960s. It grew, was transformed, and came to possess a dynamic of its own. Nation-states became involved in sponsoring terrorism—both in the West and East—but not in the manner envisioned by American defense policy makers.

Both KGB and the CIA have sponsored movements that have threatened the social harmony of the other. Yet neither side has poured a vast amount of resources into

terrorist sponsorship, and neither the CIA nor the KGB have been particularly successful in dealing with terrorist groups. Adams said the real superpower rivalry emerges
when terrorists evolve into guerrilla forces. Terrorists by themselves have not proven
to be effective in forming national strategies for the West and East.

States do play a major role in establishing terrorist groups (witness Iran's creation
of groups to export its revolution), but groups tend to grow and function on their own.
Just as Gurr and Hewitt pointed to the difficulties of maintaining a campaign, Adams
was also perplexed by the ability of large terrorist groups to maintain their operations.
If they did not enjoy overwhelming support from the superpower rivals or their client
states, from where did they get their resources? Adams found his answer in a variety of
sources with a single common denominator: no matter how a terrorist group approached its particular task, it had to have internal financial backing built into its infrastructure. Money is required to mount a terrorist campaign.

Adams examined a number of large terrorist groups to obtain his answer. In order
to obtain autonomy in the struggle for Palestine, the PLO established an economic
wing called Samed in 1970. Adams said that Samed has developed into a rational
business structure to support the PLO. It uses modern organizational theories providing
economic benefits, salaries, and incentives to the *fedayeen*. Although Samed's headquarters were destroyed in the 1983 Israeli invasion of Lebanon, operations have
moved to Tunisia, Algeria, and Syria. Samed runs farms and is rapidly building
factories. It intends to be a strong economic force in the Middle East by the twenty-first
century.

Adams also focused his attention on the Provisional IRA. He stated that it was
popular to believe that the Provisional IRA gets most of its money from the United
States. America, however, is not the prime source of its income. The Provisional IRA
maintains its coffers by running an organized crime network in Northern Ireland. This
transformation, from revolutionaries to underground gangsters, has proven to be the
best method of financing terrorism.

In what Adams called its "Capone discovery," the Provisional IRA found it could
raise vast sums of money by frightening shopkeepers and business owners into paying
protection money. The payment has two results for a typical shopkeeper. First, it
guarantees Provisional IRA protection for the business in case of trouble, but this is not
the prime motivation for the payment. The second and major purpose is to keep the
Provisional IRA from attacking the owner's property or family. The Provisional IRA
has taken in so much cash from its protection racket that it has been forced to launch a
money-laundering scheme.

In 1972 the Provisional IRA found another way to finance terrorism when it
entered the legitimate business world by purchasing a taxi company. The endeavor
succeeded, and the Provisional IRA soon realized that it could make even more money
if it forced other companies out of business. Terrorism was used to dominate the
market. The technique worked so well that the Provisional IRA has set up other front
businesses. Crime pays in Northern Ireland, as elsewhere.

Other major terrorist groups have developed alternative methods for financing
their operations. In Italy the Red Brigades turned kidnapping into an industry. According to Adams, authorities unintentionally aided the process by making the negotiation
for the return of kidnap victims routine. In Colombia, M-19 grew from a relatively

ineffective revolutionary group to an organization of 20,000 members by offering protection services to drug barons. Traditional organized crime methods have become an important factor in modern terrorism.

Adams believed that tracing the financial resources of terrorism is important for a single reason. In its battle against terrorism, the West has been focusing on the wrong target. Counterterrorism, Adams said, should concentrate on cutting off the source of terrorism. Terrorist campaigns are not waged in a vacuum; they require organization and resources. In the final analysis this means that they must be financed. Behind the structure of every large terrorist group, Adams concluded, lies a financial network. A terrorist campaign can be stopped by undermining the economic ability of a group to wage a campaign.

SUMMARY OF CHAPTER SEVEN

Terrorism is generally a group activity, and group activities require some form of social organization. The purpose of a terrorist organization is to attack established political powers. To do this it must be organized well enough to launch a campaign. Only relatively large groups have the ability to maintain a campaign of terrorism; therefore, the goal of terrorist groups is to first appear large, then to become large.

In their struggle to launch campaigns, terrorist groups employ a variety of techniques. Their actions are aimed at the general public as well as potential terrorists. Through propaganda and publicity they seek to convince all parties that the group poses a real threat. This is the first step in creating a campaign.

Most terrrorist groups never get beyond the first step. Most number less than fifty people and their campaigns last under eighteen months. Larger groups have better success rates. But regardless of the size of a terrorist group, its ultimate success depends on its infrastructure. Groups must have a substantial support network in order to pose a threat—a network that is many times larger than the number of people employed in tactical operations.

Managing the operations of a terrorist group demands the same organizational skills as are needed to run any complicated social endeavor. Conducting terrorism is not easy: it requires planning, coordination, and management. States, with a supportive bureaucracy already in place, have become involved in terrorism for this reason, but many major terrorist groups have chosen to limit the role states can play in financing and managing operations. Nations may be important in the initial establishment of a group, but major groups are successful only when they develop the ability to support themselves. James Adams argued that this was possible only through financial independence from states.

IF YOU WANT TO READ FURTHER . . .

Few books have been devoted to the organization of terrorist groups. David Rapoport's *Inside Terrorist Organizations* contains several excellent essays. Without a doubt, one of the best books on the market is James Adams's *The Financing of Terror*. Not only does Adams offer an interesting approach to the infrastructure of terrorism, but he also places the operational capabilities of terrorist groups into perspective. In a field dominated by polemics and misinformation, this is one of the most objective works on modern terrorism.

The first chapter of another outstanding book, *The Effectiveness of Anti-Terrorist Policies* by Christopher Hewitt, deals with terrorist organization in relation to the ability to launch a campaign. Rober Moss's *Urban Guerrillas* is dated but useful. Ted Robert Gurr's essay on group characteristics can be found in the first and third editions of Michael Stohl's *The Politics of Terrorism*.

PRACTICING
TERRORISM

THE TUPAMAROS OF URUGUAY
AND URBAN TERRORISM

In the early 1960s a group of revolutionaries called the Tupamaros surfaced in Uruguay. Unlike their predecessors in the Cuban Revolution, the Tupamaros spurned the countryside for an urban environment. City sidewalks and asphalt became their battleground. A decade later their tactics would inspire revolutionaries around the world, and terrorist groups would come to imitate the methods of the Uruguayan revolutionaries. The Tupamaros came to epitomize urban terrorism.

After reading this chapter, you should be able to do the following.

1. Outline the origins, development, zenith, and defeat of the Tupamaros
2. State the reasons for studying the Tupamaros even though the group has been disbanded
3. Describe the revolutionary philosophy of the Tupamaros, including their focus on urban terrorism and the influence of Carlos Marighella
4. Summarize the tactics of the Tupamaros, with special emphasis on kidnapping and bank robbery
5. Describe the organizational structure and characteristics of the Tupamaros

THE ORIGINS AND DEVELOPMENT OF THE TUPAMAROS

In the years immediately after World War II, Uruguay appeared to be a model Latin American government. Democratic principles and freedoms were the accepted basis of Uruguay's political structures. Democratic rule was complemented by a sound economy and an exemplary educational system. Although it could not be described as a land of wealth, by the early 1950s Uruguay could be described as a land of promise. All factors seemed to point to peace and prosperity.

Unfortunately, in 1954 Uruguay's promise started to fade. The export economy that had proven to be so prosperous for the country began to crumble. Falling prices on exported goods meant inflation and unemployment. Economic dissatisfaction grew, and by 1959 many workers and members of the middle class faced a bleak future. Uruguay had undergone a devastating economic reversal and many workers grew restless.

In the northern section of Uruguay, sugar workers were particularly hard hit. Sugar exports had decreased in the 1950s, and sugar workers suffered all of Uruguay's

economic woes. As a result, the workers took steps to form a national union, but several militant radicals interjected themselves in the union movement. When the sugar workers organized in 1959, the militants dominated the union and called for confrontation with the government.

By 1962 the union organizers believed they should move their organization from the rural north to Montevideo, in order to make its presence felt in the capital. Moderates joined militants in a united front and headed south. Even though their rhetoric was violent, union members felt an appearance in Montevideo would not only draw attention to their cause, but help to legitimize it.

Their logic seemed sound. Although Uruguay was predominantly rural, most of the population lived in Montevideo, a metropolis of 1.25 million. Demographically, the capital offered the promise of recognition. Unfortunately for the union, they did not achieve the type of recognition they were seeking. Far from viewing the marchers as a legitimate labor movement, the government considered them potential revolutionaries.

The sugar workers clashed with the police, and several union members were arrested. One of those taken to jail was a young law student named Raúl Sendic. Disillusioned with law school and his prospects for the future, Sendic had thrown his lot in with the sugar workers. When the police confronted the marchers in 1962, Sendic was arrested; he remained in jail until 1963. When he emerged, he had a plan for revolution.

Sendic had not seen the brighter side of Uruguayan life in prison. The stark realities of Uruguay's now-shaky political system were evident, as torture and mistreatment of prisoners were common experiences. If the population could not be kept contented by a sound economy, it had to be subdued by fear. Democracy and freedoms faded as Uruguay's economic woes increased. Sendic described the repression he saw in an article titled "Waiting for the Guerrilla," in which he called for revolt in Montevideo.

After Sendic was released from jail, several young radicals gravitated toward him.

María Gilio (1972) painted a sympathetic picture of Sendic's early followers. According to Gilio, these young people were primarily interested in reforming the government and creating economic opportunities. Although they had once believed they could attain these goals through democratic action, the current repression in Uruguay ruled out any response except violence. Gilio believed that the group of people who surrounded Sendic were humanist idealists who wanted to bring Uruguay under direct control of the people.

Others did not hold this view of Sendic and his compatriots. Arturo Porzecanski (1973) provided a more objective view of the group's next move. Sendic's group felt excluded from participation in the political system, and Sendic himself believed that violence was the only appropriate tool to change the political order. In 1963 he and his followers raided the Swiss Hunting Club outside of Montevideo. The raid was the first step in arming the group, as well as the first step in revolution.

According to Porzecanski, the group was not willing to move outside of Montevideo to begin a guerrilla war for several reasons. First the group was not large enough to begin a guerrilla campaign, because it represented radical middle-class students. Mainstream workers and labor activists had moved away from the militants before the march on Montevideo. Second, the countryside of Uruguay did not readily lend itself to a guerrilla war. Third, the peasants were unwilling to provide popular support for guerrilla forces. Finally, Montevideo was the nerve center of Uruguay. All of these factors caused the small group to believe that it could better fight within the city.

In 1963 the group adopted its official name. They called themselves the National Liberation Movement (MLN), but they would become better known by a more popular title. As they began to develop a revolutionary ideology and a structure for violent revolt, the group searched for a title that would identify them with the people. The revolutionaries sought a title with more popular appeal than the MLN acronym.

According to Christopher Dobson and Ronald Payne (1982b, 206), the MLN took its name from the heroic Inca Chieftain Tupac Amaru, killed in a revolt against the Spaniards two hundred years earlier. Arturo Porzecanski noted this story, but also suggested that the group may have taken its name from a South American bird. In any case, Sendic's followers called themselves the Tupamaros.

By 1965 their ranks had grown to fifty followers, and they were building a network of sympathizers in the city. Instead of following the prescribed method of Latin American revolution, based on a rural guerrilla operation, the Tupamaros organized to do battle inside the city, following the recent guidelines of Carlos Marighella. Terrorism would become the prime strategy for assaulting the enemy. The Tupamaros, unlike Castro, were not interested in building a conventional military force to strike at the government.

The Tupamaros had expanded to nearly three thousand members by 1970, Porzecanski estimated. Expansion brought an extremely decentralized command structure and the evolution of a grand strategy intended to result in national socialism. This program, the Tupamaros claimed, would allow the government to nationalize and distribute economic resources equitably. The Tupamaros were more interested in redistributing the wealth of Uruguay than establishing a socialist government. Rather than risk alienating the population with abstract Marxist rhetoric, they wanted to create an economy that would offer opportunities to Montevideo's working class. As they expanded, the Tupamaros constantly stressed that theirs was a working-class revolution, in an effort to attract a following.

Despite their willingness to expound the national socialist propaganda, the Tupamaros never developed an elaborate philosophical base; they were more interested in action. Ross Butler (1976, 53–59) described the growth of the terrorist group by tracking their tactics. Butler said they engaged in rather inconsequential activities in the early stages of their development. From 1964 to 1968 they concentrated on gathering arms and financial backing. After 1968, however, their tactics changed, and, according to Butler, the government found it necessary to take them seriously.

In 1968 the Tupamaros launched a massive campaign of decentralized terrorism. They were able to challenge government authority because their movement was growing, and a series of bank robberies had served to finance their operations. Armed with the power to strike, the Tupamaros sought to paralyze the government in Montevideo. They believed, as had Carlos Marighella in Brazil, that the government would increasingly turn to repression as a means of defense and the people would be forced to join the revolution.

The government was quick to respond, but found there was very little it could do. The Tupamaros held all the cards. They struck when and where they wanted, and generally made the government's security forces look foolish. They kidnapped high officials from the Uruguayan government, and the police could do little to find the victims. Kidnapping became so successful that the Tupamaros took to kidnapping foreign diplomats. They seemed able to choose their victims and strike their targets at will. Frustrated, the police turned to an old Latin American tactic. They began torturing suspected Tupamaros.

Torturing prisoners served several purposes. First, it provided a ready source of information. In fact, when the Tupamaros were destroyed, it was primarily through massive arrests based on information gleaned from interrogations. Second, torture was believed to serve as a deterrent to other would-be revolutionaries. Although this torture was always unofficial, most potential government opponents knew what lay in store for them if they were caught.

The methods of torture were brutal; María Gilio (1972, 141–172) described in detail the police and military torture of suspected Tupamaros. Even when prisoners finally provided information, they continued to be tortured routinely until they were either killed or released. Torture became a standard police tactic.

A. J. Langguth (1978) devoted most of his work to the torture commonplace in Uruguay and Brazil. The torturers viewed themselves as professionals who were simply carrying out a job for the government. Rapes, beatings, and murders were common, but the police refined the art of torture in order to keep victims in pain as long as possible. Some suspects were tortured over a period of months or even years, according to Langguth.

In the midst of revolution and torture, the Tupamaros blamed the United States for supporting the brutal Uruguayan government. Their internal revolt thus adopted the rhetoric of an anti-imperialist revolution, which increased their popular support. The Tupamaros established several combat and support columns in Montevideo, and by 1970 they began to reach the zenith of their power. Porzecanski said that they almost achieved a duality of power; that is, the Tupamaros were so strong that they seemed to share power equally with the government.

Their success was short-lived, however. Although they waged an effective campaign of terrorism, they were never able to capture the hearts of the working class. Most of Montevideo's workers viewed the Tupamaros as privileged students with no real interest in the working class. In addition, the level of their violence was truly appalling. During terrorist operations, numerous people were routinely murdered. The eventual murder of a kidnapped American police official disgusted the workers, even though they had no great love for the United States. Tupamaro tactics alienated their potential supporters.

In the end, violence spelled doom for the Tupamaros. By bringing chaos to the capital, they had succeeded in unleashing the full wrath of the government. In addition, the Tupamaros had overestimated their strength. In 1971, for example, they joined a left-wing coalition of parties and ran for office. According to Ronald MacDonald (1972, 24–45), this was a fatal mistake. The Tupamaros had alienated potential electoral support through their terrorist campaign and caused the left-wing coalition to be soundly defeated in national elections.

The electoral defeat was not the only bad news for the Tupamaros. The election brought a right-wing government to power, and the new military government openly advocated and approved of repression. A brutal counterterrorist campaign followed. Far from being alienated by this, the workers of Montevideo applauded the new government's actions, even when it declared martial law in 1972. Armed with expanded powers, the government began to round up all leftists in 1972. For all practical purposes, the Tupamaros were finished. Their violence helped bring about a revolution, but not the type they had intended.

WHY STUDY THE TUPAMAROS?

Terrorism has changed in the years since 1972, and it would seem that examples of contemporary terrorism could be used more profitably to examine our topic. This would be true of most groups from the 1960s, certainly—they appeared briefly and quickly faded into history. It is not true of the Tupamaros, however. Even though they were destroyed, their legacy of urban terrorism lives on.

Peter Waldmann (1986, 259) summed up the Tupamaros best by stating that they became the masters of urban terrorism. He believed that in terms of striking power, organization, and the ability to control a city, no group has ever surpassed the Tupamaros. They epitomized the terrorist role.

Waldmann's comments suggest that the Tupamaros merit our consideration for several reasons. First, as he stated, the Tupamaros were masters of their trade. Many revolutionary groups have sought to bring about an urban revolution, but no group has been so successful. The methods used by the Tupamaros offer the best example of revolutionary terrorism in the world. Their violent exploits made headlines around the world.

The second reason for examining the Tupamaros is much more practical. As the champions of revolutionary terrorism, the Tupamaros have been copied around the world, especially by groups in the United States and Western Europe. Many American left-wing groups from 1967 on modeled themselves after the Tupamaros. In Western Europe their structure and tactics were mimicked by such groups as the Red Army Faction and Direct Action. The Red Brigades split their activities among different cities, but essentially copied the model of the Tupamaros.

The tactics and organization of the Tupamaros have also been copied by right-wing groups. In the United States right-wing extremist organizations have advocated the use of Tupamaro-type tactics. Many revolutionary manuals and proposed terrorist organizations are based on Tupamaro experiences. In the right-wing novel *The Turner Diaries,* Earl Turner joined a terrorist group similar to the Tupamaros in Washington, D.C. The author described the mythical right-wing revolution in terms of Carlos Marighella and the Tupamaros. The right does not give credit to the left, but it does follow its example.

A third reason is that the Tupamaros reflect two major trends in the Latin American experience of terrorism. They embodied the Marighella philosophy of revolution, initiating an urban campaign without much thought to structure, strategy, or organization. And while both Marighella and the Tupamaros believed that the people would flock to the revolutionaries when government repression was employed, the opposite was true. The people endorsed repression.

The Tupamaros also illustrate the relation of class to revolution in Latin America. They sought working-class support for their terrorist campaign and employed a rhetoric of national socialism. Members of the Tupamaros were not from the working class, however; they were essentially middle class. Far from being a proletarian revolution, the Tupamaro movement tended to lend weight to Ernst Halperin's theory of upper-class competition in Latin America.

A final reason for our study is that the Uruguayan experience remains indicative of the power of modern terrorism. When the Tupamaros roamed the streets, people were afraid. Banks were robbed, officials were kidnapped, and people were murdered. Daily fear was a reality, so much so that the government was provoked into action. Like the terrorist group, the government turned to murder and torture to eradicate the Tupamaros. This may be the most frightening aspect of the experience: revolutionary terrorism served to justify repressionist terrorism.

The Tupamaros may be gone, but their legacy remains alive and well in many groups throughout the world. It would be incorrect to dismiss them as a phenomenon of the 1960s. They are a part of contemporary urban terrorism.

THE URBAN PHILOSOPHY

The fact that the Tupamaros created an urban movement is important in terms of their impact on violence in Latin America, but it also has a bearing on the way terrorist methods have developed in Europe and the United States. Historically, Latin American terrorism had been a product of rural peasant revolt. The Tupamaros offered an alternative to this tradition by making the city a battleground. They demonstrated to Western groups the impact that a few violent true believers could have on the rational routines of urban life. The urban setting provided the Tupamaros with endless opportunities.

Their revolutionary philosophy was also indicative of their pragmatism. Rather than accepting a standard line of Marxist dogma, the Tupamaros were willing to use national socialism as their political base; this demonstrated just how much they could compromise. According to one of their propaganda statements, they argued for a nationalized economy with guaranteed employment and social security. The export economy would remain intact, but profits would be shared among the people. Although this hardly represents Marxism, the Tupamaros were willing to take such a stand to attract a working-class following. Socialism under national control was popular in Montevideo.

The tactics of the Tupamaros reflected the same pragmatism. Since the physical situation of Uruguay was not suitable for guerrilla war, the Tupamaros turned to the city. Just as they modified socialism to suit the political situation, they forged new tactics for a new environment. Two of the key words in Tupamaro terrorism were flexibility and pragmatism.

The Tupamaros used the concepts of Marighella in other ways as well. The basic unit of the revolution became Marighella's firing group. Tupamaro terrorism was a matter of extremely small units engaging in individual acts of violence. Such action meshed well with Marighella's concept of a decentralized command structure as well as his belief that any form of violence supported the revolution. Tupamaro violence did not need to be coordinated; it only needed to engender fear. In a war against social order, tactics and targets were modified to meet the circumstances. The police replaced the army as the primary enemy, and financial institutions took the place of military targets. The urban war was a battle to gain resources and a psychological edge over security forces.

The foliage and cover of the jungle countryside was replaced with the mass of humanity in the city. Guerrillas hid behind trees; the urban terrorists hid among people. They were protected by congestion, mobility, and the bureaucratic rigidity of the enemy. The Tupamaros were able to appear as average citizens until the moment they struck. When the battle was over, they simply melted back into the crowd (Waldmann 1986, 260).

To successfully accomplish these tactics, the Tupamaros were forced to develop specific actions. Communication links inside the city assumed supreme importance, along with transportation. To assure these links, the terrorists had to master criminal activity. They communicated and traveled by means of an illegal network. They developed logistical support systems and safe houses to avoid confrontations with potential enemies. They traveled with false identification and collected their own intelligence from sympathizers. For all practical purposes, the Tupamaros became a secret army.

TUPAMARO TACTICS

Although many observers noted that the Tupamaros spent little time discussing their grand strategy, the group did operate under some broad assumptions. Like other extremist groups, the Tupamaros knew that their principles would have to be modified to win general support. The grand strategy centered on winning support from the middle and working classes. Because of the state of the economy and the lack of opportunity for educated people, the Tupamaros began their campaign with a good deal of sympathy in the middle class. Their primary task was to win the support of the workers, and their grand strategy reflected this. Almost without exception, Tupamaro actions were taken in the name of the working class.

The Tupamaros realized that they could not achieve popular support without the proper political circumstances. They believed they could only obtain power at a critical juncture when the political, social, and economic conditions were conducive to revolution. They called this juncture the *coyuntura*, and they aimed all revolutionary activities at this point.

John Wolf (1981, 82) said that the Tupamaros saw violence as the only method to bring about social change. The *coyuntura* would never appear unless the people were incited to revolution. Terrorist violence was to be random and frequent, but it was only a prelude to a general attack. When the conditions were set—when the *coyuntura* was right—organized popular revolution would replace terrorism.

Arturo Porzecanski (1973, 21) said the *coyuntura* was to give rise to the *salto,* or the general strike for power. The purpose of urban terrorism was to keep the idea of the *coyuntura* alive. The *salto,* however, was a separate move. Urban terrorism would be replaced by an organized people's army during the *salto*. The stages of the *coyuntura* and the *salto* reflected the ideology of Marighella.

The *coyuntura* concept was maintained through terrorist tactics. Ross Butler (1976, 54) wrote that Tupamaro tactics changed according to their ability to attract a following. Until 1968, Butler said, the Tupamaros focused on low-level activities: arson, propaganda, and exposing public corruption. As the ranks of the Tupamaros grew, they became more daring. In 1969 they shifted to bank robbery, and in 1970 they staged a $6-million robbery of a Montevideo bank. These activities were followed by a string of ambushes and kidnappings.

Porzecanski (1973, 40–45) argued that all Tupamaro tactics were designed to make the group self-sufficient. He identified eight basic tactics in his analysis of Tupamaro terrorism. The tactics gave the Tupamaros logistical support and allowed them to operate without support from foreign countries. Their terrorist activities were complemented by a transportation and intelligence network provided by supporters.

Two of the most noted Tupamaro tactics were bank robbery and kidnapping. Bank robberies fell into the category of Marighella's concept of "expropriation." That is, the purpose of robbery was to finance the terrorist organization. The Tupamaros used bank robbery as their primary tactic of waging an urban guerrilla war. The banks became both symbolic and logistical targets, and the robberies shook up Uruguayan society. Using a network of industrial, police, and military sympathizers, the Tupamaros mastered daring daylight robberies.

Kidnapping was also designed to produce both logistical support (through ransom) and propaganda value. There was as much drama in kidnapping as there was in robbery. The Tupamaros began by kidnapping local officials from Montevideo, but found they could cause more disruption by taking foreigners.

On July 31, 1970 Dan Mitrione, an American police advisor assigned to assist the

TUPAMARO TACTICS

- Assasination
- Bank robbery
- Kidnapping
- Propaganda
- Bombing
- Internal discipline
- Infiltration of security forces
- Temporary control of urban areas
- Redistribution of expropriated goods to the poor

Uruguayan government, was kidnapped on his way to work. As he was being driven away, a gun pressed against his leg was accidentally discharged. The incident and the wound caused international headlines. Mitrione's case was especially newsworthy because he had a wife and a large number of children breathlessly awaiting his return in Indiana (Langguth, 1978).

Mitrione's story ended tragically. On August 10, 1970 his body was found on the streets of Montevideo. His hands had been bound and two bullets sent through the back of his head. A Tupamaro message next to the body said he had been tried by a people's court, found guilty, and executed.

The Tupamaros kidnapped another foreign victim on January 8, 1971. Geoffrey Jackson, the British Ambassador to Uruguay, was taken and held for eight months. When it became apparent that the British government would pay no ransom for Jackson, the Tupamaros discussed executing him. Instead, they released him in a gesture of good will, hoping to offset the working-class backlash that had followed Mitrione's murder. Jackson's account of the ordeal can be found in his book, *People's Prison*.

Releasing Jackson was not out of character for the Tupamaros, even though they were known for their violence. They continually tried to maintain a Robin Hood image in their effort to win working-class support. One of their most noted actions in this role was the formation of the "hunger commandos." One Christmas Eve this unit hijacked a shipment of groceries and distributed them among Montevideo's poor. These tactics were later copied by the SLA in California when they demanded food distribution to the poor in return for the release of a kidnap victim.

Richard Clutterbuck (1975, 36) claimed that the Robin Hood tactics gained attention but failed to work. Food distribution and appeals to the working class could not neutralize violence and murder. Clutterbuck said that by 1972 the Robin Hood tactics had clearly backfired, helping to form the backlash that led to the destruction of the Tupamaros. The working class people of Montevideo saw the do-good activities as too little coming too late. Even Tupamaro humanitarian gestures were viewed with contempt because of their violent terrorist campaign.

The effectiveness of all Tupamaro tactics must ultimately be evaluated by the final result, as Clutterbuck seemed to imply. In terms of increasing support, the tactics were initially successful, but they failed in the long run. From 1965 to 1970 the ranks of the Tupamaros increased dramatically. By 1970, however, the excessive violence of the Tupamaros had had a negative impact. It alienated the middle and working classes and eventually caused many leftists to return to a nonviolent communist party. Waldmann (1986, 275–276) said the major mistake of Tupamaro tactics was that they alienated their supporters.

Tactics must also be evaluated according to the response of the enemy. Again, the Tupamaros enjoyed initial success but failed in the long run. At first Uruguay's political authorities were completely confused in their dealings with the Tupamaros. They were frustrated at every turn, as the kidnapping problem illustrates. John Wolf (1981, 21) noted that from August 1968 until the execution of Dan Mitrione in August 1971, the police were unable to locate a single kidnap victim. The tactic appeared to work.

But while this tactic gained publicity, it also provoked a harsh police reaction. Torture increased, and the police became more repressive. Ironically, the repression was greeted with public support. When forced to the brink, Uruguayan security forces turned to brutal repression—the one tactic they knew would work—and by 1972 it had become the legal norm.

In the long run, the Tupamaro tactics failed. In their own terminology, the violence changed the balance in favor of the government. Yet the tactics of the Tupamaros differ little from the tactics of every other terrorist group. The Tupamaro organizational structure proved to be much more effective than their tactics.

THE ORGANIZATION AND CHARACTERISTICS OF THE TUPAMAROS

The Tupamaros were one of the most highly organized yet least structured terrorist groups in modern history. Only groups like the PLO and the IRA could rival the organization of the Tupamaros. Yet while both the PLO and the IRA enjoy a tremendous amount of external support, the Tupamaros existed almost entirely *inside* the borders of Uruguay. Since they were virtually self-sufficient, the growth, operations, and organization of the Tupamaros is amazing. If they failed to achieve success in the long run, at least their organizational structure kept them in the field as long as possible.

The Tupamaros were nominally guided by a National Convention, which had authority in all matters of policy and operations. In reality, the National Convention seldom met more than once a year and was disbanded in the 1970s.

Christopher Hewitt (1984, 8) noted that the National Convention did not meet at all after September 1980. John Wolf (1981, 31) believed that an Executive Committee controlled all activities in Montevideo. Arturo Porzecanski, probably the most noted authority on the Tupamaros, made several references to this same Executive Committee. For all practical purposes it seems to have controlled the Tupamaros.

The Executive Committee was responsible for two major operations. It ran the columns that supervised the Tupamaro terrorist operations, and it also ran a special Committee for Revolutionary Justice. The power of the Executive Committee derived

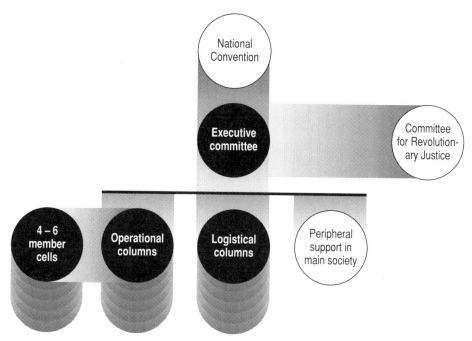

Figure 8-2   Tupamaro organization
Source: John Wolf, Fear of Fear (New York: Plenum, 1981)

from internal enforcement. The job of the Revolutionary Justice Committee was to terrorize the terrorists into obedience. If an operative refused to obey an order or tried to leave the organization, a delegation from the revolutionary judiciary would usually deal with the matter. It was not uncommon to eliminate the family of the offending party along with the errant member. The Tupamaros believed in strong internal discipline.

In day-to-day operations, however, the Executive Committee seemed to exercise very little authority. Robert Moss (1972, 222) stated that the Tupamaros lacked a unified command structure for routine functions. The reason can be found in the nature of the organization. Since secrecy dominated every facet of its operations, it could ill afford open communications. Therefore, each subunit evolved into a highly autonomous operation. There was little the Executive Committee could do about this situation, and the command structure became highly decentralized. The Tupamaros existed as a confederacy.

Operational power in the Tupamaros was vested in the lower-echelon units. Columns were organized for both combatant (operational) and staff (logistical) functions. Wolf (1981, 35) found that most of the full-time terrorists belonged to cells in the combatant columns. They lived a day-to-day existence and were constantly in conflict with the authorities. According to Wolf they were supported by larger non-combatant columns who served to keep the terrorists in the field.

The importance of the noncombatant columns cannot be overemphasized. Without the elaborate support network of sympathizers and part-time helpers, the Tupamaros could not have remained in the field. Other groups that have copied the Tupamaro organizational model have not had the ability to launch a campaign because they lacked the same support. The strength of the Tupamaros came from its logistical columns.

Wolf's analysis of the support network included peripheral support that was not directly linked to the Tupamaro organization. With Porzecanski, Wolf classified these groups into two categories. One group operated in the open and provided intelligence and background information to the noncombatant sections. The other group worked on getting supplies to the operational sections. These sympathizers provided arms, ammunition, and legal aid. Both groups gave popular support to the Tupamaros. When the government attacked the terrorists in 1972, the primary reason for their success was the destruction of the support network.

If you look at the organizational chart of the Tupamaros (see Figure 8-2), it's fairly easy to envisage the entire operation. The Executive Committee was in charge, but it ran a highly decentralized operation. Its main power came from the internal rule enforcement provided by the Committee for Revolutionary Justice. Columns were the major units, but they tended to be tactical formations. The real operational power came from the cells, which joined together for column-style operations on rare occasions. The combat striking power of the Tupamaros came from the four to six-person groups in the cells. This organization epitomized Marighella's concept of the firing unit.

One final question remains in this brief introduction to the terrorist group: Who were the Tupamaros? María Gilio's (1972, 4) sympathetic answer to the question seemed drawn from the Tupamaro rhetoric. The "soldiers" of the organization, she said, were from the working class. They joined the movement to bring democratic socialism to Uruguay. The "officers" came from the professions, to lead all classes into greater equality. Gilio admitted that critics of her book would find her sentimental and one-sided. She wrote the prescribed political apology for the terrorists.

Porzecanski (1973, 31) gave the most objective view. The Tupamaros were composed mainly of middle-class people. Their average age was twenty-seven. Although there were very few female members at the beginning of the movement, as the Tupamaros matured about 25 percent of its members were women. Students and professionals composed about two-thirds of the members, while the remaining third came from the working class.

Sergio D'Oliviera (1973) disagreed somewhat with Porzecanski. He believed that the working classes were grossly underrepresented in the Tupamaro ranks. The Tupamaros continually tried to represent themselves as members of the working class, D'Oliviera said, but the major roles were reserved for professionals and students. In reality, only a few members of the Tupamaros came from the working class. It was a movement of people aspiring to increase their status in the middle class, according to D'Oliviera.

Regardless of its demographics, the real power of the Tupamaros came from its support network. It modeled itself on Carlos Marighella's urban guerrillas, believing that terrorism would pave the path to revolution. The Tupamaros failed because the general public chose to support repression instead of revolutionary terrrorism.

SUMMARY OF CHAPTER EIGHT

The Tupamaros were spawned by Uruguay's economic woes in the 1950s and 1960s. Originally founded by Raúl Sendic in 1963, the group lacked a single leader due to its decentralized command structure. Even though the group has passed from the scene, it merits our consideration because it has had a major influence on worldwide revolutionary terrorism. Groups in both the United States and Europe have modeled themselves after the Tupamaros.

The Tupamaros came to embody urban revolution. They offered an alternative pattern for revolution in Latin America, and encouraged groups from the United States and Western Europe to attempt revolution with small urban units. The Tupamaros were modeled on the idea of Carlos Marighella and helped to spread his ideas throughout the world. They were responsible for the development of many urban terrorist tactics.

The primary reason for the initial success of the Tupamaros was their organizational structure, which had a decentralized command and small units that carried out the bulk of the operations. The small units were successful due to the immense support network they enjoyed. Even with their widespread support, the Tupamaros were essentially a middle-class movement.

IF YOU WANT TO READ FURTHER . . .

The Tupamaros lend themselves to historical analysis better than many modern terrorist groups. The most highly acclaimed study to date is by Arturo Porzecanski: *Uruguay's Tupamaros*. It is a solid, readable analysis of the movement. Christopher Hewitt said that Porzecanski is suprisingly objective given the short time that elapsed between his book and the collapse of the movement. Some of Porzecanski's data has been questioned, but the book in general is excellent.

Alain Labrousse's *The Tupamaros* gives a journalistic-type account of the circumstances. It is adequate, but does not match the quality of Porzecanski's work. María Gilio's *The Tupamaros* is a political apology for the group. She justifies Tupamaro violence as a response to repression, torture, and state terror. She was a contemporary compatriot of the Tupamaros who fled during the police crackdown and was probably killed by the right-wing government in Chile. Her book is worth reviewing.

Geoffrey Jackson's *People's Prison* tells his own story as a Tupamaro kidnap victim. It is exciting as well as being a valuable resource. A. J. Langguth's *Hidden Terrors* is an interesting book about the kidnap/murder of Dan Mitrione. Langguth does an excellent job of presenting the murder of an average American by terrorists, while graphically describing the role of torture in the Brazilian and Uruguayan governments. His book is excellent and should be read.

DEATH SQUADS IN ARGENTINA
AND EL SALVADOR

Death squads—formed from extralegal police, military, and civilian vigilante units—surface when security forces lose faith in a government or believe it can no longer control terrorists or peaceful opposition. Death squads become the unofficial means of counterterrorism, whose purpose is to terrorize the terrorists and others into submission. Death squads have appeared in several areas of the world, but they are most commonly associated with Latin America. Indeed, Latin America has given definitive meaning to the term. In this chapter we'll explore what can happen when such criminal justice and security forces go awry and overreact to terrorism.

After reading this chapter, you should be able to do the following:

1. Explain the function of death squads in Latin America
2. Describe the differences between official state repression and death-squad terrorism
3. Summarize the political factors that gave rise to death-squad terrorism in Argentina
4. Describe the results of the conflict between the ERP-Montonero factions and the Triple A from 1974 to 1976
5. Summarize the political factors that gave rise to death-squad terrorism in El Salvador
6. Compare Salvadoran death-squad methods to the Triple A's

THE FUNCTION OF DEATH SQUADS IN LATIN AMERICA

In the beginning of an article on death squads, Neil Livingstone (1983) quoted Nicolas Boilau: "How often the fear of one evil leads us into worse!" This is an apt warning for all people charged with maintaining state security. Many police agencies and security forces have responded to terrorism with terror of their own, and, as Michael Stohl (1988, 7–20) has pointed out, the state is usually a more efficient terrorist than are insurgent terrorist groups. Death squads have arisen in Northern Ireland, the Basque region of Spain, and in other areas of the world. The use of terrorism by security forces represents an overreaction to the problem of terrorism. In a democracy such a response is intolerable.

Unfortunately, a substantial portion of Latin American terrorism can be attributed to death squads. They arise when there are threats to an established regime. Death squads exist to protect the status quo. Their functions can be explained in several different ways, but the primary purpose of the death squad is always to preserve power. In Latin America they have acted without mercy to accomplish this end.

From Ernst Halperin's (1976) perspective, most Latin American violence results from a struggle for limited resources. He explains most revolutionary activity from this position, and, as we saw in chapter 4, the motivations for counterrevolution can also be examined from this vantage point. When resources are limited, the struggle for control does not cease when power is obtained. Governments in Latin America must continue to struggle for legitimacy and control long after they have obtained power. By extending Halperin's thesis, we may assume that death squads stem from this struggle.

Guillermo O'Donnell (1973) said a series of Bureaucratic-Authoritarian structures have evolved in Latin America to protect the upper classes from any form of revolution. When the threat of revolution appears, these regimes will fight ruthlessly to retain their power. Regardless of its source, revolution often becomes the primary threat to an existing government in Latin America. While revolution may be interpreted in a variety of manners, the threat it implies is seldom ignored by a Bureaucratic-Authoritarian regime. When these structures want to avoid the appearance of repression, they turn to terrorism by death squad.

In Latin America this is translated into direct action. Death squads form secretly or with unofficial government complicity, and they take it upon themselves to destroy the opposition. They may "arrest" and torture a victim, or they may follow up a detention with murder. In some cases, they simply assassinate the victim in public view. Journalists, students, family members, and anyone who might be associated with a revolutionary cause are apt to become victims.

STATE REPRESSION VERSUS DEATH SQUADS

Given the circumstances of Latin American counterrevolution, it may appear that the terrorism of death squads is little more than veiled state repression. Death squads fit into O'Donnell's concept of Bureaucratic-Authoritarianism protective devices, and some analysts have argued that they are merely an unofficial extension of state power. (Official state repression is definitely another major form of terrorism, but it is beyond the scope of this survey, which is limited to subnational group violence).

Others have agreed with this logic. Stephen Segaller (1987, 15–17) wrote that the terrorism of the death squad differs significantly from the type of terrorism employed by small extremist groups. He felt that death-squad terrorism does not reflect the problem of terrorism in the modern world, and a discussion of death squads belongs only in a context of state repression. Segaller believed that including death squads in a discussion of terrorism confuses the major issues.

Segaller's position should not be abruptly dismissed, but there are important parallels between death squads and small-group terrorism in Latin America that cannot be overlooked. First, death-squad terrorism is frequently unofficial. We are going to limit our inquiry to such illegal groups, who may have aims similar to those of the state but who are not acting in the name of the state. For example, the death squads in Argentina were most active after a military takeover in 1976, when they were sponsored by the state. Our inquiry, however, will be limited to discussing Argentine death squads prior to the military takeover.

When death squads are part of a government's campaign against terrorism, then Segaller's position is definitely valid. The topic is then state repression, not terrorism. You will see that this is precisely the case in Argentina after 1976. Yet when death squads exist apart from the government and take part in a struggle for power, they quite properly belong in a discussion of modern terrorism.

Second, when they are not official, death squads in Latin America have tended to reflect extremist positions. As George Lopez (1988) said, there is a shared ideology of repressionist terror in Latin America. Those who promote murder and torture for the sake of order are acting on an emotional counterrevolutionary basis. They operate clandestinely precisely because their attitudes and methods are extreme. Like many of their counterparts among the urban guerrillas, death-squad commandos are true-believer terrorists.

Closely related to this point is the fact that death squads must violate standard government procedures. As Álvaro Abos (1981) editorialized, death squads cannot follow legal norms because to do so would undermine their message of terrorism. He sarcastically added that there is always the "danger" of a victim being absolved when legal processes are used. Terrorism is the tool of the death squad. By acting outside of government authority, they need not be hampered by legal necessities.

Finally, because death squads operate in secrecy, they attempt to convey the same omnipotent message as revolutionary terrorists. Through their murders and violence they project an image of a powerful, pervasive force that can strike at will. No protective social or legal totem is sufficient to shield a potential victim from the wrath of the death squad. They intend to give the same symbolic meaning to violence as does any other terrorist.

To summarize, then, secret police groups like the Russian KGB often rule by terror, but state terrorism does not involve small unofficial groups acting on their own accord. When small extralegal groups take such actions, they correctly belong in a discussion of terrorism. The death squads in Latin America fit this mold when they act outside of government authority. Two examples illustrate this: Argentina in the mid-1970s and El Salvador in the early 1980s.

POLITICAL CHAOS IN ARGENTINA

In the 1970s Argentina was a land beset by the fear of insurrection, by terrorism, and by political repression. This climate gave rise to death squads. Groups of paramilitary and armed right-wing forces conducted operations in Argentina from 1974 until their zenith in 1976. In March 1976 a bloodless military coup overturned the civilian government, and officially sanctioned repression began. In the two years prior to the revolution, however, repression was the domain of the death squads.

Four political factors spawned the death squads in the 1970s. First, the Argentinean political and economic systems had been unstable since the departure of Juan Perón in 1955. Second, the established powers in Argentina lived in fear of a Cuban-style revolution, especially after 1969. Third, whenever Argentina has faced a

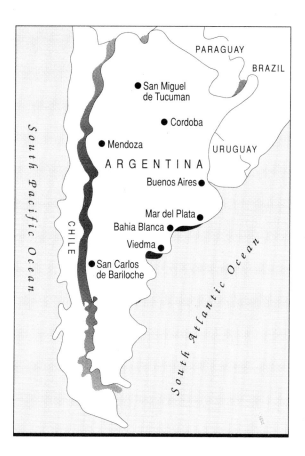

crisis, the military has traditionally intervened in order to protect its interests. Finally, in 1969 a leftist rebellion had been initiated and violence had been growing at a steady pace. Both the police and the military felt that the government was doing little to stop the violence.

Donald Hodges (1976, 7–31) maintained that any understanding of modern Argentinean politics has to be based on a military revolution that occurred in 1943. The revolution took several different courses, but when the government's power was consolidated in 1946 the President of Argentina was Juan Perón. He vowed to bring agrarian and industrial reforms to his working- and middle-class followers.

During the first part of his term, Perón was extremely successful. He was able to walk a tightrope among diverse interests. The new upper class liked Perón because he offered economic stability. The military saw Perón as one of their own. The working class witnessed Perón's support in industry and land reform. He not only brought economic gains to Argentina's lower classes, but his rule had a marked air of political stability. Perón gained control of Argentina's labor movement and was able to incorporate the left in the political structure. Until 1952, Perón was the master of Argentina. He was hailed as a hero by both the right and the left.

After 1952, however, things began to go awry. Perón faced massive economic and political difficulties. The stability that had marked the first part of his tenure gave way to chaos. With each passing year, Perón's power and decisions were subjected to greater scrutiny and criticism. In the face of growing unrest, Perón's own military forces seized the government in 1955, exiling him and banning Peronist political activity.

Despite the intentions of the military, the 1955 coup, too, fell short of solving Argentina's political and economic woes. James Kohl and John Litt (1974, 318) said the coup resulted in nearly twenty years of continued chaos. Between Juan Perón's ouster in 1955 and his return to power in 1973, Argentina had almost ten changes in national government, with most leaders assuming authority through military revolt. The situation in Argentina was clearly conducive to political violence.

During this period of perpetual political crisis, Argentina was not immune to other world events, such as the aftershocks caused by the success of the Cuban Revolution. As early as 1963 leftist organizations started to form Cuban-style guerrilla forces in Argentina, and by 1968 major efforts to form guerrilla armies were underway (Janke, 1974). Although even the Argentine Che Guevara did not believe a guerrilla war could be successful in his native land, the police and military began to fear what they perceived to be a growing communist revolutionary threat.

Guido di Tella (1983, 36–40) said that the guerrilla movement was essentially a struggle between Peronist and anti-Peronist forces, and that it was centered in the labor movement. Yet the guerrillas embraced communism and liberation theology. When they moved from the countryside to conduct a campaign of urban terrorism, daily murders and kidnappings made the threat of revolution a reality.

Peter Janke (1974) said there were two primary revolutionary forces responsible for Argentinean terrorism. The People's Revolutionary Army (ERP) embodied a host of Guevara-type guerrilla organizations, and it also became the leading element in urban terrorism. The other major group, the Montoneros, was formed by the left-wing followers of Perón. Although the ERP was able to consolidate most of the Marxist groups, the Montoneros generally operated by themselves, only forming ad hoc alliances with the ERP.

Terrorism and revolution magnified Argentina's chaos in the 1970s. In June 1970 the government of General Juan Ongania fell to a military coup. The new government of General Roberto Levingston fell to a coup the next year. General Alejandro Lanusse agreed to end military government, and he held elections in 1973. Héctor Campora, a civilian and a Perón loyalist, was elected president but resigned just six months after taking office. All would have seemed lost had it not been for the intervention of one man. Juan Perón returned from exile and was elected president by an overwhelming majority.

The military that had been so quick to intervene in the past seemed to breathe a sigh of relief. The Montoneros hailed Perón's return as a victory, and even the ERP slowed its activity. The aged Perón seemed to be able to inspire confidence across the Argentine political spectrum. Leftists believed he would bring reform, and right-wingers longed for the order associated with Peronism. Perón brought a new hope to Argentina. The hope, however, was short-lived.

According to Gary Wynia (1986), Perón's return to Argentina was a tragedy. The situation was far beyond his control, and he had to form alliances with those advocating repression in order to maintain his power. He misled the left into thinking he was their friend, but after he became president he appeared to be more of an enemy. He declared political war not only on the ERP, but on his own hopeful followers among the Montoneros. Despite their belief in Perón, leftists gradually became disillusioned with his close ties to military and police circles.

Security forces had no desire to entice the left into a governmental alliance. They were frustrated by the "softness" of the government and the Peronists. Faced with continued daily violence and government inactivity, the military and the police began to take counterrevolutionary action into their own hands. Prior to Perón's return more than a dozen members of the ERP were killed by the navy at the Trelew Naval Base on August 22, 1972. When Perón returned in August 1973, his own chief of security ordered troops to fire on Montonero demonstrators at the Ezieza airport. There were factions in the security forces who were not amenable to compromise, and Perón was forced to ally himself with those factions to maintain power.

Donald Hodges (1976, 86–101) said that the left began restructuring in the face of the security force threat and subsequent repression from Perón. The ERP was once again able to consolidate the Marxist groups under its wing, and the Montoneros rekindled a campaign of urban terrorism. By November 1974, after the government had declared martial law, both groups were back in the field. Argentina found itself in the midst of a "dirty war," a battle between two extremes of terrorism.

The ERP-Montonero campaign was not particularly coordinated, but it did have results. The ERP hoped to raise enough money from urban terrorism to finance a rural guerrilla movement. The Montoneros, on the other hand, concentrated exclusively on the cities. In 1975 alone they raised $70 million in kidnap ransoms. The terrorist campaigns were effective. Hundreds of people were killed, including off-duty police and military personnel and their families. Security forces were incensed because they felt the government was not effectively meeting the leftist threat.

Juan Perón did not live to see the ensuing tide of violence that swept through Argentina. He died in July 1974, leaving his third wife, Isabel, to assume power. Conservative columnist William F. Buckley (1974) noted that she had prepared for the presidency by working as a dancer and by her three years of formal education from the ages of five to eight. Buckley's sarcasm reflected the view of many Argentines, who had neither love nor respect for Isabel. Unpopular with the people, she was hardly the person to meet Argentina's challenges.

The police and military turned to Isabel's security chief for guidance. Kidnappings were daily events, and they were followed by bombings and murders. Left-wing terrorists were assassinating military and government officials, in some instances also murdering members of their families during their assaults. In the minds of many security force leaders, the situation seemed to be out of control. Military leaders in particular felt the time had come to purify Argentine politics: the left needed to be purged. The military and police began secretly to form an organization to wreak vengeance upon the revolutionaries.

THE TRIPLE A DEATH SQUAD, 1974–1976

The military officially took over the Argentine government in 1976. Paul Buchanan (1987) said they did so to impose a new political and economic order, and that they were forced to use repression to quell the groups who could least afford the new order. Right-wing terrorist organizations operated from 1976 to 1981 with government approval. Buchanan said these death squads reflected the nature of Latin American Bureaucratic-Authoritarian structures. They terrorized opponents of the new order.

But this legal status for right-wing terrorists was preceded by two years of clandestine counterterrorist actions, and to understand this period we must go back to Argentina prior to the return of Juan Perón. By 1972 police and military circles had begun to grow sympathetic to the idea of murdering leftists, but they did not wholeheartedly endorse it. In fact, just prior to Perón's return and during his brief tenure, many police and military officials instead favored a political solution to Argentina's woes.

It is important to understand that the formation of right-wing terrorist organizations in Argentina was not a foregone conclusion. Counterterrorism developed only when influential police and military leaders came to the conclusion that the government was totally ineffective in its dealings with terrorism. Even when the first right-wing death threats began to appear, there was no consensus about them in rightist circles. Many people in the military supported the concept of negotiating a peace with the opposition and returning Argentina to civilian rule.

During 1971 and 1972 the Montoneros and the ERP were responsible for a number of kidnappings and the murder of a former Argentine president. Military leaders felt that Argentina's leadership was not taking the proper stand against such actions. The head of naval intelligence was particularly incensed by the number of murders. Acting on his own accord, he decided to seek revenge. On August 22, 1972 he brought a number of leftist prisoners from their interrogation cells at the Trelew Naval Yard. As the captives stood in the prison yard, naval personnel suddenly opened fire. The murders reverberated throughout Argentina.

The Trelew massacre came as a shock to leftist forces. While capture and torture were to be expected, Argentina had a long history of banning capital punishment. The naval intelligence commander had acted outside of the norms of a conventional struggle, and the leftists vowed vengeance. They began methodically to murder the naval personnel responsible for the Trelew murders and succeeded in killing the head of naval intelligence in December 1972.

Guido di Tella (1983, 46–53) argued that the Montonero-ERP assassination campaign still did not galvanize the military into a death-squad stance. Many police and military officers had condemned the Trelew massacre and believed the return of Perón or Peronist control of the government would result in a more moderate stance among the radical elements of the labor movement. Violence wasn't necessary, and many officers simply rejected the idea of repression.

Other military officers were not so conciliatory, and they found sympathetic ears inside police ranks. Robert Cox (1983) said this was especially true of those who had lost friends and relatives during the assassination campaign. These officials not only supported the Trelew massacre, they thought the concept should be expanded. If the leftists were silenced or eliminated, they reasoned, Argentina's political problems would fade away. Independent groups of military officers began thinking of ways to murder leading leftists. They gradually gained the support of police commanders.

The first right-wing death threats appeared in June of 1973 (Kohl and Litt 1974,

363). A letter to guerrilla forces stated that a combined police and military death squad had collected a file of extremist names. The letter stated that upon the death of the next police officer, the first person on the leftist list would be murdered. In a later communiqué, the anonymous death squad promised to kill ten leftists for every right-leaning Peronist murdered. Although the threats were rhetorical, the potential for unofficial retaliation appeared to be real.

Yet 1973 appeared to bring a new hope to Argentina. The Montoneros had actively worked for the election of Héctor Campora, a Peronist, and Juan Perón himself was returning to Argentina. Despite the death threats, Peronism seemed to offer Argentina an alternative to violence. On June 9, 1973, the Montoneros joined the ERP in calling for war against the government, but internal support for the revolution was waning. Most of the Montoneros were excited about Perón's return and hoped to work with him.

Leftist hopes were shaken on June 20, 1973 when Perón at long last returned to Argentina, landing at the Ezeiza airport. Right-wing Peronists, led by Perón's security chief, provoked a confrontation with a group of Montoneros who had come to cheer. In the end, the right-wingers fired into the crowd and killed twenty leftists. Guido di Tella (1983, 58) believed this incident signaled the informal birth of the Triple A—the Argentine Anticommunist Alliance—and started a war between left-wing and right-wing terrorists.

The Montoneros did a turnabout, however. Instead of renewing the cry of revolt they called on the violence to end. They laid down their arms and demanded that the ERP do the same. They wanted to avoid a war, and in September they rejoiced in the election of Perón. Their comrades in the ERP were more skeptical. They kept their arms and advocated a rhetorical campaign against the government until Perón brought about economic reforms. For their part, the Montoneros sought to join Perón's new government.

History will probably conclude that the Montoneros were extremely naive. They had faith in Perón, but Perón had little faith in them. He was interested in consolidating power and regaining control of the labor movement. He advocated repression of the left and took steps to eliminate the ERP. The Montoneros continued their unilateral peace treaty, but the ERP stepped up its violence. After a series of repressive actions, Perón declared that all leftists were enemies of the state. The Montoneros were shocked. Many abandoned the Peronist ranks and renewed their campaign of terror.

The terrorist campaign had a strong effect on the military. By 1974 those favoring repression in the security forces came to believe that Perón could not stem the violence, although he seemed to be gradually siding with the forces of repression as the ERP campaign continued. Some military personnel began to take the situation into their own hands. In January 1974 they published a massive death list including Argentinean, Uruguayan, and Chilean leftists. They vowed to rid the country of all revolutionaries, and signed the threat as the Argentine Anticommunist Alliance, or the Triple A.

Donald Hodges reported that the death list was not taken seriously at first. There were so many names that murder seemed to be impractical. Many people believed the list was designed merely to frighten leftists. As the year wore on, this belief faded. When Perón died in July 1974 the sad reality struck home. The ERP was fighting hard, and most of the Montoneros had returned to the streets. Leftist terror was as frequent as it had been before Perón's return. This was too much for the police and military: the Triple A went into action.

Perón's widow, Isabel, assumed the reins of government and there is some speculation that one of her ministers, López Rega, managed the Triple A to consolidate her power (Wynia 1986, 81). Although he was in fact later found by an Argentine court to be linked to the Triple A, the conspiracy was much broader. Law enforcement officials approved of the Triple A and endorsed clandestine strikes against known and suspected leftists. Triple A military units operated under police protection. This brought about direct confrontation between left- and right-wing extremists. By 1975, Argentina was in the midst of an extremist war.

The Triple A began operations in late 1974 and by November had claimed twenty-one victims. According to *Newsweek* (1974, 53), the ERP and the Montoneros responded in kind, indiscriminately assassinating police and military officers for every one of their casualties. Violence increased dramatically in 1975, and according to Peter Snow (1979, 145), the total deaths numbered in the hundreds. By 1976 the three groups were killing an average of fifteen people a day, total.

Westerners, who expected the ERP and Montoneros to behave as terrorists, found off-duty police and military officer terrorists another matter. Government representatives simply weren't supposed to adopt the tactics of criminals. By American standards, the tactics of the Argentine police and military had always been harsh, but their official actions were not as culpable as those of the terrorists. In 1974 this changed. The Triple A became more brutal—and more effective—than the ERP and the Montoneros.

Buchanan (1987) described the tactics of the Triple A. In groups of four to six officers, they acted as if they had official authority to "arrest" their intended victims. Each police and military district had its own Triple A unit. Members would arrive at a suspect's home, almost always at night, to serve an arrest warrant. Seldom armed with legal papers or identification, they usually beat the victims in front of relatives and hauled them away. When frightened relatives called the police, the police would inevitably have no official records. The victim was said to have been "disappeared."

Actions of the Triple A were diverse. Usually a prisoner would be taken to a secret detention center to be questioned. Questioning almost always involved torture, even if the victim was later released. After the initial torture, prisoners were transferred to holding blocks. They would be routinely tortured for a number of days to set an example to other leftists. Physicians were called in to determine how much pain a victim could endure. After an indefinite period, most prisoners were killed.

Ronald Dworkin (1986), translating an official Argentine inquiry into the matter, pointed out that torture was not limited to the offending victim. Members of the victim's family were frequently arrested too, to avoid revenge on the part of relatives. During the torture sessions, children were often tortured in front of their parents. The wives and daughters of male victims were often raped within view of all prisoners. Gang rapes of female prisoners were usually the first step in their torture.

The actions of the Triple A demanded extreme secrecy and loyalty. If word of such brutal atrocities became public, members of the Triple A would have a good reason to fear. To ensure loyalty, Dworkin reported, all individual members of the Triple A were forced to participate in torture. They became full accomplices in the crimes so that any future prosecution would result in the indictment of all. Public murder was another common practice. Initiates of the Triple A were required to kill a victim in view of other members and prisoners to prove their sincerity and loyalty.

Ironically, the secret actions of the Triple A did not result in a tremendous public backlash. The public focused its disfavor instead on the left-wing terrorists. Cox (1983) said the assassinations of police and military officers roused public anger against the left, while the Triple A's actions generally went unnoticed or met with silent acceptance. And as the Triple A became stronger, public sentiment became immaterial. Those who criticized the security forces, police, or death squads were routinely "disappeared."

The next scene of this tragedy opened in March 1976. The military, enraged by Argentina's continued violence and economic problems, intervened and deposed the civilian government of Isabel Perón. They immediately began an open crackdown on leftist forces, and the death squads were legitimized. The Triple A was semilegitimized, and anyone who disagreed with the new military government was threatened with murder. In order to avoid blood feuds, the *junta* also believed it prudent to eliminate victims' relatives. Murder and repression became wholesale during the next five years.

The rest of the story is one of state repression. Terrorism became a function of the military government, and estimates of those murdered between 1976 and 1981 are as high as thirty thousand. State repression became the official method of dealing with revolution in Argentina, but other countries have operated unofficial death squads in the 1980s. El Salvador is one such nation and the focus of the next section of this chapter.

OLIGARCHY AND CLASS STRUGGLE IN EL SALVADOR

The use of death squads in El Salvador was also prompted by the fear of revolution, but El Salvador's story is somewhat different than Argentina's. Whereas Argentina's woes began with a struggle for control of a labor movement, El Salvador's internal war has been fought for control of agrarian resources. Each side in the Salvadoran struggle has embraced the rhetoric of East-West confrontation, and almost all warring parties have used some form of terrorism.

Robert Taylor and Henry Vanden (1982) began one discussion of terrorism in El Salvador by referring to the problem of definition. Their approach has merit; the situation in El Salvador clearly illustrates the problem of defining terrorism. The country is locked in a struggle between a coalition of revolutionary forces and a coalition of right-wing forces. The role of terrorism is difficult to distinguish in El Salvador, especially when the historical context of the struggle is misunderstood. As in Argentina, many sides use terrorism there to fight for their causes.

Cynthia Arnson (1982) pointed out that the roots of the revolution in El Salvador sink deep into the country's history. Although many in the United States are fond of pointing to Soviet expansionism or Cuban-style revolution as an explanation, neither of these factors plays a major role in El Salvador's conflict. The current revolutionary situation reflects a longer struggle for control of the country's agricultural resources.

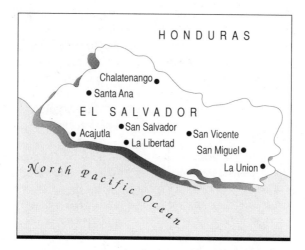

The revolution is basically about agrarian reform and land redistribution, an issue that has continued for decades.

The importance of history in the current struggle cannot be overemphasized. In the late 1800s a few of El Salvador's wealthiest families were able to wrest ownership of the land away from the local Indians. They consolidated their holdings into vast plantations, primarily producing and exporting coffee. This resulted in a tremendous income for the wealthy landholders but almost nothing for the displaced peasants.

Arnson said that by the 1920s there was growing unrest among the Salvadoran peasants, even though they were virtually powerless, and that by then they also had a leader. Agustín Farabundo Martí was an educated son of a landowner and a charter member of the Central American Socialist Party. He was concerned with the necessity to redistribute the land and wealth of the coffee exporters. His campaign made only minor headway until disaster struck in 1930. With the Great Depression, the bottom fell out of the coffee market.

Into El Salvador's depressed economy arrived a new civilian president in 1931. Under him Martí continued to organize peasants, but his efforts were thwarted by a military coup in December 1931. General Hernández Martínez came to power and promised to back the interests of the coffee oligarchy with military force. Under Martínez El Salvador's wealth was to remain in the hands of a few privileged families. This was too much for Martí; he planned a peasant revolt.

General Martínez assumes a rather important position in the history of terrorism in El Salvador due to his reaction to the revolt. Martí planned the revolt for January 22, 1932, but Martínez had gotten wind of the plot before it could develop. He arrested Martí and brutally attacked the peasants. Although Martí was executed by firing squad, the extent of the repression was seen in a wholesale slaughter of peasants. In Salvadoran history it is known as *la matanza,* "the slaughter." Most sources agreed that the death toll from Martínez's repression was in the neighborhood of thirty thousand. The army and oligarchy learned a lesson they wouldn't forget: killing peasants seemed to stop the threat of revolution.

Martínez remained in power until the mid-1940s, when he was replaced by another military government. In the following years El Salvador's peasants knew little government other than oligarchical power and military rule. The peasants become poorer and the number of landless people grew in the 1950s. Nothing seemed able to shake the elitists' rigid grip on El Salvador's poor.

News of the Cuban Revolution in 1959 spread through El Salvador's peasantry and struck fear into the hearts of the oligarchy. In the 1960s there was some talk of land reform, but the controlling elements of the military high command remembered *la matanza*. Repression could work as well as reform, and it didn't offend the oligarchy. The high command began to look for potential subversives.

The subversives appeared on the scene in the late 1950s and early 1960s. Totally disorganized, the groups ranged from guerrillas seeking land reform to communists wanting to overthrow the government. A military coup in 1967 seemed to bring some hope to these bands, but it only resulted in further repression and concentration of governmental power. Repression did not seem to work as well as it had in 1932, however. By the mid-1970s several guerrilla groups had beome quite strong, and two revolutionary groups had mounted campaigns of urban terrorism.

Before moving to a discussion of the death squads in El Salvador, it is necessary to mention briefly the role of the Roman Catholic Church in the struggle for reform. Raymond Bonner (1984, 65–84) pointed to the leading role the church played in the peasant unrest. The role of the church was twofold. On the one hand it ministered to the needs of the poor. On the other, some of its local priests and the archbishop openly sympathized with the revolutionary forces.

Such a stand failed to endear the church to El Salvador's military rulers. They dichotomized loyalties simply: if a citizen failed to support the oligarchy enthusiastically, that person was obviously a communist subversive. In this manner the Roman Catholic Church became a subversive organization, meriting the attention of the death squads.

DEATH SQUADS IN EL SALVADOR

Right-wing terrorism was a response to the revolutionary efforts of the 1970s. Cynthia Arnson (1982) described two repressionist groups that appeared during this time. ORDEN (spanish for "order") was formed by the commander of the National Guard in 1968. Its official purpose was to report on the activities of potential subversives among the peasants. Unofficially, it had begun to eliminate them by the mid-1970s. The other organization was more overt about its purpose.

The White Warrior's Union (UGB) was formed in the mid-1970s as a protective organization for the oligarchy, according to Arnson. It began a campaign of selective assassination of suspected revolutionaries, in response to leftist murders of government supporters. In 1978, after the foreign minister was kidnapped and murdered, the UGB murdered a Catholic priest. It then issued a challenge to all Jesuits, to leave the country or die. Arnson reported their slogan as "Be a patriot, kill a priest!"

In another work, Arnson (1981, 137–138) named three death squads that had come into existence by 1980. The UGB was joined by the Anticommunist Forces of Liberation (FALANGE) and the Organization for the Liberation from Communism

(OLC). ORDEN officially remained an intelligence arm of the government, but its death squads were firmly entrenched. By 1979 death-squad executions were routine.

The tactical pattern in El Salvador differed from that in Argentina. According to a report from the Americas Watch Committee and the American Civil Liberties Union (1982), people were not "disappeared" as often as they were "found." The death squads had two primary methods of disposing of their victims. Often they were found, tortured and executed, along the roadside. At other times the bodies were cast into a large dumping ground outside of San Salvador. The message was clear: the death squads hoped the sight of the bodies would serve as a deterrent to revolution.

Some people believed that the death squads were little more than a modern version of *la matanza* operated by the high command. Former El Salvador Army Captain Ricardo Fiallos (1981) said as much in testimony to the United States Congress. Fiallos said that all death-squad activities were planned by the military high command and carried out by secret groups within the security forces. He said that the groups were not reflective of military and police policies, but rather embodied the ideals of the general command.

As in Argentina, anyone who disagreed with the government could become a murder victim. Death-squad targets included labor leaders, political candidates, and potential guerrilla sympathizers among the peasants. Church officials were prime candidates, especially those who preached liberation theology—a popular Latin American version of Christianity that equates religious dogma with Marxism. And American citizens in El Salvador were not immune. A brief review of the more publicized incidents will demonstrate how the death squads operated.

On March 24, 1979 Archbishop Óscar Romero prepared for mass in the main cathedral of the capital, San Salvador. He was a frequent critic of the government, and the day before he had called on the military forces to lay down their arms and cease their attacks on the peasants. As he prepared to serve the Eucharist, a gunman rose from the altar and shot him. His murder was attributed to the death squads (Americas Watch Committe/ACLU 1982, 108–116).

ORDEN was known to supply information that resulted in the massacre of entire villages. In one incident on March 17, 1981, six hundred civilians were massacred along the Honduran border by the National Guard and ORDEN. The men, women, and older children were shot, and the younger children were thrown into the air for target practice (A Presbytery of the Honduras 1981, 148–149). On December 11, 1981, in the fourth such attack that year, then men of the village of Mozote were shot, the women raped and murdered, and the children strangled (Didion 1983, 37).

American targets of the death squads included John Sullivan, a free-lance writer who disappeared in December 1980, and Michael Hammer and Mark Pearlman. Hammer and Pearlman were representing the AFL-CIO, hoping to bring about agrarian reform. They were shot in the San Salvador Sheraton while drinking coffee with the agricultural minister. One of the assaults best known in the United States was the rape-murder of four American churchwomen by the death squads (Didion 1983, 23–24). According to an official news release from the U.S. Department of State (1981, 140–141), Sister Ita Ford and Sister Maura Clarke were American nuns who had been working with El Salvador's poor. Although they had received anonymous death threats, they ignored them. On December 2, 1980 they arrived at the San Salvador International Airport, having returned from a conference in Nicaragua.

The State Department said that the sisters were met by Sister Dorothy Kazel and lay worker Jean Donovan, two other Americans. The four women encountered some Canadian church officials at the airport and chatted with them until they left to spend the night at a parish home. According to the State Department, no one but their assailants saw them alive after they left the airport.

Their bodies were discovered on December 4, 1980 twenty miles from an area where they were supposedly stopped at a roadblock. Further investigation showed that the women had been sexually assaulted and shot. One's face had been destroyed by beating. The bodies had been left by side of the road, and they were discovered by peasants. National Guard officers ordered the peasants to bury the bodies in a common grave, and, according to the State Department, they defended their actions by stating that this was a common practice when death-squad victims were found.

These acts of terrrorism are only a sample of the massive assaults of the death squads in the early 1980s. According to Cynthia Arnson (1982), Ronald Reagan's election in 1979 was misinterpreted by the death squads as a signal that they could use any means to stop the revolution. They viewed Reagan's victory as a license to kill. Although Reagan's critics have not been enthusiastic about his policies in El Salvador, all would agree that this was a mistaken notion. In any case, death-squad actions increased.

The Americas Watch Committee and the ACLU (1982, 281) reported 12,501 murders in El Salvador in 1981. Of these, 146 were attributed to the death squads and 100 to its agents in civilian dress. An amazing 4,828 were attributed to "unknown assailants." Even if we generously assumed that half of these were the work of left-wing terrorists, the 1981 figures clearly demonstrate the impact of death-squad activity.

Richard White's analysis of extrajudicial executions revealed a pattern of repressive murder over a five-year period (1984, 44). Executions rose substantially from 1979 to 1981 and remained high in 1982 and 1983. The United States questioned the high rate of casualties from death squads, but Washington continued military, intelligence, and economic aid. Even the murder of American citizens did not stop the flow of U.S. aid to the Salvadoran government.

According to White, activities of Salvadoran death squads began dropping in 1984 due to two factors. The Reagan administration, under intense pressure from Congress, vowed to shut off all aid until death-squad terror was stopped. In addition, the nature of the insurrection had changed. The revolutionary groups formed a coalition guerrilla army called the Farabundo Martí National Liberation Front (FMLN) and attempted to launch a Cuban-style rural guerrilla movement. The Salvadoran Army, with U.S. backing, concentrated the majority of its efforts on the guerrilla war.

The future of Salvadoran terrorism is not clear. The United States seems to hope that some type of centrist party can be formed, and that El Salvador can become a democracy. The Bush administration may not echo the ideological anticommunist rhetoric of the Reagan administration, but there are no easy solutions. Some members of the guerrilla coalition have returned to San Salvador to wage their own terrorist campaigns. Rebel guerrillas have also attempted to stop elections, fearing either loss or government fraud. There seems to be no center position, and terrorism remains a tool for both right and left.

The death squads still exist in El Salvador. The mentality that spawned them and the men who carry out the majority of the executions are alive and well. They are officially outlawed by the Salvadoran government, but many government, police, and military officials allegedly belong to the death squads. They have caused far more pain and suffering than have their revolutionary counterparts, and they have killed thousands more victims. Ironically, however, the term *terrorism* is most frequently used to describe the actions of the left.

SUMMARY OF CHAPTER NINE

Death-squad terrorism frequently follows a revolutionary terrorist campaign, when members of the ruling powers perceive that normal governmental actions will not thwart the terrorist movement. They are usually officially disowned or denied by the government, but members of the death squads tend to come from official security forces.

Some experts argue that death squads do not belong in the general category of terrorism; they wish to include them under the topic of political repression. In instances where the government is officially supporting death-squad activity, this position is valid. But when they operate outside of government channels, they are simply another version of terrorism. The death squads operating in Argentina from 1974 to 1976 and the more recent ones in El Salvador belong to the latter category.

In Argentina the Triple A rose to combat the terrorism of the ERP and the Montoneros. The three groups waged an "assassination war" between 1974 and 1976. In 1976 the military took over the government and terrorism became a state affair. After 1976, small-group terrorism ceased to be the norm in Argentina.

Salvadoran death squads also grew in response to a fear of revolution, but the struggle in El Salvador is more closely associated with class stratification and land reform. Certain factions in the security forces have accepted the logic of *la matanza,* in which the opposition is brutally murdered or frightened into submission. A variety of Salvadoran death squads carry on this tradition.

IF YOU WANT TO READ FURTHER . . .

Few topics in terrorism are emotionally satisfying, but the death squads are one of its most depressing aspects. Donald Hodges's book titled *Argentina, 1943–1976* is perhaps one of the best introductory works on modern Argentine politics. It doesn't focus on the Triple A, but he provides a background for understanding terrorism in Argentina. Scholars and students alike should find it valuable. The work can be complemented by Robert Snow's *Politics in Argentina.*

Cynthia Arnson's *El Salvador: A Revolution Confronts the United States* is an outstanding overview of the situation in El Salvador. Arnson is able to summarize the history, the left- and right-wing violence, and the impact of American policy in a short, highly readable overview. Her work is outstanding. Joan Didion takes a much more emotional view of the issue in *Salvador,* but her work is very good. For a solid critique of U.S. policy in El Salvador, you may want to read Richard White's *The Morass: United States Intervention in Central America.*

The Americas Watch Committee and American Civil Liberties Union coauthored the *Report on Human Rights in El Salvador*, which is one of the best-documented accounts of death-squad activity. With meticulous research the book reveals several critical issues about the situation in El Salvador. It offers a compact fact-finding tour of the country. Ronald Dworkin's *Nunca Más* is a translation of an official Argentine inquiry into military repression. It does not discuss extralegal death squads, but it's valuable reading.

John Simpson's and Jana Bennett's *The Disappeared and the Mothers of the Plaza* is a gripping emotional description of the families of *los desaparecidos*. Simpson and Bennett recount stories from mothers who began to march in Buenos Aires demanding to know the fate of their children. It is a good account and shows the human results when security forces are unleashed with no legal controls.

Most of these works contain biases that seem to inherently support a more liberal American foreign policy. It is difficult to balance them because few sensible people want to argue in favor of death squads in an academic forum. By the same token, Latin America's problems are greater than the activities of right-wing death squads. To obtain a more balanced picture of violence and repression in Latin America, see the Suggested Readings section at the end of chapter 4.

AN OVERVIEW OF DOMESTIC TERRORISM

Terrorism in the United States has primarily been a law enforcement problem, and, according to official statistics, the level of domestic terrorist activity dropped dramatically in the 1980s. Yet U.S. law enforcement officials are not quite sure what terrorism means, and no comprehensive defense or enforcement policy addresses the issue. Domestic terrorism is shrouded in bureaucratic uncertainty and confusion. The purpose of this chapter is to introduce you to the dilemmas and misunderstandings posed by domestic terrorism and to place the subject within a general political context.

After reading this chapter, you should be able to do the following:

1. Describe the problems of conceptualizing domestic terrorism
2. Summarize Gurr's approach to domestic terrorism
3. List and define the five sources of domestic terrorism
4. Explain why the FBI emphasizes political violence when cataloguing domestic terrorism
5. Summarize the current trends in domestic terrorism using data from FBI reports
6. Outline Harris's official summary of domestic terrorism
7. Discuss abortion clinic bombings as a possible manifestation of domestic terrorism

PROBLEMS IN UNDERSTANDING DOMESTIC TERRORISM

In *Patriot Games,* Tom Clancy's best-selling novel of terrorism in Northern Ireland, the fictional American intelligence characters often have trouble coming to grips with terrorism. One of the prime reasons is their inexperience in the field. Clancy has his American protagonists look to their country for possible parallels and solutions. They are frustrated, because they simply don't exist. In the words of one of Clancy's heros, America no longer experiences terrorism. The left wing has become defunct and the right wing is dominated by religious ideologues. Compared to that of places like Ireland, terrorism in America seems minuscule.

Clancy has a point. When Americans speak of terrorism they are usually referring to incidents far from American shores. Americans may be victimized frequently by terrorist acts, but these incidents generally occur overseas. While political leaders and the media have expressed a fear of domestic terrorism, the reality is that the fear is just that—a fear and only a fear. Terrorism is something that happens in other places. Many people believe that terrorism is not an internal problem for the United States.

In one sense, this belief is justified. In another sense, it grossly confuses the issue and presents a set of problems for anyone who wishes to deal with the basic aspects of American terrorism. Several factors tend to obscure the topic and confuse attempts to address domestic terrorism. Before examining domestic terrorism, we need to think about some of those factors.

To begin, no definition or approach to American terrorism is generally accepted. The lack of a social or legal definition creates problems beyond those you reviewed in chapter 1. American police and security agencies literally do not know what terrorism is. Not only have Americans had little experience with terrorism, but this lack of experience has been exacerbated by a variety of bureaucratic and legal contradictions. Agencies charged with countering domestic terrorism often have no idea what they are looking for.

One of the main causes of confusion is terrorism's lack of legal status. There are no American statutes outlawing terrorism inside the country. When American terrorists are arrested, they are charged with a variety of common crimes. Neither federal nor state legal codes contain accepted criteria for dealing with political crime. Sometimes racketeering and organized crime statutes are applied during the prosecution of terrorist groups, but most domestic terrorists are charged with individual, unrelated violations of criminal codes. They are rarely formally examined except as they would be for traditional crimes, and the courts generally ignore the activities of violent domestic organizations. The meaning of domestic terrorism is never legally addressed. Therefore, terrorism almost always translates into some violation of the current criminal code.

This is further complicated by aspects of American policing. The Federal Bureau of Investigation has defined and classified acts of domestic terrorism, but local and state law enforcement agencies are not required to abide by that definition. Thus, when the FBI issues a report on domestic terrorism, as it has done since the mid-1970s, there are no clear criteria for categorizing criminal actions under the terrorist rubric. Even the FBI classifies some terrorist actions as common crimes.

The lack of a common approach is complemented by the lack of routinized counterterrorist policies. Although the FBI is officially the lead agency in responding to domestic terrorism, in reality a whole host of law enforcement, national defense, and civilian security bureaucracies have some responsiblity. Although many of these agencies have exchanged official rules and procedures for joint operations, the line-level workers usually have no idea what the joint responsibilities are. The FBI has a solid internal management system, but counterterrorism demands multiagency management structures and policies.

Gaining an understanding of domestic terrorism is also hampered by the anti-intellectual atmosphere common to most American police agencies. In an age in which a college education has become synonymous with technical expertise, many local police agencies view terrorism as a matter for their special weapons teams and negotiators. Most police administrators have little time for "exotic" crimes such as terrorism, and they usually see no difference between a terrorist and a barricaded suspect.

The reason for this seeming lack of concern is the status of domestic terrorism. Unlike forces in Europe and the Middle East, American police have faced very small levels of such violence at home. Which brings us back to the point Tom Clancy made in *Patriot Games:* terrorism is something that seems to occur overseas. Police and security agencies can afford to bureaucratically confuse their approaches to terrorism because it simply hasn't been much of a problem.

GURR'S ANALYSIS OF DOMESTIC TERRORISM

Ted Robert Gurr, a much-noted political scientist at Northwestern University, has written a number of works on terrorism and has also focused on domestic political violence and rebellion. With J. Bowyer Bell (1979) he did much to explain the American experience with and response to domestic terrorism. Gurr (1988) followed this study with another analysis. His work is insightful, and it is one of the best summaries of domestic terrorism.

In the article written with Bell, Gurr placed terrorism within its historical context. Terrorism, they argued, is a tactic used by the weak to intimidate the strong—and by the strong to intimidate the weak. In this sense, America has a history overflowing with terrorist activities. Various political movements have used forms of terrorism to seek political gains. At the same time, industrial giants and those holding power have historically used terrorism to maintain control over workers and unions.

Bell and Gurr began their review by looking at the late 1800s. Despite the American paranoia about radicals, terrorism in the nineteenth century was primarily aimed at protecting the status quo and the economic environment. The actions of company security police and private corporations were often terrorist in nature. They were designed to keep workers from disrupting production. Labor radicals, however, also behaved violently; the labor movement of the late nineteenth century was replete with violence. Bell and Gurr labeled this a manifestation of terrorism.

Labor violence was not the only source of early U.S. terrorism. The frontier had its own special form of violence. As the frontier expanded, the laws of the United States trailed far behind. Settlers developed their own brand of makeshift justice. At times, this type of justice spilled over into vigilante activities. Bell and Gurr referred to some aspects of the vigilante movement as terrorism. The Ku Klux Klan after the Civil War can be viewed as an example.

Although there is a long history of American political violence, Bell and Gurr separated modern American terrorism from its historical predecessors. In the 1960s, they argued, the character of American terrorism began to change. Domestic terrorism became rooted in radical politics, nationalism, and the international community's experience with terrorism. The use of terror to maintain social order was forgotten in the modern setting, and domestic terrorism was defined as a radical phenomenon.

Bell and Gurr believed that modern domestic terrorism has been entirely derived from foreign models. Both political revolutionary groups and nationalistic groups in the United States took their ideas from terrorists in the Middle East and Asia. In this sense, both types of groups saw themselves as being involved in a broader struggle of international proportions.

There was a catch to their logic, however. Bell and Gurr noted that American terrorist groups did not have the same impact as their foreign counterparts. The American public totally rejected the violence of the revolutionary groups, and popularity was never fully achieved even among their most sympathetic audiences. U.S. revolutionary terrorists ended up as small bands of social misfits who had very little impact on the political system. As a result, America has been spared the excesses of revolutionary terrorism.

Bell and Gurr issued two caveats along with their conclusion. First, even though America has avoided significant domestic terrorism, criminals and political activists have both used terrorist tactics on a local level, particularly the tactic of hostage taking. Second, nationalistic terrorists have been far more successful than revolutionaries at launching campaigns because they have an indigenous base of support. As an example, Bell and Gurr cited Puerto Rican terrorists. Although they have not had a major impact, they have enjoyed more success than revolutionary terrorists because they have a base of support.

In a later work, Gurr updated some of these ideas about domestic terrorism. He offered a typology and, following the lead of J. Bowyer Bell, outlined four types of terrorism: (1) vigilante, (2) insurgent, (3) transnational, and (4) state. He then applied this typology to contemporary terrorism in the United States. State terrorism was not an appropriate topic for discussing domestic terror, but Gurr analyzed the other three types.

Vigilante Terrorism

Gurr described vigilante terrorism as being typified by the growth of new groups on the political right and the resurgence of old ones. The purpose of vigilantes is to defend the status quo or to return to that of an earlier period. Gurr believed that the Ku Klux Klan, the Christian Identity Movement, and other white supremacy organizations are examples of vigilante terrorism that rely on right-wing rhetorical traditions. They exhibit the potential for terrorism, but with a few exceptions they do not actively engage in it.

The most enduring groups on the right are the Ku Klux Klan and the tax protest group, Posse Comitatus. They have given support to a traditional set of right-wing assumptions. The Aryan Nations and other Christian Identity groups have shared the Klan's and Posse's rhetoric, but have no single program of action. The Order is one of the few vigilante groups that has crossed the line between rhetoric and terrorism. Gurr also classified abortion clinic bombers as a form of vigilante terrorism separate from the right-wing movement.

Insurgent Terrorism

Gurr described insurgent terrorists in revolutionary terms. Black militants, white revolutionaries, and Puerto Rican nationalists fall into this category. Insurgent terrorism aims to change political policies by direct threats or action against the government. It is the political antithesis of vigilante terrorism because it attacks the status quo. Black, white, and Puerto Rican insurgent terrorism has arisen since the Second World War.

Black militancy and terrorism surfaced in the waning years of the civil rights

movement. Prior to 1966 most confrontations took the form of peaceful civil disobedience and protest marches. Violence increased through 1969 and 1970 with a
series of urban riots in cities such as Los Angeles and Detroit. Gurr believed the riots
helped give birth to black terrorist groups. Groups such as the Black Liberation Army
sprang up in reaction to police retaliation during the riots. Most black terrorism
involved attacks on individual police officers or police stations. But by 1975, Gurr
said, it was no longer a significant threat.

White revolutionary terrorism followed the same trajectory as black militancy,
according to Gurr, but it embraced a broader set of issues. White terrorism was
anticapitalist, and it arose in response to the unpopularity of the Viet Nam War. White
revolutionaries, who also adopted the cause of black revolutionaries, were generally
small cells influenced by Carlos Marighella's philosophy. They engaged in acts of
violence, and, while they gained headlines, they never mounted a true terrorist
campaign. Most groups were defunct by 1980.

As Gurr's earlier analysis with Bell indicated, Puerto Rican nationalist groups
have been the most active and enduring source of insurgent terrorism. During the
1980s eight Puerto Rican nationalist groups were active on the mainland and the island.
Gurr believed that terrorism from Puerto Rico will continue because there is no simple
solution to the political problems. The majority of Puerto Ricans do not want independence, but a substantial minority do. And some of those favoring independence
favor the use of violence: a prescription for terrorism.

Transnational Terrorism

Transnational terror occurs when nonindigenous terrorists cross national borders. Gurr
identified several sources of transnational terror in America. Some foreign nationals
have carried their fights onto U.S. soil, and some domestic groups have been inspired
by foreign events. In other cases, foreign countries may have begun to target Americans at home. All in all, however, Gurr did not believe the threat of transnational
terror was as great as has been popularly believed.

Gurr concluded that there seems to be little chance for indigenous revolutionary
terrorism in the United States, with the exception of Puerto Rican nationalist groups.
There is no revolutionary base of support, according to his analysis. Criminals and
political radicals will continue to use terrorist tactics, but their impact will be limited to
local incidents. Gurr believed there was not enough support to promote a national
terrorist campaign.

Bell and Gurr published their analysis in 1979. Gurr's 1988 version included an
analysis of the growth of right-wing extremism in the 1980s. More attention will be
devoted to this topic in the next chapter, but it is safe to say that right-wing extremists
began to move slowly toward the forefront of domestic terrorism in the 1980s. The approach these analysts used is excellent for locating the sources of American terrorism.

SOURCES OF DOMESTIC TERRORISM

If we look at the typology originally developed by J. Bowyer Bell and applied by Ted
Robert Gurr, it is possible to suggest that there are five basic sources of terrorism in the

United States. With the exeption of Puerto Rican nationalists, all domestic terrorist groups lack an indigenous base, and they tend to have localized ideological bases. Types of groups are generally defined by location. For example, white supremacy groups tend to be rural, while revolutionary groups are generally urban. Since it tends to be geographically confined, American terrorism does not affect all local police agencies in the same manner.

Domestic terrorism comes from the following sources: (1) foreign groups operating on American soil, (2) revolutionary nationalists, (3) the ideological right, (4) the ideological left, and (5) criminal groups using terrorist tactics. There are varying degrees of support for each source of terrorism, but no group of terrorists has made a tremendous social impact regardless of its source. A brief examination of these sources will help to reveal the character of domestic terrorism.

Foreign groups operating on American soil fall into two categories. First, there are nationalist groups that carry their struggles onto American soil. One of the best examples of this is the fight between the Turks and the Armenians. At the turn of the century, the Turks attempted to eliminate the Armenians through a policy of genocide. Modern-day Armenians have attacked Turks, using terrorism, in an effort to avenge their ancestors. This struggle has taken place within a variety of nations, including the United States.

Other international struggles involving terrorism also spill across borders; the Turk-Armenian conflict is but one example, but it is indicative of the illusory nature of domestic terrorism. American police find themselves responding to incidents that involve no American interests.

The second manifestation of foreign groups operating on American soil has a greater impact on national defense. In an age of clandestine wars and low-intensity conflict, foreign groups may target the United States on American soil. According to one confidential police report in 1988, a Nicaraguan group has been operating in such a manner. This report maintained that a small group of Sandinistas had infiltrated the United States to sell drugs and commit armed robberies in order to raise money for the Nicaraguan government.

While small, the group was heavily armed and extremely well trained, according to the police intelligence report. Operatives traveled in a family-type vehicle, while heavily armed support units trailed the car. If the operatives were stopped by police, members of the backup unit would assault the police officers.

Although such reports draw the attention of law enforcement officers, the alleged Nicaraguan operation is extremely small. Hugh Stephens (1987) made a more unsettling point about potential terrorism. He argued that by targeting facilities such as ports, small groups of foreign terrorists could paralyze American maritime interests. Indeed, the potential for terrorist acts in the United States is frightening.

Nationalist terrorism in the United States mainly stems from Puerto Rican separatists. As Gurr demonstrated, Puerto Rico accounts for the greatest amount of indigenous domestic political terrorism. Other nationalist groups, such as radical American Indian groups, engage in terrorist activities, but they lack an extended base of support. The political questions raised by the Puerto Rican movement represent the greatest threat.

The ideological right reemerged in the 1980s as a source of domestic terrorism.

FIVE SOURCES OF DOMESTIC TERRORISM

- Foreign groups
- Revolutionary nationalists
- Ideological right
- Ideological left
- Criminals

Source: Jonathan White, *Holy War* (Gaithersburg, MD: IACP, 1986)

The extremist right has always been a factor in American politics, but it waxes and wanes according to economic conditions and political sentiment. Along with farm foreclosures and an economic downswing, the conservativism of the 1980s helped to create the conditions for extremist groups to resurface.

The ideological left has not enjoyed success in the climate of the 1980s. Unlike those on the right, left-wing terrorists have not fared well in recent times. According to James Stinson (1984), left-wing groups were forced to merge into a loosely bound confederation of terrorist groups. Only three groups had a major impact on the 1980s: the Weather Underground, the Armed Resistance Unit, and the United Freedom Front. But these groups were composed almost exclusively of 1970s "holdovers."

Perhaps the most frequent yet least effective form of domestic terrorism has emanated from criminal groups. Gangs and organized criminals emulate political terrorists, but most actual terrorism comes from criminals facing capture. Their most frequent tactic is to take hostages. Unlike politically motivated terrorists, such criminals can be dealt with using standard police procedures. As Bell and Gurr argued, their tactics are usually copied from a political terrorist groups enjoying a higher media profile.

FBI reports on domestic terrorism supply one of the few records of the American experience with terrorism from all five sources. They indicate that terrorism has not developed into a major domestic problem, and that it seems to be decreasing. An examination of these reports illustrates this trend.

FBI SUMMARIES OF DOMESTIC TERRORISM

The FBI is legally designated as the lead law enforcement agency in the response to domestic terrorism. As a federal agency with general law enforcement powers, the FBI is in a position to respond to terrorism from a national perspective. In the 1980s Congress enlarged the scope of antiterrorism legislation, both expanding the FBI's role and increasing its authority in matters of international terrorism.

Research conducted by James Stinson (1984) suggests that this emphasis on the FBI's role needs further examination. Stinson argued that local police agencies almost always constitute the first force responding to a terrorist incident. In addition, local police agencies often must confront criminals who are using terrorist tactics, even

A BREAKDOWN OF TERRORIST INCIDENTS
WITHIN THE UNITED STATES AND PUERTO RICO 1980–1986

State/Territory	Number of Incidents	Percentage
New York	63	33.16
Puerto Rico	57	30.00
Florida	19	10.00
California	15	7.89
Washington, D.C.	14	7.37
Idaho	5	2.63
Michigan	3	1.58
Illinois	2	1.05
Massachusetts	2	1.05
New Jersey	2	1.05
Texas	2	1.05
Colorado	1	.53
Nevada	1	.53
Oregon	1	.53
Pennsylvania	1	.53
Tennessee	1	.53
Virginia	1	.53
TOTAL	190	*100.01

*Due to rounding, percentages may not add to 100.0
Source: FBI, *Analysis of Terrorist Incidents in the United States* (Washington, D.C.: Government Printing Office, 1986), 47.

though these incidents are not classified as terrorism by the FBI. Despite the Bureau's mandate, confusion seems to exist about the roles of the various law enforcement agencies with regard to terrorism. Policy makers need to define the functions of local, state, and federal agencies in responses to terrorism.

One method that can clarify the issue is to look at the type of terrorism the FBI faces. While the Bureau places many forms of activity under the category of traditional crime, political violence generally has been classified as terrorism. That is why the FBI has taken the lead in the response to terrorism: it is an extension of its national security role. Local police have no such role, officially.

The FBI's role in national security has gradually evolved over the years. Although it is forced to compete for organizational space with other federal agencies and carries on an especially heated rivalry with the Central Intelligence Agency, the FBI has gradually assumed responsibility for counterespionage. Since World War II, the FBI has expanded its national security activities to include foreign and domestic political threats. J. Edgar Hoover encouraged this expansion, and since the CIA was barred from gathering domestic intelligence, the FBI seemed to be the perfect agency to handle the job.

Understanding their role in national security does much to illuminate the FBI response to domestic terrorism. To be sure, the Bureau has retreated from the enthusiastic expansion of its intelligence activities in the Hoover era, but its role in monitoring political threats has remained intact. In addition to carrying out law enforcement tasks, the FBI has been held responsible for domestic political security. And the FBI conceives of domestic terrorism as an exclusively political threat. Almost all nonpolitical terrorism is classified as traditional crime and falls to local and state agencies or to other federal police units.

In 1977 the FBI began issuing annual reports on domestic terrorism. Supporters claimed that these reports revealed the patterns of terrorism in America. Critics maintained that the reports failed to account for many terrorist incidents because the classification system was skewed. There is merit in both positions, if you consider the FBI's limited concept of its national security mission. When the FBI issues domestic terrorist incident reports, they are only talking about manifested *political* violence. If you do not expect the reports to discuss criminal terrorism, you will find that they are fairly accurate summaries.

In 1977 the FBI Analysis of Terrorist Incidents in the United States began with a summary of groups, a synopsis of the major incidents, and a graphic analysis of tactics, geographical locations, and victims. The reports have become more sophisticated through the years, and they are now compiled by a specialized antiterrorist research section. Still, the format has remained basically stable.

The FBI reports indicate two major trends. First, left-wing political terrorism underwent a transformation in the late 1970s as left-wing groups began a period of gradual decline. Nationalist Puerto Ricans expanded operations but the traditional revolutionary groups—the white and black insurgents described by Gurr— consolidated in larger organizations and then gradually disappeared. They had unified out of weakness, not strength; the leftists needed help. Left-wing activities in the early 1980s were at times dramatic, but the number of incidents declined as the number of groups did.

The second major trend was more obvious and rather ironic. As the country's awareness of terrorism increased in the 1980s, the number of actual domestic political incidents decreased. From more than 200 incidents in 1977, the number of terrorist attacks has declined fairly steadily through the 1980s. Keep in mind, however, that these incidents only refer to political violence, not the broader category of criminal terrorist tactics.

Beginning in 1986, the FBI formalized and limited its definition of terrorism. In the preface to the 1986 report terrorism was called "the unlawful use of force or violence against persons or property . . . in furtherance of a political or social objective." The FBI divided American terrorism into two categories: international terrorism, which was conducted inside U.S. boundaries by foreign groups, and domestic terrorism, which was exclusively indigenous. It added two more operational definitions to its 1986 report. First, a terrorist incident was an act that violated criminal laws and whose goal was coercion. Second, the term *incident prevention* was coined for the successful interdiction of terrorist activity prior to an incident.

While these definitions appeared to clarify some issues covered in the reports, they were still far from precise. The FBI's definitions were still sufficiently broad to include the activities of street gangs and organized criminals, which they had no intention of investigating. The FBI reports on domestic terrorism have continued to be summaries of strictly political violence that can be tied to a specific political group.

This is not to suggest that the definitions served no purpose. They did help to clarify some issues. For example, academics might quibble about their distinction between "domestic" and "international" terrorism, yet the FBI was on the right track in tying types of terrorism to their source. In very practical terms, the FBI is looking for terrorism that originates either inside or outside of U.S. borders. Each type of terrorism has its separate set of legally acceptable guidelines. As Paul Wilkinson (1986, 37) said, terrorism is either external or internal. For the FBI the differences are pragmatic, not theoretical.

A graphic representation of externally originated incidents from 1980 to 1986 indicates the pattern of external terrorism in the United States (see Figure 10-1, a and b). To the surprise of those fearing a strike from the Middle East, by far the major source of externally motivated terrorism has been anti-Castro Cubans, followed by Armenians and Croatians. In other words, the external threat has not come from the most common international sources of terrorism.

Further analysis of externally motivated terrorism reveals another trend. While the

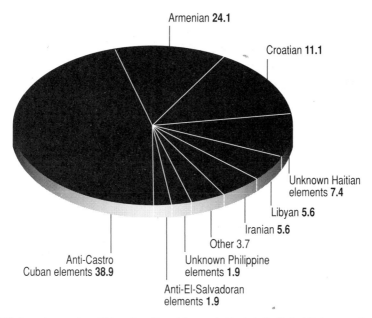

Figure 10-1a   An overview of international terrorist group incidents in the United States according to group classification, 1980–1986

Due to rounding, percentages may not add to 100.0

Source: FBI: *Analysis of Terrorist Incidents in the United States* (1986), p 53

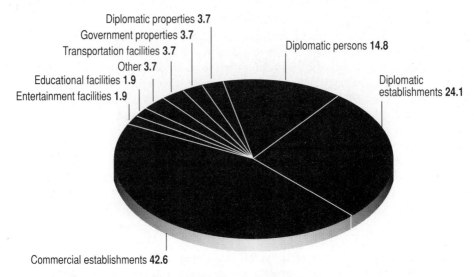

Diplomatic properties **3.7**
Government properties **3.7**
Transportation facilities **3.7**
Other **3.7**
Educational facilities **1.9**
Entertainment facilities **1.9**

Diplomatic persons **14.8**

Diplomatic establishments **24.1**

Commercial establishments **42.6**

Figure 10-1b   An overview of international terrorist group incidents in the United States according to target, 1980–1986

Due to rounding, percentages may not add to 100.0
Source: FBI: *Analysis of Terrorist Incidents in the United States* (1986), p 53

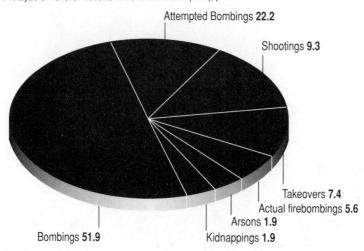

Attempted Bombings **22.2**

Shootings **9.3**

Takeovers **7.4**
Actual firebombings **5.6**
Arsons **1.9**

Bombings **51.9**   Kidnappings **1.9**

Figure 10-2   An overview of international terrorist group incidents in the United States according to type, 1980–1986

Due to rounding, percentages may not add to 100.0
Source: FBI: *Analysis of Terrorist Incidents in the United States* (1986), p 54

United States has been frantically developing hostage rescue forces, the major tactic used by international groups on American soil is bombing (see Figure 10-2). Takeovers, seizures of physical property with or without hostages, have only accounted for 7.4 percent of all internationally sponsored domestic terrorist incidents.

The analysis of incidents also provides insight into internally based terrorism. The most active indigenous groups have been Puerto Rican nationalists (see Figure 10-3a

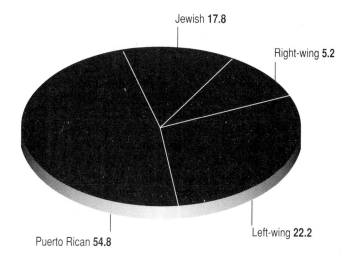

Figure 10-3a   An overview of domestic terrorist group incidents in the United States according to group classification, 1980–1986

Due to rounding, percentages may not add to 100.0
Source: FBI: *Analysis of Terrorist Incidents in the United States* (1986), p 56

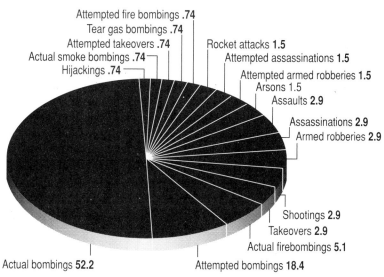

Figure 10-3b   An overview of domestic terrorist group incidents in the United States according to type, 1980–1986

Due to rounding, percentages may not add to 100.0
Source: FBI: *Analysis of Terrorist Incidents in the United States* (1986), p 56

and b). Their most common tactic, as is true in domestic terrorism in general, has been bombing.

The FBI reports also contain detailed target summaries and geographical displays (see Figure 10-4). Note that when Puerto Rico is excluded, New York City is the locale for over half of all urban terrorism incidents.

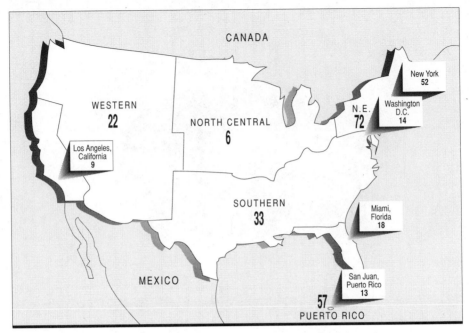

Figure 10-4   Terrorist incidents by region, 1980–1986

*AN OVERVIEW OF DOMESTIC TERRORIST GROUP INCIDENTS IN THE UNITED STATES ACCORDING TO TARGET, 1980–1986	
Target	*Percentage*
Government buildings and properties	19.9
Commercial establishments	12.5
Diplomatic { establishments	6.6
Diplomatic { property	2.9 } Total
Diplomatic { persons	2.9 } 12.4
Military	11.0
Public utilities	5.9
Banks and armored trucks	5.1
Residences	5.1
Transportation facilities	4.4
Educational facilities	3.7
Recreation and entertainment facilities	3.7
Other	3.7
Press and media	2.9
Public safety and personnel	2.9
Vehicles	2.2
Persons (other than diplomatic)	2.2
Postal facilities	2.2

*Due to rounding, percentages may not add to 100.0
Source: FBI, *Analysis of Terrorist Incidents in the United States* (1986), p. 57.

TERRORIST INCIDENTS ATTRIBUTED TO
DOMESTIC TERRORIST GROUPS IN THE UNITED STATES, 1980–1986

The following is a tabulation of domestic terrorist incidents recorded in the United States beginning with calendar year 1980.

Date	Total incidents attributed to a domestic terrorist group or individual	Killed	Injured	Total domestic terrorism sub-program preventions
1980	16	0	4	*
1981	26	1	1	*
1982	37	5	26	0
1983	20	6	4	4
1984	13	0	0	6
1985	7	2	10	17
1986	17	1	19	5

*This statistic was not maintained in 1980 and 1981.

TERRORIST INCIDENTS ATTRIBUTED TO
INTERNATIONAL TERRORIST GROUPS IN THE UNITED STATES, 1980–1986

The following is a tabulation of international terrorist incidents recorded in the United States beginning with calendar year 1980.

Date	Total incidents attributed to an international terrorist group or individual	Killed	Injured	Total international terrorism sub-program preventions
1980	13	1	15	*
1981	16	0	3	*
1982	14	2	0	3
1983	11	0	0	2
1984	0	0	0	3
1985	0	0	0	6
1986	0	0	0	3

*This statistic was not maintained in 1980 and 1981.
Source: FBI, Analysis of Terrorist Incidents in the United States (Washington, D.C.: Government Printing Office, 1986), 60.

FIVE GROUPS RESPONSIBLE FOR DOMESTIC TERRORISM IN THE 1980's

- White leftists
- Puerto Rican leftists
- Black militants
- Right-wing groups
- Jewish extremists

Source: John Harris, "Domestic Terrorism in the 1980's," (*FBI Law Enforcement Bulletin*, October 1987)

HARRIS'S ANALYSIS OF FBI DATA

In October 1987 the FBI devoted an entire issue of its *Law Enforcement Bulletin* to the problem of terrorism. Some of the articles were little more than an attempt to improve the prestige of the FBI in the eyes of the local law enforcement forces and federal bureaucrats, but others contained excellent summaries. A report by John Harris (1987, 5–13) was especially enlightening on the topic of domestic terrorism; it provided an excellent synopsis of several years of official reports.

According to Harris, five types of groups were responsible for domestic terrorism in the 1980s. These groups included (1) white leftists, (2) Puerto Rican leftists, (3) black militants, (4) right-wing extremists, and (5) Jewish extremists. Like the FBI reports on domestic terrorism, Harris's article did not include criminal incidents involving terrorist tactics. He limited his topic to the problem of political terrorism.

White Leftists

Harris agreed with other analysts that law enforcement interest in white leftist groups had waned by 1980. Although such groups had dominated the early part of the 1970s, their activities had dwindled by 1980. Law enforcement officials had all but forgotten the left when a Brinks armored car was robbed on October 20, 1981. One guard was killed and another wounded, and when police stopped the suspect's vehicle, two New York state troopers were ambushed and murdered.

At first officials believed the robbery was the work of black radicals, but investigations revealed that a network of white leftist groups had masterminded it. According to Harris, the Brinks armored car robbery signaled the return of the white left.

For the most part these groups were made up of older members from earlier revolutionary groups. Harris wrote that the United Freedom Front (UFF) was the most active of all the groups. The UFF was involved in a series of bombings, but also engaged in a variety of other activities throughout the Northeast. By 1985 most of the members of the UFF were in custody and awaiting trial.

Harris believed that other white leftist groups are not as strong as their rhetoric suggests. He also believed that some groups have operated under a variety of names. For example, the Armed Resistance Unit (taken into custody in 1988) may have operated as the Red Guerrilla Forces and the Revolutionary Fighting Group. Regardless, leftist activity again began to dwindle in 1987.

Puerto Rican Leftists

Puerto Rican nationalists have been extremely active during the 1980s. Harris stated that they have attacked military installations in addition to conducting a number of bombings and pulling off the largest armored car robbery in American history. Of fifty-six terrorist acts committed since 1980, most have been attributed to the Macheteros and the Volunteers for the Puerto Rican Revolution (OVRP).

Ronald Fernandez (1987) explicated the reasons for Puerto Rican nationalist terrorism in the United States. Puerto Rico was colonized by the Spanish shortly after the European discovery of America, and the Spanish ruled the island for nearly three centuries. In 1898 this changed when the United States captured Puerto Rico in the Spanish-American War.

At first the Puerto Ricans welcomed the United States as liberators, believing they were going to be granted independence. The were disappointed. Instead, the United States granted Puerto Rico commonwealth status. Its special relationship to the United States grew with the increasing military importance of the island.

Currently, the population is divided by three opinions. Some desire Puerto Rican statehood. Others want to create an independent country. Still others are leftists who want an independent country with a Marxist government. The United States has not responded to any of these groups, which provides the basis for dissatisfaction and armed revolt. Fernandez did not mention Ted Robert Gurr's summary of the paradox: no matter which group is satisfied, two other groups will be disappointed.

Terrorism has become one means of revolution, according to Fernandez. Two groups have been active in the United States for a number of years. The Armed Forces of the Revolution (FALN) is the oldest Puerto Rican nationalist terrorist group. More recently, the Macheteros have emerged in both Puerto Rico and the United States. Like Gurr, Fernandez believed that Puerto Rican terrorism will continue.

It was beyond the scope of Harris's analysis to offer a explanation for Puerto Rican violence, and he quite correctly limited his approach to a descriptive analysis of Puerto Rican groups. Yet the problem of Puerto Rican nationalism will not simply evaporate. Law enforcement officers must continue to respond to Puerto Rican terrorism, but at some point American policy makers need to resolve the status of Puerto Rico to the satisfaction of its people. This will not be easy.

Black Militants

Harris believed that the number of black groups operating in the 1980s has been extremely limited. Far from launching a general strike at society, black terrorism has been aimed at other black people. Most of it has focused on settling disputes among the black Muslim sects. One black Chicago street gang drew the attention of federal officials for allegedly offering its service to Libya, but no terrorist acts were committed. Other blacks individually joined groups of white leftists. In the 1980s, there seemed to be no pattern of black racial terrorism.

Right-Wing Groups

This was not true of the far right. Like other analysts, Harris noted the reemergence of the extreme right in the 1980s. He also pointed to the difficulty of plotting their activities. While right-wingers routinely engage in violent rhetoric, they do not routinely endorse terrorism. They do not leave communiqués or claim credit after an incident; thus, in terms of confirmed incidents, left-wing terrorism has outdistanced right-wing terrorism in the 1980s.

Confirmed instances of terrorism may be deceiving, however. The doctrines of the right-wing groups may lead them to activities far beyond rhetoric. The right is philosophically united by an antigovernment ideology and by anti-Semitism. Many are bound together, as you will read in the next chapter, by a racist religious creed called Christian Identity. Their extremist beliefs exhibit a potential for violence.

Harris acknowledged this within his analysis of data. Officially, the right has been responsible for less than one dozen acts of terrorism in the 1980s. They have actually behaved in a much more violent fashion, Harris said, but their acts are typically reported as routine crimes. In other words, since right-wing extremists tend not to link acts of violence directly with political activity, the FBI's system of monitoring political violence does not cover their activities.

The list of right-wing extremist groups is long. The major ones associated with violence have been The Order; Posse Comitatus; and The Covenant, the Sword, and the Arm of the Lord (CSA). Although two members of The Order allegedly plotted to assassinate presidential candidate Jesse Jackson in 1988, most of its members are in jail. The leaders of Posse Comitatus have gone into hiding, and the CSA was raided and disbanded in April 1985.

Yet these groups represent only the tip of a very large right-wing movement. If the movement continues to engage in rhetorical violence without developing a support network for terrorism, its members are constitutionally free to believe what they want to believe. If they practice violence, it's another matter. As Harris points out, their official terrorist activity is low, but their potential for terrorism is quite high indeed.

Jewish Extremists

Harris concludes his analysis by examining Jewish extremist groups. In the 1980s Jewish groups were responsible for twenty acts of terrorism. Harris said their most frequent tactic was bombing and that the most active group was the Jewish Defense League (JDL). Persons or organizations believed to be anti-Semitic are the most frequent target of these extremists.

The JDL is headquartered in New York City, and most acts of Jewish terrorism occur in the metropolitan area. The JDL has a nationwide organization, however, with chapters in several American cities. Ironically, the JDL operates much like its anti-Semitic counterparts in the extremist right. According to Harris, they engage in quite a bit of rhetorical violence, but their actual acts of terrorism are relatively few. Terrorism is conducted by a small, hard-core element, Harris said.

Harris believed that incidents of terrorism are cyclical, and that the United States is now in a downward spiral. He also believed that a new generation of terrorists will surface with a new agenda for violence. Whether he is right or wrong, the overall pattern of domestic terrorism is clear. The United States has remained relatively unscathed. Terrorism has been a foreign relations problem, not a domestic political problem.

ABORTION CLINIC BOMBINGS AND TERRORISM

During the 1980s the United States witnessed almost forty bombings of abortion clinics in various states. There is no easy resolution to the abortion debate, as proponents of each side believe they are morally correct. The side favoring the right to choose an abortion feels it is defending Constitutional rights. Those against abortion often believe they are following the will of God. No matter which side dominates, the other side may react violently. Such has been the case with America's newest terrorists, the abortion clinic bombers.

David Nice (1988) attempted to produce a theory of violence by examining trends in abortion clinic bombings. He stated that the literature reveals several explanations for violent political behavior. One theory suggests that social controls break down under stress and urbanization. Another theory says that violence increases when people are not satisfied with political outcomes. Violence can also be reinforced by social and cultural values. Finally, violence can stem from a group's strength or weakness, its lack of faith in the political system, or its frustration with economic conditions.

Nice matched trends in abortion clinic bombings against these theories of violence. By examining thirty bombings from 1982 to 1985 he found some patterns. First, bombings tended to be regionalized. With the exception of two in Washington, D.C., the bombings occurred in eight states, only three of which had more than four bombings. Nice compared the social factors in the detonation areas to the theories about violence.

Nice concluded that abortion clinic bombings were related to several social factors. Most of the bombings occurred in areas of rapidly expanding population and declining social controls. That meant that bombings tended to occur in urban areas. The slowest growing states in America did not experience bombings, while half of the fastest growing states did.

Bombings also reflected a method of communicating frustration with political processes and outcomes. Bombing is a means of taking direct action. Nice noted that most bombings took place where the rate of abortions to live deliveries is relatively high. Abortion bombers feel compelled to action by social and political circumstances. They feel they are making a positive impact on the political situation. Nice also noted that bombings predictably occur more frequently in states that have a highly active militant antiabortion constituency.

States that experience bombings also exhibit a greater toleration for crimes against women. Clinic bombings are highest in areas where cultural and social violence against women is more acceptable. States that have passed laws against domestic violence experience fewer bombings than states with no such laws.

Bombings are also a sign of weakness. Areas that have strong concentrations of antiabortion sentiment do not experience as much bombing when such sentiment is not accompanied by activism. In addition, Nice said, when high populations of Roman Catholics, Baptists, or Mormons are present, bombings decline. When potential bombers feel outnumbered, however, they may take action because they feel weak.

In summary, Nice found that abortion clinic bombings were positively correlated with every theory of violence, save the theory of economic deprivation; there was no relation between abortion clinic bombings and economic conditions. He concluded that antiabortion violence appears in areas of rapid population growth where the abortion rate is high. As social controls decrease and desires to substitute political controls increase, bombings develop into a form of political action.

This returns us to the point made in chapter 1 about labeling and the term *terrorism*. If you strongly believe that abortion is immoral, you might refer to abortion clinic bombers as misguided. If you strongly believe that every women has a right to choose an abortion, you may call them terrorists. This issue does not *cause* terrorism, but if you were to bomb your opponents' facilities, you would certainly be taking illegal action. After discovering the social conditions under which bombings generally occur, Nice called them "political violence." The FBI, on the other hand, refers to abortion clinic bombings as criminal felonies in the annual Uniform Crime Report. It does not report the bombings as terrorism, even though they fit its own definition.

SUMMARY OF CHAPTER TEN

The United States has not experienced the same level of terrorism as have many countries in other parts of the world. This often leads to confusion for many Americans, especially those in law enforcement agencies, who do not know how to approach terrorism. The lack of experience in domestic terrorism exacerbates problems in comprehending the issues.

Gurr and Bell provided one of the better descriptions of domestic terrorism. Historically, terrorism in the United States was used as a repressive tool to maintain power and stability. This changed in the 1960s when American terrorism began to take on an international revolutionary flavor. Despite this trend, revolutionary terrorism failed to become popular in the United States. Gurr and Bell believed that Puerto Rican nationalism and criminals using terrorist tactics have been the main manifestation of domestic terrorism.

There are five sources of domestic terrorism: (1) foreign groups operating on American soil, (2) revolutionary nationalists, (3) right-wing extremists, (4) left-wing revolutionaries, and (5) criminals. The annual reports on domestic terrorism issued by the FBI are one of the best sources of information concerning most of these categories. The FBI discussion, however, is limited to political violence.

Domestic terrorism in the 1980s has also been limited. Summarizing several FBI reports, Harris identified domestic terrorism by the type of group engaged in violence. Puerto Rican nationalists were the most active group in the 1980s. Right-wing extremists pose an enormous potential for violence, yet it has been difficult to link their activities to terrorism. Harris believed the 1980s have experienced a downward trend in a cycle of domestic terrorism.

Abortion clinic bombings grew during the 1980s. They are not typically treated as terrorism by some analysts, and official reports of domestic terrorism do not list them. On the other hand, abortion clinic bombings do meet the definition the FBI has established for terrorism.

IF YOU WANT TO READ FURTHER . . .

The FBI annual reports on domestic terrorism are not exciting reading, yet they contain a great deal of information. They are available to the public, and you should review them if you are interested in domestic terrorism. They are probably the best factual summaries of domestic political violence available. You can find the reports at most government depository libraries. Look under FBI, "Summary of Domestic Terrorism."

An excellent guide to journals and professional reports can be found in the National Criminal Justice Reference Service Document Retrieval Index. While the majority of the articles describe SWAT tactics or negotiation techniques, it is by far one of the better resources on domestic terrorism. In addition, the NCJRS index provides the information you'll need to order documents when they're not available in your local library.

Another good resource on the topic is the International Association of Chiefs of Police *Clandestine Tactics and Technology* series. It now numbers over eleven volumes and contains dozens of studies by practitioners and scholars. The only problem is that it has restricted circulation; it is difficult to obtain copies unless you are currently an active law enforcement officer.

New scholary works on domestic terrorism have appeared in recent years. Prior to 1978, most concentrated on crime, violence, and rioting. Terrorism came into focus only after that time. *Violence in America,* edited by Hugh Graham and Ted Robert Gurr, will be helpful in grasping the issues. Frederic Homer and Ted Robert Gurr have published two separate articles worth reading in Michael Stohl's *The Politics of Terrorism.* James Poland also has a good section on domestic terrorism in his *Understanding Terrorism.* John Wolf's *Fear of Fear* assumes that you already have an understanding of domestic terrorism, but it contains useful sections for police investigation.

Finally, although it is not directly related to terrorism, another book by Ted Robert Gurr deserves mention. *Why Men Rebel* outlines some of the theories of violent political action. Gurr's approach has not become dated because he is looking for a political explanation for violence. It is productive to apply Gurr's thesis to the American experience of domestic terrorism. If you applied his comments to the abortion clinic bombing issue, for example, you would gain a deeper understanding of politically motivated violence.

HOLY WAR, AMERICAN STYLE

Religious violence is most frequently associated with Middle Eastern terrorism, and many Americans may think that America has moved beyond the threat of internal religious violence. Yet the United States currently is home to a religion known as Christian Identity, and some of its followers have issued a call for a holy war against the sources of American social ills. The prime sources of these ills, in the minds of Identity Christians, are Jews and racial minorities. Their religion has become the melting pot of a loose confederation of extremists. Most of the calls to violence have been rhetorical, but in the 1980s a portion of domestic terrorism was attributable to Christian Identity. It has become a source of law enforcement concern.

After reading this chapter you should be able to do the following:

1. Explain the difference between extremism and terrorism
2. Outline the origins of the modern right-wing movement
3. Describe various types of right-wing organizations
4. Summarize the theology of Christian Identity
5. Discuss the dangers posed by Identity theology

DIFFERENCES BETWEEN EXTREMISM AND TERRORISM

The problems of terrorism and extremism in America often appear to be similar. Extremist violence in American history is nothing new. It has featured in such events as the taxation-inspired Whiskey Rebellion shortly after the Revolutionary War and John Brown's abolitionist raid on Harper's Ferry in 1859. The labor movement—and the capitalist reaction to it—has been rife with violence over the past century and a half. The violence of more recent years has frequently been characterized as an extension of a long American tradition of extremist violence.

There is a danger when extremism is equated with violence, though. Terrorism is a form of violence under all circumstances, but this is not necessarily true of extremism. Extremists may become violent, and when they do they are a law enforcement concern. Yet rhetorical extremism simply represents an attitude. Bear this in mind while reading this chapter: many unpopular views are presented here, but people are free to hold unpopular views in a democracy.

The Constitution clearly says that there is a difference between opinions and actions. Court interpretations of the First Amendment have consistently reinforced the rights of individuals to hold beliefs, no matter how offensive and unpopular they are. This is the essence of freedom of speech, and it is a critical issue in law enforcement. When discussing domestic terrorism it is not permissible to equate extremism with violence. Merely harboring a set of unpopular views is not a crime.

In America *action* is the critical issue. Sometimes this is not fully understood by opponents of right-wing extremists. All citizens have the right to say or do what they like provided they neither engage in nor provoke criminal actions. When the line between rhetoric and criminality is crossed, the police can take responsive measures. If there is no criminal action, there is no crime.

This poses a problem for any agency having a counterterrorist function in the United States. Extremist groups frequently call for violence. The call itself is not a crime unless investigators can prove there is a direct link between the rhetoric and a resulting crime. When an officer has reasonable suspicion that such a link exists, police may investigate. But no action can be taken based solely on the extremist position of a group. The distinction is critical.

THE ORIGINS OF RIGHT-WING EXTREMISM

Right-wing extremism is part of the history of the United States. On the surface it endorses basic American values such as individualism and self-determination. These themes have remained fairly constant in right-wing dogma, but James Coates (1987) said its underlying values are different. Historically these values have featured anti-Semitism and anti-Catholicism. Coates believed they were reinforced by the perception of America as a Protestant nation and by a literal interpretation of the Book of Revelation.

Allen Sapp (1985) described the origins of the movement as based on Anglo-Israelism, the idea that the lost tribes of Israel were scattered when a revolt against the Romans failed around 60 A.D. Before Roman wrath the tribes fled north, crossing the Caucasus mountains and sweeping through Western Europe. In a series of invasions they conquered the lands that stretched from Italy to Ireland. In this manner the lands of Western Europe became the lands of the Israelites.

The United Kingdom had a special role in the new order. God gave the tribe of Mannasah the British throne and charged it with spreading the Gospel throughout the world and bringing all people under the subjugation of Christianity. All Europeans were chosen by God, according to Anglo-Israelism, but the British became the most favored of all.

That special role was transferred to America when the British colonists arrived. By the late 1800s, American followers of the movement believed the United States to be the new Israel, the land God promised to Moses in the Bible. Americans, the descendants of the Israelites of old, were called upon to bring God's kingdom into being. The Declaration of Independence and the Constitution were holy covenants between God and his new people. America was destined to lead the world from a morally sanctified position.

Many of the tenets of Anglo-Israelism spilled over beyond the extremist right. Mainstream religions frequently overlooked or rejected their theories about the lost tribes of Israel, but many fundamentalists had no doubt that they dwelled in God's chosen country. By the twentieth century many fundamentalist churches openly sanctioned the belief that America was God's chosen leader of the world.

The followers of Anglo-Israelism had an influence on mainstream Protestantism, but they did not dictate its course. Anglo-Israelism has remained an unorthodox view throughout the twentieth century. It did make inroads among other extremists, however. Specifically, by the 1920s members of the Ku Klux Klan and other right-wing extremists were proving to be a sympathetic audience for Anglo-Israelism. There were never formal denominational arrangements, but right-wing extremists found comfort in the belief that they were chosen by God.

In the last three decades Anglo-Israelism has blended with a new right-wing theology called Christian Identity. The movement was spawned by the Reverend Wesley Swift, a right-wing anti-Semitic preacher from California, shortly after World War II. Swift preached the message of Anglo-Israelism with a few added features. He brought overtones of racism and religious superiority to its theology.

Swift made several claims as an extension of Anglo-Israelism. Since Europeans were white, Swift deduced that God must be white, because Adam was created in God's image. It followed that the Israelites of old were also white. Swift encouraged followers to use Old Testament laws, festivals, and terminology to identify with the Israelites of old. Accordingly, he reverted to the Israelite name for God, Yahweh, and he used it often.

Richard Holden (1986) claimed that Swift invented many of the other portions of his theology. Swift simply spoke off the top of his head or made up passages of the Bible as he "read" to a radio audience. In addition to promulgating Anglo-Israelism, Swift claimed that Yahweh was at war with the Jews because they had killed Jesus. Only the children of Satan could accomplish this, so Swift relegated the role of devil to the descendants of the Jews. Catholics were no better, because they had perverted Yahweh's faith and had endorsed ideas of racial equality. Swift found an eager audience among right-wing political extremists.

When Swift died his Identity message was carried on by a number of theological disciples, including Richard Butler of Aryan Nations, William Potter Gale and James Wickstrom of Posse Comitatus, and Robert Miles of the Mountain Church of Jesus Christ. These men have helped to blend Identity theology with the traditional hate message of the Ku Klux Klan and a notion of white supremacy.

Another important right-wing group is of slightly more recent origin. In 1958 George Lincoln Rockwell founded the American Nazi Party, and the Nazis have since provided a haven for many extremist concepts. The group split several times, and Rockwell himself was assassinated. As is true of the Klan, there is no centralized Nazi party in the United States. By the 1970s, various groups of Nazis had found common ground with the Klan: Klan members started to wear Nazi regalia at their gatherings, and Nazis began burning crosses. Both groups increasingly attended Christian Identity churches.

In 1978 America began an agricultural economic crisis from which it has not yet recovered. Corporate farms began replacing individual family farms, and a group of traditional Americans was displaced. When rural Americans asked why large banks had the right to foreclose on farms, a group of extremists had an answer. The banks were controlled by Jews, they said. Farm foreclosures were nothing less than satanic confrontation, but the old order was dead, and Yahweh was about to usher in a new kingdom. God needed help, however, and Yahweh was calling his chosen people to the battle of Armageddon. The economic crisis was a call to battle. To some the simplicity of the right-wing response made far more sense than did complicated economic answers.

TYPOLOGIES OF RIGHT-WING GROUPS

The past decade has witnessed a new stage of development in the American extremist right, and some groups have moved from extremist rhetoric to terrorism. Many groups reached their zenith in 1984 when a loosely bound coalition endorsed a common program and violence reached its height. Since 1984 there has been a decrease in the total numbers of right-wing followers but an increase in potential violence. Violent actions by right-wing extremists in the 1980s brought about a new form of indigenous terrorism with a theological base.

The right-wing movement gained strength via its unification through religion. Allen Sapp (1986) examined a major right-wing document calling for revolution and found it contained themes common throughout the right. The Nehemiah Township charter was developed and signed in Hayden Lake, Idaho, the home of the Aryan Nations. Its purpose was to establish a new government separate from the Jewish-dominated United States government. It called for a separate white country, racial purity, and government under Yahweh. Christian Identity was at the heart of the document. Several Nazis, Klansmen, and Identity theologians signed the document. Many survivalists, people who live in paramilitary mercenary training communes throughout the country, also joined in the call for revolution.

A proposed new constitution by Posse Comitatus (Holeck, 1985) had a similar theme. The forces of white Christianity were losing ground to the Zionist Occupation Government (ZOG). The only hope of restoring the original rights of white people was to form a new government excluding blacks and condemning Jews to extinction. James Wickstrom (1983) preached that such a holy mission could only be accomplished through the unification of Identity followers.

Among the militant right-wing groups—those that sometimes cross the line from rhetoric to terrorism—there are other common themes. Jews cannot be stopped peacefully, according to their line of logic. God's kingdom and the battle of Armageddon will only come about through militant preparation and active strikes against ZOG. Police forces are the tools of ZOG, and the militants believe themselves to be above American law. They serve Yahweh in a higher order.

But even though many have adopted common themes and revolutionary documents, each right-wing group has its own specific agenda. Posse Comitatus began as a tax protest group and suggested that the highest level of office in the land should be the county sheriff. The Klan and Nazis have remained splintered and factionalized. Survivalist groups like The Covenant, the Sword, and the Arm of the Lord (CSA) have kept themselves apart from mainstream society. The majority of Christian Identity churches simply reject violence. Some analysts have looked for patterns to describe this jumble of right-wing organizations.

Coates's Typology

James Coates (1987) examined the common themes of the militant right and their variations. Despite the homogeneity of their basic response to social problems, Coates believed the groups could be classified by behavioral patterns. He developed a typology of right-wing groups in an effort to categorize their activities.

Coates's first category was terrorist groups. In it he placed The Order, or the Silent Brotherhood. The Order began with close ties to the white supremacy movement and the Identity church. A small group of would-be revolutionaries planned and executed a series of robberies in 1983 and 1984 to help finance a right-wing revolution. In strategy they followed the dictates of Carlos Marighella, and they may have been inspired by Andrew MacDonald's novel, *The Turner Diaries*.

Some analysts believe that the hard-core membership of The Order came from the CSA and Aryan Nations, although Richard Butler of Aryan Nations has repeatedly denied this. The Order's robberies were followed by three murders, including that of a Denver-based radio talk show host. The Order also planned a massive counterfeiting scheme to finance further operations and hopefully disrupt the American economy. In 1984 the group's leader, Robert Matthews, was killed in a shoot-out with FBI agents. By 1985 most members of The Order were in jail.

The Order lives on as a symbol for other right-wing revolutionaries. Richard Butler referred to it as a group of virile young white men who could no longer tolerate the system. Another group called Bruder Schweigen Strike Force II appeared in Idaho in 1986. The have allegedly been linked to several bombings in the town of Coeur d'Alene. The Order's most romanticized portrait has been an anonymous book published in Cohoctah, Michigan, by the Mountain Church of Jesus Christ.

In *Wann Alle Bruder Schweigen,* an unsigned author from the Mountain Church portrayed The Order as comparable to the gods of Norse mythology. The author was apparently influenced by Wagner's operas and his heroic character Siegfried. Robert Matthews, The Order's leader, was cast as Siegfried. Called by Odin, the king of the Norse gods, he left Valhalla to do Odin's will. In Wagner's opera Siegfried sought to do battle with Odin's enemies and was killed. In the Mountain Church version, Siegfried fought ZOG and was killed by demons (FBI agents). Various characters in the right-wing movement are represented by Norse gods in the story; two characters appear to be Richard Butler and Robert Miles.

Like Wagner's character, Matthews was doomed. He faced a heroic death and his spirit was carried by the Valkyrie maidens back to the sanctuary of Valhalla. Norse gods—apparently Richard Butler and Robert Miles—then promised the soul of Matthews that his death was not in vain and that vengeance would be wreaked upon ZOG. *Wann Alle Bruder Schweigen* is a right-wing tragedy, but it is designed to be a story of inspiration. It calles for Aryan Warriors to fight the battle against ZOG.

Wagnerian allegories aside, the real Order was a terrorist group. *Wann Alle Bruder Schweigen* was a propaganda tract designed to gather more right-wing support. Neither the FBI nor the media have referred to such instances of political violence and propaganda as terrorism, but Coates did. He believed that The Order and its support network constituted domestic terrorism.

Coates identified five other types of extremist groups, all of which support some form of violence. He classified them as (1) Identity churches that support violence, (2) tax protest groups such as Posse Comitatus, (3) "lone wolves" fighting the system without a support group, (4) survivalists, and (5) compound dwellers.

Suall's and Lowe's Typology

Irwin Suall and David Lowe (1987) offered a different typology of right-wing behavior. Seeking to avoid direct comparisons with conservatism or those on the political right, they called these extremists "hate groups." They argued for four categories of such groups. The first one stems from the Ku Klux Klan and its variants. The second and third are militant Christian Identity groups and Nazis. The final type of extremist group is called a "hybrid" group. Suall and Lowe believed hybrids to be sophisticated extensions of old-style hate groups.

The Ku Klux Klan is experiencing an overall national decline in membership, according to Suall and Lowe. Several regional groups have remained strong, however, and the Klan's real strength has always lain in close-knit local organizations. So although the major national Klans are not strong, individual pockets of local Klans are threatening in limited areas.

Christian Identity is organizationally similar to the Klan with two major exceptions. First, Identity theology pervades the whole right-wing movement. Although Christian Identity churches are not united, they provide ideological links among groups. Second, many organizational contacts are made by Aryan Nations, the major arm of Christian Identity. The Hayden Lake group apparently sees itself as the organization that can unite the right.

An undercover video by journalist Peter Lake (1984) reinforced the view of Suall and Lowe. Lake pretended to join the Aryan Nations and became its official historian. In Lake's video recordings Richard Butler appears to be the man wishing to unite the right-wing movement. He does so through appeals for unification among Nazis and Klansmen, and by preaching Identity Christianity. Butler leads the Church of Jesus Christ Christian.

Nazi groups come next in the Suall and Lowe typology. Nazis have changed since their group was founded in America in 1958. Each party is local and goes by its own particular name. There is no standard identification, and the Nazis lack national, regional, and local strength. Some groups have attempted to contact Nazis in Germany. Nazi groups engage in ritualistic displays of uniforms, symbols, and military organization.

Hybrid groups are a new phenomenon, according to Suall and Lowe. They have been built on the ruins of Ku Klux Klan and Nazi groups and are generally devoid of symbols. They are attempting to gain a respectable political base by portraying themselves as conservatives.

Suall and Lowe make no distinction between violent groups and the hybrid groups, but the latter's efforts to join mainstream politics returns us to the problem discussed at the beginning of this chapter. Hybrid groups would seem to fall into a category of political expression, and freedom of speech and politics are protected by the Constitution. There is a difference between a group advocating a political position and one advocating violence. Suall and Lowe pointed out that some members of the extremist right have come to grasp this distinction. Accordingly, they have modified their plan, and emphasize rhetoric over action. This has ironically resulted in a call for greater violence among the militants.

In general, right-wing extremist groups are in a state of decline. Suall and Lowe attributed this to aggressive law enforcement and legislation banning paramilitary training. The greatest future dangers appear to be the remaining militants and the increasing number of Skinhead groups, cult-like groups of young men and women aged 15-20, generally centered in urban areas. Skinhead groups have been growing in American urban centers and have been embraced by some elements of the white supremacy movement. Young members of the white supremacy movement have been quick to advocate violence, and older members have done little to mute their war cries.

Sapp's Typology

Allen Sapp (1985) also introduced a typology that classified right-wing groups in three categories. White supremacists formed the base of the right-wing movement. This included groups like the Aryan Nations, the Nazis, and the Ku Klux Klan. Survivalist groups formed another segment. The final group comprised the Christian Identity movement. If the supremacists form the base, Christian Identity forms the bulk.

Sapp concluded that all typologies of the extreme right help analysts to understand the various segments of the movement, but that the classification systems are artificial. There are no clear lines dividing the various types of extremist groups, and there is no predictive method to infer when a group will move from rhetoric to violence. Additionally, members of one type of group tend to belong to other types of groups.

Sapp said that such joint memberships blur the distinctions among extremist groups. It is often difficult to tell which group is being discussed or represented. This is all the more difficult when their potential for violence is examined. A group like The Order can easily be classified as a terrorist organization, but it drew its membership and support from other, nonactive extremist organizations that advocated and applauded The Order's violence. It is often difficult to tell where rhetoric stops and crime begins.

THE THEOLOGY OF CHRISTIAN IDENTITY

In 1984 a Springfield, Missouri television station went to Licking, Missouri to cover the annual Freedom Festival, sponsored by the Christian Patriots Defense League. Television coverage of the participants revealed a *Who's Who* of right-wing extremism. Tactical manuals were displayed in booths, and classes on developing a revolution were offered. Amidst the violent rhetoric and calls for revolution, the strains of the Christian hymn "Shall We Gather at the River?" could be heard coming from a tent. The Christian patriots had gathered to prepare for Armageddon.

The Freedom Festival is a religious event as well as a political meeting. It follows the model of the Aryan National Congress held by Richard Butler in Hayden Lake, Idaho. Both the Aryan National Congress and the Freedom Festival have the spirit of an old-time camp meeting. In between hymns and political lectures, the faithful are told to prepare to do God's will. Armageddon awaits.

In theology, various arguments are used to explain the origins of life and the human relationship to God. Identity theology has proposed several theories of an ontological nature. Robert Miles spoke of a cosmic battle between Good and Evil. The forces of Evil were driven to earth in this account, so God created humans in His image to fight those evil life forms. The good people were white and were created along with Adam. The evil people—technically they are less than people—were Jews and the nonwhite races they attempt to seduce (Holden, 1986).

A more conventional theory follows the standard biblical account: God created heaven, earth, and then Adam. Phillip Finch (1983) recorded a version of this account that he gained in discussion with an Identity preacher. The minister said that God created all life in the first three days, including humanlike creatures. After this God created Adam in God's own image. Adam was white and was given dominion over all the earth, including the lesser races.

Posse Comitatus minister James Wickstrom (1983) tried to simplify this complicated bit of ontology. He stated simply that whites are pure and constitute a race. The "mud" races are also pure. The Jews, however, are a mixture. They "mix their seed" with other races to produce other species. This is the ontological world of Christian Identity.

Identity theologians arrive at these conclusions by reinterpreting history through the spectacles of Anglo-Israelism. The Old Testament, in their eyes, is the history of Adam and his descendants, and the stories of the Old Testament reflect Yahweh's promises to the Israelites in their battle with Satan. Satan's disciples and servants are the Jews, the enemies of the Israelites.

Christian Identity's view of history contrasts with the standard Old Testament interpretations by Judaism, Christianity, and Islam, in which Yahweh's chosen people are the Jews, and Abraham is the common father of Jews, Christians, and Muslims alike. In Identity's version, Abraham made a covenant with God for divine protection of the white Israelites. Abraham, Isaac, Jacob, and their descendants are the ancestors of white Europeans and Americans. Jews have tried to confuse the issue by claiming the Old Testament heroes for themselves.

This historical reinterpretation of the Old Testament allows Identity Christians to restate the human nature of Jesus Christ. Jesus is presented as an Israelite, not a Jew. In fact, to refer to Jesus, or any other Israelite, as Jewish is to commit the greatest sacrilege in Identity theology. Reflecting the views of Anglo-Israelism, Identity theologians insist on a strict dichotomy between Israelites and Jews.

Identity Christians believe that the New Testament begins in tragedy but gets better. A human Israelite, Jesus, was tricked and crucified by the Jews. Satan had apparently won. Yahweh had his own tricks, however, and brought Jesus back to life. The real purpose of the Resurrection was to strike back at the Jews. The followers of Identity Christianity believe that Jesus is coming back to wreak havoc among the followers of Satan.

The end of the New Testament, the Book of Revelation, is crucial to Identity theology. Even among mainstream Christians, there are varying interpretations of the work. Some view it as a literal description of the end of the world; in theological language, this type of study is known as eschatology. Other Christians see it as a symbolic account, while still others view it as a clandestine literary attack on the Roman Empire. Identity followers accept the eschatological view.

Eschatology is indispensable to Identity theology and largely explains its relationship to violence and terrorism. Richard Holden (1986) wrote that Identity followers feel they are called to a holy war against the forces of darkness. They must take up the sword and prepare for the militant coming of Jesus. Armageddon is not only at hand, militant Identity Christians feel, but they must create it. The final battle of creation, Armageddon, is in the hands of a few true-believer Christians who must destroy the Jews and the enemies of Christ.

Identity Christianity's call to holy war, of course, conflicts with the basic pacifism of more mainstream Christianity. Identity Christians therefore must restate basic Christian principles to issue their call (White, 1986b). Most importantly, the Christian principle of love must be revised.

Identity Christians resort to a conspiracy theory to explain the current plight of their churches and the social ills of the country. Free white Americans would not have given in to Jewish interests had they not been duped. James Wickstrom (1983) said the Jews began by gaining economic control of the country. This was followed by their propagation of myths of racial equality. An Aryan Nations tract titled "The Death of the White Race" agreed. Racial mixing, racial equality, drugs, and crime are all the result of a Jewish conspiracy. In the Identity Christians' view, the devil is one crafty fellow.

THE DANGER OF A CALL TO HOLY WAR

Some Identity Christians take the rhetoric of violence seriously. A CSA defense manual written about 1982 provided instructions for conducting terrorism. The manual told followers how to prepare ambushes, how to fortify their homes against police entrance, and how to fight in an urban environment. Tactical instructions were frequently interrupted by quotations from the Bible or Identity theology.

A number of other survivalist groups seem to be preparing for a war that will go beyond rhetorical pronouncements. These groups have not turned violent yet, but they have advocated violations of criminal law. They include the Arizona Patriots, the Iowa Society for Educated Citizens, and the Oregon Militia. The central question for law enforcement is, Will such groups turn to violence and crime?

The future of right-wing extremism is unclear, but the call for violence and extremism is clear in the literature. For example, Eustace Mullins of the Aryan Nations (1984) wrote that the holocaust of World War II was a Jewish myth, but that it should become a reality. A publication by the Western Front in California called for individual attacks on blacks and Jews. Many publications of the Aryan Nations contain similar themes.

In 1988 a federal jury ruled that most of these right-wing pronouncements were rhetorical, and Christian Identity's message was protected. By finding a number of right-wing extremists not guilty of attempting to overthrow the United States government, the jury clearly judged the call for holy war rhetorical. Right-wing extremism did not equate with domestic terrorism.

Yet some individual factions of the movement can hardly be considered rhetorical and nonviolent. In 1986 Coeur d'Alene, Idaho, was subjected to a bombing campaign by a group modeled after The Order, and money from The Order's 1984–1985 crime spree may now be in the hands of right-wing organizations. The Aryan Nations is currently seeking stronger ties with urban Skinheads. These young neo-Nazis are establishing patterns of racial and religious violence (National Public Radio 1988).

There is no doubt that rhetoric can breed violence. According to an unpublished police intelligence report (Kansas Bureau of Investigation 1984), survivalist groups like Posse Comitatus have frequently crossed the line between rhetoric and violence. Police stations have been attacked and opponents threatened and killed. One prosecuting attorney in Kansas added that armed survivalists have frequently confronted sheriffs' agencies during farm foreclosures.

An officer assisting at one farm foreclosure in a southern state confidentially walked the author through a confrontation with survivalists. A group of police and sheriffs' officers were serving foreclosure papers on a farm when they encountered twenty armed men from a northern survivalist group. The group was entrenched in the front yard and armed with illegal military weapons. The police retreated.

According to the same officer, a stronger police force returned the next day with military advisors. The survivalists were gone, along with the farmer's family and personal belongings. The house was booby-trapped, and military demolitions experts were required to secure it. Details in the officer's description matched the details of other such encounters. Armed confrontations go beyond the bounds of rhetoric and Constitutional protections.

A document seized by local law enforcement officers during the 1985 arrest of a number of extremists also raises concerns. According to the "Committee of the States Assembled in Congress," some right-wing groups were planning a campaign of domestic terrorism. The "Committee of the States" document outlined procedures for attacking police, communication, and government service installations. A manual that received wider circulation, titled *The Road Back,* contained similar instructions as well as procedures for booby-trapping highways.

Whether such calls will lead to significant violence is unclear. There is danger both in the violence itself and overreation by police forces. Ted Robert Gurr (1988) said that economic dissatisfaction and concern over social changes could be a breeding ground for terror on the right. The call to a holy war is particularly disturbing. Norman Cohn (1957, 307) argued that eschatology and violence are an unstable combination; religious terrorists can be the most deadly of all. When a deity calls for battle, warriors need not be concerned with human restraints on violence. They fight in a holy war.

SUMMARY OF CHAPTER ELEVEN

This chapter focused on the extreme right and its potential for domestic terrorism. When approaching domestic terror, we must remember that extremism is not terrorism, and that the Constitution grants citizens the right to maintain and foster unpopular political beliefs. Law enforcement agencies may take action only when calls for violence can be linked to a specific crime.

The call for right-wing revolution in America is a holy call. It has its roots in historical movements such as the Ku Klux Klan and is based on religious and racial prejudice. Protestant superiority has been promoted by the theology of Christian Identity and Anglo-Israelism. Religious views have been incorporated into the contemporary Ku Klux Klan, Nazi, white supremacy, and survivalist movements.

Christian Identity theology is based on the belief that a white God has called white Americans to a holy war with the forces of the devil. Jews are believed to be the children of Satan. Identity theology reads the Bible as a record of the Aryan struggle against the Jews. Identity Christians await the second coming of a militant white Jesus.

The majority of Identity Christians are not violent and do not advocate the overthrow of the American government. Potentially violent extremist organizations, however, have taken up the eschatological cry of Christian Identity. Some Identity-inspired groups have engaged in localized terrorism. The most dangerous potential outcome is that an extremist group will engage in significant acts of violence, believing they are called upon to do so by God.

IF YOU WANT TO READ FURTHER . . .

It is difficult to obtain good works on the extreme right and its potential for terrorism. This is primarily because books contain either a violent call for revolution or a vehement attack on the right. The University of Kansas has on file several hundred tracts of right-wing hate literature and "mayhem manuals." Various right-wing presses such as those at Aryan Nations also turn out hate material.

The Anti-Defamation League of B'nai B'rith has published several attacks on right-wing groups. The most famous is *Hate Groups in America*. Other accounts include *The Ku Klux Klans, The Ku Klux Klan Tries for a Comeback,* and *The KKK and the Neo-Nazis*. Scholarly critics of the ADL claim that the group has distorted its criticism through its own hatred of hate groups.

Two pieces of journalism take you inside the movement. Phillip Finch's *God, Guts, and Guns* is very good. James Coates's *Armed and Dangerous* is more recent and provides a broader view. Both works are extremely readable; they lack scholarly rigor, but they are still informative.

Scholars at Central Missouri State University have blazed a trail into the relationship between right-wing extremism and domestic terrorism. Richard Holden's *Postmillennialism as a Justification for Right-Wing Violence* is available through the International Association of Chiefs of Police (IACP) Clandestine Tactics and Technology series. Other works from Central Missouri State have yet to be produced, but they will prove informative if they do appear.

ABU NIDAL, HIZBOLLAH,
AND ISLAMIC JIHAD

At the end of chapter 5 we began to examine some of the international aspects of Middle Eastern terrorism. In this chapter we'll discuss the methods three Middle Eastern groups have used to "internationalize" their activities. This facet of terrorism poses one of the most complex challenges to those formulating counterterrorist policies. On the one hand it is a law enforcement problem: criminal activity occurring on an international level. At the same time this type of terrorism has a national security aspect. An examination of the terrorist groups Abu Nidal, Hizbollah, and Islamic Jihad will illustrate the difficulty in designing a tactical response to international terrorism.

After reading this chapter, you should be able to do the following.

1. Compare analytical viewpoints on international aspects of PLO activities
2. Discuss the international activities of the Abu Nidal group
3. Describe the relation between the civil war in Lebanon and Shiite terrorism
4. Examine the tactical aspects of Islamic Jihad
5. Discuss transnational terrorism with regard to the policy issues facing the United States

INTERNATIONALISM AND THE PLO

The history of the Palestinian Liberation Organization has been dominated by factionalism and a clash of ideologies. Regardless of the PLO's segmentation, the United States government, along with several Middle Eastern analysts, generally classifies the activities of the PLO as terrorism. The PLO is viewed as an international gang of terrorists, and peaceful factions within it are ignored.

Closer examination reveals that this view may not be entirely justified. While there are terrorist groups in the PLO, the organization has a variety of other functions. Some analysts view the PLO as a political group, not a terrorist organization. No matter which view is taken, evidence shows that PLO factions have engaged in terrorist activities that have thrust the PLO into international affairs.

The international aspects of Middle Eastern violence have created a problem for security forces in the West. The battle over the Palestinian question and other Middle Eastern issues has moved beyond the Middle East. The problem was exacerbated in the

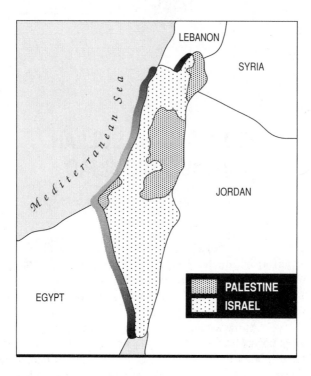

1980s as Western Europeans and Americans began to be targeted by terrorist groups, even though Arabs remained the primary target. Violence spread to Europe, and some analysts wondered if it was coming to America. Western security forces have been called upon to respond.

You may recall at the end of chapter 5 a brief discussion of Middle Eastern terrorism occurring outside of the Middle East. A question that now suggests itself is, Why has Middle Eastern terrorism expanded?

Part of the answer is that the PLO has been forced to appeal to the international arena. Palestinians are a displaced people. They are scattered throughout the Middle East, and those who remain in Palestine live under Israeli occupation. With no legitimized home country, the PLO has been forced to make its case without a national base. When internal fighting develops among PLO factions, conflict takes place in an international arena. Factional groups use the same type of terrorism against their rivals inside the PLO as they use against Israel and its allies. Several analysts have addressed such problems in the PLO's position.

Helene Cobban (1984) approached the problem in her excellent study of the PLO. Although the PLO is popularly portrayed as a large, monolithic terrorist organization, Cobban pointed out that its unique position contradicts the stereotype. Deprived of a home base, the PLO was forced to form itself as a confederation of various Palestinian interest groups. Several powerful groups developed inside the PLO, according to Cobban, and many became rivals.

According to Cobban, the PLO's fragmented nature has produced a variety of conflicting organizational demands. The Palestinians are not uniformly distributed in a single area or country. To be successful, however, PLO leadership must give the impression that it can represent all Palestinians, regardless of their current nationality. A PLO leader such as Yasser Arafat must convince the Palestinians that he is qualified to lead, while supressing violent internal challenges to his leadership. At the same time he must contend with various nations who wish to subvert the goal of the PLO or who, like Syria and Iraq, wish to take it over. These foreign relations have helped to push the homeless PLO into international affairs.

PLO leadership faces a grave challenge, then. Direct control by Arafat or anyone else is practically impossible because the organization is physically dispersed among many countries. Factions within the PLO have played up to different Middle Eastern states in their attempts to challenge Arafat. Arafat in turn has been forced to respond by creating his own militant groups and temporary internal and external alliances.

David Rapoport (1988, 46–50) believed that the internal problems of the PLO have resulted from its inability to establish a national base. The Palestinians are a displaced people, Rapoport said, and must therefore compete from an international posture.

According to Rapoport, there are five reasons for the international profile of the PLO. First, the PLO has been thrust into the international arena due to political circumstances. Aside from its plans to operate in other countries, the PLO really has no choice but to be an international organization. Its homeland has been taken, and other Arab states have not granted it sanctuary. Regardless of what its people might prefer, the PLO is defined internationally.

Second, Rapoport stated, the PLO has been able to take advantage of these circumstances to some extent by appealing to an international audience. The PLO has gained international recognition as the representative of the Palestinian people. Official recognition has extended beyond the Middle East to include over eighty members of the United Nations. In this sense, the PLO has played up to and gained support from many nations.

The third reason cited by Rapoport is that the PLO needs military support. Arafat and other PLO leaders believe that success for the Palestinians will only come about with diplomatic and military support from other Arab states. The PLO must therefore play to the ambitions of those states without being consumed by any single nation's interests. The PLO transcends national organization in this matter, defining itself as a separate Arab power supported by various Arab states.

Internal competition for PLO leadership provides the fourth reason for its international posture. The deadly rivalry between factions in the PLO brings the group into continual public view. This is magnified whenever competing nations ally themselves with one of the PLO factions, and, as the competition has been extremely violent, terrorism emanating from the conflicts grows to international proportions.

Rapoport cited the distribution of the Palestinian population as the final reason for PLO internationalism. Fully 60 percent of all Palestinians live outside of Palestine. The majority of those who reside in their traditional homeland live under the watchful eye of Israel's security forces. Palestinians living outside of Israel are perpetually displaced.

Rapoport believed that the PLO has paid a price for its international posture.

Internationalism has placed the PLO in competition with every state in the Middle East. The major problem, according to Rapoport, is that by identifying with no particular Arab state the PLO has become a quasistate of its own, yet it lacks the resources other states use to bolster their status.

One analyst believed that the PLO's international posture resulted from the nature of the Arab-Israeli conflict. Ilan Peleg (1988, 525–548) implied that the PLO became an internationally based group as a result of Arab-Israeli struggles. The PLO's terrorism was originally designed to focus international attention on an issue and bring a Viet Nam–style conflict to Israel. In the 1970s the goal of its terrorism changed, primarily due to the PLO's relations with other Arab states.

Peleg's conclusion was very similar to those of Cobban and Rapoport. The PLO is dependent on Arab governments for its existence, but PLO leadership consistently attempts to act independently of any government. This has created a climate in which Arab governments play to the interests of factions inside the PLO—and vice versa. According to Peleg, this has resulted in a history of violent internal and external relationships transcending national boundaries.

The international aspect of the PLO is important because it has fostered the development of several splinter groups. The Popular Front for the Liberation of Palestine and other groups emerged in the early going. By the mid-1970s Abu Nidal's group, the most violent of all Palestinian factions, began to surface in Iraq.

Abu Nidal became one of the masters of international terrorism. He seemed to understand both the international position of the PLO and the value of terrorism on a transnational level. Abu Nidal became an ominous extension of the Palestinian international posture

ABU NIDAL AND INTERNATIONAL TERRORISM

Abu Nidal and the activities of his group provide one of the best examples of international terrorism originating in the Middle East. The group was born of the PLO's need to operate in an international arena. Abu Nidal founded a maverick organization when he broke with Arafat in 1974 while on PLO business in Iraq.

His group began planning operations of its own out of Baghdad around 1976, and eventually Abu Nidal began selling his services to the highest bidder. By the 1980s the violence he spawned brought a new dimension to international terror. He built a truly international terror network, and police around the globe were forced to respond to it.

Ilan Peleg (1988, 538–540) traced the origins of Abu Nidal to militant Iraqi rejectionism, an attitude that emerged in 1969. Rejectionism is a Middle Eastern political term meaning unilateral refusal of any peaceful settlement with Israel. Rejectionists rule out any settlement that acknowledges Israel's right to exist. This stance is the basis of the Abu Nidal group.

At the end of the 1967 war the Arabs were in full retreat. Resources and blood would be required to continue the struggle with Israel, as militarists in Israel proved to be no easy match. Some Arab leaders began to talk of a more moderate approach; peace might be more acceptable than continued bloodshed.

Initial Arab proponents of peace suggested that if Israel could recognize the need for a Palestinian homeland, perhaps the Arabs could recognize the need for a sovereign

Jewish state. It seemed to offer a basis for discussion. Moderates within Israel and Arab countries began cautiously to explore alternatives to war.

The mere thought of peace with and recognition of Israel was repugnant to many people in the Arab world, however. Militant governments rejected any possibility of a peaceful solution, and they joined with extremist segments of the PLO to form an ad hoc organization called the Rejectionist Front. Arafat, trying desperately to maintain his fragile coalition, tried to appease both peace seekers and rejectionists. Rejectionists viewed these attempts as a sign of weakness.

Iraq was one of the more militant Rejectionist countries. Like extremists in the PLO, they were appalled by Arafat's apparent softness toward Israel. The Iraqis also expressed a growing concern over Syrian influence in the PLO and Syrian designs on Lebanon. In 1969 the Iraqis established a PLO splinter group called the Arab Liberation Front to give themselves a voice in the PLO. Militant *fedayeen* began to gather in Baghdad under Iraqi protection. According to Peleg, in 1974 the Arafat-influenced Palestinian National Council accepted a plan calling for diplomatic overtures toward Israel to discuss the possible coexistence of a Palestinian and an Israeli state. The Iraqis were incensed by the idea, and the concept of rejectionism was born. Iraq would accept no movement toward peace. They vowed to continue the fight, and they searched for someone to lead the militant *fedayeen* who were congregated in Baghdad. They found him in the person of Sabri al-Bana.

Yossi Melman (1986) said that al-Bana came to Baghdad in 1974 on a recruiting mission for Arafat. One of the founding members of Fatah, al-Bana was searching for new *fedayeen* as well as a new PLO base in Baghdad. He was completely disillusioned with the 1974 decision of the Palestinian National Council, so when the Iraqis began to explore his feelings toward rejectionism they found him an enthusiastic listener. They soon gave him permission to create his own terrorist organization with Iraqi support.

Peleg said the Iraqis had much to gain from al-Bana. His knowledge of tactics and organization was complemented by his ability to lead. After assuming the code name Abu Nidal, al-Bana set about building a new terrorist organization of the same name. He raised and trained 150 to 200 terrorists under Baghdad's protection. While he was willing to employ his force for the good of Iraq, his main goal was the destruction of Israel. Al-Bana believed that the only acceptable method to accomplish both goals was to launch a campaign of terrorism on a worldwide scale. The Abu Nidal terror network had been born.

David Schiller (1988, 90–107) stated that the growth of the Abu Nidal group should have come as no surprise to anyone familiar with the Palestinian struggle. Schiller believed that the entire movement, from 1920 to the present, has been characterized by violent disagreements and terrorism. He viewed the factionalism that spawned Abu Nidal as nothing more than a reflection of the nature of Middle Eastern terrorism and Abu Nidal as just another of the major characters trying to gain control of the PLO.

While the birth of the Abu Nidal group may have mirrored standard Middle Eastern terrorism, the exploits of the Abu Nidal group drew more attention than did those of its rival terrorist organizations. Abu Nidal was particularly ruthless. Making no distinction among targets or the types of people in and around targets, Abu Nidal became noted for the harsh brutality of its murderous attacks. Its international exploits gained the most attention: the world was a battleground for Abu Nidal.

Schiller pointed out that Abu Nidal first broke into the world of terrorism by striking an international target: in the mid-1970s his group hijacked a British airliner en route from Dubai to Tunis. In 1975 he tried to unite all radical *fedayeen* against Arafat; when he failed, he turned his terrorists against PLO members following Arafat's line and the Arab states that supported them. His group also joined the Iraqis in their feud with Syria. Assassination became the signature of the Abu Nidal organization.

Things changed in June 1976, when the Syrians intervened in Lebanon against the PLO. During the same month, Egypt began to encourage moderate Arabs to make peace with Israel. It was a dark time for Abu Nidal, and Schiller said he emerged from this episode with a new mission. Abu Nidal formed Black June—the name commemorated the month in which the more moderate states endorsed a potential peace plan—and when the Syrians took direct action against the PLO he then launched an all-out campaign against Arab moderates.

In a Western magazine interview Abu Nidal said his first goal was to eliminate Zionism, but his second was to destroy the reactionary regimes in Syria, Jordan, and Lebanon. Abu Nidal had widened his war. Israelis, Arabs, and Westerners alike became his targets. In Schiller's words, violence started to spiral.

In 1977 U.S. President Jimmy Carter achieved a coup in Middle Eastern affairs. Inviting both Israeli Prime Minister Menachem Begin and Egyptian President Anwar Sadat to Camp David, Carter presided over the drafting and signing of a long-term peace accord. Although many people in the Middle East and around the world rejoiced at the signing of the Camp David Peace Accord, the rejectionists flew into a rage. Indeed, Abu Nidal felt betrayed by the Egyptians. He expanded his campaign of terrorism to include Egypt and promised vengeance against the United States.

In the meantime, the targets of Abu Nidal's attacks were not inactive. A growing number of counterstrikes were carried out against Abu Nidal terrorists, especially by rival groups within the PLO. These acts were yet another step up in the mounting crescendo of terrorist violence.

Abu Nidal's adversaries were also willing to use the world as a stage. Fighting ranged from Great Britain to Pakistan. Police officers responding to the increased violence frequently became its victims, even though most of them were not associated with the struggle.

Rapoport (1988, 44) pointed to another international connection with Middle Eastern terrorism. By 1974 German radicals were becoming increasingly bored with their anti-American campaign due to the end of the Viet Nam War. In the mid-1970s they searched for a new cause and found it in the Palestinian question. The Red Army Faction established links with the PLO, and sent some of its members to train at PLO camps. This paved the way for other European radicals to join in. As Abu Nidal grew, Baghdad became one of the most popular international training centers for terrorists.

The expansion of Middle Eastern terrorism brought a strange unification of revolutionary doctrine to Europe by the late 1970s. European radicals embraced the Rejectionist Front and gained techniques and intelligence from Middle Eastern terrorist groups. Abu Nidal was able to take advantage of these European links to create an infrastructure in Europe. By the 1980s Abu Nidal had become an organization capable of embracing a myriad of ideologies. It was now a truly international terrorist organization.

At the heart of this willingness to embrace different dogmas was the hard-core pragmatism of Abu Nidal himself. Ideology notwithstanding, al-Bana demonstrated that he could make the most shocking and unexpected moves to benefit his terrorist organization. Schiller said nothing demonstrated this more than Abu Nidal's shift between 1979 and 1980, when he left a structure in Baghdad to create a new command post in Syria. Al-Bana had joined hands with his old enemy, Syria.

After the 1982 Israeli invasion of Lebanon, Abu Nidal established training centers and support camps in Lebanon. The group's activities increased, and the terrorist organization became linked to both Iraqi and Syrian intelligence circles. Schiller said Abu Nidal's base increased further by the mid-1980s when Libya was added to its list of supporters. In exchange for Libyan support, the organization was willing to do Khadaffy's bidding.

Yossi Melman (1986, 6–7) wrote that the group has come to be characterized by a compartmentalized infrastructure. That means that several nations are supporting independent command structures within the organization. Unlike the PLO, however, Abu Nidal has not splintered, so this simply gives the group additional striking power. The structure of the organization is based on isolation and secrecy. Its infrastructure is based in Iraq, Syria, Lebanon, Libya, and Western Europe. Even though al-Bana's health is questionable (some intelligence sources believe he is dead), the organization continues.

Arabs have been one of the most frequent targets of Abu Nidal, but a growing number of Westerners and Americans have fallen to the group's wrath. This has meant a twofold problem for security forces. On a diplomatic policy level, it is difficult to isolate the command structure of the organization and its logistical network. Any military or diplomatic action taken against the group may have to come through unconventional channels in order to be effective.

A similar problem confronts the police. In Western Europe, for example, police and security forces are responsible for responding to foreign-inspired terrorism, but they cannot deal with the origin of its activities. Security force responses to this paradox have ranged from an organized national protest by French police to calls for a joint European–American police force to deal with terrorism. This has resulted in growing police cooperation in the West.

In the 1980s Abu Nidal came to epitomize international terrorism. The group has bombed houses of worship, carried off assassinations, and attacked airports across three continents. It has done so with the enthusiastic but clandestine support of client states. The United States has not been attacked on its own soil, but Americans are increasingly becoming the victims of groups such as Abu Nidal.

Despite its superior organization and activity, the Abu Nidal group has no monopoly on international terrorism originating in the Middle East. Two Shiite groups, Hizbollah and Islamic Jihad, have been associated with both state-sponsored and transnational terrorism. An examination of these groups should enhance our understanding of international terrorism.

IRAN, LEBANON, AND SHIITE TERRORISM

Just as the Abu Nidal group was engendered by the Palestinian conflict, Shiite terrorism has its origins in other Middle Eastern political strife. On one hand it is tied to the 1978–1979 Iranian Revolution and the Persian Gulf War. On another, it can be linked directly to the Israeli invasion of Lebanon in 1982. During the Reagan administration violence resulting from both conflicts was commonly called "state-sponsored terrorism," and a variety of diplomatic and military tactics were employed to stop it. It may be possible, however, to view the Shiite hostilities in another light.

The name Hizbollah literally means The Party of God. According to Dilip Hiro (1987, 113–181; 240–243), Hizbollah grew out of the Iranian Revolution as an extension of the Revolutionary Guards. The Revolutionary Guards were the military wing of the Ayatollah Khomeini's organization. Hizbollah assisted the Revolutionary Guards by attempting to purify the revolution. It attacked all forms of Western thought and sought to consolidate Khomeini's gains.

Hizbollah was one of two types of parties that emerged from the revolution. The first type was a formal political organization with known membership. The other type, according to Hiro, was an organization that functioned via informal groups and secret or unknown members. Hizbollah was the second type of group. It members were recruited from poor urban districts and were generally young males with a fanatical devotion to the Ayatollah Khomeini. Hizbollah's essential structure has not changed.

Hiro said the members of Hizbollah were not only interested in carrying out the goals of the revolution but also concerned with the social conditions of Islam in general. This helped to account for their loose organizational structure. The Party of God was more a meeting of similar minds than a group interested in a rigid, formal structure. Shiaism was the heart of Hizbollah, and Shiites throughout the Middle East were the concern of the group. The Shiites of Lebanon were no exception.

Relations between Lebanese and Iranian Shiites had been close since the 1950s, according to Hiro. When conflict broke out in Lebanon in 1975, Al-Amal, a Shiite militia, was formed to protect Lebanese Shias. Al-Amal was trained by the PLO, but it developed and maintained strong Iranian contacts. It grew in strength, and its members watched the Iranian Revolution with growing interest.

Nabih Berri was elected General Secretary of Al-Amal in 1980. This caused concern among the more radical members of Amal, including those who supported the Iranian Revolution, because they believed that Berri was a constitutionalist and too conservative. The radicals left Amal for the Syrian-controlled Bekka Valley where they formed a new group, Islamic Amal, and awaited further developments. They did not have long to wait.

In 1982 the Israeli army invaded Southern Lebanon, supposedly to destroy PLO bases there. Jonathan Randal (1984) believed that the invasion was motivated more by Israeli adventurism and desire to intervene in the Lebanese civil war. The PLO bases were a problem, but the Israelis were more concerned to counter Syrian interests in Lebanon and establish a Lebanese government sympathetic to Israel. According to Randal, this invasion had a variety of unexpected outcomes.

One was a closer identification of the United States with Israeli foreign policy. Israel occupied Southern Lebanon and seemed to do so with U.S. support. The American–Israeli alliance intensified when American military forces supported Israeli-backed factions in the Lebanese civil war. The military targets of American actions were frequently Shiites, which got the attention of Iran. By late 1982 the Iranian Revolutionary Guard sent volunteers to Lebanon under the auspices of Hizbollah.

There they linked up with the dissident members of Islamic Amal in Baalbek and prepared to do battle with the United States and Israel.

Once situated in Baalbek, Hizbollah came under the leadership of Hassan Fadlollah. He began to entice young Shiite militants to Hizbollah's banner. Inspiring and charismatic, Fadlollah preached an apocalyptic message: Israel and its allies could be destroyed through martyrdom. His young followers were intrigued by the idea, and a series of small groups with a common idea began to gather around Fadlollah. Suicide attacks could be used to drive the infidels from Lebanon. A confederation of suicidal terrorist cells began to build within Hizbollah.

To understand the movement of Hizbollah to Lebanon it is necessary to return briefly to the Iranian Revolution. Shahram Chubin (1987) explained the movement by looking at the changing power structures resulting from the Persian Gulf War. Chubin said the Iranian Revolution was not simply an ideological shift but rather signaled a change in the balance of power in the Persian Gulf. In addition, it put a challenge, if not an end, to American political and military dominance in the region.

This shift brought three new facets of Iranian foreign policy to light. First, the Iranians resolved to reject and fight Western dominance in the Middle East. Second, all foreign relations would be based on principles of Islam. Third, the government was to seek closer links with Shias outside of Iran. This called for increased Iranian involvement in the Gulf states and in Lebanon.

Hizbollah became the perfect tool for developing closer relations with fellow Shiites. It also became an important psychological weapon for intimidating enemies. With the fanatical devotion of its followers Hizbollah could challenge enemies on new levels. At the same time, Chubin pointed out, Hizbollah was not officially Iranian, so the government could deny direct links or control. Hizbollah could assist Iran with its foreign policy goals, but the Iranian government could deny responsibility for the group's actions. Ideally Hizbollah was an international Islamic organization above nationalist politics. In reality it was something else.

Chubin argued that Hizbollah developed into Iran's weapon of terrorism. Revolutionary Guards came to the Bekka Valley under the auspices of Hizbollah. Under Fadlollah's guiding hand, Hizbollah gave birth to a new organization, Islamic Jihad. Islamic Jihad represented the groups of young militant Shiites who had gathered around Fadlollah. It was not a single group, but a conglomeration of militants who referred to their small cells by a variety of names. Islamic Jihad became a perfect organization for untraceable terrorism.

Amir Taheri (1987, 4–10; 136–197) claimed that the name Islamic Jihad was selected by Khomeini. The group was the antithesis of Abu Nidal. According to Taheri, the Abu Nidal group maintained links with the Palestinian cause but linked itself to the foreign policy of Iraq, Syria, and Libya. In some ways it had become a mercenary group renting itself out to the highest bidder. Islamic Jihad rejected such notions. It was a religious group, led by religious figures and recruited from fundamentalists.

Taheri stated that after the first suicide bombing in 1983 Hizbollah employed the name Islamic Jihad to cover all of the terrorist groups under its control. Hizbollah maintains a militia and has a number of political functions as well as directing terrorist activities. Islamic Jihad became an umbrella group to protect the terrorist functions and semiautonomous terrorist cells. Taheri said it became a clearinghouse for terrorist activities.

Islamic Jihad launched a devastating suicide bombing campaign in Lebanon in 1983. In 1984 its activities spread to Kuwait and Tunisia, and it became clear that the struggle was not just for Lebanon but for the Islamic Revolution. By 1986, in Taheri's estimation, fighting had moved to Europe. This brand of international terrorism is endorsed because it involves a holy war against all parties resisting the Islamic revolution. Taheri referred to it as the "holy terror."

Robin Wright (1986, 84–86) wrote that the structure of Islamic Jihad was different than anything the West had ever faced before. Most groups could be identified by an infrastructure and a support network. This was not the case with Islamic Jihad. It was a dynamic network distributing information from the secrecy of Baalbek. It contained a fluctuating number of secret organizations and cells. While U.S. officials talked of state-sponsored terror, this group had no clear links to Iran. Islamic Jihad is a hidden army.

THE TACTICAL ASPECTS OF ISLAMIC JIHAD

The West found the tactics of Islamic Jihad to be as dynamic and as frightening as its organizational structure. In 1983 a tactical twist on car bombings appeared: instead of blowing up abandoned vehicles, suicidal terrorists would drive them right into the target. After an initial attack on the American embassy in Beirut, Islamic Jihad car bombs began to appear throughout the Middle East and Europe. The development of specialized hostage rescue teams in the United States, Great Britain, and West Germany forced Islamic Jihad to search for new hostage taking tactics. Airplanes were hijacked, but hostages were either dispersed or military support was used to secure the area surrounding the aircraft. Kidnapping also developed as an attractive alternative to massive hostage taking.

Tactical innovation came as a surprise to the West. In a special article prepared for the *New York Times,* Philip Taubman (1984) wrote that the United States had very few solid leads on the Islamic Jihad despite enhanced intelligence efforts. In a related article Eric Pace (1984) described the innovative use of car bombs in the Middle East. The West seemed at a tactical loss when dealing with Islamic Jihad. What neither reporter could know was that the worst was yet to come.

The strength of Islamic Jihad lay in its secretiveness and ability to manipulate followers. The cry of the Iranian Revolution had been one of martyrdom, and that cry spread to Lebanon. Unlike other terrorists, members of Islamic Jihad were willing to combine sacrifice with secrecy. The organization was able to capitalize on its pool of suicidal volunteers. While most terrorist groups could only attack unguarded civilian targets, Islamic Jihad went after well-defended military positions with a pool of martyrs. Their success caused more than one military force to retreat.

The use of suicide bombers frightened and baffled the West, but it was logically explicable in terms of the conflict, according to Maxwell Taylor and Helen Ryan

(1988). Taylor and Ryan examined the role of fanaticism in Shiite terrorism and concluded that the use of suicide bombers was particularly successful in Lebanon. A suicide bomber became an inexpensive guided missile ensuring the success of an attack.

After a series of bombings in 1983 and the retreat of the U.S. Marines from Beirut, the weakness of Western defensive systems was completely exposed. Military forces from France, Israel, and the United States had employed a fairly sophisticated security system appropriate to peacekeeping situations in Western diplomacy. In several instances suicide bombers penetrated these defensive perimeters and struck targets with relative ease. Taylor and Ryan suggested that this demonstrated a fundamental weakness of technologically based defense: none of the defenders had predicted the role of suicide in the Lebanese conflict.

Taylor and Ryan argued that it was necessary to define terrorism in Middle Eastern terms rather than to extrapolate from Western norms. From the Western perspective suicide attacks seem rooted in illogical fanaticism. Yet this interpretation does not fit the Shiites fighting in Lebanon. Bombing was a logical policy—in fact, one of the few policies that worked against established military power. Since delivery of the bombs had to be guaranteed if the policy were to work, it was also logical to employ sacrificial warriors as delivery sources.

From a policy standpoint, Taylor and Ryan concluded, suicide bombings were hardly the work of abnormal fanatics. The bombings were successful and rational. They created fear among the Israelis and the Western peacekeeping forces, and forced Shiite opponents to make policy changes. In particular, the United States was forced to retreat and the Israeli occupation of Southern Lebanon became extremely costly. Taylor and Ryan believed that kidnapping tactics could be viewed from the same perspective.

It is interesting to speculate about Taylor's and Ryan's conclusion regarding hostage taking in Lebanon. Terrorist groups within Islamic Jihad began toying with the idea in 1983, and by the next year they launched a wholesale kidnapping campaign. At one point they held more than forty Western hostages. Hizbollah and Islamic Jihad saw that they could not only gain the attention of the West with kidnappings, but even influence the behavior of Western governments.

The kidnapping policy of Islamic Jihad had several practical functions. It could be used to punish a country for acting against the Shiites. Hostages could be released for propaganda value, or, when an enemy took action against Islamic Jihad or its supporters, hostages could be executed. Finally, threats of harm to hostages or additional kidnappings could be used to influence another government's actions.

Research on the policy results of kidnapping is not complete, but two events in 1987 and 1988 revealed the extent to which the West took kidnapping seriously. In January 1988 a West German official gave a speech to the European Economic Community admitting that his government had refused to extradite an accused terrorist to the United States for fear of further kidnappings in Beirut. This came on the heels of an entire summer devoted to U.S. Senate hearings on the Reagan administration's dealings with Iran to free Americans held in Lebanon. Like suicide bombings, hostage taking violated the protocol of Western conflict, but it produced results.

TRANSNATIONAL TERRORISM AND AMERICAN POLICY

When groups such as Abu Nidal and Islamic Jihad are examined it becomes clear that there are many different types of terrorism, and that a single policy cannot embrace all the appropriate approaches to them. In addition, the activities of Abu Nidal and Islamic Jihad have forced Western European police agencies to redefine their roles. If such activities were to spread to America, an event most analysts believe to be unlikely, American police would be caught in the same dilemma.

America and Western Europe have often been stymied by transnational terrorism from the Middle East. Security forces had grown accustomed to the earlier attacks on innocent, unfortified civilian targets and had prepared responses accordingly. Islamic Jihad changed the nature of the conflict by attacking heavily fortified military positions. Experts in the West had always believed terrorists were too weak to engage in such tactics; suicide bombers proved them wrong. Analysts such as Jeffery Wright (1984) have even begun to suggest that terrorism has become a new mode of warfare.

Robert Kupperman of the Georgetown Institute for Strategic Studies was interviewed on NBC's "Today" show in December 1988 following the bombing of an American passenger plane over Scotland. Although it was a typically brief television interview, Kupperman managed to make a critical point. He stated that the United States faced two policy choices when dealing with transnational terrorism from the Middle East. It had to be approached either as a justice problem—meaning investigation, arrest, and punishment—or as a national security problem.

Had NBC given Kupperman more time to elaborate, his analysis would have been most interesting. The United States has long been in search of a policy to deal with this kind of terrorism. Over the last seven years policies have ranged from firing on terrorists from a naval battleship to empowering the FBI to arrest terrorists outside of U.S. jurisdiction. American policy toward transnational terrorism has not been consistent.

If the problem of transnational terrorism is a military one, as Wright suggested, then different military policies will need to be developed to counter terrorist threats. Larry Cable (1987) has stated that more innovative policies need to be found in such instances. Conventional concepts of conflict will not work, according to Cable.

Others believe that transnational terrorism should be handled as violations of criminal and international law. U.S. Senate hearings on the hijacking of a cruise ship, the *Achille Lauro,* concluded that hijacking was a violation of international law (U.S. House 1985); Congress expanded the enforcement power of the FBI as a result. The FBI was granted power to forcibly seize suspected terrorists menacing Americans in other countries, charge them with violation of American laws, and bring them to the United States for trial (U.S. Senate 1985).

The law granting the FBI that power was tested in March 1989. In a unique trial, Fawaz Younis was charged with air piracy. He was allegedly the leader of a group of hijackers who took over a Royal Jordanian Airlines flight on June 11, 1985. Americans were aboard the flight, which gave the FBI power to arrest him under the 1985 law.

On September 13, 1987 Younis was lured aboard a yacht in the Mediterranean by secret agents. They informed him that the yacht contained arms and ammunition for an upcoming terrorist campaign. The agents sought Younis's support and direction.

Younis boarded the boat to find a surprise: instead of the promised terrorists, FBI agents greeted Younis and welcomed him to the free world. Younis was charged with a violation of American criminal law in international waters and flown to Andrews Air Force Base.

Interestingly enough, the defense did not base its case on a challenge of the law that allowed an extrajurisdictional arrest with no other government's cooperation. It also did not complain that Younis had been kidnapped by FBI agents. Instead, the defense argued that Younis was innocent because he was only following the orders of Al-Amal. The defense did not question America's authority to arrest on the charge of air piracy. In another twist, the U.S. government relocated fourteen witnesses from the Middle East, gave them legal alien status, and hid them, under the U.S. Marshals Service Witness Protection Program.

This policy has not been without its critics. Some analysts strongly disagree with the use of American law enforcement power outside of American territory. Aside from the fact that its legality was questionable, it opened a Pandora's box of potential policy disasters. These analysts straightforwardly argue to keep American police at home.

Larry Cable's analysis of changing conflict took a middle position. According to Cable (1987), it is not necessary to define every terrorist incident as either a violation of law or a matter of national security. States use force when relating to one another, and terrorism is nothing new. Cable argued that the amount and type of force used are critical in determining the type of response. He felt that a competent intelligence-gathering network should provide information to democratic decision-making bodies. The use of force in international relations must be understood apart from rhetoric about criminal justice or low-intensity conflict.

Grant Wardlaw (1988, 237–259) agreed in an article on state-sponsored terrorism. He argued that the concept of terrorism is not clear enough and that it is responded to politically rather than judiciously. When judging how to respond to an incident, the type of terrorism must be examined as well as the nature of the threat posed by the particular group. Wardlaw believed that the West, especially the United States, had overstated the dangers of terrorism and the difficulty of controlling it.

Even though individual acts of terrorism are horrific, Wardlaw argued, it is necessary to avoid overstating their importance. Major powers may feel psychologically threatened by terrorism, but they are often being challenged by minor powers too weak to play the international relations game by traditional rules. Unless a nation's approach to terrorism is well defined and discerning, Wardlaw believed, policies would degenerate into ideological dogma and be nonfunctional.

The arguments concerning policy setting are particularly applicable to transnational terrorism from the Middle East. The types of terror differ, as evidenced by Abu Nidal and Islamic Jihad. A single approach or a single policy definition may not suffice. When dealing with acts of transnational terror, it is necessary to gather information and realistically assess the actual and potential threats. Simply dichotomizing the problem of transnational terrorism as either a criminal justice or a national security issue does not solve it. As Larry Cable suggested, the solution may well lie in establishing closer links between intelligence gathering and democratic decision making.

SUMMARY OF CHAPTER TWELVE

The Middle East can be used to illustrate the problem of transnational terrorism and the problems it poses for the West. In this chapter two sources of Middle Eastern terrorism were analyzed for that purpose. The transnational aspects of the PLO were examined by the terrorist splinter group Abu Nidal, and the effects of the Iranian Revolution were surveyed through Hizbollah and Islamic Jihad.

Abu Nidal grew out of the international character of the PLO. Denied a homeland, the PLO was forced into an international posture. When terrorist organizations inside the PLO acted, they reflected this international orientation. Abu Nidal evolved from a split in the *fedayeen* and became a separate network for terrorism. It has headquarters in the Middle East and Europe and has gained attention through its international acts of terrorism.

Hizbollah and Islamic Jihad originated with the Iranian Revolution and Iran's intervention in the war in Lebanon. Hizbollah is an umbrella organization covering many groups, including Islamic Jihad, a confederation of Shiite terrorist groups. Headquartered in the Bekka Valley of Lebanon, both groups are extremely secretive. Unlike Abu Nidal, Islamic Jihad has incorporated the fanaticism of young believers in its operations and used them against military targets in suicide attacks.

The transnational aspects of Middle Eastern terrorism have posed a policy dilemma for the United States. Some believe the problem should be approached as a national security matter; others see it as a criminal justice issue. Cable argued that this simple dichotomy is not useful. Wardlaw believed that until the approach to the problem is refined, counterterrorist policies will be based on ideology.

IF YOU WANT TO READ FURTHER . . .

If you are searching for works on the Middle East, you should review the suggested reading list at the end of chapter 5. You can augment it with sections from other works, among the best of which is James Poland's *Understanding Terrorism*. In one section Poland presents a case study of the Middle East that is thorough, easy to understand, and particularly appropriate for approaching transnational terrorism.

Ilan Peleg has an excellent article in Michael Stohl's *The Politics of Terrorism*. It is based on the Arab-Israeli conflict and assumes you know something of the background, but it is highly recommended. David Rapoport's *Inside Terrorist Organizations* is a fairly new work that is outstanding. It contains several high-quality essays, including Rapoport's own analysis of the PLO's internationalism, Schiller's work on Abu Nidal, and a brilliant essay by Wardlaw on state-sponsored terror. Those new to the field may have some difficulty reading it, but the book is excellent.

IRELAND AND THE SECURITY PROBLEM

Few places in the world have witnessed a long-term conflict like the one in Ireland. Hatred has been brewing there for the past few centuries, and revolts have taken place in many forms. In the twentieth century Ireland has been the scene of an ongoing indigenous terrorist campaign. In this chapter we'll examine terrorism in Northern Ireland from a security standpoint. Ireland offers a different perspective because the functions of the police and military there have been combined in an antiterrorist campaign. Security policies have not been without heated controversy, and the experiences in Northern Ireland serve to demonstrate the complexities and the paradoxes of practical counterterrorism.

After reading this chapter, you should be able to do the following.

1. Sketch a brief history of the Anglo-Irish conflict
2. Outline the development of the Irish Republican Army
3. List the events that rejuvenated the IRA in the late 1960s and early 1970s
4. Discuss the policies of internment and trial without a jury
5. Summarize the development of tactical policies among criminal justice forces in Northern Ireland
6. Describe terrorism in Northern Ireland from a criminological perspective

AN INTRODUCTION TO THE ANGLO-IRISH CONFLICT

In August 1969 the British Army was ordered to increase its presence in Northern Ireland in an effort to quell a series of riots. While the army had maintained bases in Northern Ireland for quite some time, riotous situations in Londonderry and Belfast were suddenly far beyond the control of the local police and the handful of British regulars stationed in the area. On August 18 army reinforcements began arriving, hoping to avoid a long-term conflict. Their hopes were in vain. The army would soon become embroiled in a new outbreak of a war that has spanned centuries.

Ireland has not been ruled by the Irish since a series of Viking incursions in 800 A.D. Giovani Costigan (1980) wrote that Irish culture originated with Celtic

invasions three centuries before Christ. The Irish settled in tribal groups and government was maintained through kinship and clans. No Celtic ruler or political authority
ever united Ireland as a single entity.

Around 500 A.D. the Irish were introduced to Christianity and became among the
most fervent converts in the world. The medieval church played a large role in uniting
Ireland, but the traditional Gaelic tribal groups still remained separate. They submitted
to a central religion, not a central political system.

The relations among the Gaelic tribes became important when Viking raiders
began to attack Ireland around 800 A.D. The divided Irish were dominated by their
Viking rulers, and the Norsemen used Ireland as a trading base and center of com-
merce. The Vikings built several Irish cities, including Dublin.

Viking rule of Ireland was challenged in 1014 when a tribal chieftain, Brian Boru,
was declared High King of Ireland. He led a united tribal army against the Vikings and
defeated them at Clontarf. Fate ruled against the Irish, however. At the end of the
battle, as Brian knelt in prayer, he was assassinated. Dreams of a united Ireland
crumbled with Brian Boru's death, and the clans and tribes soon divided leadership
again.

Costigan believed this paved the way for a gradual Norman invasion of Ireland.
The Normans were the descendants of William the Conqueror and had ambitions for
extending their domains. With the Irish divided and the Viking influence limited,
Normans began to stake out territorial claims on the island with the permission of the
Norman king. The Normans were particularly successful in Ireland because they used
new methods of warfare. By 1172 the Norman king of England had assumed the rule of
Ireland.

The Normans and the Irish struggled in a way that was not reflective of the modern fighting. The Normans could not maintain the field force necessary to control the Irish peasants, and the Irish did not have the technology that would allow them to attack smaller Norman forces barricaded in castles. Therefore, the Normans built castles to control Irish cities while Irish peasants generally dominated rural areas. This situation continued until the sixteenth century.

The Protestant Reformation of the 1500s had a tremendous impact on Ireland. Wanting to free himself from the ecclesiastical shackles of Rome, the English king, Henry VIII, created an independent Church of England. He followed up by creating a similar church in Ireland, but the Irish Catholics could not stomach this move. They began to rebel against the English king, and the troubles created by the Reformation have literally continued until the twentieth century in Ireland.

The problems of the early Reformation were magnified by Henry's daughter Elizabeth. Not content with merely ruling Ireland, Elizabeth I carved out the most prosperous agrarian section and gave it to her subjects to colonize: this resulted in the creation of the Plantation of Ulster. English and Scottish Protestants eventually settled there, displacing many of the original Irish inhabitants. This created an ethnic division in Ireland fueled by religious differences and animosities.

Costigan believed that the 1600s in Ireland were dominated by three major issues. First, the Plantation of Ulster was expanded and Irish peasants systematically displaced. Many of them perished. Second, Oliver Cromwell came to Ireland to quell a revolt and to stop Catholic attacks on Protestants. He literally massacred thousands of Irish Catholics, thanking God for granting him the opportunity to kill such a large number of his enemies. Cromwell's name still stirs hatred among Catholics in Ireland as a result.

The third issue of the 1600s also involved Catholic and Protestant struggles, and the image of the conflict is still celebrated in ceremonies today. From 1689 to 1691 James II, the Catholic pretender to the British throne, used Ireland as a base from which to revolt against William of Orange, the English king. In August 1689 Irish Protestant skilled workers, called "Apprentice Boys," were relieved by the English after defending Derry through a long siege by the pretender. The following year William defeated James at the battle of the Boyne River.

The revolt was over, but the Protestants were now forever in the camp of the House of Orange. The Protestants have flaunted these victories in the face of the Catholics since 1690. Each year they gather to militantly celebrate the battle of the Boyne and the Apprentice Boys with parades and demonstrations. It fuels the fire of hatred in Northern Ireland and demonstrates the division between Protestants and Catholics. The current troubles, in fact, started in 1969 when riots broke out in Londonderry and Belfast following the annual Apprentice Boys' parade.

The 1700s and early 1800s were characterized by waves of revolt, starvation, and emigration. Irish nationalists rose to challenge English rule, but they were always soundly defeated. Each generation seemed to bring a new series of martyrs willing to give their lives in the struggle against English rule.

Among the best-known revolutionaries was Thomas Wolfe Tone. From 1796 to 1798 Wolfe Tone led a revolt based on Irish nationalism. He tried to appeal to both Protestants and Catholics in an attempt to form a unified front against Great Britain. Wolfe Tone argued that Irish independence was more important than religious differences. In the end his revolt failed, but he had created a basis for appealing to nationalism over religion.

Despite the efforts of people like Wolfe Tone, religious animosity did not die in Ireland. During the late 1700s Protestants and Catholics began to form paramilitary organizations. Divided along religious lines, these defense organizations began violently to confront one another. The Orange Orders were born in this period. Taking their name from William of Orange, these Protestant organizations vowed to remain unified with Great Britain. The Orange lodges soon grew to dominate the political and social life of the North of Ireland.

The early 1800s brought a new level of political struggle to Ireland. In 1801 the British Parliament passed the Act of Union, designed to incorporate Ireland into the United Kingdom. Struggle over the act began to dominate Irish politics. Unionists, primarily the Orange Protestants in the North, supported the act while republicans, who became known as the Greens, argued for a constitutional government and an independent Ireland. Daniel O'Connell led the republican movement in the early part of the century, and Charles Stewart Parnell, a Protestant, created a democratic Irish party to support the cause in the late 1800s.

The struggle for republicanism accompanied one of the saddest periods in Irish history. Displaced from the land, Irish peasants were poor and susceptible to economic and agricultural fluctuations. Historian Cecil Woodham-Smith (1962) documented that Ireland had undergone a series of famines in the 1700s as peasants in the country began to rely on the potato as their main crop. In 1845 the crop failed, and agricultural production among the peasants came to a standstill until 1848. Even though thousands of Irish people began to starve, wealthy farms in the North exported other crops for cash.

The 1845–1848 famine devastated Ireland. Its effects were felt primarily among the poor, especially among the Irish Catholics. In an era in which other industrialized nations were experiencing a tremendous rise in population, Ireland's was cut by a quarter. As famine and disease took their toll, thousands of Irish people emigrated to other parts of the world. During this period unionists in the North consolidated their hold on Ulster.

In the years following the famine some members of the British Parliament sought to free Ireland from British control. They introduced a series of home rule acts designed to give Ireland independence. Charles Stewart Parnell and other republicans supported home rule, but they faced fierce opposition from unionists. The unionists were afraid that home rule would shift the balance of economic power in the North. They believed that continued union with Great Britain was their only option for economic success. Unionists were supported in British military circles.

Even though Parnell was a Protestant, most republicans were Catholics living in the southern portion of Ireland. Unionists tended to be Protestant skilled laborers, industrialists, and landlords in the North. The religious aspect of the conflict remained and was augmented by deep economic divisions.

One other aspect of the evolving conflict needs to be emphasized. By the nineteenth century both the unionists and the republicans were fully Irish. This means that neither side comprised transplanted settlers from another country. Unionist Protestants in the North had lived in Ireland for generations. They were as Irish as their

Catholic counterparts. The unionists were able to call on British help, but the struggle in Ireland began to take on the earmarks of an intra-Irish conflict.

THE IRA AND THE GROWTH OF THE IRISH REPUBLIC

By the twentieth century the struggle in Ireland had become a matter of the divisions between unionists and republicans. A host of other conflicts was associated with this confrontation, but the main one was the unionist–republican struggle. The unionists often had the upper hand because they could call on support from the British-sponsored police and military forces. The republicans had no such luxury, and they searched for an alternative.

Costigan believed that the republican military solution to the Irish conflict was born in New York City in 1857. Irish Catholics had emigrated from their homeland to America, Australia, Canada, and New Zealand, but they never forgot the people they left behind. Irish immigrants in New York City created the Irish Republican Brotherhood (IRB) as a financial relief organization for relatives in the old country. After the American Civil War some Irish soldiers returning from the Federal Army decided to take the struggle for emancipation back to Ireland. The IRB gradually evolved into a revolutionary organization.

J. Bowyer Bell (1974) has written the definitive treatise on the origins and development of the Irish Republican Army (IRA). He stated that it began with a campaign of violence sponsored by the IRB in the late 1800s. Spurred on by increased Irish nationalist feeling in the homeland and the hope of home rule, the IRB waged a campaign of bombing and assassination from 1870 until 1916. Its primary targets were unionists and British forces supporting the unionist cause. Among their greatest adversaries was the British-backed police force in Ireland, the Royal Irish Constabulary (RIC).

By 1916 the situation in Ireland had changed. The British had promised home rule to Ireland when World War I came to an end. While most people in Ireland seemed to believe the British, unionists and republicans secretly armed for a civil war between the North and South. They believed a fight was inevitable if the British granted home rule, and each side was determined to dominate the government of a newly independent Ireland. And some forces were not willing to wait for home rule.

With British attention focused on Germany, leaders of the IRB believed the time was ripe for a strike against the unionists and their British supporters. In Easter of 1916 Patrick Pearse and James Connolly led a revolt in Dublin. Pearse was a romantic idealist who felt the revolt was doomed from the start but believed it necessary to sacrifice his life to keep the republican spirit alive. Connolly was a more pragmatic socialist who fought because he believed a coming civil war was inevitable.

The revolt enjoyed local success because it surprised everyone. Pearse and Connolly took over several key points in Dublin with a few thousand armed followers. Pearse proclaimed an Irish Republic from the halls of the General Post Office and asked the Irish to follow him. The British, outraged by what they deemed to be treachery in the midst of a larger war, also came to Dublin. The city was engulfed in a week of heavy fighting.

While Pearse and Connolly came to start a popular revolution, the British came to fight a war. In a few days Dublin was devastated by British artillery. Pearse recognized the futility of the situation and asked for terms. Bell pointed out the interesting way Pearse chose to approach the British: he sent a message using a new title, Commanding General of the Irish Republican Army, to the general in charge of British forces. The IRB had transformed itself into an army: the IRA.

What Pearse and Connolly could not achieve in life they could in death. Irish opinion was solidly against the IRA, and most Irish people held Pearse and Connolly responsible for the destruction of Dublin. The British, however, failed to capitalize on this sentiment. Rather than ride the wave of public opinion, they cracked down on all expressions of republicanism. Dozens of republicans were executed and thousands sentenced to prison. The promise of home rule seemed forgotten. Most Irish people were appalled by the harsh British reaction, and the ghosts of Pearse and Connolly rose in the IRA.

Michael Collins commanded the IRA at the end of the First World War. A master of guerrilla strategy, Collins continued a campaign of terror against unionists and the RIC. The British responded by sending a hastily recruited military force—called the Black and Tans due to their unmatched uniforms—and Ireland became the scene of a dreadful war. Both sides accused the other of atrocities, but murder and mayhem were the tactics of both sides.

Meanwhile, home rule had not been forgotten by more moderate groups. Politicians in Britain and in Ireland sought to bring an end to the violence by formulating the steps to grant Irish independence. The main stumbling block was the North. Protestant unionists were afraid of being abandoned by the British. In 1921 the situation was temporarily solved by a treaty between Britain and Ireland. Under the terms of the treaty Ireland would be granted independence while the northern section around Ulster would remain under British protection until it could peacefully be integrated into Ireland. Southern Ireland became the Free State—the Republic of Ireland. The majority of people in Ireland accepted the treaty. Michael Collins also accepted the treaty, but the IRA did not.

When the treaty between Ireland and Britain was ratified in 1921, a civil war broke out in the newly formed Republic. The IRA fought government forces, claiming that Irish independence had to extend to all Irish people. They rejected British control of the North. Yet the IRA was a house divided. When one of its leading members, Eamon de Valera, left the IRA to join the government, the IRA was hopelessly fragmented. Its demise was hastened by de Valera's ruthless campaign of arrest against his former colleagues.

For their part, the British wanted nothing to do with the civil war in the southern areas. They tightened their hold on Northern Ireland and bolstered its strength with a new police force, the Royal Ulster Constabulary (RUC). The northern unionists were delighted when the British established a semiautonomous government in Northern Ireland and gave it special powers to combat the IRA. The unionists used this power to gain control of Northern Ireland and lock themselves into in the British orbit. Ireland became a divided country.

As the fortunes of the IRA waned, two important trends emerged. Bell recorded the first by pointing to the split in IRA ranks. By the 1930s some members of the IRA wanted to follow the lead of their political party, *Sinn Fein*. They felt that the IRA should express itself through peaceful political idealism. They believed they should begin working for a united socialist Ireland in the spirit of James Connolly.

Another group of IRA members rejected this philosophy. They believed that the purpose of the IRA was to fight for republicanism. They would never be at peace with the British or the unionists until the North was united with the South. They vowed to carry on the fight. Even though the IRA had been virtually destroyed by the de Valera government, these members formed a Provisional wing of the IRA in the 1930s. They launched an abortive terrorist campaign in Northern Ireland from 1956 to 1962, but they were truly reborn during civil rights disturbances in 1969. The failure of the civil rights movement in Northern Ireland can be directly linked to modern Irish terrorism and the rise of the IRA.

THE IRA REJUVENATED

Alfred McClung Lee (1983, 59–97) recorded another trend in Ireland. Internally, the IRA split into a traditional Official branch and a more militant Provisional wing. Externally, he noted, the economic situation in Northern Ireland consolidated in favor of the Protestant unionists. From 1922 to 1966 the government in Northern Ireland systematically reduced the civil rights of Catholics living in the North. During the same period the economic power of the unionists increased.

According to Lee, the political and economic conditions in Northern Ireland provided the rationale for a major civil rights movement among the Catholics. While the movement had republican overtones, it was primarily aimed at increasing adequate housing and education among Ulster's Catholic population in an attempt to improve economic growth. The civil rights movement was supported by both Protestants and Catholics, but the actions of the Northern Irish government began to polarize the issue. Increasingly it became recognized as a unionist-republican confrontation, and the old battlelines between Protestants and Catholics were redrawn. By 1969 the civil rights movement and the reaction to it had become violent.

The IRA had not been dormant throughout the civil rights movement, but it had not played a major role. The leaders of the civil rights movement were peaceful republicans, for the most part. The IRA could not play a leading role because it had virtually destroyed itself in an earlier campaign against the government of Northern Ireland. Some type of miracle would be needed to rejuvenate the IRA.

The reason for IRA impotence could be found in the second generation of Provisionals. Wanting to follow in the footsteps of their fathers, the Provisionals began to wage a campaign against the RUC in Northern Ireland. They established support bases in the Republic and slipped across the border for terrorist activities. Although they initially enjoyed support among republican enclaves in the North, most Irish people, unionists and republicans alike, were appalled by IRA violence. Even the Officials criticized the military attacks of the Provisionals.

Faced with a lack of public support, the Provisional IRA called off its offensive in the North. By 1962 almost all of its activities had ceased. Some Provisionals joined the civil rights movement; others rejoined former colleagues in the Official wing. Most members, however, remained in a secret infrastructure and prayed for a miracle to restore their ranks and prestige. In 1969 their prayers were answered.

The government in Northern Ireland reacted with a heavy hand against the civil rights workers and demonstrators. Max Hastings (1970, 40–56) wrote that peaceful attempts to work for equal rights were stymied by Northern Irish militancy. Catholics were not allowed to demonstrate for better housing and education; if they attempted to do so, they were attacked by the RUC and its reserve force, known as B-Specials. At the same time no attempts were made to stop Protestant demonstrations. The Catholics believed that the RUC and B-Specials were in league with the other anti-Catholic unionists in the North.

Issues came to a head in the summer of 1969. Civil rights demonstrators planned a long, peaceful march from Londonderry to Belfast, but they were gassed and beaten by the RUC and B-Specials. On August 15, 1969 the Protestants assembled for their traditional Apprentice Boys celebration. Just a few days before, the RUC had enthusiastically attacked Catholic demonstrators; on August 15, however, it welcomed the Protestant Apprentice Boys with open arms. The Catholics weren't surprised: many B-Specials had taken off their reservist uniforms to don orange sashes and march with the Protestants.

Protestant marchers in Londonderry and Belfast armed themselves with gasoline bombs, rocks, and sticks. They not only wished to celebrate the seventeenth-century victory in Derry, they were thrilled by the recent dispersal of the civil rights marchers and hoped to reinforce their political status by bombarding Catholic neighborhoods as they marched by. When the Protestants began taunting Catholics, violence broke out. By nightfall, Belfast and Londonderry were in flames. Three days later the British sent the army in as a peacekeeping force. Ironically, the army became the miracle the IRA so desperately needed.

According to most analysts and observers, the early policies and tactics of the British Army played an important role in the rebirth of the IRA. In an article on military policy J. Bowyer Bell (1976, 65–88) criticized the army for its initial response. He said the British Army came to Ulster with little or no appreciation of the historical circumstances behind the conflict.

According to Bell, when the army arrived in 1969 its commanders believed they were in the midst of a colonial war. They evaluated the situation and concluded that there were two "tribes." One tribe flew the Irish tricolor and spoke with deep-seated hatred of the British. The other flew the Union Jack and claimed to be ultrapatriotic subjects of the British Empire. It seemed logical to ally with friends who identified themselves as subjects.

Bell believed this policy was a fatal flaw. Far from being a conflict to preserve British influence in a colony, the struggle in Northern Ireland was a fight between two groups of Irish citizens. Neither side was "British," no matter what their slogans and banners claimed. The army should have become the peaceful, neutral force, but it mistakenly allied itself with one of the extremist positions in the conflict. That mistake became the answer to IRA prayers.

Bell argued that the reaction of republican Catholics fully demonstrates the mistake the army made. The unionists greeted the army with open arms, but this was to be expected. Historically the army had rallied to the unionist cause. Surprisingly, however, the republicans also welcomed the army. They believed that the RUC and the B-Specials were the instruments of their repression and that the British Army would not continue those restrictive measures. It was not the army of the past, in republican eyes—it was a peacekeeping force. The republicans believe the army would protect them from the unionists and the police.

Such beliefs were short-lived. As the army made its presence felt in Ulster, republicans and Catholics were subjected to the increasing oppression of army measures. Catholic neighborhoods were surrounded and gassed by military forces searching for subversives, and the soldiers began working as a direct extension of the RUC. Londonderry and Belfast were military targets, and rebels fighting against the government were to be subdued. As confrontations became more deadly, republican support for the army vanished.

Feeling oppressed by all sides, Catholics and republicans looked for help. They found it—partly—in the form of the IRA. The Officials and Provisionals were still split during the 1969 riots, and the IRA was generally an impotent organization. According to Iain Hamilton (1971), the method of British intervention provided a basis for reconciliation within the IRA. Internal squabbles pushed aside, the Officials and Provisionals focused on their new common enemy, the British Army. The new IRA policy emphasized the elimination of British soldiers from Irish soil and brushed aside internal political differences.

Robert Moss (1972, 16–18) remarked that the army found itself in the middle of the conflict it had hoped to forestall. Alienated nationalists offered support for the growing ranks of the IRA. Each time the army overreacted, as it tended to when faced with civil disobedience, the republican cause was strengthened.

Reporter Simon Winchester (1974, 171–180) noted another outcome of the conflict: as IRA ranks grew, Orange extremist organizations also began to swell. While crackdowns by army patrols and incidents of alleged torture by intelligence services increased the ranks of the IRA, unionist paramilitary organizations grew in response. The army also began taking action against the unionist organizations and then truly found itself in the midst of a terrorist conflict.

In 1972 the British government issued a report on the violence in Northern Ireland. Headed by Leslie Scarman (1972), the investigation concluded that tensions inside the community were so great that once they had been unleashed little could be done to stop them. The policies of the police and the army had done much to set those hostile forces in motion. The report concluded that normative democracy could not return until the people in Northern Ireland had faith in all government institutions, including the security forces. The report indicated that a legal method was needed to resolve the violence.

OUTLAWING TERRORISM: INTERNMENT AND DIPLOCK COURTS

Partly as a continuation of Scarman's research and partly because of the continued violence, the British attempted to seek a legal answer to the problems of terrorism in Northern Ireland. Lord Chief Justice Diplock was dispatched to Northern Ireland to examine the possibility of using criminal law to combat terrorism. In 1972 Diplock's committee issued a report, complete with recommendations. It became the basis of one of the most controversial policies in Northern Ireland.

Under Diplock's recommendations the police and courts in Ulster were given increased powers to deal with the problems posed by terrorism. The administrative powers in the criminal justice system were greatly expanded by legislation that followed the Diplock report. Security forces were given the power to arrest and intern without warrant or trial. Courts were given the power of secret trial and testimony. These policies have been controversial, to say the least.

A special form of martial law lies at the base of security policy in Northern Ireland. The Special Powers Act was first enacted by the semiautonomous parliament in Northern Ireland after the outbreak of civil war. It granted expanded powers to police officers and allowed courts to operate on a secret basis. The act was renewed each year until 1933, when it became a permanent part of Northern Ireland's legal code.

John Finn (1987) said there was little doubt that the purpose of the 1922 Special Powers Act was to limit the power of Irish Catholics in the North. Civil rights activists of the 1960s sought to have the act repealed, and the British government convened a special panel to do so. In 1973 the government charged Lord Chief Justice Diplock with developing a set of more impartial laws that could deal effectively with terrorist organizations.

Finn argued that Diplock's committee proceeded on the assumption that the Northern Irish criminal justice system could not deal with the problem of terrorism. Terrorism had resulted in three legal problems. First, common law rules of evidence tended to protect terrorists. Second, under normal criminal procedure, witnesses and victims could be threatened by members of Protestant or Catholic terrorist organizations. Finally, the Diplock committee feared favoritism in juror selection and trial verdicts.

The result of the Diplock investigation was to invoke a new Emergency Powers Act in 1973. Unlike the previous Special Powers Act, the EPA came directly from Britain. The major strategies behind the act, according to Finn, were to shift the burden of proof from the state to the defendant, and to shift more control away from the judicial branch of government and channel it toward the executive branch.

The EPA was amended in 1978 and has remained the law of the land in Northern Ireland. It gives security forces the right to treat suspected terrorists differently than normal suspects or criminals. Its critics, such as Alfred McClung Lee (1983, 63–70), have maintained that it is used to legally continue discrimination in the North and to serve the existing power structure. Emergency powers translated into state power under unionist control. The supporters of the Diplock report hold a different view, believing that certain freedoms could be maintained while responding to terrorism in a democracy. Regardless, certain powers have been restricted since the signing of the 1985 Anglo-Irish Peace Accord.

The heart of the EPA controversy is revealed in several important sections of its language. The act gave the government key powers: the powers of police search and seizure were expanded, and the police were enabled to stop and question citizens without reasonable suspicion. While they weren't given arrest authority, military forces operating in support of the police were also allowed to stop and question civilians and to detain suspected terrorists for the police. Far more controversial were the practices of internment—arresting a suspect without formal charges—and trial without a jury. Protection against such governmental powers is generally assumed by citizens of most Western nations.

Finn examined the issues of internment and trial without a jury and compared them against public confidence and support for the legal system in Northern Ireland. He argued that although internment had been a feature of Northern Irish justice from 1921 to 1975, in 1975 the concept underwent a substantial change. The power to intern moved from the judicial branch of government to the executive branch.

In effect, internment became an administrative process. Officials responsible for the security of Northern Ireland could issue an administrative order to detain a suspected terrorist. No criminal charges had to be filed because the suspect was not under arrest. The suspect could be held for twenty-eight days unless a police official decided there was a reason for further detention.

Finn stated that suspects were entitled to a hearing before a judicial officer, but he did not believe this was part of the judicial process. At such hearings suspects were routinely given vague reasons for their detention. Additionally, the British Secretary of State or his deputies were allowed to intervene at any point. They also appointed the judicial officers who reviewed the cases in private. Finn stated that this demonstrated the administrative nature of internment. It was not a judicial process based upon individual rights and impartial review.

Finn also focused attention on the trial processes in Northern Ireland. The Emergency Powers Act established nonjury trial processes with relaxed rules of evidence. Courts conducting these trials have commonly been referred to as Diplock courts after the British chief justice. They are used for trials of accused terrorists.

Unlike more emotional supporters and critics of the Emergency Powers Act, Finn analyzed the impact of internment and special trials through an examination of public attitudes toward the courts and government. He concluded that internment was too harsh, that it deviated too much from the norms of democratic society and was accepted by neither Protestants nor Catholics. It is interesting to note that the British government has since abandoned the practice of internment and has refused to reinstate it even under strong political pressure.

Finn found that public condemnation of the Diplock courts was not quite so strong. His analysis demonstrated that the public was able to discern a difference between common criminals and terrorists. In Northern Ireland people were willing to accept a different class of trial for terrorists, provided that common law norms were not grossly violated by emergency legislation. In terms of policy, Finn implied that people in Northern Ireland were willing to accept reasonable restrictions of liberty provided they were subject to impartial judicial review.

Finn's conclusions make an important point about public policy. If security forces are to be successful in Northern Ireland, they must not act as if they are imposing the will of a foreign power. This means that they must reflect the will of the local population. D. G. Boyce (1984, 149–170) shared this view. Successful counterterrorism depends on swinging local public opinion against political violence, Boyce argued. The policies of the government must demonstrate that peace lies in equality and justice and not in the extremes offered by militant Protestant extremists or the IRA. Security forces can neither politically nor morally afford to alienate the Northern Irish population.

If we briefly reconsider the 1972 Scarman Report, you may recall that the committee concluded that peace could not come to Northern Ireland until the public gained confidence in governmental institutions. The Emergency Powers Act was designed to stop violence, but some aspects of it may have had a negative effect on public confidence. Another factor to consider in the equation is the actions of government units empowered by the emergency legislation. Security forces were charged with the task of combating violence. Their tactics also had an impact on counterterrorist policy.

THE EVOLUTION OF SECURITY FORCE TACTICS IN NORTHERN IRELAND

From a criminal justice standpoint one important factor has dominated the experiences of security forces in Northern Ireland since 1969: the police and military have been used in combined operations. This means that security in Northern Ireland has fallen into the exclusive domain of neither the police nor the military. Both organizational structures have been forced to learn a variety of nontraditional roles. The learning process has been painful and often has been developed through trial and error. Like other aspects of Irish policy, it has been surrounded by controversy.

When the first troops arrived in Belfast and Londonderry in August 1969 they were hardly prepared for the tasks that faced them. Aside from the political misunderstanding reported by Bell, the troops were thrown into an urban peacekeeping role with little or no preparation. In other words, combat troops were utilized essentially as an extension of police power. Since these troops had limited knowledge of police functions, they tended to approach hostile situations as if they were engaging an enemy. Most accounts recorded that overreaction was not uncommon.

Robert Moss (1972, 24) wrote that the British government quickly began to realize this situation. As rioting and demonstration gave way to a campaign of terrorism, it appeared that the presence of the army would be needed for quite some time. This meant preparing troops for a different type of duty. Units assigned to Northern Ireland began to receive special training in peacekeeping duties.

It might be best to examine the military response in a series of phases. These are rough outlines that obscure details, but they can illustrate the evolution of the military's tactics. In 1969 the army simply responded to riots; then it attempted to isolate republican neighborhoods. From 1970 to 1973, Peter Janke (1974) reported, the army was used to create a more neutral peacekeeping force. Despite this goal, the army engaged in massive roundup operations against IRA suspects and still approached Northern Ireland as if it were a military target. Policies and actions during those periods isolated Catholic communities and increased the strength of the IRA.

From 1973 to 1978 army policy changed drastically. According to retired British Colonel James Deerin (1978, 670–675), the army learned from its previous mistakes. Rather than approaching Ulster as a war zone, the army conceived of its role as one of police support. Troopers were not soldiers, Deerin said; they were an extension of police security. He added that this role was learned by trial and error from overreaction during the early years of military involvement.

In 1978 army policy changed, not so much through internal evaluation as through a change in British attitudes toward Northern Ireland. The British government increasingly viewed Ireland as an Irish problem, but it would not abandon Ulster for fear of a civil war (Kelley 1982, 227). Prime Minister Margaret Thatcher followed this policy of "Ulsterization" by reducing the number of British troops and increasing the number of Irish security forces throughout 1985. The signing of the Anglo-Irish Peace Accord temporarily solidified this process.

Military policy cannot be understood apart from police policy. As Janke noted, the military became involved in the conflict because they were believed to be more neutral than the police. When the initial disturbances were quelled, however, it was necessary to return civil security activities to the police. The problem was that the public lacked confidence in the police. The Catholics in particular believed that the police were merely representatives of the Protestant cause.

Based on the recommendations of several official inquiries, the British government took a series of steps to restore faith in the RUC and to make it a neutral civil power. It was a long-term process that began in the early 1970s and has continued up to today. Two general strategies were utilized to accomplish the objective. First, the B-Specials and other overtly Protestant aspects of the RUC were officially dissolved. Second, the RUC and other organizations in the justice system began to recruit Catholics for enforcement, judicial, and security roles.

According to Deerin, the RUC became the mainstay of security forces in Northern Ireland. Although it was armed with emergency powers, its primary job was to respond to terrorism as a violation of criminal law. When the army modified its role to one of police support in 1973, the RUC became completely responsible for counterterrorist operations. Military force was only called on for support during hazardous calls and for additional security patrols during emergencies. Military personnel were constrained by strict rules of engagement very similar to the police guidelines.

In the area of investigation the police and military began to cooperate fully. The RUC used standard criminal investigation techniques and began building files on known and potential terrorists. The army gathered information through military intelligence sources. Military procedures became controversial, however, when abuses of interned suspects were reported. Some international observers concluded that the army tortured several IRA suspects to gain information in the early 1970s.

The 1980s saw a more subtle and effective form of persuasion. Security forces began to use known terrorists as their sources of information. Finn made mention of the technique: informants have been used to infiltrate extremist factions among both republicans and unionists. Known as "supergrasses," they are allowed to give secret testimony in Diplock courts. Many people have been convicted without other corroborative evidence. The use of supergrasses has been extremely controversial, but it has been effective.

The 1980s also witnessed the growth of a rather unique unit in the British order of battle. As the number of British troops in Northern Ireland was reduced with the

"Ulsterization" of the conflict, the number of Irish troops increased. The British created an Ulster-based military unit in the early 1970s whose eventual purpose was to replace the British Army.

Deerin reported that the Ulster Defense Regiment (UDR) was originally created to back up the British Army with a civilian reserve force. Unlike the B-Specials, the UDR was to be composed of both Protestants and Catholics and to remain under direct control of the army. The UDR initially operated under a strict set of guidelines. It was deployed neither in riot control nor in Catholic areas of Belfast and Londonderry. The majority of reservists patrolled one or two nights per week and met monthly for weekend drills. They were activated in the summer for training.

As the British Army began to reduce its presence, the UDR gradually assumed a more and more prominent role. According to Robert Pockrass (1985), by 1985 the heavily armed patrols of the RUC and the UDR had taken the place of many British units. Pockrass patrolled with the RUC for a number of months. In his estimation, the security of Northern Ireland had evolved into a mainly police function with the UDR playing a reserve role.

There is still not enough evidence to evaluate the political success of the security forces in Northern Ireland. During their early employment both police and military forces were plagued by misunderstanding and overreaction. There is no doubt that many human rights abuses occurred. On the other hand, security force policy evolved and eventually helped to calm a tremendously complex, violent situation. Additionally, the increased competence of security forces seemed to result in a less confrontational attitude, according to analysts like Deerin.

Currently, however, the security forces still operate in a volatile emotional climate. They have support from some sectors of Northern Irish society, and they are detested by others. While apologists such as Deerin praise their efforts at bringing peace, others are extremely critical. For example, Denis Faul and Ray Murray (1976a), two Catholic priests from Northern Ireland, have charged the British Army with the intentional slaying of Irish children. Others, such as Alfred McClung Lee, claim that security forces cannot avoid being repressive because the state is repressive.

Yet in this debate the violence of terrorists is often dismissed. There are extremists in Northern Ireland who have a long record of murder and mayhem. Members of the IRA and the equally violent Irish National Liberation Army have waged campaigns of bombings, assassinations, and crippling assaults. Their counterparts in the unionist camp, such as the Protestant Ulster Volunteer Force and the Ulster Defense Association, have been only too quick to respond. Since 1969 over 2,300 people have been killed in Ireland due to terrorist violence. Before leaving our discussion of Northern Ireland, it would be fruitful to look at the criminological aspects of terrorism.

A CRIMINOLOGICAL ANALYSIS OF IRISH TERRORISM

Robert Pockrass (1987) conducted an in-depth study into the nature of terrorism in Northern Ireland. He examined the patterns of violence from 1969 to 1984 by relating the motivations of the killers to the selection of their victims. Specifically, he asked what types of people became victims and why they were killed.

Pockrass believed that at bottom, Irish violence was cultural. Other revolutionary countries have experienced more violence, he argued, but Irish violence is a kind of national expression. It is glorified in poetry, literature, and song. It is the celebrated event of the past, and the expected outcome of the future. The sad reality of such a cultural expression is seen in the number of people killed by terrorist violence.

Pockrass argued that Irish violence could best be understood by focusing on the motivation behind it. Feeling that too often terrorists are dismissed as abnormal, he suggested that their actions be evaluated in terms of outcome. In other words, he believed that terrorists operate with a goal in mind. When analysts focus on the goal, they may not be able to decipher all of the motives behind terrorist activity, but they can often determine the primary motive. This could lead to better predictive models of terrorism.

Pockrass identified four categories of terrorism in Northern Ireland. Sectarian violence involved interreligious conflicts—that is, the fighting between Protestants and Catholics. Interorganizational violence included the internal struggles of unionist and republican terrorist organizations. The final categories were terrorist attacks on non-combatants and similar attacks on security forces. He related each type of violence to the motivation behind it.

Sectarian violence went through an evolutionary development. In 1969 it was primarily mob action. In the riots that engulfed Northern Ireland that August, mobs of Catholics confronted mobs of Protestants. Violence was random and dominated by the psychology of the mob. This was not terrorism.

According to Pockrass, terrorism entered sectarian conflicts when individuals abandoned mob rioting around 1971 and started hunting for selected targets. Random mob violence had not been extremely deadly; terrorism changed that situation. As attacks became individualized, the amount of violence increased along with its effectiveness.

The initial purpose of rioting and terrorism was to convey an illusion of power. By participating in a mob or selecting an individual victim from the other side, Catholics and Protestants sought to intimidate each other by fear. As individual terrorist murders increased, Pockrass said, the motivation began to change. In some cases murders were committed to force a change in policy. Others were committed for revenge. In analyzing sectarian murder, pure hatred and a desire to kill also played a leading role.

Interorganizational violence was motivated by other factors. Both republican and unionist terrorist groups used murder as a means of enforcing internal discipline. It was also used to take revenge against an informant and to set examples for potential informants. The use of supergrasses by security forces has resulted in a number of deadly internal killings.

Attacks on noncombatants seem to have three motives. First, killing public officials increases the aura of power around terrorists. Second, the sophistication of many of the attacks also brings attention to the cause. Finally, revenge has become an important motive. Pockrass noted that a number of off-duty correctional and judicial personnel have been targeted. Corrections officers have been murdered for alleged cruelty toward inmates, and judges for their sentencing. The IRA and INLA even assassinate Catholic judges, because they view them as national traitors.

In the 1980s the increasing trend in Northern Ireland has been to attack members of the security forces. Pockrass maintained that this has primarily been a tactic favored by republican terrorists, because they see themselves as fighting a war for national liberation. Unionist terrorists have also attacked security forces, but generally in response to being attacked. Republican terrorists have rechanneled most of their efforts since 1976 into attacks on the security forces.

Given the motivation of political conflict, there are other reasons for attacking security forces. Indiscriminate attacks against civilians threatened a potential backlash from the population. As random violence declined, the lines of terrorism became more clearly demarcated. The RUC and its supporters were defined as the enemy by republican terrorists. Republican organizations hoped to force a withdrawal of RUC forces and support similar to the British withdrawal in 1921.

Pockrass said that this analogy breaks down when tested. The RUC and UDR are not British forces; they are Irish, and they have nowhere to retreat. The terrorists can only hope that they will become demoralized or emigrate from Northern Ireland to join the British. Neither possibility seems likely.

There are greater dangers in waging battle with organized security forces rather than civilians. Pockrass pointed to other areas of the world to show the desirability of civilian targets for terrorists: it's much safer to attack an unarmed civilian population than an armed security force. Therefore, terrorism in Ireland has taken an interesting turn. Terrorist weapons have grown in size and sophistication. In addition, a number of police officers have been assassinated while off duty. The IRA leadership believes such tactics will eventually lead to victory.

One of the lessons to be learned from Pockrass's analysis of terrorist murders is that the motivations behind Irish terrorism have changed since 1969. The historical root of the violence remains, but terrorism has evolved—as have the counterterrorist measures taken by security forces. Both sides have made substantial changes since August 1969 when the army returned to Ulster.

SUMMARY OF CHAPTER THIRTEEN

Terrorism in Northern Ireland is the product of a long history of violence and a struggle for independence. The Irish have not had complete control of their country since the Viking incursions. Norman barons replaced the Vikings and paved the way for an eventual English foothold in Ireland.

Current troubles can be traced directly to the Reformation. The Irish resisted English attempts to replace Catholicism with Anglican theology. This was followed by English attempts to colonize Ireland and by several Catholic revolts. A pattern of Anglo-Irish conflict developed, spanning three centuries.

The IRB was created in the mid-1800s to serve as a relief organization for the poor. It soon became an instrument of terrorism, and Orange organizations were formed to counter it. Groups such as the UVF can be traced to these Orange organizations. The IRB gave birth to groups such as the IRA and INLA. The IRA was an instrumental force in the Black and Tan War, but it was virtually destroyed by the new government in the Free State.

Current troubles in Northern Ireland originated in a civil rights movement in the

1960s. After Protestant marches and rioting among Catholic and Protestant mobs in 1969, the British Army was sent to Ulster. The northern communities were polarized by the insensitivity of the military response, and terrorist organizations and violence grew in Northern Ireland.

Security force policy in Northern Ireland has evolved in response to that violence. Controversial emergency powers gave the police additional authority, but the police alone were not strong enough to combat terrorism. The RUC was augmented by military force, and tactical responses emerged from a joint approach. The 1980s were characterized by an emphasis on the Irish—rather than British—nature of the struggle and by increasing terrorist attacks on security forces. The 1985 Anglo-Irish Peace Accord has appeased neither Orange nor Green extremists.

IF YOU WANT TO READ FURTHER . . .

There are several excellent history books covering the development of the violence in Ireland. If you don't enjoy reading history, you may find Leon Uris's novel *Trinity* a painless way to explore Irish history and terrorism. For the more stout of heart I wholeheartedly recommend Giovani Costigan's *A History of Modern Ireland*. It's fun, fairly objective, and easy to read. Another good book is J. C. Beckett's *A Short History of Ireland*. Raymond Corrado and Rebecca Evans have an outstanding brief summary of the conflict in Michael Stohl's *The Politics of Terrorism*.

The best analysis of the IRA is J. Bowyer Bell's *The Secret Army*. It is probably the definitive history of the terrorist group. You can complement it by reading Tim Pat Coogan's *The IRA*. Maria McGuire will take you inside the IRA with *To Take Arms*. The political groups in Northern Ireland can readily be sorted out using W. D. Flackes's *Northern Ireland: A Political Directory*.

There are many good works on Ireland that deal with the problems of terrorism. Alfred McClung Lee's *Terrorism in Northern Ireland* takes a look at the social costs of terrorism while casting a critical eye over social policies in Britain. Max Hasting's *Barricades in Belfast* gives a view of the civil rights movement. A critical look at martial law can be found in *Governing Without Consensus* by Richard Rose. More popular works and articles by Jack Holland and Conor Cruise O'Brien are informative.

INDIGENOUS TERRORISM
IN WESTERN EUROPE
AND THE CRIMINAL JUSTICE RESPONSE

The experiences of Great Britain in Northern Ireland exemplify one of the longest campaigns against terrorism in Western Europe, but they don't include all of the issues involved in European terrorism. The nations of Western Europe have faced a number of challenges from terrorist groups since the 1960s. Terrorism in Europe has ranged from long-term nationalist campaigns to criminal activities. Governments in Western Europe have responded in a number of ways, and they have developed innovative techniques for police, military, and intelligence-gathering units. Before reviewing some of the major security issues in Part III, we need to take a brief look at modern terrorism in Western Europe.

After reading this chapter you should be able to do the following.

1. Give an overview of the nature of Western European terrorism
2. Describe the West German experience with terrorism and the response to it
3. Summarize Pisano's thesis on subversion and violence in Italy
4. Discuss nationalist and ideological terrorism in Spain
5. Outline the varieties of Western European approaches to counterterrorism

AN OVERVIEW OF EUROPEAN TERRORISM

There is no single type of terrorism in Western Europe. Groups range from small-time criminal elements using terrorism for financial gain to relatively large nationalist groups. Leftists and rightists alike have engaged in ideological terrorism, while African mercenary terrorists have recruited soldiers in Europe and plotted the overthrow of foreign governments. In Great Britain animal protection groups have used terrorism in an attempt to stop the consumption of meat. Europeans have experienced a variety of terrorist activities over the past twenty years.

Raymond Corrado and Rebecca Evans (1988, 373–444) examined Western European terrorism and concluded that it has developed into a variety of forms having no single ideology to unite them. They used two case studies, one of the IRA and one of the German Red Army Faction (RAF), to demonstrate their point.

According to Corrado and Evans, indigenous European terrorism has developed from two bases: ideology and nationalism. Both sources are linked to the past, and terrorism in Western Europe has shared a common evolutionary ancestry from the time of Napoleon. After World War II, however, the structure of European terrorism began to change. Prior to the war terrorism was usually fueled by communism, fascism, or nationalism. After the war the demand for violent political solutions temporarily ceased, along with the practice of terrorism.

Terror began to reemerge in the 1960s. Corrado and Evans believed that this renewed growth was a response to Western European modernization and industrialization. The theory is that modern Western civilization has destroyed family life and communities with its emphasis on materialism, wealth, and industrial production. The ideological terrorists of the 1960s, both on the left and the right, were expressing their frustration with the social structures imposed by a modern industrial society. Nationalist terrorists also embraced this theme. Idealist and nationalist terrorists sprang from diverse interests, but their concern with the evils of modernization was shared.

Analysts who search for conspiracies among terrorist groups have been quick to dismiss this bifurcation of terrorist types. For example, John Reese (1986) believed that nationalists and idealists were linked by common backgrounds and common goals. According to Reese, not only do both types of groups want to rebel against current political structures, they also share a common vision of the structure they would like to impose. For Reese, Western European terrorism was essentially socialist in nature and ultimately inspired by communism.

Analysts sharing this perspective frequently cite the similar rhetoric of extremists and nationalists practicing terrorism. The RAF and the Red Brigades speak of communism and socialism as the eventual outcome of their revolution. Much of the rhetoric of the nationalist Basque Homeland and Nation (ETA) calls for a similar outcome. This serves as evidence of a united "brotherhood of blood" in some scholars' views.

Corrado and Evans argued that the fundamental difference between ideological and nationalist terrorists, could be found in their goals. Ideological terrorists in Europe reject the economic and social structure of industrial capitalism; they want a new order. Nationalists, on the other hand, frequently embrace capitalism and work to achieve materialistic goals. They desire economic opportunity within a strong national identity.

In Corrado's and Evans's analysis, although European terrorists are not united by a common goal of revolution, they are bound by another external factor. The political situations that created the frustrations of the 1960s did not provide social outlets for dissenting political groups, including violent revolutionaries and nationalists. As a result frustration was frequently expressed through violence. According to Corrado and Evans, violence became the tie that bound the nationalists and the revolutionaries.

In the 1980s the situation changed. The pluralism of Western democracies opened the door to peaceful participation in the political system and offered opportunities for change. Violence no longer seemed an attractive method for expressing grievances. As pluralistic governments worked to relieve frustration, the attractiveness of terrorism waned, and terrorists lost their support base.

Today the factor that binds nationalist and ideological terrorists in Europe is this common lack of support. Neither group of extremists enjoys much popularity, and both have increasingly lost ground in recent years. Idealists had very little support from the beginning. Nationalists had more support, but the breakup of ethnic constituencies weakened their position. The forces supporting a pluralistic democracy seem to have far more strength at present.

As a result, Corrado and Evans believed, future incidents of European terrorism will be sporadic. Terrorist groups have lost the base needed to support a terrorist campaign. In addition, the changes in European social structures have blurred class and ethnic distinctions. Corrado and Evans felt that European terrorists have failed to grasp the full import of the social and political weakness of their position.

Dennis Pluchinsky (1982, 40–78) did not share the conclusions of Corrado and Evans. He believed that Western Europe had become a major terrorist battleground due to external factors and localized indigenous support for terrorism. Pluchinsky stated that internal support for European terrorism was significant but that it was primarily potential support. Furthermore, the main areas of indigenous terrorism were Spain, Northern Ireland, Turkey, and Italy. Other Western European states have faced less serious indigenous threats.

A greater threat was posed by what Pluchinsky called "supraindigenous" terrorism. By this he meant the extension of local terrorist activities beyond local boundaries, a step beyond indigenous terrorism. He cited international terrorism as a third problem for Europeans, and he defined it as terrorist groups carrying out the majority of their assaults outside of their country of origin.

A final type of terrorism that Pluchinsky saw developing in Western Europe was state-sponsored terrorism: states using terror to strike at targets as small as political exiles or as large as other states. He believed that Western Europe was becoming a battleground for state-sponsored terrorists.

Pluchinsky's primary concern for Western Europe was its potential role as a battleground. While some forms of terrorism seem to be limited to a single geographical area, Pluchinsky believed that Western Europe suffered a variety of expressions of terrorism. Each time a government brings one variety into check, a new strain appears in another country or region. Unlike Corrado and Evans, Pluchinsky felt there was no indication that this problem would vanish in the near future.

Stephen Segaller (1987, 36–40) took yet another view. He argued that what European terrorists shared was a tactical link. The varieties of terrorism were not as important as the way violence was manifested. Segaller argued that all forms of European terrorism shared a common method of operation.

According to Segaller, modern European terrorism was strongly influenced by the styles of Latin American violence and revolution. Shared revolutionary attitudes imported this influence, and, while it did not result in a union of terrorist movements, it brought about a general sense of solidarity against a common enemy, as well as a common tactical style. Western European democracies became the enemy, along with the economic system that supported them. Since 1970 nationalists and idealists alike have chosen European governments as their common target. They chose a common method of revolution, too.

Variations on the urban guerrilla theme became the norm within almost all Western European terrorist movements. Whether they were on the left or the right, European terrorists were influenced by the writings of Carlos Marighella and tried to establish organizations following his suggestions. The success of Uruguay's Tupamaros was an important influence: both fascists and radicals sought to model their organizations after the Tupamaros.

Segaller said that while European terrorists longed for a Marighella-style revolution, they never achieved it because they were too weak. He believed that this weakness has been realized, especially among left-wing terrorists. Faced with their shrinking power, revolutionary terrorists throughout Europe have retreated into a shell. They united to become stronger, but they sought unification because each group was so weak.

Left-wing Western European groups began joining together around 1985. Members of the Communist Combat Cells of Belgium went to Paris searching for the French terrorist group Direct Action. Shortly afterward, the leadership of Italy's Red Brigade also made overtures toward Paris. West Germany's Red Army Faction expressed an ideological union with these groups. Direct Action published several communiques claiming that a new left-wing unified terrorist movement had formed. Some analysts, like Segaller, believe this is a demonstration of weakness. Others see it as a move toward a higher level of terrorist sophistication.

David Rapoport (1988, 43–50) also noted this trend in Europe. He believed that German terrorists in the 1980s were so weak that they even lacked an ideological base. Antigovernment, antinuclear, and anti-NATO causes were not strong enough to motivate supporters. Therefore German terrorists had to embrace a political cause apart from the German political experience. They found it in the Middle East. Ironically, extremists from both the left and the right took up the Palestinian cause to provide a reason for their continued existence.

Christopher Dobson and Ronald Payne (1982b, 18–43) expanded on the European fascination with the Middle East. They argued that terrorists all over Europe found friendly support in terrorists in the Middle East. A number of diverse political terrorists identified with the Palestinians, as terrorists ranging from the IRA to neo-Nazi idealists trained in Middle Eastern camps and received weapons and supplies from Arab governments.

While Dobson and Payne were more closely allied to those analysts looking for international networks of terrorists, the arguments of Rapoport and Segaller seem to lend weight to Corrado's and Evans's thesis that Western European terrorists have little support. Revolutionary European terrorist groups lack an indigenous base for a campaign. Only nationalistic terrorists have developed a broad base for support. Pluralistic European societies have found alternatives to expressing frustration through violence, except for nationalist minorities in Northern Ireland and Spain. The turn to the Palestinian issue demonstrates the paucity of violent revolutionary ideology and themes in Europe, and European police authorities believe the radical left's new-found union was based on common weakness.

Still, as Pluchinsky argued, indigenous terrorism cannot be dismissed, and ethnic minorities continue to struggle for national identity and economic opportunities. In addition, transnational terrorism continues to use Europe as its adopted battleground. Even though terrorism has become a sporadic problem, Europe remains a major center of terrorist activity.

To be sure, there are many forms of European terrorism outside of Ireland.

European experiences with terrorist groups not only illustrate the possibility of spreading conflicts, they can be used to show a variety of different police responses. A brief review of the different modes of European terrorism can enhance our understanding of the topic.

THE WEST GERMAN EXPERIENCE WITH TERRORISM

The Federal Republic of Germany (FRG) has experienced three forms of indigenous terrorism since 1968. Left-wing terrorism emerged from a radical student movement in 1967. It has been manifested primarily through the Red Army Faction (RAF), the Red Cells (RZ), and the June 2 Movement. Right-wing terrorism emerged as a response to the leftist radicals and as a continuation of the fascist past. Criminals have formed the third brand of West German terrorism, copying the tactics of political terrorists in their commission of crimes.

Schura Cook (1982, 154–178) argued that modern German terrorism evolved through several stages. At first, young Germans imported American culture and along with it the youthful rebellion of the 1960s, which was adopted by German radicals. This was followed by a period of hypersensitivity to U.S. injustices and a corresponding naivete about the very real pain caused by political terrorism. Finally, a campaign of terrorism emerged when militant radicals became willing to sacrifice individual victims to an idealistic cause.

The Baader-Meinhof Gang (BMG) has commonly been described according to the stages outlined by Cook. As the forerunner of the RAF, the BMG originated among a group of militant extremists at the Free University of Berlin. On April 3, 1968 Andreas Baader and his girlfriend, Gudrun Ensslin, decided to move beyond student protests and confrontations. They set fire to two department stores with incendiary bombs. The BMG was born of this action.

Jillian Becker (1977) documented the history of the BMG from 1968 to 1976. Although she gave the BMG credit for too many aspects of German terrorism, she painted an entertaining picture of the German revolutionaries. According to Becker, the group was made up of chic radicals in Berlin's university circles. Leftist students were content to challenge the system with propaganda, demonstrations, and other tolerable social dissent until they gathered around a militant core: Andreas Baader and his girlfriend. The core expanded to include a few dozen others, including Ulricke Meinhof.

In Becker's analysis, the revolutionary purity of Baader was questionable. He seemed to be motivated by the antisocial behavior of his radical clique and their loose attitudes toward group sex. In addition, he enjoyed the thrill of robberies and the criminal life. He was more of a criminal than a revolutionary, in Becker's estimation.

Ulricke Meinhof, in contrast, was dedicated to an idealistic revolutionary cause. Before meeting Baader she was active among leftist students and helped publish an underground newspaper combining revolutionary ideology with soft pornography. In the late 1960s she became acquainted with Baader and the two gravitated toward one another as they moved through radical circles. Horst Mahler, a lawyer who joined the student movement, helped provide the catalyst for violence. When Baader and Ensslin suggested a campaign of direct action, Meinhof joined the cause.

After beginning a low-level campaign of action, Becker stated, the BMG moved to bigger and better concepts. Inspired by the writings of Carlos Marighella the group turned to bank robbery as a means of expropriation. The group financed itself through a series of robberies, and while Meinhof remained dedicated to the revolutionary cause, Baader seemed to enjoy the high-profile life of a major criminal.

Baader did little to change this image. He not only wanted to wage a terrorist campaign, he wanted to wage it in style. Before bank robberies, for example, he urged the group to steal automobiles to use as getaway cars. As he only wished to travel in style, he insisted that his compatriots steal BMWs. This became the trademark of BMG bank robberies—so much so that the BMW was popularly dubbed the Baader-Meinhof *Wagen*.

Such exploits necessarily drew the attention of law enforcement authorities. After initial failures, the German police slowly began to close in on the gang. By 1972 the leading members of the group, including Baader and Meinhof, were in jail. The German government increased its security to contain the terrorists, and the campaign of bombings, robberies, and murders seemed to be at an end. According to a *New York Times* special, Baader and Meinhof were doomed to failure because they could generate no public support (Lasky 1975).

Despite the arrests, the group began to exhibit a most resilient quality. Hans-Josef Horchem (1985, 63–68) pointed to this Phoenix-like quality in an article on German terrorism. Following the arrests of the key leaders in 1972, the group launched a series of bombings attacks. In 1973 they established a new infrastructure and fought to release their jailed comrades. The Baader-Meinhof Gang would begin a cycle of collapse and resurrection lasting until the present time.

Prior to their arrests, Badder and Meinhof had changed the name of their group to the Red Army Faction. Although they continued to be known popularly as the Baader-Meinhof Gang, the new name was accepted by their followers. While the FRG built a special prison for Baader and Meinhof, free members of the RAF refused to sit idly by. They selected new leaders and prepared for a new terrorist campaign.

Meinhof eventually committed suicide by hanging herself. Baader and other leaders shot themselves in 1977 after an attempt to rescue them failed. The guns were smuggled into prison by attorneys representing members of the gang. Subsequent investigation revealed that several attorneys were in league with the terrorists and involved in supplying jailed members with contraband and maintaining a network between them and the outside organization. It seemed to work. Over the next twenty years leading members of the RAF were continually apprehended, but the organization perpetually rose from its ashes.

The RAF reached a turning point in 1977. Until that time members were painted as misunderstood romantics of the revolutionary left. They were glamorized and their criminal exploits sensationalized. Their image was exploded when allies of the group hijacked an airliner in October 1977 and brutally murdered the pilot. Several subsequent murders turned public opinion against the RAF.

In a later publication, Horchem (1986) related the experiences of the RAF to the broader problem of German terrorism. His analysis helps to place the development of the RAF in perspective. The Baader-Meinhof Gang was one of three modern expressions of German left-wing terrorism. The RAF was eventually joined by two other groups called the June 2 Movement and the Red Cells. Each group operated independently of the other, although the June 2 Movement was absorbed by the RAF in 1980.

Horchem said that the RAF was the oldest and most brutal terrorist organization in the FRG. Since 1977 its goal has been the destruction of the U.S. military establishment and its West German allies. To accomplish that it needed to destroy the corporate system, which supports the military establishment. Horchem identified the ideological basis of the group as the writings of Baader and of the lawyer Horst Mahler.

Horchem stressed the RAF's unique ability to regenerate itself. In 1972 the original leadership of the RAF was jailed. By 1973 a new infrastructure had been created, but its leaders were jailed in 1974. Yet in 1976 the group was active again, and its activities peaked in 1977. Although it lost favor in 1977 due to a series of murders, the group was resurrected in 1981, 1983, and 1985. In the late 1980s it focused almost exclusively on an anti-NATO campaign, with a new generation of terrorists.

According to Horchem, the group's ability to recover from counterstrikes can be attributed to its structure. The RAF maintains three membership tiers: legitimate citizens, active terrorists, and jailed members. The organization is cemented by the legitimate members, who maintain contacts between those in jail and those conducting operations.

Horchem believed that the RAF underwent a major change in 1985. Due to the unpopular murders in 1977 the RAF had been in a state of decline until 1984. It began a three-phase revitalization plan in that year. First, the focus of the group shifted almost exclusively to anti-NATO operations. Second, jailed members staged a hunger strike. Third, the active terrorists began a massive bombing campaign. By 1985 the RAF was back in operating order.

Another factor assisted the RAF in 1985. Faced with possible extinction in West Germany, the RAF looked for allies and found them in the French terrorist group Direct Action. Some analysts believe that the interplay between the RAF and Direct Action has been overemphasized, and some police groups believe that their collaboration points to the weakness of the RAF. Nonetheless, the fact remains that after that alliance the RAF was able to continue as an active terrorist group into the nineties.

The June 2 Movement was born of the same political climate as the Baader-Meinhof Gang. Terrorists of the former were highly critical of the latter's stylish approach to revolution, and of their intellectual elitism as well. Members of June 2 believed that revolution should begin and end with the common people, and they sought to open their ranks to workers and nonintellectuals. Ultimately, however, the weakness of both groups forced a reconciliation. In 1980, June 2 merged with the RAF.

West Germany's most active terrorists in the 1980s had no links with the RAF. David Th. Schiller (1987) noted that the Red Cells (RZ) have surpassed the 1960s Marighella-style leftists in activity. According to Schiller, the RZ denounced the RAF for its intellectual arrogance and sought support from the urban homeless and unemployed. Some strong leaders emerged from the group, but the RZ was typified by small tight-knit groups. Internally, they referred to their organization as a family.

In the 1970s some RZ members drifted into the Palestinian movement. Along with other German leftists and some fascist groups, members of the RZ received training from the Popular Front for the Liberation of Palestine. The PFLP lent financial and logistical support to the RZ, who, when they returned to Germany, added prominent Jewish and Israeli targets to their hit list.

In 1977 the RZ underwent a major change. West German public opinion had hardened against terrorism as a result of the RAF's murder campaign. The RZ therefore made a change in tactics. Rather than focusing on major violent activities or sensationalized media events, the RZ began to focus on low-level terrorism—small activities designed to disrupt everyday social norms.

Schiller said the RZ had instituted these tactics by the 1980s. Calling for small-scale revolts, the RZ suggested that everyone could be a terrorist. They still applaud major actions, but they encourage citizens to sabotage construction sites, place glue in the locks of bank doors, and place obscene telephone calls to the powers that be. Schiller believed that these actions changed the character of German terrorism.

The loose structure of the RZ made it very difficult to penetrate. Police began to get a picture of its extent in 1978 when they encountered an RZ bomber who had been severely wounded in a premature explosion. Questioning led police to a vast cache of arms and explosives. While the RZ encouraged "after-hours terrorism," their armaments suggested they were capable of something far greater. Schiller said that in the late 1980s hardly a week went by without a major terrorist incident. The RZ, he said, deserved the majority of credit.

Other ideological terrorists in contemporary Germany come from right-wing and paramilitary organizations with fascist overtones. *Der Spiegel* (1980), a German news magazine, estimated the total number of right-wing activists to be around fourteen hundred. Dobson and Payne (1982b, 183) placed the figure at around twenty thousand in more than seventy groups. German groups, however, may inflate their numbers just as right-wingers tend to do in America. Obtaining an objective count is clearly difficult. Horchem's (1986) analysis suggested that the number of right-wing extremists who are actually violent is quite small.

The number of right-wing terrorists is not quite as interesting as are the ideological links they have formed. Like their counterparts on the left, fascist terrorists detest the results of German capitalism and West Germany's close relations with the United States. They are national socialists; that is, they want a socialist economy under the direct control of a strong central government as in the days of Hitler. They part with the left, however, in their extreme hatred of communism and strong belief in nationalism. Ironically, their tactics, allies, and support networks follow the patterns established by left-wing terrorists.

The Middle East has become an important training ground for small right-wing terrorist groups. Horchem believed that a number of fascist groups trained in various locations in the Middle East between 1970 and 1981. In addition, right-wing groups have acted as European agents for such organizations as Black September. The right-wingers have been intrigued by the anti-Israeli and anti-American positions of many Middle Eastern terrorist groups. Ironically, fascist terrorists have been trained by the same organizations that trained the RAF and RZ.

German right-wing terrorism has been more limited than terror from the left. Peter Merkl (1986, 241–245) believed that fascists were generally more selective about their targets. Rather than engaging in indiscriminate violence, they targeted individuals.

Jews, Russians, and Americans were selected for attack. There have been exceptions and occasional public bombings, but in general terror on the right has been limited.

Merkl examined the activities of the Military Sports Group Hoffman to demonstrate his point. The group was started by Karl Heinz Hoffman in the late 1970s and soon achieved a reputation for intensive military training. This drew the attention of German law enforcement authorities, who began to monitor the group. It seemed to follow the pattern of other neo-Nazi groups, and the police watched it with interest.

Horchem (1986) said that Hoffman went to Beirut in 1979 to receive training from the former leader of Black September. He took fifteen colleagues with him, and they underwent extremely rigorous training in PLO camps. Hoffman severely beat one of his compatriots for a breach of discipline, and the offender has subsequently disappeared. Four members of the group deserted after Hoffman's disciplinary tantrum, but the remaining members returned to Germany in the summer of 1980.

According to Horchem, two Germans were murdered on the orders of Hoffman in 1980. Merkl stated that this provoked a crackdown from the German police. When they went into action, almost all the Military Sports Group's members were arrested; Hoffman was among those taken into custody. In 1982 two other members were arrested in Rome. The group seems to have become defunct through arrest and conviction.

Merkl believed that small right-wing groups fit into categories similar to that of the Military Sports Group. They resemble 1930s-style Nazi SS action groups, and they alienate a large portion of German society. Their fight is intended to purify Germany, expel all foreigners, and reunite the country. Some fascists have set off bombs in public places, but most analysts and law enforcement authorities believe these actions to have been the work of individuals. Neo-Nazi groups select their targets with greater care than that.

Criminal groups have mimicked the tactics of the Federal Republic's political terrorists. Horchem believed the Guerrilla Diffusa to be one such organization. He believed that criminals use political rhetoric to mask pure crime. In 1984 a number of German criminals were arrested who stated that they belonged to Guerrilla Diffusa. The name continued to pop up throughout the 1980s, but Horchem believed it to be only camouflage. Guerrilla Diffusa, he concluded, is without political significance.

Schiller was not so quick to dismiss the organization. He believed that Guerrilla Diffusa was not an organization, but rather a way of conducting terrorism. He believed it was an expression of the low-intensity terror campaign advocated by RZ. It represented informal terrorism. According to the RZ's low-intensity concept, any small act against the state is an act of terrorism; crime is no exception. Guerrilla Diffusa might be a criminal organization, but Schiller felt it also might be indicative of a revolutionary pattern.

PISANO'S ASSESSMENT OF SUBVERSION AND VIOLENCE IN ITALY

West Germany is not the only European nation to suffer from ideological terrorism. Italy, too, has been the scene of major violence since the 1960s. Leonard Weinberg (1986, 146–159) cited several reasons for Italian political violence. He stated that Italy met all the preconditions necessary for an atmosphere of violence. Italian politics tend toward abstract solutions of problems and only became pragmatic during times of crisis. And even every pragmatic action is endlessly debated by those who fear a return to Italy's fascist past. As a result, very little is accomplished by means of Italian politics.

According to Weinberg, the Italian inability to conduct normative political functions has become a catalyst for violence. Italy has been unable to respond effectively to technology and the resultant social changes. This has led to a breakdown of traditional forms of authority and brought about a constant struggle for power. Unlike German terrorism, Italian terrorism is the result of a weak political structure.

Vittorfranco Pisano (1987) reflected this theme in an outstanding analysis of political violence in modern Italy. He believed that the political structure of Italy has contributed to the rise of Italian terrorism and an accompanying crime wave. All political violence in Italy is interrelated: since the government doesn't work, violence becomes a means of political expression.

Pisano cited several problems in governing Italy. First, Italy's relatively recent national status has not laid the foundation for unification among the various regions of the country. Disunity is enhanced by a weak constitutional government imposed by the victorious Allies after World War II. Democratic pluralism does not work within this framework because no one has executive authority. Pisano said this problem is exacerbated by a multiparty system and close government links to both the private sector and trade unions. No one has the voice or power to invoke final authority.

Pisano stated that Italy has been engulfed in crime and terrorism as a result of political anarchy. In the absence of a parliamentary majority and executive authority, avenues for political expression in Italy are closed. One of the few remaining ways to achieve goals is violence, manifested in terrorism and crime. Pisano distinguished terrorism from common crime by stating that the former is pure politically motivated violence, while criminal activities are aimed at a profit.

Another reason for the plethora of Italian terrorism is that Italian history is replete with examples of violent political expression. Pisano stated that terrorism has long been a traditional method of resolving political disputes. In the early part of the century fascist terrorism dominated the country. After the fall of the fascists, left-wing terrorism grew, especially in the form of left-wing death squads in the 1940s. Disorders in 1968 brought a resurgence of left- and right-wing terrorism. According to Pisano's research, Italy was the scene of almost sixteen thousand terrorist incidents from 1968 to 1985.

Pisano said that Italian terrorism is best understood by dividing it into three categories: (1) left-wing terrorism, (2) right-wing terrorism, and (3) criminal violence. As with many typologies, such a distinction is somewhat artificial, yet it allows us to understand the sources of Italian terrorism. All three types of groups have been active in the twentieth century, but the left has dominated the scene most recently.

From 1968 to 1985 the most active terrorist groups came from the left. Pisano identified nearly three hundred groups and stated that most of them had a Marxist–Leninist orientation. The best-known group is the Red Brigades (BR). It was formed in Milan when Renato Curio broke away from a left-wing working-class political organization and began talking violent revolution. In 1970 he gathered more militant followers and announced plans for a terrorist campaign. He was joined by Margherita Cago, who later became his wife. The future militants called their organization the Red Brigades; Curio's first group of militants became known as the Historical Nucleus.

Pisano stated that the BR's violent communist ideology made no mystery of its strategy for revolution. Curio and Cago sought to make the cities unsafe for any government official or sympathizer. They believed that a climate of violence would help bring about a revolution in Italy and eventually in all of Europe. Members of the BR saw themselves as the vanguard of a worldwide communist revolution. They believed sensational violence would be their key to the future.

The organization of the Red Brigades was rather unique in European terrorism. They came closer to matching the Tupamaro model than did any other group in Europe. They were bound in a loose confederation, with a central committee meeting periodically to devise a grand strategy. While the Tupamaros operated only in Montevideo, the BR had a variety of urban centers. Each unit, therefore, became a fairly autonomous organization within its own area. The BR managed to establish independent headquarters in several major Italian cities.

The structure of the BR made it extremely difficult to penetrate. Police might penetrate a group in one city but have little effect on units in other towns. Since each unit was generally autonomous, there was no single command structure for the authorities to combat. Decentralization was the key to the Red Brigades. They killed, kidnapped, took foreign hostages—including an American general—, and even kidnapped and killed the Italian Prime Minister. They were responsible for hundreds of terrorist incidents.

Despite their decentralization, Pisano noted a tactical innovation common to divergent BR units. The BR used standard terrorist tactics but developed a twist to their delivery. Instead of launching a series of seemingly unrelated crimes, the BR would attack in clusters. Several attacks were designed to occur simultaneously or in sequence. This intensified their effect, and cluster assaults added to the aura of BR attacks.

Pisano divided the evolution of the BR into three stages. From 1970 to 1974 the group learned terrorism. Pisano described this as a demonstration phase. The heyday of the BR was from 1975 to 1981, when it launched a massive terrorist campaign. In 1982 a downward spiral began. This was due to a number of factors, including a police crackdown and the loss of public sympathy among the left. From 1983 to 1986 Pisano credited the BR with only five attacks.

Even though the BR has been in remission, their impact has been felt via spin-off groups, other Italian terrorists who have attempted to followed the tactics of the Red Brigades. In addition, Italy has been plagued by resurgent right-wing terrorism. While fascist groups have not enjoyed the organizational structures and support of those on the left, Pisano noted that they have developed their own special techniques for terror.

Right-wing terrorists could not compete with the left during the early 1970s. As a result, Pisano said, the fascists turned to indiscriminate public bombings. They began randomly to set off explosives in crowded public areas. This policy backfired, however, as the public became enraged and demanded the destruction of fascist groups. Right-wing terrorists were forced to abandon their bombing policy and follow the example of the left.

Pisano identified six major right-wing groups, but he cautioned against placing too much emphasis on the names and identities of fascist terrorists. Like groups on the left, many right-wing terrorist groups exist for only a brief period. Larger groups also frequently change their names or invent code names for tactical reasons. There is no accurate count of Italian terrorist groups.

The leading group on the right is the New Order/Black Order (ON). Pisano said the group was created in the 1950s under the name New Order. It was forced underground by the police and reemerged in 1973 as the Black Order. It is estimated to have over two thousand followers, and the actual number of violent terrorists is unknown. ON has taken responsibility for a number of bombings but has been involved in few deaths.

Far more violent is the Armed Revolutionary Nuclei (NAR). The NAR is a relatively new group that emerged in the late 1970s. From 1977 to 1982, Pisano reported, the NAR was responsible for fifteen murders and forty-seven woundings. The NAR was best known for a bomb set off in Rome in 1979 that wounded twenty-three people.

Pisano argued that certain new trends were appearing in right-wing terrorism in the mid-1980s. Groups were linking themselves closely with organized criminal gangs, and there also appeared to be some clandestine liaison with government officials. Specifically, some members of the government seemed to support the objectives of the right-wing groups. The right could also be more closely linked to nationalist and separatist movements. Pisano believed both the left and the right were working to destabilize the government but could never join forces due to ideological differences.

Pisano believed that organized crime in Italy has contributed to its climate of violence and political instability. Organized criminals are not terrorists, but their anarchy encourages an environment of violence. He cited as an example kidnapping, which has become a virtual industry in Italy. Ironically, legitimate businesses have contributed to it by providing kidnap insurance, which automatically provides for payment to kidnappers.

Even though the general level of political violence in Italy declined in the last portion of the 1980s, Pisano believed that the final solution to the problem is to restructure the Italian political system. He argued that Italy must move out of its state of perpetual crisis management and develop pragmatic methods of policy implementation. Until this occurs, political violence and subversion will continue.

NATIONALIST TERRORISM IN SPAIN

Apart from the IRA, the Basque region of France and Spain has been the other major nationalist terrorist campaign in Europe. The Basque region is primarily located in Spain, though it extends over the Pyrenees into France. Basque separatists believe they should be allowed to develop a homeland in Spain, and since the 1950s Basque separatism has been an important issue in Spanish politics. Many Americans are not aware of the Basque lands because they are unaware of the evolutionary nature of many European nations. Robert Clark (1979) said the Basque region of Spain has always had its own language and culture. It has not existed as an independent kingdom since 1035, but it has maintained its own culture separate from Spain. This changed when Francisco Franco, the fascist Spanish dictator, forcibly campaigned against Basque national identity. A 1950s resurgence of nationalism there reflected a centuries-old tradition of unique language and culture.

Edward Moxon-Browne (1987) examined the Basque separatist movement and its relation to terrorism. He maintained that current problems are the result of a gradual loss of national identity that began in the nineteenth century when Madrid assumed greater control of the region, and that was accelerated by industrialization in the early twentieth century. After the Spanish Civil War (1936–1939), the victorious Franco completely incorporated the Basque region into Spain and banned its language and expressions of national culture. Regaining them became the focus of the modern struggle.

Terrorism grew out of the nationalist movement. Moxon-Browne said the Basque Nation and Liberty (ETA) was formed as an offshoot of a nationalist political party in the 1950s. The ETA was composed of young, frustrated nationalists who wanted regional autonomy. It was not originally violent, but its members turned to violence when Franco tried to repress the movement. In 1966 the ETA voted to follow the example of the Third World and engage in armed revolution. In 1968 they started a terrorist campaign.

A more militant group, the ETA-M, broke away from the ETA in 1974. It described itself as the military wing of the ETA, and, according to Moxon-Browne, was responsible for the worst atrocities of the 1970s and 1980s. Both groups have waged a campaign under the name ETA. The campaign reached its zenith between 1977 and 1980 and declined steadily throughout the 1980s.

Robert Clark (1984) studied the characteristics of Basque terrorists, and Moxon-Browne used these as a basis to describe the characteristics of the ETA. Membership matches the composition of the local population, although most terrorists are males. The ETA is primarily a working-class movement, as are many nationalist terrorist groups. Its members were not necessarily raised in a Basque family, but they were raised in Basque enclaves and feel a strong ethnic identity. The overwhelming majority feel they are fighting for all the members of their community.

One of the most interesting characteristics of the ETA is that its members do not view terrorism as a full-time activity. According to Moxon-Browne's research, they keep up some type of employment while serving in the ETA. In addition, most members only engage in terrorism for about three years. After this they return to their full-time occupations.

Clark (1984) said that the eventual goal of Basque terrorism is regional independence. In this sense they are very similar to the IRA. Another parallel is that the majority of Basques do not support the terrorist campaign, even though most support nationalism and some form of independence. In these circumstances, one of the prime tasks of the Spanish government becomes denying the legitimacy of violence.

Moxon-Browne believed the government was beginning to accomplish these objectives by fostering democracy. The Spanish government could open avenues for peaceful resolution of the problem, he argued, by creating opportunities for democratic expression. In spite of this, ETA members feel they have been betrayed by the major powers in Spain: the church, the military, and financial interests. Militants in the ETA do not think democracy will work unless the three major social institutions in Spain agree to recognize Basque nationalism.

The ETA believes itself to be at war with Spanish power, not with the people of Spain. Moxon-Browne said its targets have been extremely selective as a result. The ETA concentrates on high-profile symbolic targets. They attack with guns; assassination is their primary tactic. One to six people are killed in most of their assaults. Most casualties are among police, military, and national guard units. There has been a notable lack of business and civilian targets. Off-duty policy officers and political leaders are the favorite targets for murder.

Jose Trevino (1982, 141–153) examined ETA target selection through an analysis of a Basque police force. In an effort to win the support of the people in the Basque region, Spain has increased the representation of Basques in local police forces. The purpose is to get the Basque community to identify with the forces of order; hopefully this will lessen the number of officers who are murdered.

Trevino approved of the concept, but he did not believe that the ethnic transformation of the police force would end the ETA campaign. Spanish authorities, keeping a low-profile, maintain control of the police. This is not acceptable to extremists in the ETA. Trevino believed they would continue their campaign and that Spanish command officers would become all the more attractive as potential murder victims. It is interesting to note that Moxon-Browne found a high number of command casualties among the Spanish police and military. Trevino's conclusion might indicate that attacks would continue, with rank-and-file officers becoming less susceptible to attack.

Despite the continued campaign, Basque terrorism has decreased in recent years. Moxon-Browne cited three reasons. First Spain and France began cooperating to combat the ETA in the late 1980s. Second, the increasingly Basque police force has reduced the number of assaults on rank-and-file officers and created closer liaisons with the community. Third, discussions about increased autonomy have defused much of the heated atmosphere.

The Basque problem cannot be solved by security forces, who merely carry out the policies of the Spanish government. In this sense there are parallels between the Basque region and Northern Ireland in terms of ethnic terrorism as well as ideological terrorism. In all areas of Europe where terrorism has surfaced, security forces have been called upon to deal with the problem. They have a limited role, however. Unable to solve the problems, they are still required to maintain social order. They don't provide political solutions, but they do provide temporary stability.

EUROPEAN APPROACHES TO COUNTERTERRORISM

European criminal justice systems have approached the problem of terrorism in different ways, but common themes can be gleaned from their experiences. In almost all instances the approach to terrorism has been through legal channels. Great Britain may have pioneered the way by reintroducing emergency powers legislation to Northern Ireland. This has been reinforced recently by the Prevention of Terrorism Act. This legislation has outlawed terrorism throughout the United Kingdom, and has mandated guidelines for citizens, the media, and security forces. In a similar manner, the

Federal Republic of Germany, Italy, and Spain have approached problems through legislation.

Horchem reported that West Germany began enacting antiterrorism laws after the Baader-Meinhof campaign got under way. In 1971 laws strengthening penalties for hijacking, kidnapping, and hostage taking were passed. In 1976, as a result of the Baader-Meinhof lawyers assisting terrorists while in prison, the rights of defense attorneys were limited. They could even be barred from trials if they were suspected of assisting terrorists. By 1978 West Germany had also made it illegal to belong a terrorist group, and the search-and-seizure powers of law enforcement personnel were increased.

Italy also passed similar legislation but approached the problem in a different manner. Pisano said that terrorism was not directly outlawed, but rather that the laws for crimes linked to terrorism were enhanced. In 1979 and 1980 Italy increased the power of laws defining conspiracy and crime leading to disorder and terrorism. Penalties for terrorism were increased, but in 1982 clemency was also formalized. Repentant terrorists could be pardoned if they provided the state with intelligence information. The degree of clemency was dependent upon the value of the information.

The Spanish government also increased the power of its criminal code. Moxon-Browne wrote that 1978 antiterrorist legislation passed in Spain was to be renewed only after annual review, but that it was passed permanently in 1980. Since that time the power of the legislation has been increased further yet. The Spanish government is allowed to declare emergencies based on political situations. There are three levels of emergency powers, ranging from limitations on traffic flow to martial law.

As follows from this legal approach to terrorism, police agencies have become the primary force used against terrorism. Local German police departments are backed up by federal departments for constitutional protection, border protection, and general criminal investigation. Military forces are not used, but the Federal Border Guard, a paramilitary unit with police powers, is employed extensively against terrorism. Its most visible unit is the Federal Border Guard Unit 9 (GSG-9).

Pisano reported that the operational structure of Italian policing has been changed by terrorism. He stated that there were five national police forces in addition to local police. In 1979 legislation creating greater cooperation between the three most prominent police forces was passed. The most visible force, according to M. Daniel Rosen (1982, 42–48), is the Carabinieri. In the 1980s its efforts were coordinated with the two other national police agencies to fight terrorism and organized crime.

As we discussed, the police in the Basque region are being integrated in an attempt to increase Basque membership. The Spanish police remain the central authority, however, and the government views ETA terrorism as a national police problem. The military has not been involved directly, but since high-ranking officers have frequently been the target of the ETA, confrontations between the military and terrorists are not unusual.

Spain has also witnessed a disturbing trend among extremists within the military and police forces. Faced with ETA terrorism and violence from GRAPO, a militant wing of the Spanish communist party, reactionary police and military officers have formed secret death squads. The Warriors of Christ the King was formed in the 1970s. This was followed in the 1980s by the Spanish Anticommunist Alliance. According to

Dobson and Payne (1982b, 214–215), these groups are modeled on the Triple A in Argentina and bear a secret loyalty to Spain's fascist past.

The use of police forces has been augmented by a reliance on intelligence. Throughout Europe military intelligence continues to play a role in counterterrorism, but the ability of the police to collect criminal intelligence has now been enhanced. The Germans use a large information system in Bonn to correlate all terrorist intelligence in the country. Italy's system was forced upon the police by legislation. It has had some dramatic results, but Pisano questioned its overall effectiveness. Military and police forces share intelligence in Spain.

Intelligence gathering is an extremely sensitive area, fraught with internal dysfunctions. Traditional military and political intelligence-gathering organizations do not trust the police. They are concerned with national security and generally treat police units as inferior. The police, on the other hand, frequently become exasperated with national security intelligence personnel, who routinely disregard laws and individual rights.

Intelligence gathering is one of the most important aspects of counterterrorism, but the division between intelligence and police organizations remains. Each one has been charged with a different task. This is most easily understood by looking at the relationship between the FBI and the CIA in the United States. While the agency chiefs generally profess complete cooperation, operational personnel in each agency commonly speak of the other with utter contempt. The situation between police and intelligence personnel in Europe is similar.

Despite these tenuous relations, the European intelligence and police organizations together have revealed an important characteristic of indigenous terrorism. While some commentators such as Stephen Segaller (1987, 36–40) have expressed a growing concern about the unification of European terrorist groups, European police and intelligence investigations suggest the reality is not all that threatening.

For example, Horchem pointed to the links between the RAF and a French terrorist group, Direct Action. The link developed in 1985 when the two groups launched a brief series of related operations. This move was cited as evidence that the radical left in Europe was uniting. The primary co-conspirators were believed to be the Red Brigades, the RAF, and a Belgian group called the Communist Combat Cells (CCC). They were united under the leadership of Direct Action.

Police and intelligence systems have indicated, however, that unity among the groups is symbolic at best. The RAF has remained autonomous and the CCC was probably a direct extension of Russian anti-NATO operations. Pisano said Italian police believe that the BR fled to France out of weakness. Law enforcement agencies believe terrorism is in remission.

Many European police officers believe this is partly due to their own cooperative ventures in counterterrorist investigation. While animosity exists between police and intelligence systems, European police agencies have begun routinely sharing information across borders. Europeans and Americans have long cooperated with each other through INTERPOL, but terrorism brought the need for more direct links.

West German, British, and French police units began meeting together regularly in 1985, the same year that the Direct Action unification was under way. They were joined by other European police departments. By 1987 French and Spanish police began sharing information about the ETA. While the long-term effects of this collaboration have yet to be analyzed, terrorism has resulted in unprecedented European police cooperation. It will not solve the problem of terrorism, but it has enhanced the response of security forces.

SUMMARY OF CHAPTER FOURTEEN

Indigenous terrorism exists not only in Ireland, but on the continental mainland as well. Each European country has experienced its own brand of terrorism, which generally comes from ideological and nationalist groups. The problem of European indigenous terrorism arose in the 1960s but declined in the late 1980s. This may be due to the creation of alternative outlets to social stress among European democracies.

Terrorism in West Germany began in the 1960s with a radical student movement. The main group involved in terrorism at that time was the RAF. By the late 1980s, the RZ seemed to have taken the place of the RAF. The RZ's idea of terrorism is to mount a grass-roots campaign and encourage everyone to be a terrorist. Right-wing terrorists in Germany have attempted to organize, but they have not achieved the operational success of the left. German criminals have mimicked the tactics of political terrorists.

Italian terrorism has its roots in political frustrations and the inability of the government to deal with social problems. The Red Brigades can be linked to the 1960s student movement, but grew in a pattern different than that of Germany. It developed a decentralized organization headquartered in cities around Italy. Italian right-wing groups are also a result of dissatisfaction with the government, and attempt to produce the same disorders as the left wing. Criminal activity, especially kidnapping, is also a reflection of political tension, and organized crime is at least as great a problem as terrorism.

Indigenous terrorism in Spain is essentially the outgrowth of a nationalist campaign by the ETA, a terrorist movement seeking a separate Basque nation. The ETA has targeted security forces as its primary enemy. Right-wing death squads have appeared in Spanish police and military ranks, partly as a response to ETA assassinations.

The European response to terrorism has focused on criminal justice. Every major terror campaign has been followed by attempts to legally contain terrorism in Germany, Italy, and Spain. Law enforcement activity comprises most security force action. Intelligence organizations assist police agencies, but the flow of information is hampered by interagency rivalries and prejudices. Much information has been gained through international police cooperation, nonetheless.

IF YOU WANT TO READ FURTHER . . .

Several books focus on the problem of indigenous terrorism in Europe. A very good overview can be obtained from a volume edited by Yonah Alexander and Kenneth Myers. Entitled *Terrorism in Europe,* the book is composed of a series of articles. Some of the authors assume that you have a good historical background, but the essays are all worthwhile. Stephen Segaller's *Invisible Armies* gives a complete run-down on European terrorism.

Jillian Becker's *Hitler's Children* is fun to read; it's like reading a novel. Its main problems are its early publication date and the fact that many of Becker's conclusions do not match the findings of terrorist researchers. For an in-depth look at German terrorism, you should read the articles by Schiller and Horchem cited in this chapter.

Vittorfranco Pisano's study of violence in Italy is outstanding. It's loaded with information, but easy to understand. It also draws out important criminological and public policy implications. Titled *The Dynamics of Subversion and Violence in Contemporary Italy,* it should be read if you have even the slightest interest in Italian politics.

There are two definitive works on the Basques in English, and both are by Robert Clark. If you want to learn about the ETA, I would strongly recommend both of them. *The Basques* deals with the history of Basque nationalism and violence, focusing especially on Franco's repression. *The Basque Insurgents* is a study of the ETA.

ISSUES
IN
TERRORISM

SOME CONTROVERSIAL ASPECTS
OF COUNTERTERRORISM

In Part II you reviewed selected cases that illustrated different types of and approaches to terrorism. Part III will address some important issues arising from those cases. In this chapter we'll explore some of the controversial areas of security policies and operations. There are no obvious solutions to the problems posed in this chapter; its purpose is only to introduce ideas for your consideration. The impact of the mass media and the future of terrorism will be examined in separate chapters.

After reading this chapter, you should be able to do the following.

1. Explain why counterterrorism is controversial
2. Discuss the different opinions on repression as a technique for preventing terrorism
3. Describe the debate about the elimination of social factors that cause terrorism
4. Outline the arguments for and against using laws to regulate terrorism
5. Summarize the issues involved in the use of military force in counterterrorism
6. Discuss the effect of police secrecy on terrorist investigations
7. Summarize Stinson's conclusions about target hardening
8. Discuss the problem of worldwide conspiracy theories

REPRESSION, TERRORISM, AND THE ORIGIN OF CONTROVERSY

Any policy designed to improve security measures against terrorism will generate controversy. The reason is that enhanced security limits civil liberties. Improved security entails greater powers for security forces, and this increases the power of the state.

If we knew what caused terrorism, the situation would not be so volatile. With all of the issues studied so far, the reader must realize there is no single cause for terrorism. Security policies, therefore, tend to spark debate because they imply that security procedures are the answer to all forms of terrorism. Analysts have offered a variety of opinions on the latter topic, but policy research is in its infancy. Any approach involving counterterrorism is controversial, and all approaches tend to be dominated by ideology rather than hard data.

The lack of research data on counterterrorism has invited a proliferation of assumptions and common beliefs. One of the most common approaches to counterterrorism is based on the assumption that repression is the antithesis of terrorism. In other words, the quickest and most effective method to stop terrorist campaigns is to clamp down on the liberties of a society experiencing terrorist violence. Behind this lies the assumption that terrorists need a free society in which to operate.

Walter Laqueur (1987, 7) is one who argued that terrorism could be destroyed through repressive measures. He felt that the pool of potential terrorists was not unlimited, and that the elimination of the majority of terrorists would reduce incidents. Neil Livingstone (1983) agreed, arguing that repression is the enemy of terrorism. Terrorists cannot operate in a repressive state, according to Livingstone.

Some analysts have pointed to the lack of terrorism in the Eastern Bloc prior to 1990 as evidence for the repression argument. Until recently, the Soviet Union and its Eastern European allies suffered minimal amounts of terrorism because they did not tolerate the freedom necessary to support terrorist organizations. Walter Laqueur also pointed to Khomeini's Iran to illustrate the point. Iran had little internal terrorism, Laqueur argued, because its citizens had been frightened into submission.

But there is a flip side to the argument. Analysts who believe that repression does not destroy terrorism point out that although repression seemed to work in Argentina, by 1989 new leftist revolutionary groups had formed. In El Salvador the unbridled use of death squads not only failed to stop terrorism, but it can be argued that repression actually increased the ranks of the insurgents there.

In our examination of the IRA and ETA we saw that repressive measures were of questionable efficacy. In Ireland the near-defunct IRA was able to rebuild when British soldiers overreacted in 1969. In the Basque region of Spain repression by police forces increased Basque nationalist fervor. In both cases the repression of local nationalist populations was successfully used as a recruiting device by terrorist organizations.

In one of the more recent empirical studies of the effectiveness of repressionist measures, Christopher Hewitt (1984) came to a twofold conclusion. He examined the use of repressionist measures by British security forces on Cyprus in the 1950s and concluded that repression could in fact deter terrorism, but that it had a short-term effect. As repressionist measures continued, they had less and less impact on the amount of terrorism. Repression did not provide a long-term solution, according to Hewitt's research.

Limitations on political activities seem to require the support of the people. In the West government is based upon the assumption that the population is controlled by its own consent. This implies that terrorist policies cannot be based on repression. In the West it may be assumed that a government must mobilize public opinion against a terrorist campaign in order to legitimize restrictions on freedoms. Repression outside of democratic norms is not acceptable.

There is a fairly practical guideline to be gained from this debate for police and other security forces. Stated simply, law enforcement agencies in the West are expected to respond to terrorism within democratic parameters. Repression will not be tolerated by the mores of the culture. The danger is that frustrated groups of soldiers or police officers might decide to take matters into their own hands. Death squads in Argentina and El Salvador emerged when some members of the security forces lost faith in their political leadership.

ELIMINATING THE SOCIAL FACTORS CAUSING TERRORISM

The impulse to counter terrorism with repression is a conservative one. An equally controversial solution has been proposed from the liberal viewpoint. The argument is simple. Some analysts believe that social injustices and the denial of equal participation in a political system are at the root of terrorism. They believe that if the causes were eliminated, terrorism would no longer have a motivation to develop. Terrorism could be eliminated by attacking poverty and injustice. Proponents of this position have argued that counterterrorist policies should be aimed at improving social conditions and opening avenues of political expression.

Such arguments are very similar to those of the "environmental" school of criminology. They are based on the assumption that terrorism, like crime, is spawned by social conditions. Terrorists, like criminals, are the product of their environment, and they turn to violence because they have no other avenue to express their frustration. The ultimate treatment for the problem is to destroy the environment that produces violence.

Several analysts support this premise. Richard Rubenstein (1987) said that instead of attempting to profile the people involved in terrorist activities, we should ask why they engage in violence. He found his answer in the social conditions that bred violence. Rubenstein believed that improving those conditions would eliminate terrorism.

The environmental position was also argued by others. Alfred McClung Lee (1983) believed that the lack of opportunities for meaningful political expression and democratic change were at the root of violence in Ireland. Raymond Corrado and Rebecca Evans (1988) argued that Western European terrorism was diminishing because all but the most violent political extremists had legitimate political avenues through which to express their frustrations. Terrorists, they argued, could not build political support under such conditions.

Once again, Christopher Hewitt (1984) offered an empirical analysis of this premise that throws a wrench into the works. He argued that when governments seek to improve the conditions that are commonly held to produce terrorism, it often produces an unintended effect. Faced with government "concessions," terrorists may increase their activities because they feel the government is weakening. Treating the social conditions producing terrorism may therefore increase terrorism in the short run.

Hewitt added, however, that there is another, long-term aspect to such actions. By responding to causes such as poverty, suppression of political expression, and lack of economic opportunity, governments may defuse potential sources of violence. Hewitt argued that this was a long-term solution. Changes in government policies, he said, affect terrorism in many unintended ways. Initial reforms may increase violence, but the long-term effect of reform may be to defuse the problem.

Not all analysts accept this logic. Walter Laqueur (1987, 6) maintained that social conditions had very little to do with terrorism. He returned to the repressionist argument to make his point. In the twentieth century, Laqueur wrote, evidence indicates that the more repressive a government becomes the less terrorism it suffers. Social conditions are relatively immaterial. Laqueur pointed to ETA terrorism as an example. Basque terrorism, he argued, did not burst forth until the repressive hand of Franco was lifted.

No doubt the causes of terrorism will be the subject of numerous future debates. Neither side has firmly demonstrated its point. Rather than coming to a conclusion useful for counterterrorist policies, the debate has mainly illuminated the political biases of the participants. One side favors eliminating social injustice and the other a more rigorous tactical policy.

OUTLAWING TERRORISM

One of the methods of countering terrorism in Western society has been to focus on the illegality of its actions. Several Western governments have attempted to regulate terrorism by legal means. We have seen examples of this in the Emergency Powers and Prevention of Terrorism acts in Great Britain and Northern Ireland. The Spanish have also invoked a form of emergency legislation to deal with the Basques, and the Germans have enacted a variety of laws in their efforts against terrorism. The basis for these actions is a belief in the efficacy of the legal system.

At first glance it would appear that a legal approach to terrorism would not be too controversial. Laws are passed by legislative assemblies in keeping with democratic traditions. For the most part concepts of constitutionality and individuals' rights are emphasized. Judicial review is incorporated into most antiterrorist legislation, except for the most extreme cases. Terrorism treated as a criminal act rather than a political behavior would seem to be compatible with the democratic process.

The controversy about antiterrorist legislation arises from concerns about civil liberties. The legal solution has become controversial because some critics have maintained that governments have overreacted to the problem of terrorism. They have argued that antiterrorist legislation is based on a political agenda rather than on an objective assessment of the terrorist threat.

Among the staunchest critics of antiterrorist legislation is Beau Grosscup (1987). He was not so concerned with the overreaction of specific legislation, such as the Emergency Powers Act in Ireland, as he was to the whole concept behind such legislation. Grosscup believed that antiterrorist legislation reflected the political will of a philosophical paradigm called neoconservatism.

According to Grosscup, neoconservatism emerged from the Thatcher and Reagan governments. Its central thesis is that most of the problems in the West, including terrorism, have been caused by a breakdown of cherished values and the permissiveness of liberal politics. The agenda of neoconservatism has been to return society to a more orderly course. This necessarily involved legislation of some moral issues to ensure the success of the neoconservative agenda.

Conservative analysts, too, have expressed concern about antiterrorist legislation, not so much from an acceptance of Grosscup's thesis, but from fear of losing civil liberties (McFarlane 1985). Some members of the British government have cast a critical eye toward measures in Northern Ireland, fearing the limitations on freedom imposed by antiterrorist legislation. CIA Director William Webster has issued several warnings about the danger of overreacting to terrorism at the expense of American liberties. Such warnings from conservative politicians hardly fit Grosscup's theories of neoconservatism.

The empirical voice of Christopher Hewitt has noted that terrorism decreases when terrorists are placed in jail. Whether this means that antiterrorist legislation is needed is another issue, however. If jailed terrorists do not engage in terrorism, the process of getting them to jail is still subject to question. The debate centers on an unresolved issue: Should terrorists be jailed under special laws, or should they be charged with standard criminal violations?

THE USE OF MILITARY FORCE AGAINST TERRORISM

Military units have come into play against terrorism in three ways. First and most frequently, military force has been used as an extension of police force. Second, when terrorist groups have been deemed to originate with entire states or geographical areas, military force has been used to strike at terrorist base camps. Third, military force has seen the evolution of counterterrorist commando units. These have been used primarily in hostage rescue operations, but they have also been employed as specialized strike units.

The assumption behind the use of military force is a belief that the terrorist problem has become too great for the civil power of the state. When military forces are employed, in other words, governments feel civilian police forces and the courts are no longer capable of dealing with violence. The terrorists have grown too strong, and police power must be augmented.

Four factors are at the heart of controversy over military counterterrorist activities. First, in Western democracies civil governments have an aversion to the use of military force to ensure domestic peace. The function of the military is not to enforce civil law. In some places, such as the United States, the use of the military in a police role is outlawed.

The second factor is a history of overreaction on the part of military forces. In Latin America, for example, the use of military power to back civil power is often associated with the rise of repression. When military force is used to augment police power, the manner in which it is employed and the duration of its use become critical.

Another controversial aspect of military power is the use of armed forces in retaliatory strikes and in specialized tactical units. Once again, ideology often dominates the arguments for and against such retaliation. One side claims that retaliatory strikes deter terrorism by setting an example; the other believes revenge ultimately creates more terrorism.

There is another area in which military force is the focus of policy debate. When specialized commando units are utilized against terrorists, they raise questions concerning the proper use of force and the role of the military. Few question the deployment of elite hostage rescue units; the debate concerns unconventional military tactics designed to strike at terrorist groups.

No unit better illustrates this last issue than the Twenty-second Special Air Service (SAS) Regiment operating within the British Army. According to John Akehurst (1982), the SAS evolved from British commando units of the Second World War. P. Dickens (1983) said that after the war SAS tactics evolved to meet changing military threats. James Ladd (1986) and Tony Geraghty (1982) said that SAS tactics were designed to offer unconventional military solutions to nontraditional military threats. As the threat of international terrorism grew after World War II, the SAS began to focus on counterterrorist strategies.

By 1975 the SAS had developed state-of-the-art hostage rescue techniques and methods for protecting dignitaries. Tony Geraghty said these functions were developed in the Counter Revolutionary Warfare Wing. Bodyguards and hostage rescue units began to pattern themselves after the SAS, and SAS troops and advisors were involved in several spectacular hostage rescue raids from 1977 to 1980. Their activities have been strongly applauded throughout the West.

There is another aspect to SAS activities, however. Geraghty noted that the SAS was sent to Northern Ireland in about 1975. They have remained ever since, and they have also been deployed against the IRA in other parts of Europe. Geraghty said that the SAS mission has been shrouded in secrecy and that its troops have learned to fight a most unconventional war. Christopher Dobson and Ronald Payne (1982a, 19–50) believed the SAS has become extremely effective against the IRA by intimidating terrorists.

The SAS became the master of the counterterrorist ambush, and the IRA was completely taken aback by its tactics. While the IRA understood the practices of the regular troops and of the RUC under the Emergency Powers Act, the SAS presented a more frightening reality of counterterrorist warfare. The IRA could not compete with the SAS.

Many IRA terrorists were never able to reach their own ambush areas when the SAS was in the countryside. The IRA began to claim that the SAS was a "killer squad" and an example of British terrorism. They had to scream something; they were certainly no match for the SAS.

SAS policies were ruthless and frightening to the IRA. Unlike the police, SAS troopers often killed terrorists during IRA operations. Individuals were shot while picking up weapons or planting car bombs. IRA "roadblocks" were destroyed by SAS ambushes. In 1987 the IRA planned to strike an RUC station for the purpose of killing several police officers. Unbeknownst to the terrorists, intelligence sources had gotten wind of the plot and the police were replaced by SAS troopers in RUC uniforms. Few of the would-be murderers from the IRA left the area alive.

One of the most widely reported events was an SAS ambush on Gibralter in 1988. Three alleged members of the IRA were involved in a plot to set off a bomb during a parade. As they were making preparations, according to news reports, undercover SAS personnel ambushed the terrorists. The terrorists were killed by well-aimed small arms fire. According to all three major American television networks, one of the terrorists was shot repeatedly after falling to the ground.

The unconventional warfare tactics of the SAS have raised a storm of controversy.

Supporters quickly point to the deplorable terrorism of the IRA and the inability of ordinary security forces to make proactive strikes against the terrorists. Critics take a different view. The clear implication of many critics is that SAS policies are acceptable under wartime conditions, but that as the IRA represents a threat to civil peace it should be countered by civil law. Unsurprisingly, Irish republicans lead the critics of the SAS. Denis Faul and Raymond Murray (1976b) claimed the SAS was a death squad.

Grant Wardlaw (1982, 87–102) examined the role of the military in counterterrorist operations, paying particular attention to the SAS. According to Wardlaw, a police force is more suitable for counterterrorist operations than are military units. The police have been better prepared for these activities in Western societies than in others because their organizations have been militarized. The police can adopt military training and tactics when extra power is needed while still maintaining their orientation to civil law.

Wardlaw acknowledged that there are times when the police simply cannot handle a terrorist situation. The threat may become too great, or the police may not be prepared for a rapidly developing terrorist threat. In these cases the military should be brought in subject to civil regulations, norms, and controls. Wardlaw believed that the use of military force often exaggerates the threat of terrorism. He also shared others' concerns about the use of military force to enforce civil law. Military force may be required at times, but its use should be minimized.

SECRECY AND SHARED INFORMATION

Another controversial aspect of counterterrorism is directly related to the internal workings of police agencies. This issue is hidden from those unfamiliar with police operations, and it is not generally discussed by terrorist analysts. It is also closely related to the abilities of the police to respond to crime. Stated simply, the police are reluctant to share information inside and outside of their organizations. This has a negative impact on all criminal investigations, and the effects spill over into counterterrorism.

Abraham Blumberg (1979) judged the problem to originate with the bureaucratic nature of modern policing. Blumberg maintained that police agencies exhibit all the characteristics of bureaucracies: they are highly centralized hierarchical structures under rigid authority. Routine patrol cannot be regulated in such an environment, but routine management at the police station can. Information becomes the basis for such regulation, and control of information translates into power. Therefore, in order to obtain and maintain power police officers develop a fetish for secrecy.

Peter Manning (1976) explained how secrecy maintains social power. The police, Manning said, claim to have a monopoly on understanding and controlling social violence. When the reality of police work is examined, however, they can do neither. If the police admitted they could neither explain nor control crime, they would lose public confidence and support; to avoid this, they act as if they can. Manning called this the manipulation of appearances. The police manipulate their activities to give the appearance that they control violence. The weakness of their position is camouflaged by perpetual secrecy and lying. The police learn to hide information.

Secrecy is dysfunctional for conducting counterterrorism. Aside from the fact that it could be used to cover unauthorized repression, secrecy hampers the police in their response to terrorism. Manning argued that investigative capacity is directly linked to the ability to gather and use information. Secrecy works against the effective use of information. While this issue has not been the subject of extensive public debates, it is a key internal police dilemma.

The effectiveness of sharing counterterrorist information can be demonstrated through the activity of European police agencies in the late 1980s. A variety of factors was responsible for the recent decline of European terrorism, but it is interesting to note that the decline was accompanied by a willingness of police agencies to share information. Organizationally, governments provided more incentives for sharing rather than hoarding information.

STINSON'S ANALYSIS OF SECURITY

In 1984 the Detroit Police Department hosted a joint police–military international conference on counterterrorism. One of the prominent speakers at the meeting was security specialist James Stinson. He has conducted a number of studies of terrorist tactics and was the principal investigator of several Middle Eastern bombings. Stinson compared the methods of tactical assaults on targets with the defensive measures used to protect them. His conclusions sparked a heated debate among security experts.

Stinson (1984) argued that America tends to approach counterterrorism in the same way it does crime prevention. For the past twenty years American police agencies have preached that it is necessary to deny criminals the opportunity to commit a crime. In terms of physical security this means that it is necessary to add security measures to potential targets. For example, merchants might add additional locks, special doors, alarm systems, or even security guards to protect their assets. This process is known as target hardening.

Counterterrorism has been approached the same way. Stinson argued that Americans have come to equate security with fortification. Targets are physically hardened to prevent terrorist assaults. Many analysts have cautioned against such an approach because it allows terrorists to maintain the initiative. Their feeling is that terrorists who encounter a hardened target will simply seek a weaker one. Stinson agreed with this conclusion, but he offered a more provocative analysis.

According to Stinson, target hardening has very little effect on the success or failure of a terrorist assault. This is not because terrorists shy away from hardened targets, but rather because terrorists have a very high success rate in attacks on extremely secure targets. Stinson suggested that physical security has very little to do with stopping terrorist threats.

He supported his analysis with sobering data based on the bombings of several American military and diplomatic installations in the Middle East. When no physical security was present, terrorists had no problem attacking the target. Stinson said they enjoyed a 100-percent success rate. Yet when heavy security was present—including barracades, identification checkpoints, armed guards, surveillance systems, and interdiction teams—terrorists successfully attacked their targets 85 percent of the time.

Physical security only slightly diminished the ability of terrorists to launch a successful assault.

Stinson argued that defensive systems needed to be proactive; target-hardening techniques for the most part are passive. He suggested that the concept of target hardening has to be expanded beyond physical security. He believed that behavioral models, such as those employed by the West Germans, should be used to help predict potential targets. He also believed that intelligence systems should concentrate on identifying and interdicting terrorists before they are able to strike. Stinson felt this would reduce terrorism.

Critics of Stinson's approach point to two problems with his analysis. First, prediction is difficult. Predictive behavior models for terrorist activities provide intelligence, but in no way are they sophisticated enough to pinpoint the detailed probabilities needed to counteract an assault. Just as it is impossible to predict the types of people who will become terrorists, it has not been possible to develop a predictive model of terrorist groups.

The second controversial aspect of Stinson's remarks hinges on the meaning of "success." For example, the Macheteros once fired a rocket at the FBI office in San Juan. The office was fortified and there was very little damage. The Macheteros held this to be a major victory against imperialism, but the janitors who cleaned up a few pieces of broken glass thought it only a mess. The extent of terrorist successes is highly debatable. Stinson's critics argue that physical security measures make people feel safe, and that when people feel safe from terrorism, terrorists can have no victory.

Stinson's findings have been examined and debated within the security community. At first glance, he seems to be highly critical of physical security. (A security executive once complained to me, "Stinson thinks 85 percent of what I do is worthless!") This is not this case, however, because proactive security does not imply that target hardening should be abandoned. Stinson simply suggested that passive security be reinforced with active security. Despite the initial reactions, this hardly seems controversial.

THE TERRORIST INTERNATIONAL?

Modern terrorism is the result of complex social activity on several levels. Different types of terrorism are manifested in various ways. Despite this, some analysts have sought to demonstrate that terrorism originates from a single source. Rather than focusing on the complex issues surrounding terrorism, these analysts tend to explain terrorism as a phenomenon linked to a single activity. They see no difference between criminal and political terrorism, and they believe that most terrorism can be linked to the threat of international communism.

This approach is acceptable to some analysts in the United States who see American interests as threatened by international communism. This is especially true among certain law enforcement and intelligence groups who believe internal and external communism is one of the greatest threats to American democracy. By viewing terrorism as an anti-Western activity and as a new form of war, the complex nature of terrorism is readily simplified. They believe the West is under conspiratorial attack.

Examples of this position are easy to find. Roberta Goren (1984) completed a work on the link between international terrorism and the Soviet Union. In its foreward Jillian Becker claimed that Goren's work demonstrated the communist conspiracy. Robert Conquest also supported the view.

In 1984 the Western Goals Foundation produced a video program titled "No Place to Hide." The tape has been used in several criminal justice courses on terrorism. In the video several law enforcement informants, terrorist experts, and Congressional representatives argue that the Soviet Union is at war with the United States and that terrorism is its principal form of combat. The narration blames everything from the tragic demonstration at Kent State University to the attempted assassination of Pope John Paul II on an international communist terrorist conspiracy.

In the early 1980s Claire Sterling (1986) released *The Terror Network*. The book enjoyed tremendous popular success and has been reprinted as a mass market paperback. In it, the Rome-based journalist declared that almost all international terrorism could be linked to Russian sponsorship.

According to Sterling, the Soviets came to realize that they could manipulate left-wing terrorism to fulfill their own political agenda. Right-wing terrorists were not related to Soviet intentions (a point contested by some conspiracy theorists), but left-wing terrorists were nothing less than a direct extension of Soviet foreign policy. For the Soviets, Sterling argued, terrorism has become a substitute for war.

If the proponents of Soviet strategy and conspiracy theory are correct, the way the majority of Western analysts conceive of terrorism is wrong. If the Soviet Union is ultimately responsible for international terrorism, then we must radically change the way terrorism is approached. Terrorism would not be the outcome of complex social reality, but rather the deliberate action of a state determined to rule the world. The conspiracy thesis would have a tremendous impact on the approach to terrorism if it were accepted.

In terms of counterterrorism, the West's approach to the Soviet Union would need to change dramatically. Western governments would be forced to enlist their own client states to engage Soviet surrogates. Police forces would need to be completely militarized, and civilian criminologists would need to stop looking for the causes of terrorism and start searching for Communists. Unfortunately for those seeking an easy answer, the world of terrorism is not as simple as the conspiracy theorists would have us believe. If nothing else, recent events in the USSR illustrate this.

Soviet connections with the PLO and the Cuban Directorate of Government Intelligence (DGI) are no secret. But the United States is also engaged in similar practices through its links to the Mujahedin in Afghanistan and the Contras in Nicaragua, for example. While the Soviets have spelled out their military support for revolutionary organizations in their doctrine, both East and West use clandestine forces and surrogates. But forging relationships that foster unconventional warfare is a far cry from controlling the striking power of international terrorism.

James Adams (1986) may have provided the best criticism of the theory when he examined Sterling's thesis. Adams wrote that when *The Terror Network* first appeared William Casey, the late director of the CIA, read the book and brought it to a staff meeting. According to Adams, Casey instructed his deputies to do everything possible to publicize the book. Sterling's message about the Soviet involvement in terrorism, Casey said, was a message that the CIA had been trying to prove for years.

Adams stated that Casey's advisors and deputies began to grow uneasy at his request. One advisor asked him to check the sources of evidence in Sterling's book. Then a deputy pointed out that most of Sterling's thesis was based on a disinformation campaign conducted by the CIA. In short, the CIA had created a large body of phony documentary evidence to prove that terrorism was the result of an international communist conspiracy. Sterling had cited most of that evidence, according to Adams. Casey dropped his order to publicize the book.

Grant Wardlaw (1988) offered more biting criticism. He argued that in the first part of the eighties, conservative ideological analysts pointed to state sponsorship as the primary source of terrorism, ultimately linking terrorism to the Soviet Union. As relations between the United States and the USSR began to thaw, the conservative spotlight gradually moved away from the Soviets to focus on Iran and Libya. Proponents of state-sponsored theories then believed those nations to be the primary culprits.

Wardlaw argued that the search for state sponsors has done much to confuse the issues surrounding terrorism. The argument for sponsorship lacks clarity, he wrote, and definitions of terrorism are always politically motivated. He cited Syria as an example. Wardlaw believed that the Syrians were responsible for more terrorism in the last half of the 1980s than most other states, yet the United States focused on Iran and Libya because they were more visible and acceptable targets. Americans had a diplomatic need for Syria and did not wish to offend it by labeling it a terrorist state.

In order to understand terrorism and to develop workable counterterrorist security tactics, it is necessary to consider each case of violence individually. No two terrorist campaigns are the same. It is possible to glean general security principles by comparing various manifestations, but the practice of counterterrorism must be based on an in-depth assessment of each individual threat. Blind faith in a KGB international terror network does not facilitate this understanding, but hinders it.

SUMMARY OF CHAPTER FIFTEEN

This chapter reviewed some selected controversies that terrorism poses for security forces. Counterterrorist tactics and policies are bound to be controversial, because we cannot point to a single cause of terrorism and we are not sure what security policies prevent it. As a result, counterterrorist discussions and actions are often guided by ideology.

The topics examined in this chapter were (1) repression as a control, (2) social injustices as a cause, (3) legal attempts to control terrorism, (4) the function of military units in counterterrorism, (5) the effects of police secrecy, (6) the effectiveness of physical security measures, and (7) the conspiracy theory. With the exception of the conspiracy theory, it is difficult to determine which positions on these topics are correct due to the dominance of ideology over pragmatism.

IF YOU WANT TO READ FURTHER . . .

Many of the controversial aspects of terrorism are raised in most books on the subject. If you are interested in the tactical aspects of counterterrorism, one of the best books is Grant Wardlaw's *Political Terrorism*. Wardlaw examines the nature of counterterrorist actions from a security and criminological standpoint. He leaves few stones unturned and develops several interesting conclusions.

The best empirical analysis of policy is *The Effectiveness of Anti-Terrorist Policies* by Christopher Hewitt. Although he focuses on the broad issue of government policy, Hewitt's findings are particularly important to criminal justice and security agencies. His book is a refreshing change of pace from a myriad of ideological works.

If you're interested in the military aspects of special counterterrorist units, several popular books provide a surprising amount of tactical detail. Of those readily available, I recommend the following: James Ladd's *SAS Operations,* Philip Warner's *The Special Air Service,* Tony Geraghty's *Inside the SAS,* and Peter Koch's and Kai Hermann's *Assault at Mogadishu.* Koch and Hermann provide a great deal of information on the elite German border guard unit GSG-9.

TERRORISM AND THE MEDIA

One of the most controversial current topics of terrorism analysis is the way the print and electronic media cover terrorist acts. Police and other government forces operate with a set of objectives diametrically opposed to the goals of reporters covering an event. In addition, experts have heatedly debated the effects of electronic coverage on terrorism, and there are several competing schools of thought on the effectiveness and impact of newspaper coverage. Regardless of which side of the question you favor, reporting terrorism will remain controversial because the media has become part of the terrorist event. The purpose of this chapter is to summarize some of the issues inherent in the relationship between the media and terrorism.

After reading this chapter, you should be able to do the following.

1. Outline the three positions on the relationship of the media to terrorist events
2. Explain contagion theory within the context of terrorism and the media
3. Using the findings of Schmid and de Graaf, discuss terrorism as a form of political communication
4. Discuss the problems of censorship and the First Amendment to the U.S. Constitution

SECURITY FORCES VERSUS REPORTERS

Within the ranks of everyday police or military operations it is not uncommon to hear many statements criticizing the media. Chiefs of police and military commanders generally do not seem to respect media figures and reporters, and their attitudes are reflected by their line personnel. Specialized command units are often created in police agencies to portray a favorable image to reporters, and military units are similarly assigned to public relations. Reporters, newspapers, and television news teams are generally not trusted.

Police and security forces officially represent the social order, and they are charged with the maintenance of stability. They see themselves as servants of the public interest in America and other Western democracies. Additionally, they believe they make decisions for the public good. They perceive themselves to be the forceful extension of democracy.

Members of the media, on the other hand, have two competing and often contradictory roles. They control the flow of information while simultaneously making the news entertaining enough to "sell." M. Cherif Bassiouni (1981) pointed out the potential conflict these competing purposes bring to terrorist scenarios. The police or security forces are charged with bringing the situation to a successful conclusion. Their job is primarily to preserve order and protect lives. The press has the job of transmitting information while making the story interesting to the consumer. During live coverage the media must also facilitate interaction between the scene and the audience.

Bassiouni (1982) argued that the police must respond to terrorist situations by lessening their drama and psychological impact. News producers, however, see the drama of terrorism as the perfect attention grabber. Bassiouni pointed out that terrorism defies security force goals while catering to the goals of the media.

The issue of terrorism brings the animosity between the police and the media to a head. It is a reflection of a deeper conflict between those in government and those in the media. Government officials seldom enjoy having their decisions analyzed and criticized to a mass audience, yet that is one of the major functions of media presentations. Tensions run high in terrorist situations, especially when the event is ongoing or when hostages are involved. Television and newspaper reporters usually arrive at the scene of a terrorist incident within minutes of security forces. Distrust and distaste often dominate their interactions from the start.

This predicament gives rise to three different points of view on terrorism and the media. First, some members and supporters of the press see the media as a quasiconstitutional force keeping the government in check. A second point of view is that of some analysts who agree about the democratic role of the press, but who want to limit it during the coverage of terrorism. They see the media as terrorism's ally. A third faction feels the opposite is true: the media may exploit terrorism, but they rarely convey messages favorable to terrorists. We'll briefly examine each position.

Members of the news media generally have no intention of endangering lives or escalating terrorism. Abraham Miller (1982, 133–147) pointed to internal codes controlling journalistic excess. These guidelines indicate that news organizations expect their reporters to behave responsibly. Under no circumstances are they to interfere with security forces or to assist terrorists, even inadvertently. Journalists, interestingly enough, seem to fear manipulation by terrorists as much as they do government control.

The media claim to have the right to have access to and to report all findings. Some analysts and government officials claim this right hampers governmental decision making. Reporters have defended their position by saying that in a democracy all the people have a right to influence decision making. They can only do this, some media defenders have claimed, when they are given unrestricted information.

Several terrorist analysts vehemently disagree with the position taken by the media. According to Yonah Alexander (1984, 135–150), terrorism is a new type of struggle, and terrorists have made the media their ally. Modern terrorists view communication as a potential weapon, and they seek to exploit it by eliciting media exposure. Willingly or unwillingly, the media have become the tool of terrorism.

Other critics have gone even further than Alexander. Norman Podhoretz (1981), for example, said modern reporters are in subtle, informal collusion with terrorists. Terrorists and journalists are in business for mutual benefits, Podhoretz said. The media do not consciously conspire with terrorists, but they play to each other's needs. Yoel Cohen (1983) shared this view. The PLO, he said, would not exist were it not for media coverage and media sympathy. The media in turn make a profit by reporting PLO violence.

In separate works, J. Bowyer Bell (1978) and H. A. A. Cooper (1977a, 140–156) agreed that the media produced terrorist theater. The drama of terrorism makes for great news stories: it is filled with action and is entertaining. In this sense, the press has become an ally of terrorism. Yet both Bell and Cooper questioned the effectiveness of this relationship. Subsequent research has indicated that the coverage of terrorism is not helpful to terrorist groups. Terrorists want to use the media for propaganda purposes, but the media focus on violence. News reports rarely explain the causes of the terrorists, and they almost never portray terrorism in a favorable light.

Quite a bit of research indicates that the press makes a poor terrorist ally. Gabriel Weimann (1983) found that reporting terrorist events increases the public's knowledge about terrorism but builds little sympathy for terrorists. Michael Kelly and Thomas Mitchell (1981) also found that news reports focus mainly on violence, which paints a negative picture of terrorism. L. John Martin (1985) agreed, implying that a negative media image causes terrorist propaganda efforts to backfire.

Other researchers have questioned the effectiveness of the electronic and printed media in serving the needs of terrorists. David Paletz, Peter Fozzard, and John Ayanian (1982a; 1982b) conducted two studies on the way the media handles terrorism. They examined coverage of the Red Brigades, the IRA, and the FALN by both television and newspapers. In their television study the researchers focused on the three major American network nightly news programs. They searched for the method of reporting as well as any biases. They concluded that television generally ignores the motivations for violence, focusing instead on the activity itself.

The method of coverage used by network television was found to have a negative effect on terrorism. The purpose of terrorism is to communicate a message about its goals and objectives. Network TV doesn't do this. In fact, the audience is appalled by terrorist violence. Paletz et al. concluded that television engenders no sympathy for terrorists because coverage clearly portrays terrorism as an illegitimate form of violence.

The three researchers approached newspapers in a similar manner. In an analysis of the *New York Times* they found a coverage pattern similar to that of television. Although the *Times* provided greater depth in the issues surrounding the terrorist event, the acts of terrorism were generally delegitimized. They also found another trend in press coverage: it tended to legitimize the government instead of the terrorists. Far from being a tool for terrorism, the media served the interests of the government. Paletz et al. claimed the perspectives of news stories depend on the source, and in the majority of terrorist stories examined, governments were the source. Reporters are under pressure to produce quickly, so over 75 percent of their stories came from government sources. This meant that reporters also picked up the labels that government sources applied to the terrorists. The terrorists seldom fared well.

THE CONTAGION EFFECT OF MEDIA COVERAGE

Some analysts are not as concerned about the content of press coverage as they are about its role in spreading terrorist violence. Does the coverage of terrorism inspire more violence? In other words, Is it contagious? Some analysts believe it is. This has been a hotly debated issue leading to discussions of censorship.

Allan Mazur (1982) was convinced that media reports have a suggestive effect on violent behavior. His study compared bomb threats in the nuclear industry to the amount of press coverage nuclear power plants received. He began by noting that news reports of suicides increase the actual number of suicides, and he wondered if he might find a similar pattern in the nuclear industry.

Mazur examined bomb threats against nuclear power facilities from 1969 to 1980, comparing them to the amount of coverage devoted to nuclear power on television and in newspapers. He found that the number of threats proportionately matched the number of news stories. When coverage increased, bomb threats increased, and the converse was also true. When coverage decreased, bomb threats decreased.

Mazur concluded that the media can affect public behavior through suggestion. Coverage of problems in the nuclear industry seemed to suggest that there was a need for a general public response. Some people chose to make their statements violently. He was not sure if the media alone caused the response, or if their reports combined with another factor. He was positive about the contagion effect, however.

M. Cherif Bassiouni (1981) located the problem of contagion in the arena of police–media relations. He believed that media coverage had several contagious effects. Media reports promote fear and magnify the threat in the public mind. That fear spreads. The media also influence the way terrorists select their targets; to spread violence, terrorists select targets for maximum publicity. The media have become the vehicle for the psychological impact of terrorism. From this standpoint, terrorism is contagious: media-reported terrorism causes more terrorism.

Bassiouni applied the contagion hypothesis to criminal and political terrorism. Researchers, he believed, have not derived any conclusive data, but the contagion theory is popularly accepted, especially in law enforcement circles. Although the evidence remains inconclusive, Bassiouni decided there must be some basis to the contagion theory.

Philip Schlesinger (1981) was not willing to go quite so far. He believed that the contagion theory was merely a hypothesis of terrorist researchers. Schlesinger did not reject the notion that terrorism could be contagious, but he denied that current evidence proves the point. Contagion theory is used to support censorship, Schlesinger argued, and analysts who subscribe to it are attempting to force their opinions on those who can control the media.

TERRORISM AS A FORM OF COMMUNICATION

One of the most comprehensive research studies on terrorism and the media came from Alex Schmid and Janny de Graaf (1982), two noted terrorist analysts from the Netherlands. They said the lack of understanding of the media's role in terrorism is due to a lack of research. They sought to fill in some blanks by conducting a systematic study of the relationship between the media and insurgent terrorism.

The purpose of the study was to examine the links among terrorist violence, the Western news media, and the political actors. Schmid and de Graaf hoped such information would help to bring peaceful resolutions to violent situations. Their study has been hailed as a landmark of empirical research on terrorism and the media.

They began their examination by looking at the nineteenth-century Western anarchists, whose violence, they argued, resulted from political frustration. The anarchists were frustrated because they could not make their voices heard. Anarchists began using violence to communicate their political stance and to force governments to respond to their demands. They found that resorting to violence publicized their presence.

Schmid and de Graaf said the twentieth century changed the nature of insurgent terrorism. In the nineteenth century terrorists had used selective assassination; in the twentieth, they opened a new technological arsenal of weapons. In addition, their choice of victims changed from selected government or industrial symbols to neutrals selected at random. This policy enhanced the communicative ability of terrorism, especially when it was combined with the revolution in the electronic media.

Modern communications and the mass media have helped shape the nature of modern conflict. Schmid and de Graaf argued that in the past warring parties limited their strategy to major battlefields. Rapid communications, however, allow reporters to travel to the war zone and bring the battlefield to the general public. As a result public opinion has become a major aspect of modern warfare, and mobilizing public opinion is deemed a necessary strategy to achieve victory. This attitude is reflected in terrorism.

Some terrorist groups have successfully exploited this factor, while others have been less opportunistic. Schmid and de Graaf believed that the way the media is used depends on the cultural conventions of a country. In Latin America, they argued, terrorists routinely seize broadcasting stations because government censorship is common. The Palestinian *fedayeen,* on the other hand, have taken full advantage of the Western press. The United States is a media-saturated nation, and the American media generally give any type of terrorist a forum. In Western Europe terrorists use the media in an attempt to build public empathy.

The relationship does not only benefit the terrorists. Schmid and de Graaf stated that the media have been able to exploit terrorists for their own needs. It is difficult to define terrorism, but the media has done so by applying labels to terrorist actions. They are selective about calling violent events terrorism, but when they do the public is provided with a de facto definition. The media labels terrorism and covers it according to its own needs.

The Dutch researchers gave several reasons for Western news coverage of terrorism. The two leading reasons are the commercial profits obtained by reporting sensationalized violence and the public's inherent interest in terrorism. People also turn to the media for vicarious experiences, so terrorism has become a form of thrilling entertainment. Audiences also enjoy the rebellious aspects of terrorism and may safely identify with these rebels. Finally, television routinely favors violent over nonviolent stories.

The Western news media have few moral qualms about their desire to report terrorism, because they see themselves as neutral purveyors of information. Schmid and de Graaf pointed to the irony of this belief. The thesis of a news story, they wrote, depends on the source. Stories generally reflect the source's perspective. The press is far from objective, in part because it is manipulated by its sources. Ironically, the greatest source of terrorist information is the government. Therefore, most Western news items reflect a governmental perspective.

Still, no one element—governmental or terrorist—has managed to control the media entirely. This has resulted in all types of outcomes from media reports on terrorism. Relatively minor violence may be exacerbated. The act of reporting may change the character of what is being reported. In hostage situations reports may jeopardize operations and lives. The media may magnify the threat of terrorism to the government, and, conversely, reports of violence may encourage more terrorism. Quite often the public identifies with neither the government nor the terrorists, but focuses on the victims. Given this myriad of possible effects, Schmid and De Graaf believed, the media have a responsibility to the public.

They placed the blame for increased terrorism on the media. Violence, they concluded, breeds violence. Terrorists learn their tactics and copy methods from the mass media. Media coverage also serves as a motivation for terrorism. The most serious outcome is that violence seems to increase during media coverage. The mass media have become the perfect instrument of violent communication.

Schmid and de Graaf concluded that the media must live up to their responsibility to Western civilization. Their job is not simply to report; they should become effective agents of positive social change. Their job should be to illustrate social problems and positive solutions rather than engaging in competition for the public's attention. Schmid and de Graaf suggested that specially elected regulatory bodies should be created to ensure that the media follow this path.

CENSORSHIP AND FREEDOM OF THE PRESS

The questions raised by Schmid and de Graaf ultimately lead to questions of censorship. Few officials want direct censorship of the press, but many agree with British terrorist expert Major General Richard Clutterbuck (1975) that the press should be a neutral factor. Officials and conservative analysts don't want to limit free speech and writing, but they are very concerned about the media playing into the hands of terrorists. Therefore, it is not surprising that we hear calls for varying degrees of media control.

Schmid and de Graaf devoted an entire chapter to the issue of censorship. The original purpose of free speech, they argued, was to allow a person to present a view. With the rise of capitalism in the 1800s and the corporate consolidation of the media, newspapers and eventually television news assumed the responsibility for protecting individual freedom of speech. Freedom from censorship came to equal the media's right to report the news.

In today's society the control of information is far more important than it was in the past. Schmid and de Graaf argued that the media have been given a very powerful position in the modern world as the gatekeepers of public information. The media are responsible to the large corporate conglomerates who own them for their activities. Since their reporting and interpretations have the potential to cause disasters, Schmid and De Graaf suggested that it might be appropriate to hold the media accountable to another, more disinterested source.

Attitudes toward censorship tend to take one of three forms. A small minority of analysts have suggested some form of governmental control. Another group has urged the media to develop more stringent internal guidelines. A third group has argued that the media are already bound by internal controls that serve established governments.

Christopher Kehler, Greg Harvey, and Richard Hall (1982) discussed the first two viewpoints from a Canadian perspective. A free press is an unquestioned Canadian right, deriving from a cultural history shared with America.

Still, Kehler et al. argued that some form of media regulation is necessary because media coverage of terrorist events endangers lives. There have been instances where the press has negotiated with terrorists; where press corps members have entered lines of fire and secured zones; and some cases where hostage rescue forces have been pictured on live television as they moved in for an assault. They felt the government had a legal right to regulate, but that it would be better if the broadcast industry developed responsible standards of its own. Internal regulation is more beneficial than governmental regulation.

At the same time, they pointed out, the public does have a passive system to redress injuries that result from negligent news coverage. When the media behaves negligently, victims have the right to sue. There is little history of such cases, because the concept is in its embryonic stage. But if media news coverage violates standards of responsible reportage and someone is injured as a result, a tort claim may be pursued.

Juanita Jones and Abraham Miller (1979) suggested that government restrictions on dissemination of news does not violate the press's rights during emergency conditions. They compared hostage situations against the First Amendment to the U.S. Constitution and viewed the problem through case law history. They argued that this is not an abstract problem, because lives hang in the balance during hostage crises. They believed that reporting and the freedom to report are not the only critical concerns in such crises: the impact of the media on the event and media interference with police operations have also become central issues.

Jones and Miller said the press could legally be excluded from certain areas during hostage situations. Especially when police procedures call for secrecy in an attempt to save lives. However, the Supreme Court will not allow blanket denial through a set of preconditions. Limitations to access are supported only when they are justified by the circumstances. A total or standard ban on news access is not acceptable.

Hostage situations especially bring the point to bear. Jones and Miller said the police have a right to place restrictions on the press. The media's behavior at a hostage incident is a matter of conduct, not speech. Denial of access and specific regulations for the protection of hostages are acceptable, and such actions have been upheld in the courts. It is a form of censorship acceptable under the First Amendment, and it denies neither free speech or free press.

Jones and Miller took pains to demonstrate that they were not trying to stop reporting. Miller's (1982) additional work provides further evidence of this. The researchers believe that the police only want the media to behave in a responsible manner. The police can help to encourage this by providing the media with realistic and timely information. If the police and media could come to an understanding of each other's position, Jones and Miller believed many confrontational issues could be mollified.

Philip Schlesinger (1981) took a different view and argued that the media in Western democracies favor government stability. Schlesinger centered his argument on the concept of legitimization. He argued that the media have worked to delegitimize terrorist violence.

Schlesinger examined the role of security forces in Northern Ireland. He concluded that the British press has acted "responsibly" in terms of covering the government's position. That is, the press supported the government while condemning anti-government violence. He felt that such actions only reflected "responsibility" as defined by the government.

Schlesinger argued that terrorism is approached by the media on official and unofficial levels. Language is crucial because it can serve to either support or deny the legitimate right of a political position to exist. Officially, media language is used to criminalize terrorism. Unofficially, it can serve to criminalize the issue that motivates terrorists.

The language of news reporting has become secondary to the way in which governments have been portrayed by the media. Schlesinger said that when the first incidents of modern terrorism started to break out in Northern Ireland, reporters went to locations and tried to print and broadcast objective reports. Such reports were often as critical of government policy as they were of terrorists. This enraged the government, especially the security forces engaged in dangerous activities.

The government soon came to Richard Clutterbuck's conclusion that the media was a neutral weapon. It could be used for or against terrorism. The best way to take advantage of the weapon was to cooperate with the media. Schlesinger said this process was accompanied by strong pressures for the press to behave within guidelines deemed to be responsible by the government. It has evolved into a *de facto* form of censorship, and the British government has found an ally in the press.

Schlesinger's conclusions are by no means readily accepted. Some distinguished terrorist experts have scoffed at his suggestions, while others who believe the media ends up being sympathetic to governmental authority structures reject the notion that the power of the media has been compromised. Recent censorship efforts on the part of the Thatcher government, for example, would suggest that the Prime Minister does not believe the press to be her best ally in Northern Ireland.

Still, Schlesinger's position is one of many controversial aspects surrounding the media and terrorism. Even voluntary guidelines are subject to scrutiny from those who think they should be stronger and those who think they should not exist. Noam Chomsky and Edward Herman (1977, p. 85) pointed out that control of the media can legitimize government terrorism. Others are aware of this, Abraham Miller believed, including police chiefs.

Regardless of any of the analytical positions taken about the media, security forces are faced with practical problems during terrorist events. Joseph Scanlon (1981 and 1982) addressed the issue, and he suggested some practical guidelines for operating with the media during a terrorist incident. Scanlon believed that if reporters are treated honestly and given the whole story, they will usually avoid interfering with police and security measures.

Scanlon focused on the problem of terrorism as a live event. He did not feel that the majority of reporters were irresponsible, but argued that media presence was a tactical consideration, and that it often interfered with the successful resolution of the event.

Scanlon gave several suggestions for managing the media during a terrorist incident. The media should be pooled and given valid information. He emphasized that the media should be given as much information as possible with the understanding that critical tactical items could not be utilized until their publication or broadcast posed no threat to the public. If members of the media threaten operations or lives, they should be detained until their reporting no longer endangers an event. Scanlon was hesitant to recommend the use of police power against the media, however, and he believed that media actions during terrorist events should be voluntary.

Western governments tend to approach the media with fear and mistrust. In terrorist incidents police and military forces reflect this attitude. When lives hang in the balance, security forces should be able to expect cooperation from the media. After the event, however, the media are free to analyze and give critical opinions. This is a cherished aspect of freedom, and it's something that many terrorists would like to take from us.

SUMMARY OF CHAPTER SIXTEEN

This chapter introduced one of the most controversial aspects of counterterrorism, the relation of the media to terrorism. Approaches to the topic are sharply debated. Police and security forces generally dislike the media and hold reporters in contempt. However, they usually do not officially call for limitations on a free press and will attempt to manipulate the press for their own ends.

Terrorism has become a form of political communication. Schmid and de Graaf examined this issue with one of the strongest studies of the media and terrorism. They concluded that the media give terrorism a forum and there must be some attempt to regulate that forum in the public interest. Their book also dealt with most of the major issues raised in this chapter.

While terrorists attempt to use the media, the effectiveness of this strategy is questioned. Some analysts believe the media are a catalyst to violence, and others believe that sensationalized reporting of violence has blown the problem of terrorism out of proportion. Another group of analysts believe that the media have been relatively ineffective in achieving terrorist goals. Violence is reported, but terrorist goals and objectives are generally ignored.

The contagion effect refers to the theory that reporting terrorist violence causes more terrorist violence. Some analysts subscribe to this theory, although they admit is has not been proven. Other analysts dismiss the idea due to lack of evidence.

The issue of censorship is an area where most analysts agree. Few seem to advocate direct censorship. There are a variety of lesser degrees of media control that are frequently advocated. It may be possible to invoke some of these without violating individual rights and the freedoms of speech and press. Internal methods of self-regulation are the most frequently recommended method of dealing with the press. Even these are controversial, however, because they foster cooperation with the government.

IF YOU WANT TO READ FURTHER . . .

There are three excellent books that examine the problem of media relations. Alex Schmid and Janny de Graaf, *Violence as Communication,* is outstanding. In a short volume they raise most of the critical issues. It's easy to read, very informative, and their research is thorough and complete. In short, the work is excellent.

Abraham Miller's *Terrorism, the Media, and the Law* is also a high quality work. Miller weaves a host of strong articles together with informative commentary. The book is limited to hostage situations, but that strengthens the work because Miller has a readily definable unit of analysis. It can be complemented with M. Cherif Bassiouni's *Terrorism, Law Enforcement, and the Mass Media.*

TECHNOLOGY, TERRORISM, AND THE FUTURE

Many analysts have speculated about the future of terrorism. In doing so, they produce models and hypothetical scenarios based on past and current trends in terrorism. Many of their theoretical speculations end by focusing on a most frightening prospect: the combination of modern technology with terrorism. In a technological society we are vulnerable both to assaults on technology and assaults by weapons of mass destruction. So far these have only been potential threats, but should they materialize, technological terrorism could pose a challenge to criminal justice and political systems that would make the manifestations we've reviewed thus far pale by comparison. In this chapter we'll examine the potential of technological terrorism, with special emphasis on domestic vulnerability.

After reading this chapter, you should be able to do the following.

1. Describe the possible future of terrorism in terms of technological targets and weapons
2. Summarize Brian Clark's thesis concerning technological terrorism
3. Describe America's vulnerability to technological terrorism
4. Explain the state of security in the energy industry
5. Discuss the likelihood and nature of nuclear terrorism

TECHNOLOGY AND THE FUTURE OF TERRORISM

Technological terrorism is one of the more frightening scenarios we can imagine. Modern societies are susceptible to two methods of technological terror. The first would be the employment of mass destruction weapons or the conversion of an industrial site, for example a chemical plant, into a massively lethal instrument through sabotage. The other method would be to attack a source that supplies technology or energy. The results of either type of attack could be catastrophic. Technology looms as a potentially sinister partner in the evolution of terrorism.

When analysts examine potential directions for terrorism, they can seldom avoid discussing the threats to and from technology. This does not mean that technological terrorism is inevitable, nor that governments cannot cooperate to solve future problems of terrorism. It does mean that of all the potential problems of terrorism, multiplying its force by technological means seems to be a grave threat.

Grant Wardlaw (1982, 173–184) made a good point about the future at the conclusion of an excellent study of terrorism. Prediction, he wrote, is an occupation fraught with uncertainty and danger. Keeping the "soft" nature of futuristic analysis in mind, Wardlaw still maintained that it is necessary and important to speculate about future trends in terrorism. In fact, Wardlaw argued, speculation should be an activity of as many analysts as possible.

Other analysts have shared Wardlaw's concern for the future of political violence. Richard Falk and Samuel Kim (1984) approached the problem strategically. They viewed the threat as one not so much of localized violence but of a social failure to think about all forms of violence from a global perspective. Walter Laqueur has speculated about a "Sarajevo effect," in which a terrorist incident expands into a war. He referred to the assassination of the Austrian Archduke in Sarajevo in August 1914. This act led to the start of World War I. J. Bowyer Bell (1985, 41–52) also raised this point. A single terrorist act is usually unlikely to create a major war, Bell said, but the practice of terrorism can be a prelude to greater conflict.

In almost all speculations, analysts eventually turn their attention to technology. The greatest danger looming in the future of terrorism, according to Wardlaw, is the potential destructive power of modern weaponry. Instruments of mass destruction could be used to produce the ultimate form of terrorism. Wardlaw said the essential question was whether terrorists would use such weapons. If they did, the face of terrorism and the nature of governmental response to the problem would change.

Trends in modern terrorism are disturbing, Wardlaw said, because of the increasingly nihilistic spirit among terrorist groups. Groups that engage in thrill killing and that devalue human life may not be deterred by the prospect of massive deaths. Many terrorist groups are calling for worldwide revolution, but this is not a concrete goal. Faced with this fact, individual terrorists are abandoning their national and group identifications to focus on abstract reasons for violence. Technology in the hands of such people, Wardlaw argued, is volatile.

Wardlaw was not the first to predict the potentially devastating effects of technology and terrorism; many other analysts have raised the issue. The literature tends to focus on (1) attacks on technological installations, (2) the use of Chemical-Biological Weapons (CBW), and (3) the use of radioactive material and nuclear weapons. Nuclear terrorism seems to dominate the literature, yet terrorism in any of these areas could produce devastating effects.

BRIAN CLARK'S VIEW OF TECHNOLOGICAL TERRORISM

Brian Clark (1980) joined the ranks of those talking about the future of terrorism in a book titled *Technological Terrorism*. This often overlooked work was written from a fairly conservative viewpoint, and Clark took few pains to hide his biases. Despite this, he produced an overview that outlines most of the potential problems posed by technology and terrorism.

Clark believed that the importance of terrorism has been understated. Terrorism as

BRIAN CLARK'S THESIS

- Technology creates new opportunities for terrorism.
- Technology will make terrorism a major problem of the future.
- America is especially vulnerable to technological terrorism.
- American bureaucracies have failed to take protective measures against technological terrorism.

Source: Brian Clark, *Technological Terrorism* (Old Greenwich, Conn.: Devin-Adair, 1980)

a weapon used to obtain a criminal or political goal, he wrote, will become a problem that will make many other social problems shrink to insignificance. Political terrorism will emerge as the foremost world problem, Clark claimed, when terrorists begin to take advantage of technology.

Clark argued that terrorism has crossed the threshold into a technocratic age. He wrote his book to demonstrate the potential magnitude of the problem, and to charge the American government with insufficient preparation. He also wanted to demonstrate the political and social implications of large-scale technological terrorism. In short, his book was designed to be a warning.

Clark leveled three charges against technological industries. First, he said, the nuclear waste material is not adequately protected and can easily be stolen. Second, he believed that chemical production facilities are vulnerable and that CBW agents can be stolen in a manner similar to nuclear waste. Third, Clark felt the transportation system for dangerous chemical and nuclear agents lacked proper safeguards. These areas leave America vulnerable, he maintained.

Clark acknowledged that his view was not accepted by all, citing comments by J. Bowyer Bell to show the other side. Clark admitted that many analysts did not believe that terrorism was extremely significant; however, he rejected their arguments on the basis of the coming threats from technology. The potential lethality of technology has rendered those arguments meaningless, he implied. Terrorism will become supremely important through the use of technology. In Clark's mind, it's only a matter of time.

Clark's thesis was quite clear. The level of technology in modern society has placed the nation at risk. Technology is a neutral tool that can be used for good or evil. The only method of ensuring social goodness is to develop adequate industrial security measures and to enforce them rigorously. Neither the federal government nor American industries take such measures today, Clark charged. This leaves America vulnerable to technological terrorism.

AMERICA'S VULNERABILITY TO TECHNOLOGICAL TERRORISM

The United States is one of the most technologically advanced superpowers in the world. Technology has opened new doors to the future, which many Americans have taken for granted. Other national competitors have taken advantage of America's nonchalant attitudes toward technology at times, but the united States stands as one of the masters of new industrial and technological techniques. Along with Japan and Western Europe, the United States is a technologically oriented society.

The irony of America's success with technology is that the country has become vulnerable to attacks on technology and by technology. You don't have to agree with Brian Clark's political position to understand that America is dependent upon technology. While the military has taken some pains to shield defense and weapons systems from interference, civilian industry has fallen behind. Given America's dependence on technology, this has created a window of opportunity for terrorists.

There is no clear way to react to the problem of technological vulnerability. Some analysts, like Clark, have called for rigid new safeguards and massive new security efforts. Others believe that a calm assessment of potential threats is more in order (Heim, 1984). Analysts do not agree about the extent of the threat, and most of them focus on weapons of mass destruction.

A study by B. J. Berkowitz et al. (1972) was one of the first to examine the implications of mass destruction weapons in the hand of terrorists. Its conclusion was that civil chaos would result. According to the study, several attempts were made by radical groups to employ some level of CBW attack from 1967 to 1970. Although this information is dated, the threat still remains.

The Berkowitz study pointed to several areas of vulnerability. Metropolitan water supplies are subject to contamination. Although poisons would dissipate in a large volume of water, general public reaction would be one of panic. In addition, criminal organizations have attempted to produce chemical weapons for extortion and assassination. Berkowitz et al. also pointed out attempts to steal or produce CBW weapons in Europe and the United States.

Robert Mullen (1978) also examined modern society's vulnerability to technological weapons. The capacity for mass destruction is a recent historical development; in the past, killing many people required many people to do the killing. Technology has changed this. Mass destruction terrorism can be inferred from CBW and nuclear weapons.

Mullen stated that terrorism based on massively destructive weapons involves skills that few terrorist groups possess. Technical weapons require technical skills and support networks. Many groups lack these capacities, but Mullen said the past may not be indicative of the future. The capability for mass destruction exists.

Robert Kupperman and Darrell Trent (1979) dealt with some of the issues posed by technological threats. Kupperman (1985) examined the issue again, with a specific focus on organizational responses to technological threats, and he described the potential threat technological terrorism posed for America. Both Kupperman and Trent struck a middle ground, however, between complacently ignoring the problem and overreacting to it.

In Kupperman's and Trent's analysis, responsible policies should be developed to meet the potential threat. The response should be one of policy analysis and application. Industrial and technological safeguards will work only if they are accompanied by proper emergency procedures. Kupperman and Trent suggested models for restructuring U.S. federal bureaus and emergency planning networks.

Unlike many analysts, Kupperman and Trent believed the analytical literature on

ANALYSTS SPECULATE ON THE FUTURE OF TERRORISM

Analyst	View
• Grant Wardlaw	• There is an increasing nihilism among terrorist groups. Technology offers the ultimate weapon.
• Walter Laqueur	• There is danger of a "Serajevo Effect": a single incident or campaign could spread to war.
• J. Bowyer Bell	• A "Serajevo effect" probably will not develop from terrorism. Incidents need to be placed in perspective.
• Robert Kupperman	• Planning for technological terrorism is essential.
• Brian Jenkins	• Terrorism will continue as a mode of conflict. Social deterrents may eliminate technological terrorism.
• Paul Wilkinson	• Western democracies may have to accept minimal levels of terrorism.

terrorism to be fairly complete. They did not see the need to add to the theoretical body of knowledge. Instead, they argued that Walter Laqueur had appropriately described the historical and social background of terrorism, and that Brian Jenkins had adequately analyzed current and future trends. The only gap in the literature was in the area of technology.

The authors were trying to get policy moving in the direction of counterterrorism; technology provided their motivation for writing. Kupperman and Trent believed the problem of technological terrorism has generally been ignored, and that the U.S. government is woefully underprepared to deal with a technological threat. Accordingly, they described several horrifying potential scenarios for terrorism (without giving terrorists clues on weapons construction or utilization). They hoped the devastating nature of the scenarios would grab the attention of policy makers.

Kupperman and Trent believed that social deterrents are insufficient to rule out the use of mass destruction weapons. Increased possession of nuclear and chemical weapons has been accompanied by their use or threatened use. Nation-states have legitimized the use of mass destruction weapons, hence paving the way for terrorists to adopt them. The analysts concluded that it was time to start realizing the truly destructive nature of such weapons.

The most common type of terrorist weapon is a bomb. It has been historically popular, it is easy to deliver, and it poses a difficult puzzle for police to solve. Kupperman and Trent said that when groups mature they move toward more sophisticated weaponry, but that in their initial stages bombs are cheap and effective tools. The danger, they stated, was an enhancement of bombs through CBW or nuclear capacities.

Kupperman and Trent argued that either type of weapon could be used for psychological impact, and they predicted the public would react with panic if either nuclear or CBW agents were introduced by terrorists. They believed that because nuclear bombs are difficult to make or steal, terrorists would achieve the same psychological impact by spreading radioactive materials. If accompanied by an effective means to spread the toxins, chemical and biological weapons have a similar potential.

Attacks on technological targets are another way to achieve mass destruction without the need for technological weapons. In addition, Kupperman and Trent pointed to the ability of terrorists to paralyze the economy by attacking targets necessary for production and service. Electrical power grids are important from this standpoint, and the most likely targets are transmission lines and transformers. Gas and petroleum lines are even more vulnerable, and conventional and nuclear power plants present tempting targets. They also considered the vulnerability of computer networks.

Counterterrorism must begin with a reorganization of the federal bureaucracy, in the Kupperman and Trent analysis. Without discussing the specifics for each agency, their recommendations can be summarized in two steps. First, the analysts wanted a few key federal agencies to have definite responsibility for emergency situations. The role of individual agencies should be spelled out in policy guidelines, and bureaucratic managers should be held responsible for their agencies' abilities to deal with potential terrorism.

In their second series of recommendations, Kupperman and Trent wanted the government to develop realistic management plans to coordinate the response of its various units. There is a need to develop a small, knowledgeable crisis staff to direct operations in the event of a technological attack. It is not necessary to become preoccupied with the counterterrorist functions of each agency, according to the researchers, because mass destruction terrorism is a low-probability occurrence. On the other hand, preparing for an event with key managers can serve as both a deterrent and a practical method to restore normalcy in the event of an attack.

Some security specialists have focused on the idea of prevention. Indeed, it comprises the philosophy of such organizations as the American Society for Industrial Security. Prevention of technological terrorism is a corollary to safeguarding technological materials. Robert Kindilien (1985) made this argument with reference to the nuclear power industry. Enhanced security will reduce the risk of losing dangerous material and waste. American industry is currently vulnerable to such losses. Kindilien said it is necessary to assess risks and attack them with an aggressive security system.

Another point about U.S. vulnerability has been raised by many analysts. If a mass destruction threat were to develop, the initial public reaction would probably be one of panic. A fear of chemical weapons and radioactivity pervades popular culture. If the American public believed a major city were in jeopardy, there is reason to believe that fear would sweep the nation. In a climate of fear, cherished liberties can be destroyed.

Russell Ayers (1975) and John Barton (1980) have raised this issue. In this sense, the corollary to technological terrorism is another threat; in reacting to potential mass destruction, security and police powers would be increased. In many societies this has been closely correlated with a decline in civil liberties. The ideal function of the American justice system is to protect individual rights, but historically, in times of panic, the government and the police have forgotten this. There is good reason to believe that technological terrorism would create panic, and civil rights often fall by the wayside in such situations.

Another potential target of technology and terrorism is the energy industry. Oil and gas are America's chief means of energy. An article placed in an addendum to the Kupperman and Trent analysis raised the problem of securing the energy industry. The transportation and storage of fossil fuels, the analysis claimed, is not as safe as people tend to assume.

SECURITY PROBLEMS IN THE ENERGY INDUSTRY

America relies on energy to support its technology, so the interruption of energy supplies could be construed as a national security threat. If a nation or terrorist group could shut off America's energy, it could close down major portions of the economy. Secure energy production, transportation, and storage are all critical to the United States.

Kupperman and Trent stated that electrical systems are quite vulnerable. Attacks on key power transformers could stop the flow of electricity to large segments of the country for quite some time. Damage to key generating facilities would also have long-term effects. Currently, the threat is localized. Power stations and transformers have been subject to industrial sabotage, but this has had only local, short-term effects.

Maynard Stephens (1979, 220–223) assessed the vulnerability of America's oil and natural gas systems. The interruption of oil and gas delivery would have the most devastating economic impact of any attack on energy, Stephens argued. The reason is that oil and gas form America's greatest source of energy. Seventy-five percent of U.S. energy needs are filled by oil and gas. While electrical power grids have backup supplies, there is no method of continuing service if oil and gas lines are destroyed.

The efficiency of the systems is the major problem, according to Stephens. Industry and government planners designed America's pipeline for maximum flow and distribution of the product. As a result, oil and gas are channeled over hundreds of miles in a highly efficient and concentrated set of pipelines. But this very efficiency has weakened the security of the system: an attack on a major line would magnify the scope of the attack.

Stephens's main worry was the lack of federal and state concern about protecting the gas and petroleum industries. He claimed the government had taken almost no protective measures. Since domestic terrorism in America has not often been manifested, threats to the oil and gas industries appear to be abstract, Stephens said.

Yet, Western Europe has experienced attacks on its energy systems, as have a number of nations in Latin America. And terrorism poses only a portion of the problem: energy distribution systems are subject to military attack. Intelligence agencies began working with the Department of Energy in 1987 to protect the distribution system from potential terrorist and military threats (Associated Press, 1989).

THE THREAT OF NUCLEAR TERRORISM

The most frequently discussed aspect of future terrorism, however, is not energy but nuclear targets, which seem to have a psychological impact far more frightening than others. This may be due to the widespread fear of nuclear weapons or to the fact that a greater body of knowledge on the topic is available to the general public. Regardless, it is frequently impossible to discuss the future of terrorism without examining the potential impact of nuclear weapons or radioactive material.

One of many analysts who have addressed the question of nuclear terrorism, B. David (1985), made four critical points about the issue. First, nuclear terrorism and CBW terrorism are usually discussed together. Second, true nuclear terrorism requires either a difficult production process or the theft of radioactive materials or weapons; CBW agents are easier to produce and obtain. Third, a key to responding to nuclear terrorism is to discern the motivation of a group that might be willing to use weapons of mass destruction. Finally, there are still social sanctions against employing such weapons.

Martha Crenshaw (1977) raised other points. First, she was concerned about the proliferation of nuclear materials on an international level. The abundance of nuclear materials, she believed, increases the likelihood of nuclear terrorism. Second, the spread of the nuclear power industry increases the potential for attacks on power-generating stations and for the theft of waste material.

Brian Jenkins (1975; 1980; 1986; 1987) has approached the question of nuclear terrorism cautiously and provided several answers. He gave his first answer in 1975, admitting that his conjectures were purely speculative. His answer has been slightly revised through the years, but his initial response has been partially validated by fifteen years of developments in terrorism. Basically Jenkins said that we don't know whether terrorists will use nuclear weapons, but that there is no reason to assume that they will automatically evolve in that direction.

Jenkins said that nuclear terrorism is possible, but he was reluctant to see it as a major threat. He believed that terrorists are rational creatures and that nuclear terrorism is irrational. Nuclear weapons would not work in low-level operations, and once the weapons were deactivated there would be no incentive for governments to continue to honor any negotiated promises. Social restraints tend to make nuclear devices impractical.

The possibility of nuclear terrorism cannot be dismissed, however. Jenkins pointed out that many Americans believe that nuclear terrorism is more likely than a nuclear confrontation between the superpowers. Trends in nuclear-related terrorism have reinforced public beliefs. Jenkins equated attacks on nuclear facilities with nuclear terrorism and his data indicated that attacks on the nuclear industry and on weapons facilities are declining. Yet attacks continue, accompanied by the general trend toward an increased level of violence. If nuclear terrorism is not inevitable, it is certainly not impossible.

Nuclear terrorism could take a variety of forms. Jenkins said terrorists could attack nuclear facilities and use the entire area as a weapon. They could also simply steal material or ask a ransom for it. Terrorists could fabricate a nuclear hoax, and the ensuing panic might be as dangerous as a threatened explosion. In the simplest case terrorists could spread radioactive material; in the most complex case they might detonate a device. The term *nuclear terrorism* is employed frequently, but for a variety of potential activities.

Several people have commented on Jenkins's position. Paul Leventhal and Yonah Alexander (1986, 33–53) recorded a speech by Jenkins on nuclear terrorism and some experts' reactions to it. One member of the audience, David Mabry of the U.S. Department of State, agreed with Jenkins about the rationalism of terrorists. Terrorists, he said, do not kill for the sake of killing; they have a political motivation for their actions.

Mabry disagreed with Jenkins's assessment of the probability of nuclear terrorism, though. Given the increasing violence of terrorist groups, the lure of nuclear terrorism is becoming too great. State sponsors of terrorist groups have greater access to nuclear weapons, further increasing the possibility of such terrorism. Mabry was convinced that Iran and Libya would not hesitate to utilize nuclear weapons in a terrorist incident. Finally, since bombing is the most popular terrorist act, nuclear bombing might simply be viewed as its logical extension.

Yural Ne'eman, a physics professor and former Israeli cabinet minister, also disagreed with Jenkins. He was critical of Jenkins's reluctance to distinguish attacks on nuclear facilities from the use of nuclear materials in terrorism. They are not the same thing, Ne'eman said, and they certainly were not positively correlated. In other words, declining rates of attacks on nuclear facilities had no connection with the probability of a use of nuclear material in terrorism.

Ne'eman also believed that most terrorism was state sponsored. Far from the individual groups that Jenkins imagined, Ne'eman saw most terrorists as an extension of national governments. Ne'eman agreed with Mabry that Iran and Libya were prime candidates for the use of nuclear weapons. He also added Iraq to the list and completely dismissed Jenkins's notion that terrorists would be somehow constrained by a sense of morality.

Neil Livingstone and Terrell Arnold (1986, 1–11) addressed the issue of state sponsorship in another forum. Both analysts agreed with Ne'eman's position on state-sponsored terrorism. They also pointed to evidence applicable to the nuclear debate when they claimed that the Red Army Faction had developed a CBW capability. Technological terrorism is not a future issue; a major terrorist group has already exhibited its capability of using it.

Larry Collins and Dominique Lapierre (1980) wrote a terrorist thriller titled *The Fifth Horseman* that featured state-sponsored technological terrorism. The premise of the book was that Moamar Khadaffy had managed to construct a hydrogen bomb. He placed the weapon in New York City by clandestinely shipping it to the United States with a semiautonomous terrorist group. An army of bureaucrats, emergency personnel, and police officers searched for the device while Khadaffy negotiated with America's president about Libyan demands. America was paralyzed in its response for a variety of diplomatic reasons.

The premise of the novel is exciting, and the book is fun to read. In the real world, however, there are some problems with the scenario. If any nation were to sponsor nuclear terrorism against the United States, it would run the risk of full American military reprisal. Mass destruction could obviously be construed as an act of war; American military forces have been deployed for terrorist events of far less significance than a nuclear explosion.

Several analysts have hinted at this military constraint. Frank Forrest (1976) raised the issue by naming nuclear terrorism as one of a set of factors leading to war. Stanley Berard (1985) addressed the same reality, repeating most of the social deterrence arguments of Jenkins. Nuclear terrorism may be possible, but state sponsorship is questionable. The sponsor would have to remain anonymous, and terrorism without a message serves no purpose.

Still, as Jenkins has indicated, the possibility of nuclear terrorism cannot be ruled out. As the West prepares for the future of terrorism, the United States has taken a number of steps to prepare for emergencies. On the international level concerns have been raised about nuclear proliferation. Senator Alan Cranston (1986, 177–181) called for controls on exports of Western nuclear technology. Senators Sam Nunn and John Warner (1987, 381–393), the ranking members of the U.S. Senate Armed Services Committee, urged U.S.–Soviet cooperation in preventing nuclear terrorism.

On the domestic scene, concern has prompted action on several of the proposals of Kupperman and Trent. According to Christopher Dobson and Ronald Payne (1982b, 51–76) an array of federal agencies has joined forces to combat all acts of domestic terrorism. Donald A. DeVito and Lacy Suiter (1987, 416–432), both directors of state emergency planning agencies, suggested that the Federal Emergency Management Agency (FEMA) be used as the clearinghouse for bureaucratic coordination. Terrorism, they said, demands emergency planning. FEMA has taken a leading role in preparing for effective interaction among local, federal, and state governments. It is supported by a variety of federal regulatory bodies and law enforcement agencies.

In terms of combating nuclear terrorism, one of the most important units is the Nuclear Emergency Search Team (NEST). According to Mahlon Gates (1987, 397–402), NEST teams were created by the Atomic Energy Commission in 1975 after a host of nuclear emergencies, including a police hunt for an alleged homemade nuclear bomb in Boston in 1974. The purpose of NEST teams is to assist with nuclear security and to locate nuclear weapons, materials, and devices.

NEST teams would become active in any domestic incident involving nuclear terrorism. Notification of the emergency would go from the FBI to the Department of Energy. NEST units are then dispatched to assist law enforcement personnel, in cooperation with the FBI. Their job is to locate potential devices, neutralize them, and assist with proper cleanup. Gates rated the teams favorably, indicating that they can rapidly provide local and federal law enforcement with nuclear expertise.

Not everyone agrees with Gates's assessment, nor are all analysts convinced that the government is prepared for nuclear terrorism. Critics of federal emergency policies continually emerge. Recent oil spills off the coasts of Alaska and New Jersey, they argue, demonstrate the government's inability to respond to massive emergency disasters. Critics feel that FEMA behaves according to bureaucratic norms, and that it cannot deal with the problems of disasters such as nuclear terrorism. At this point, critics lack the evidence to support their position because nuclear terrorism is potential terrorism. As of this writing it is an issue of the future.

SUMMARY OF CHAPTER SEVENTEEN

Terrorism analysts frequently attempt to predict the course of terrorism. When they examine the future, they view the greatest potential problem of terrorism as technology. Technology can be used to enhance terrorist weapons; also, modern societies are vulnerable to assaults on their technological facilities.

Brian Clark believed that we have entered a new age of technological terrorism, and he raised several concerns about America's ability to deal with it. Clark maintained that our technological industries—especially the nuclear industry—are not secure. He believed nuclear material can be routinely stolen and that we have failed to safeguard CBW agents and energy transport systems.

America is vulnerable to a variety of terrorist scenarios involving technology. To date they are potential scenarios. Kupperman and Trent suggested that an effective counterterrorist policy should be based on an analysis of potential mass destruction and management plans to thwart that potential. They believed mass destruction by terrorists to be a low-probability event, however. Other analysts demonstrated that the energy industry was vulnerable and a more likely target than mass destruction of population.

The threat of nuclear terrorism dominates much of the literature on the future. Jenkins did not believe that it was likely, but he would not rule out the possibility. Others believed that we are on the threshold of an age of nuclear terrorism. The United States has assigned the responsibility of preventing nuclear terrorism to a host of federal and state bureaucracies.

IF YOU WANT TO READ FURTHER . . .

A number of excellent works on technology and terrorism go beyond the introductory statements of this chapter. Brian Clark's *Technological Terrorism* is an excellent though opinionated examination and critique of the federal response. Three books of readings are also very good: Augustus Norton's and Martin Greenberg's *Studies in Nuclear Terrorism* and two works edited by Paul Leventhal and Yonah Alexander, *Nuclear Terrorism* and *Preventing Nuclear Terrorism*. An outstanding comprehensive view of the world's nuclear problems is Louis René Beres's, *Apocalypse: Nuclear Catastrophe in World Politics*.

One of the better reviews of technological terrorism and preparations for the future is Robert Kupperman's and Darryl Trent's *Terrorism: Threat, Reality, and Response*. While most works of this period are becoming dated, Kupperman and Trent provide an excellent projection of possible future courses of terrorism and policy response. Their text is followed by a set of well-chosen readings that tend to emphasize their points. The technical descriptions of nuclear and CBW scenarios, in particular, are outstanding.

WORKS CITED

Abos, Álvaro. (1981). "Circles of Violence." *This Magazine* (May/June): 8–16.

Adams, James. (1986). *The Financing of Terror*. New York: Simon & Schuster.

Akehurst, John. (1982). *We Won a War*. London: Russell.

Alexander, Yonah. (1984). "Terrorism, the Media, and the Police." In Henry Han (ed.), *Terrorism, Political Violence and World Order*. Landham, MD: University of America Press.

Alexander, Yonah. (1976). "From Terrorism to War: The Anatomy of the Birth of Israel." In Yonah Alexander (ed.), *International Terrorism*. New York: Praeger.

Alexander, Yonah and Kenneth A. Myers (eds.). (1982). *Terrorism in Europe*. New York: St. Martin's Press.

Alexander, Yonah and Alan O'Day (eds.). (1984). *Terrorism in Ireland*. New York: St. Martin's Press.

Americas Watch Committee/American Civil Liberties Union. (1982). *Report on Human Rights in El Salvador*. New York: Vintage Books.

Andics, Helmut. (1969). *Rule of Terror*. New York: Holt, Rinehart & Winston.

Arnson, Cynthia. (1982). *El Salvador: A Revolution Confronts the United States*. Washington, D.C.: Institute for Policy Studies.

Arnson, Cynthia. (1981). "The Frente's Opposition: The Security Forces in El Salvador." In Marvin E. Gettleman et al. (eds.), *El Salvador*. New York: Grove Press.

Aryan Nations. (n.d.). "The Death of the White Race." Hayden Lake, ID: Aryan Nations.

Ayers, Russell W. (1975). "Policing Plutonium: The Civil Liberties Fallout." *Harvard Civil Rights–Civil Liberties Law Review* 10: 369–403.

Bakunin, Mikhail. (1987). "Revolution, Terrorism, Banditry." Reprinted in Walter Laqueur and Yonah Alexander (eds.), *The Terrorism Reader*. New York: Meridian Books.

Balsinger, David W. (1988). "Narco-Terrorism Shooting Up America." *Scoreboard* (n.v.): 14–16.

Barton, John H. (1980). "The Civil Liberties Implications of a Nuclear Emergency." *New York University Review of Law and Social Change* 10: 299–317.

Bass, Gail and Brian Jenkins. (1983). "A Review of Recent Trends in International Terrorism and Nuclear Incidents Abroad." Santa Monica, CA: The Rand Corp.

Bassiouni, M. Cherif. (1982). "Media Coverage of Terrorism." *Journal of Communication* 32: 128–143.

Bassiouni, M. Cherif. (1981). "Terrorism and the Media." *Journal of Criminal Law and Criminology* 72: 1–55.

Bassiouni, M. Cherif (ed.). (1983). *Terrorism, Law Enforcement, and the Mass Media*. Rockville, MD: NCJRS.

Beam, Louis. (1985). "Klan Alert." Hayden Lake, ID: Aryan Nations.

Becker, Jillian. (1977). *Hitler's Children*. Philadelphia: Lippincott.

Becker, Jillian. (1984). *The PLO*. New York: St. Martin's Press.

Beckwith, Charlie and Donald Knox. (1985). *Delta Force*. New York: Dell.

Bell, J. Bowyer. (1974). *The Secret Army: A History of the IRA, 1916–1970*. Cambridge, MA: MIT Press.

Bell, J. Bowyer. (1976). "Strategy, Tactics, and Terror: An Irish Perspective." In Yonah Alexander (ed.), *International Terrorism*. New York: Praeger.

Bell, J. Bowyer. (1985). "Terrorism and the Eruption of Wars." In Ariel Merari (ed.), *On Terrorism and Combating Terrorism*. Landham, MD: University of America Press.

Bell, J. Bowyer. (1978). "Terrorist Scripts and Live Action Spectaculars." *Columbia Journalism Review* 17: 47–50.

Bell, J. Bowyer. (1975). *Transnational Terror*. Washington, D.C.: American Enterprise Institute.

Bell, J. Bowyer and Ted Robert Gurr. (1979). "Terrorism and Revolution in America." In Hugh D. Graham and Ted Robert Gurr (eds.), *Violence in America*. Newbury Park, CA: Sage.

Bell, J. Bowyer. (1978). *A Time of Terror*. New York: Basic.

Berard, Stanley, (1985). "Nuclear Terrorism: More Myth Than Reality." *Air University Review* 36: 30–36.

Beres, Louis. (1980). *Apocalypse: Nuclear Catastrophe in World Politics*. Chicago: University of Chicago Press.

Beres, Louis. (1983). "Subways to Armageddon." *Society* 20: 7–10.

Beres, Louis. (1979). *Terrorism and Global Security*. Boulder, CO: Westview.

Berkowitz, B. J. et al. (1972). "Superviolence: The Civil Threat of Mass Destruction Weapons." Santa Monica, CA: Advanced Concepts Research.

Blumberg, Abraham S. (1979). *Criminal Justice: Issues and Ironies*. New York: New Viewpoints.

Bodansky, Yoseff. (1986a). "The Rise of Terrorism in the USA." The Maldon Institute (unpublished draft).

Bodansky, Yoseff. (1986b). "Terrorism in America." Paper presented at EITWAT (Equalization on the War Against Terrorism), New Orleans, LA (September).

Bolz, Francis. (1984). Hostage negotiation training, Grand Rapids Police Department, Grand Rapids, MI (May).

Bolz, Francis A. and E. Hershey. (1980). *Hostage Cop*. New York: Rawson, Wade.

Bonner, Raymond. (1984). *Weakness and Deceit: U.S. Policy and El Salvador*. New York: Times Books.

Boyce, D. G. (1984). "Water for the Fish, Terrorism and Public Opinion." In Yonah Alexander and Alan O'Day (eds.), *Terrorism in Ireland*. New York: St. Martin's Press.

Buchanan, Paul G. (1987). "The Varied Faces of Domination: State Terror, Economic Policy, and Social Rupture During the Argentine 'Proceso', 1976–1981." *American Journal of Political Science* 31: 336–380.

Buckley, William F. (1974). "Argentine Terror." *National Review* (4 March): 286.

Burton, Anthony. (1976). *Urban Terrorism*. New York: Free Press.

Butler, Ross E. (1976). "Terrorism in Latin America." In Yonah Alexander (ed.), *International Terrorism*. New York: Praeger.

Cable, Larry. (1987). "Piercing the Mists: Intelligence and Policy in Constrained Lethality and Ambiguous Conflicts." Paper presented at the International Studies Association Section on Military Studies Conference, Atlanta, GA.

Cable, Larry. (1986). "Soviet Low-Intensity Operations and NATO." Paper presented at the International Studies Association Section on Military Studies Conference, Harvard University (November).

Chomsky, Noam and Edward S. Herman. (1977). *The Washington Connection and Third World Fascism*. Boston: South End Press.

Chubin, Shahram. (1987). "Iran and Its Neighbours: The Impact of the Gulf War." *Conflict Studies* 204: 1–20.

CISPES. (1981). "El Salvador: A Political Chronology." In Marvin E. Gettleman et al. (eds.), *El Salvador*. New York: Grove Press.

Clark, Brian. (1980). *Technological Terrorism*. Old Greenwich, CT: Devin-Adair.

Clark, Robert. (1984). *The Basque Insurgents*. Madison, WI: University of Wisconsin Press.

Clark, Robert. (1979). *The Basques*. Reno, NV: University of Nevada Press.

Cloward, Richard and Lloyd Ohlin. (1960). *Delinquency and Opportunity*. New York: Free Press.

Clutterbuck, Richard. (1975). *Living with Terrorism*. London: Faber & Faber.

Coates, James. (1987). *Armed and Dangerous: The Rise of the Survivalist Right*. New York: Hill & Wang.

Cobban, Helene. (1984). *The Palestine Liberation Organization: People, Power, and Politics*. Cambridge, England: Cambridge University Press.

Cohen, Yoel. (1983). "The PLO: Guardian Angels of the Media." *Midstream* (February): 7–10.

Cohn, Norman. (1957). *The Pursuit of the Millennium*. London: Secker and Warburg.

Collins, Larry and Dominique Lapierre. (1980). *The Fifth Horseman*. New York: Avon Books.

Collins, Larry and Dominique Lapierre. (1973). *O Jerusalem*. New York: Pocket Books.

Committee of the States Assembled in Congress. (c. 1985). "Special Orders." Unpublished.

Coogan, Tim Pat. (1971). *The IRA*. London: Fortune.

Cook, Schura. (1982). "Germany: From Protest to Terrorism." In Yonah Alexander and Kenneth A. Myers (eds.), *Terrorism in Europe*. New York: St. Martin's Press.

Cooper, H. A. A. (1977a). "Terrorism and the Media." In Yonah Alexander and Seymour Finger (eds.), *Terrorism: Interdisciplinary Perspectives*. New York: John Jay.

Cooper, H. A. A. (1978). "Terrorism: The Problem of the Problem Definition." *Chitty's Law Journal* 26:105–108.

Cooper, H. A. A. (1977b). "What Is a Terrorist? A Psychological Perspective." *Legal Medical Quarterly* 1: 8–18.

Corrado, Raymond and Rebecca Evans. (1988). "Ethnic and Ideological Terrorism in Western Europe." In Michael Stohl (ed.), *The Politics of Terrorism*. New York: Dekker.

Costigan, Giovani. (1980). *A History of Modern Ireland*. Indianapolis, IN: Bobbs-Merrill.

The Covenant, the Sword, and the Arm of the Lord. (1982). *Defense Manual*. Zorapath-Horeb, AR: CSA.

Cox, Robert. (1983). "Total Terrorism: Argentina, 1969 to 1979." In Marcha Crenshaw (ed.), *Terrorism, Legitimacy, and Power*. Middletown, CT: Wesleyan University Press.

Cranston, Alan. (1986). "The Nuclear Terrorist State." In Benjamin Netanyahu (ed.), *Terrorism: How the West Can Win*. New York: Avon Books.

Crenshaw, Martha. (1977). "Defining Future Threats: Terrorists and Nuclear Proliferation." In Yonah Alexander and Seymour Finger (eds.), *Terrorism: Interdisciplinary Prespectives*. New York: John Jay.

Crenshaw, Martha (ed.). (1983). *Terrorism, Legitimacy, and Power*. Middletown, CT: Wesleyan University Press.

Crozier, Brian. (1975). "Terrorist Activity: International Terrorism." Hearings before the Subcommittee to Investigate the Administration of the Internal Security Act and Other Internal Security Laws of the Committee on the Judiciary. 79th Congress, 1st session, Washington, D.C.: United States Senate.

David, B. (1985) "The Capability and Motivation of Terrorist Organizations to Use Mass-Destruction Weapons." In Ariel Merari (ed.), *On Terrorism and Combating Terrorism*. Landham, MD: University of America Press.

Debray, Regis. (1967). *Revolution in the Revolution?* Westport, CT: Greenwood.

Deerin, James B. (1978). "Twilight War." In U.S. Congress, *Northern Ireland: A Role for the United States?* (Report by two members of the Committee on the Judiciary, based on a factfinding trip to Northern Ireland, the Irish Republic, and England.) 95th Cong. (Aug./Sept.) Washington, D.C.: Government Printing Office.

Der Spiegel (October 6, 1980): 37–46.

DeVito, Donald A. and Lacy Suiter. (1987). "Emergency Management and the Nuclear Terrorism Threat." In Paul Leventhal and Yonah Alexander (eds.), *Preventing Nuclear Terrorism*. Lexington, MA: Lexington books.

di Tella, Guido (1983). *Argentina Under Perón*. New York: St. Martin's Press.

Dickens, P. (1983). *SAS: The Jungle Frontier*. London: Arms and Armour.

Didion, Joan. (1983). *Salvador*. New York: Simon & Schuster.

Dobson, Christopher and Ronald Payne. (1982a). *Counterattack: The West's Battle Against the Terrorists*. New York: Facts on File.

Dobson, Christopher and Ronald Payne. (1982b). *The Terrorists*. New York: Facts on File.

D'Oliviera, Sergio. (1973). "Uruguay and the Tupamaro Myth." *Military Review* 53: 25–36.

Doyle, Kate and Mark Statmen. (1988). "A Dirty War." *The Nation* 246: 701.

Duff, Ernest and John McCamant. (1976). *Violence and Repression in Latin America*. New York: Free Press.

Dworkin, Ronald. (1986). *Nunca Más: The Report of the Argentine National Commission on the Disappeared*. New York: Farrar, Straus & Giroux.

Ehredfeld, Rachel. (1986). "Narco-Terrorism." Paper presentated at EITWAT Equalization in the War Against Terrorism, New Orleans, LA (September).

Falk, Richard A. and Samuel S. Kim. (1984). "World Order Studies: New Directions and Orientations." In Henry Han (ed.), *Terrorism, Political Violence, and World Order*. Landham, MD: University of America Press.

Fall, Bernard B. (1967). *Ho Chi Minh on Revolution*. New York: Praeger.

Fanon, Frantz. (1982). *The Wretched of the Earth*. New York: Grove Press.

Faul, Denis and Raymond Murray. (1976a). "Majella O'Hare Shot Dead by British Army." Dungannon, Northern Ireland: St. Patrick's Academy.

Faul, Denis and Raymond Murray. (1976b). "SAS Terrorism: The Assassin's Glove." Dungannon, Northern Ireland: St. Patrick's Academy.

Fellner, Jamie. (1988). "Invitation to a Murder: Colombian Death Squad Message." *Harper's* (February): 58–59.

Fernandez, Ronald. (1987). *Los Macheteros: The Wells Fargo Robbery and the Violent Struggle for Puerto Rican Independence*. Englewood Cliffs, NJ: Prentice-Hall.

Fiallos, Ricardo Alejandro. (1981). "The Death Squads Do Not Operate Independent of the Security Forces." In Marvin E. Gettleman et al. (eds.), *El Salvador*. New York: Grove Press.

Finch, Phillip. (1983). *God, Guts, and Guns*. New York: Seaview Putnam.

Finn, John E. (1987). "Public Support for Emergency (Anti-Terrorist) Legislation in Northern Ireland: A Preliminary Analysis." *Terrorism* 10: 113–124.

Fleming, Marie. (1982). "Propaganda by the Deed: Terrorism and Anarchist Theory in Late Nineteenth-Century Europe." In Yonah Alexander and Kenneth A. Myers (eds.), *Terrorism in Europe*. New York: St. Martin's Press.

Fleming, Peter A., Michael Stohl, and Alex P. Schmid. (1988). "The Theoretical Utility of Typologies of Terrorism: Lessons and Opportunities." In Michael Stohl (ed.), *The Politics of Terrorism*. New York: Dekker.

Forrest, Frank R. (1976). "Nuclear Terrorism and the Escalation of International Conflict." *Naval War College Review* 29: 12–27.

Fraser, James and Ian Fulton. (1984). "Terrorism Counteraction." Fort Leavenworth, KS: U.S. Army Command and General Staff College, FC 100-37.

Freedman, Lawrence, et al. (1986). *Terrorism and International Order*. New York: Routledge and Kegan Paul.

Gates, Mahlon E. (1987). "The Nuclear Emergency Search Team." In Paul Leventhal and Yonah Alexander (eds.), *Preventing Nuclear Terrorism*. Lexington, MA: Lexington Books.

Geraghty, Tony. (1982). *Inside the SAS*. New York: Ballantine.

Gettleman, Marvin E. et al. (eds.). (1981). *El Salvador*. New York: Grove Press.

Gilio, María Esther. (1972). *The Tupamaros*. London: Secker and Warburg.

Goren, Roberta. (1984). *The Soviet Union and Terrorism*. Winchester, MA: George Allen and Unwin.

Graham, Hugh D. and Ted Robert Gurr. (1979). *Violence in America: Historical and Comparative Perspectives*. Newbury Park, CA: Sage.

Grosscup, Beau. (1987). *The Explosion of Terrorism*. Far Hills, NJ: New Horizons.

Guevara, Ernesto (Che). (1968). *Reminiscences of the Cuban Revolutionary War*. New York: Monthly Review Press.

Gurr, Ted Robert. (1988). "Political Terrorism in the United States: Historical Antecedents and Contemporary Trends." In Michael Stohl (ed.), *The Politics of Terrorism*. New York: Dekker.

Gurr, Ted Robert. (1988). "Some Characteristics of Political Terrorism in the 1960s." In Michael Stohl (ed.), *The Politics of Terrorism*. New York: Dekker.

Gurr, Ted Robert. (1970). *Why Men Rebel*. Princeton, NJ: Princeton University Press.

Hacker, Frederick J. (1976). *Crusaders, Criminals, and Crazies*. New York: Norton.

Halperin, Ernst. (1976). *Terrorism in Latin America*. Newbury Park, CA: Sage.

Hamilton, Iain. (1971). "From Liberalism to Extremism." *Conflict Studies* 17: 5–17.

Han, Henry H. (ed.) (1984). *Terrorism, Political Violence, and World Order*. Landham, MD: University of America Press.

Harris, John W. (1987). "Domestic Terrorism in the 1980s." *FBI Law Enforcement Bulletin* 56: 5–13.

Harris, Jonathan. (1983). *The New Terrorism*. New York: Simon & Schuster.

Hastings, Max. (1970). *Barricades in Belfast*. New York: Taplinger.

Heikal, Mohammed. (1975). *The Road to Ramadan*. London: Collins.

Heim, M. (1984). "Reason As a Response to Nuclear Terrorism." *Philosophy Today* 28: 300–307.

Heinzen, Karl. (1987). "Murder." Reprinted in Walter Laqueur and Yonah Alexander (eds.), *The Terrorism Reader*. New York: Meridian Books.

Herman, Edward. (1983). *The Real Terror Network*. Boston: South End Press.

Hewitt, Christopher. (1984). *The Effectiveness of Anti-Terrorist Policies*. Landham, MD: University of America Press.

Hiro, Dilip. (1987). *Iran Under the Ayatollahs*. London: Routledge & Kegan Paul.

Hodges, Donald C. (1976). *Argentina, 1943–1976*. Albuquerque, NM: University of New Mexico Press.

Holden, Richard. (1985). "Historical and International Perspectives on Right-Wing Militancy in the United States." Paper presented at the annual meeting of the Academy of Criminal Justice Sciences, Las Vegas, NV (March).

Holden, Richard. (1986). *Postmillennialism As a Justification for Right-Wing Violence*. Gaithersburg, MD: IACP (International Associations of Police).

Holeck, Carl. (1985). "The Re-establishment of a Constitutional Republic Known As These United States of America." Omaha, NB: Constitutional Party.

Horchem, Hans-Josef. (1985). "Political Terrorism—The German Perspective." In Ariel Merari (ed.), *On Terrorism and Combating Terrorism*. Frederick, MD: University of America Press.

Horchem, Hans-Josef. (1986). "Terrorism in West Germany." *Conflict Studies*, 186.

International Security Council. (1986). *State Sponsored Terrorism*. Tel Aviv, Israel: ISC.

Ivianski, Zeev. (1988). "The Terrorist Revolution: Roots of Modern Terrorism." In David C. Rapoport (ed.), *Inside Terrorist Organizations*. New York: Columbia University Press.

Iyad, Abu. (1978). *My Home, My Land: A Narrative of the Palestinian Struggle*. New York: Times Books.

Jackson, Geoffrey. (1972). *Peoples' Prison*. London: Faber & Faber. (Published in the United States in 1974 as *Surviving the Long Night*. New York: Vanguard.)

Janke, Peter. (1983). *Guerrilla and Terrorist Organizations*. New York: Macmillan.

Janke, Peter. (1974). "Terrorism in Argentina." *Royal United Service Institute for Defence Studies Journal* (September): 43–48.

Jenkins, Brian. (1987). "The Future Course of International Terrorism." *The Futurist* (July/August): 8–13.

Jenkins, Brian. (1985). *International Terrorism: The Other World War*. Santa Monica, CA: The Rand Corp.

Jenkins, Brian Michael. (1986). "Is Nuclear Terrorism Plausible?" In Paul Leventhal and Yonah Alexander (eds.), *Nuclear Terrorism*. New York: Pergamon Press.

Jenkins, Brian. (1983). *New Modes of Conflict*. Santa Monica, CA: The Rand Corp.

Jenkins, Brian Michael. (1980). "Nuclear Terrorism and Its Consequences." *Society* (July/August): 5–16.

Jenkins, Brian. (1984). "The Who, What, When, Where, How, and Why of Terrorism." Paper presented at the Detroit Police Department Conference on "Urban Terrorism: Planning or Chaos?" (November).

Jenkins, Brian. (1975). "Will Terrorists Go Nuclear?" Santa Monica, CA: The Rand Corp. (original predictions)

Jenkins, Brian Michael. (1987). "Will Terrorists Go Nuclear?" In Walter Laqueur and Yonah Alexander (eds.), *The Terrorism Reader*. New York: Meridian Books. (original predictions with comments and revisions)

Jenkins, Brian and Gail Bass. (1983). "A Review of Recent Trends in International Terrorism and Nuclear Incidents Abroad." Santa Monica, CA: The Rand Corp.

Johnpoll, Bernard K. (1976). "Perspectives on Political Terrorism in the United States." In Yonah Alexander (ed.), *International Terrorism*. New York: Praeger.

Joll, James. (1980). *The Anarchists*. Cambridge, MA: Harvard University Press.

Jones, Juanita and Abraham Miller. (1979). "The Media and Terrorist Activity: Resolving the First Amendment Dilemma." *Ohio Northern University Law Review* 6: 70–81.

Juergensmeyer, Mark. (1988). "The Logic of Religious Violence." In David C. Rapoport (ed.), *Inside Terrorist Organizations*. New York: Columbia University Press.

Kansas Bureau of Investigation. (1984). "Special Report by the Crime Analysis Unit on the Posse Comitatus." Unpublished.

Kehler, Christopher P., Greg Harvey, and Richard Hall. (1982). "Perspectives on Media Control in Terrorist-Related Incidents." *Canadian Police Journal* 6: 226–243.

Kellen, Konrad. (1979). "Terrorists—What Are They Like? How Some Terrorists Describe Their World and Actions." Santa Monica, CA: The Rand Corp.

Kelley, Kevin. (1982). *The Longest War*. Westport, CT: Lawrence Hill.

Kelly, Michael J. and Thomas H. Mitchell. (1981). "Transnational Terrorism and the Western Press Elite." *Political Communication and Persuasion* 1: 269–296.

Ketcham, Christine C. and Harvey J. McGeorge. (1986). "Terrorist Violence: Its Mechanics and Countermeasures." In Neil C. Livingstone and Terrell E. Arnold (eds.), *Fighting Back*. Lexington, MA: D.C. Heath.

Kindilien, Robert E. (1985). "Nuclear Plants Confront Modern Terrorism." *Security Management* 29: 119–120.

Kissinger, Henry A. et al. (1983). *The Report of the President's National Bipartisan Commission on Central America*. New York: Macmillan.

Koch, Peter and Kai Hermann. (1977). *Assault at Mogadishu*. London: Corgi.

Kohl, James and John Litt (eds.). (1974). *Urban Guerrilla Warfare in Latin America*. Cambridge, MA: MIT Press.

Kropotkin, Peter. (1987). "The Spirit of Revolt." Reprinted in Walter Laqueur and Yonah Alexander (eds.), *The Terrorism Reader*. New York: Meridian Books.

Kupperman, Robert. (1985). CBS television interview.

Kupperman, Robert. (1988). CNN television interview.

Kupperman, Robert. (1985). "Government Response to Mass Destruction Threats." In Ariel Merari (ed.), *On Terrorism and Combating Terrorism*. Landham, MD: University of America Press.

Kupperman, Robert and Darrell Trent. (eds.) (1979). *Terrorism: Threat, Reality, and Response*. Stanford, CA: The Hoover Institute.

Labrousse, Alain. (1973). *The Tupamaros*. Harmondsworth, England: Penguin.

Ladd, James. (1986). *SAS Operations*. London: Hale.

LaFeber, Walter. (1983). *Inevitable Revolutions*. New York: Norton.

Laffin, John. (1987). *The PLO Connections*. London: Corgi.

Lake, Peter. (1984). Video files of the Ontario Provincial Police made available to the author through the courtesy of the Detroit FBI office.

Lakos, Amos. (1986). *International Terrorism: A Bibliography*. Boulder, CO: Westview.

Langguth, A. J. (1978). *Hidden Terrors*. New York: Pantheon.

Laqueur, Walter. (1987). *The Age of Terrorism*. Boston: Little, Brown.

Laqueur, Walter. (1976). *Guerrilla: A Historical and Critical Study*. Boston: Little, Brown.

Laqueur, Walter and Yonah Alexander (eds.). (1987). *The Terrorism Reader*. New York: Meridian Books.

Lasky, Melvin J. (1975). "Andreas and Ulricke." *New York Times Magazine* (May 11): 73–81.

"The Last Letter of Gordon Kahl." (n.d.) Cohotah, MI: The Mountain Church.

Lee, Aldred McClung. (1983). *Terrorism in Northern Ireland*. New York: General Hall.

Leiken, Robert S. (1982). *Soviet Strategy in Latin America*. New York: Praeger.

Leventhal, Paul and Yonah Alexander (eds). (1986). *Nuclear Terrorism*. New York: Pergamon Press.

Leventhal, Paul and Yonah Alexander (eds.). (1987). *Preventing Nuclear Terrorism*. Lexington MA: Lexington Books.

Lewy, Guether. (1974). *Religion and Revolution*. New York: Oxford University Press.

Livingstone, Neil C. (1983). "Death Squads." *World Affairs* 116: 239–248.

Livingstone, Neil C. and Terrell E. Arnold. (eds.). (1986). *Fighting Back*. Lexington, MA: D.C. Heath.

Lopez, George A. (1988). "Terrorism in Latin America." In Michael Stohl (ed.), *The Politics of Terrorism*. New York: Dekker.

MacDonald, Andrew (William Pierce). (1985). *The Turner Diaries*. Arlington, VA: National Vanguard.

MacDonald, Ronald. (1972). "Electoral Politics and Uruguayan Political Decay." *Inter-American Economic Affairs* 26: 24–45.

Mallin, J. "Terrorism As a Military Weapon." *Air University Review* 28.

Manning, Peter K. (1976). *Police Work: The Social Organization of Policing*. Cambridge, MA: MIT Press.

Marighella, Carlos. (1971). *For the Liberation of Brazil*. Translated by John Butt and Rosemary Sheed. Harmondsworth, England: Pelican.

Marighella, Carlos. (1969). *The Minimanual of the Urban Guerrilla*. Unpublished copy of the United States Army Military Intelligence School.

Martin, L. John. (1985). "The Media's Role in International Terrorism." *Terrorism* 8: 44–58.

Mazur, Allan. (1982). "Bomb Threats and the Mass Media: Evidence for a Theory of Suggestion." *American Sociological Review* 47: 407–410.

McFarlane, Robert C. (1985). "Terrorism and the Future of Free Society." *Terrorism* 8: 315–326.

McKinley, Michael. (1984). "The International Dimensions of Terrorism in Ireland." In Yonah Alexander and Alan O'Day (eds.), *Terrorism in Ireland*. New York: St. Martin's Press.

Melman, Yossi. (1986). *The Master Terrorist*. New York: Avon Books.

Merari, Ariel (ed.). (1985). *On Terrorism and Combating Terrorism*. Frederick, MD: University Publications of America.

Merkl, Peter. (1986). *Political Violence and Terror*. Berkeley, CA: University of California Press.

Miller, Abraham. (1982). *Terrorism, the Media, and the Law*. New York: Transnational Publishers.

Miller, David. (1984). *Anarchism*. London: Dent.

Monti, D. J. (1980). "The Relation Between Terrorism and Domestic Civil Disorders." *Terrorism* 4: 123–141.

Moss, Robert. (1972). *Urban Guerrillas*. London: Temple Smith.

Moxon-Browne, Edward. (1987). "Spain and the ETA." *Conflict Studies* 201.

Mullen, Robert K. (1978). "Mass Destruction and Terrorism." *Journal of International Affairs* 32: 63–89.

Mullins, Eustace. (1984). *The Secret Holocaust*. Hayden Lake, ID: Aryan Nations.

National Advisory Committee on Criminal Justice Standards and Goals. (1976). *Report of the Task Force on Disorders and Terrorism*. Washington, D.C.: Government Printing Office.

National Public Radio. (1988). Report on Aryan Nations' links with the Skinheads (December).

Nechaev, Sergey. (1987). "Catechism of the Revolutionist." In Walter Laqueur and Yonah Alexander (eds.), *The Terrorism Reader*. New York: Meridian.

Netanyahu, Benjamin. (1986). *Terrorism: How the West Can Win*. New York: Avon Books

Newsweek. (November 4, 1974), p. 53.

Nice, David C. (1988). "Abortion Clinic Bombings As Political Violence." *American Journal of Political Science* 32: 178–195.

Nima, Ramy. (1983). *The Wrath of Allah*. London: Pluto.

Nelson, Anthony. (1986). "Terrorism: The Intelligence System." United States Defense Intelligence Agency: Unpublished document.

Nunn, Sam and John W. Warner. (1987). "U.S.–Soviet Cooperation in Countering Nuclear Terrorism: The Role of Risk Reduction Centers." In Paul Leventhal and Yonah Alexander (eds.), *Preventing Nuclear Terrorism*. Lexington, MA: Lexington Books.

O'Donnell, Guillermo. (1973). *Modernization and Bureaucratic-Authoritarianism*. Berkeley, CA: University of California Press.

Pace, Eric. (1984). "Car Bombing Has Become Favored Tactic of Terrorists in the Middle East." *New York Times* (September 21): A13.

Paletz, David L., Peter A. Fozzard, and John Z. Ayanian. (1982a). "The IRA, the Red Brigades, and the FALN in the *New York Times*." *Journal of Communication* 32: 162–171.

Paletz, David L., John Z. Ayanian, and Peter A. Fozzard. (1982b). "Terrorism on Television News: The IRA, the FALN, and the Red Brigades." In William C. Adams (ed.), *Television Coverage of International Affairs*. Norwood, NJ: Ablex.

Peleg, Ilan. (1988). "Terrorism in the Middle East: The Case of the Arab-Israeli Conflict." In Michael Stohl (ed.), *The Politics of Terrorism*. New York: Dekker.

Pisano, Vittorfranco S. (1987). *The Dynamics of Subversion and Violence in Contemporary Italy*. Stanford, CA: The Hoover Institute.

Pluchinsky, Dennis. (1986). "Middle Eastern Terrorist Activity in Western Europe: A Diagnosis and Prognosis." *Conflict Quarterly* 3: 5–26.

Pluchinsky, Dennis. (1982). "Political Terrorism in Western Europe: Some Themes and Variations." In Yonah Alexander and Kenneth A. Myers (eds.), *Terrorism in Europe*. New York: St. Martin's Press.

Pockrass, Robert M. (1985). "Out and About: The Royal Ulster Constabulary and the Campaign Against Terrorism." Paper presented at the annual meeting of the Academy of Criminal Justice Sciences, Las Vegas, NV (March).

Pockrass, Robert M. (1987). "Terroristic Murder in Northern Ireland: Who Is Killed and Why." *Terrorism* 9: 341–357.

Podhoretz, Norman. (1981). "The Subtle Collusion." *Political Communication and Persuasion* 1: 84–89.

Poland, James M. (1988). *Understanding Terrorism: Groups, Strategies, and Responses*. Englewood Cliffs, NJ: Prentice-Hall.

Porzecanski, Arturo C. (1973). *Uruguay's Tupamaros*. New York: Praeger.

Post, Jerrold M. (1987). "Rewarding Fire with Fire: Effects of Retaliation on Terrorist Group Dynamics." *Terrorism* 10: 23–36.

A Presbytery of the Honduras. (1981). "My Lai in El Salvador: The Sumpul River Massacre." In Marvin E. Gettleman et al. (eds.), *El Salvador*. New York: Grove Press.

Radu, Michael S. (1987). "Terror, Terrorism, and Insurgency in Latin America." In Walter Laqueur and Yonah Alexander (eds.), *The Terrorism Reader*. New York: Meridian Books.

Randal, Jonathan C. (1984). *Going All the Way*. New York: Vintage Books.

Rapoport, David C. (ed.). (1988). *Inside Terrorist Organizations*. New York: Columbia University Press.

Reese, John. (1986). Unpublished briefing presented at EITWAT (Equilization in the War Against Terrorism), New Orleans, LA (September).

The Road Back. (n.d.) Macaba.

Rosen, M. Daniel. (1982). "At War with the Red Brigades." *Police Magazine* (March): 42–48.

Rosenbaum, David M. (1977). "Nuclear Terror." *International Security* 1: 140–161.

Rosie, George. (1987). *The Directory of International Terrorism*. New York: Paragon House.

Rubenstein, Richard E. (1987). *Alchemists of Revolution*. New York: Basic Books.

Russell, Charles A. and Bowman H. Miller. (1978). "Profile of a Terrorist." In J. D. Elliot and L. K. Gibson (eds.), *Contemporary Terrorism*. Gaithersburg, MD: IACP (International Association of Chiefs of Police).

Saltman, Richard B. (1983). *The Social and Political Thought of Michael Bakunin*. Westport, CT: Greenwood.

Sapp, Allen. (1985). "Basic Ideologies of Right-Wing Extremist Groups in America." Paper presented at the annual meeting of the Academy of Criminal Justice Sciences, Las Vegas, NV (March).

Sapp, Allen. (1986). "The Nehemiah Township Charter: Applied Right-Wing Ideology." Paper presented at the annual meeting of the Academy of Criminal Justice, Orlando, FL (March).

Scanlon, Joseph. (1981). "Coping with the Media: Police Media Problems and Tactics in Hostage Taking and Terrorist Incidents." *Canadian Police College Journal* 5: 129–148.

Scanlon, Joseph. (1982). "Domestic Terrorism and the Media: Live Coverage of Crime." *Canadian Police College Journal* 8: 154–178.

Scarman, Leslie. (1972). Tribunal of Inquiry. "Violence and Civil Disturbance in Northern Ireland in 1969." Belfast, Northern Ireland: Her Majesty's Stationery Office.

Schiller, David Th. (1988). "A Battlegroup Divided: The Palestinian Fedayeen." In David C. Rapoport (ed.), *Inside Terrorist Organizations*. New York: Columbia University Press.

Schiller, David Th. (1987). "Germany's Other Terrorists." *Terrorism* 9: 87–99.

Schlesinger, Philip. (1981). "Terrorism, the Media and the Liberal-Democratic State: A Critique of Orthodoxy." *Social Research* 48: 74–99.

Schmid, Alex P. (1983). *Political Terrorism: A Research Guide to Concepts, Theories, Data Bases, and Literature*. New Brunswick, CT: Transaction.

Schmid, Alex P. and Janny F. A. de Graaf. (1982). *Violence as Communication*. Newbury Park, CA: Sage.

Scotti, Tony. (1983). "Is the Media Really Covering Terrorism?" *TVI Journal* 4: 2–4.

Segaller, Stephen (1987). *Invisible Armies: Terrorism into the 1990s*. San Diego: Harcourt Brace Jovanovich.

Shaked, Emmanuel. (1986). "A Review of Counterterrorist Operations, Including Hostage Rescue." Paper presented at EITWAT (Equalization in the War Against Terrorism), New Orleans, LA (September).

Shultz, Richard. (1984). "The Role of External Forces in Promoting and Facilitating Internal Conflict." In Stephen J. Cimbala (ed.), *National Security Strategy*. New York: Praeger.

Simpson, John and Jana Bennett. (1985). *The Disappeared and the Mothers of the Plaza*. New York: St. Martin's Press.

Sloan, Stephen. (1981). *Simulating Terrorism*. Norman, OK: University of Oklahoma Press.

Snow, Peter G. (1984). "Latin American Political Violence: The Case of Argentina." In Henry H. Han (ed.), *Terrorism, Political Violence and World Order*. Landham, MD: University of America Press.

Snow, Peter G. (1979). *Political Forces in Argentina*. New York: Praeger.

Stephens, Hugh. (1987). "Maritime Defense at Home: The Influence of Jurisdictions." Paper presented at the International Studies Association Section on Military Studies, Atlanta, GA (September).

Stephens, Maynard M. (1979). "The Oil and Natural Gas Industries: A Potential Target of Terrorists." In Robert Kupperman and Darrell Trent (eds.), *Terrorism: Threat, Reality, and Response*. Stanford, CA: The Hoover Institute.

Sterling, Claire. (1986). *The Terror Network*. New York: Dell.

Stevenson, William. (1976). *Ninety Minutes at Entebbe*. New York: Bantam Books.

Stinson, James. (1984). "Assessing Terrorist Tactics and Security Measures." Paper presented at the Detroit Police Department Conference on "Urban Terrorism: Planning or Chaos?" (November). See also James Stinson (1981). "Unconventional Threat Assessment." *The Role of Behavioral Sciences in Physical Security*. Washington, D.C.: Defense Nuclear Agency. DNA-TR-83-32.

Stohl, Michael (ed.). (1988). *The Politics of Terrorism*. New York: Dekker.

Suall, Irwin and David Lowe. (1987). "Special Report—The Hate Movement Today: A Chronicle of Violence and Disarray." *Terrorism* 10: 345–364.

Taheri, Amir. (1987). *Holy Terror*. Bethesda, MD: Adler and Adler.

Taubman, Philip. (1984). "U.S. Said to Know Little About Group Despite Intelligence Efforts." *New York Times* (September 21): A13.

Taylor, Maxwell and Helen Ryan. (1988). "Fanaticism, Political Suicide, and Terrorism." *Terrorism* 11: 91–111.

Taylor, Robert W. and Henry E. Vanden. (1982). "Defining Terrorism in El Salvador: 'La Matanza'." *Annals of the Academy of Political and Social Science* 463: 106–118.

Thackrah, John. (1987). *Encyclopedia of Terrorism and Political Violence*. London: Routledge & Kegan Paul.

Thomas, Hugh. (1977). *The Cuban Revolution*. New York: Harper & Row.

Thorton, Thomas P. (1964). "Terror As a Weapon of Political Agitation." In H. Eckstein (ed.), *Internal War*. New York: Free Press.

Time. (November 23, 1987): 37–37.

Tololyan, Kachig. (1988). "Cultural Narrative and the Motivation of the Terrorist." In David C. Rapoport (ed.), *Inside Terrorist Organizations*. New York: Columbia University Press.

Trevino, Jose A. (1982). "Spain's Internal Security: The Basque Autonomous Police Force." In Yonah Alexander and Kenneth A. Myers (eds.), *Terrorism in Europe*. New York: St. Martin's Press.

United Kingdom. (1980). *Northern Ireland (Emergency Provisions) Act 1980*. London: Her Majesty's Stationery Office.

United States Congress. (1984). Hearings Before the Committee on Foreign Affairs. "Recent Developments in Columbian Narcotics Control." Washington, D.C.: Government Printing Office.

United States Department of Defense. (1983). "Report of the DOD Commission on the Beirut International Terrorist Act, October 23, 1983." Washington, D.C.: Government Printing Office.

United States Department of State. (1985). "Combating International Terrorism." Policy Circular 667 (March 5). Washington, D.C.: Government Printing Office.

United States Department of State. (1986). *Human Rights in Nicaragua*. Washington, D.C.: Government Printing Office.

United States Department of State. (1981). "Press Release." In Marvin E. Gettleman et al. (eds.), *El Salvador*. New York: Grove Press.

United States Drug Enforcement Administration. (1985). "Cocaine Review." *The Quarterly*. DEA (quarterly intelligence trends) 12: 8–14.

United States House of Representatives. (1985). *Aftermath of the Achille Lauro Incident*. Hearing before the Committee on Foreign Affairs and Its Subcommittee on International Operations. Washington, D.C.: United States House of Representatives.

United States House of Representatives. (1980). "FBI Oversight." Hearings before the House Subcommittee on Civil and Constitutional Rights. Washington, D.C.: United States House of Representatives.

United States House of Representatives. (Dec 9, 1980). "Increasing Violence Against Minorities." Hearings before the Subcommittee on Crime. Washington, D.C.: United States House of Representatives.

United States Marshals Service. (1988). Unpublished circular for domestic terrorism briefing.

United States Senate. (1985). *Bills to Authorize Prosecution of Terrorists and Others Who Attack U.S. Government Employees and Citizens Abroad*. Hearing before the Subcommittee on Security and Terrorism of the Committee of the Judiciary. Washington, D.C.: United States Senate.

Waldmann, Peter. (1986). "Guerrilla Movements in Argentina, Guatemala, Nicaragua, and Uruguay." In Peter Merkle (ed.), *Political Violence and Terror*. Berkeley, CA: University of California Press.

Walker, Samuel. (1985). *Sense and Nonsense About Crime: A Policy Guide*. Pacific Grove, CA: Brooks/Cole.

Wann Alle Bruder Schweigen. (n.d.). Cohoctah, MI: The Mountain Church.

Wardlaw, Grant. (1982). *Political Terrorism: Theory, Tactics, and Counter-Measures*. London: Cambridge University Press.

Wardlaw, Grant. (1988). "Terror As an Instrument of Foreign Policy." In David C. Rapoport (ed.), *Inside Terrorist Organizations*. New York: Columbia University Press.

Weimann, Gabriel. (1983). "Theater of Terror: Effects of Press Coverage." *Journal of Communication* 33: 38–45.

Weinberg, Leonard. (1986). "The Violent Life: Left and Right Wing Terrorism in Italy." In Peter Merkl (ed.), *Political Violence and Terror*. Berkeley, CA: University of California Press.

Weisband, Edward and Damir Roguly. (1976). "Palestinian Terrorism: Violence, Verbal Strategy, and Legitimacy." In Yonah Alexander (ed.), *International Terrorism*. New York: Praeger.

Western Front. (n.d.). "The Hidden Tyranny." Sacramento, CA: Western Front.

Western Goals Foundation. (c. 1984). "No Place to Hide." Western Goals Foundation.

White, Jonathan R. (1986a). "The Development of Offensive Strategies in Counterterrorism." Paper presented at the International Studies Association Section on Military Studies Conference, Harvard University (November).

White, Jonathan R. (1986b). *Holy War: Terrorism As a Theological Construct*. Gaithersburg, MD: IACP (International Association of Chiefs of Police).

White, Jonathan R. (1987). "The Principles of Hostage Rescue Operations: A Comparative Analysis of Mogadishu and Nimrod." Paper presented at the annual meeting of the Academy of Criminal Justice Sciences, St. Louis, MO (March).

White, Richard Alan. (1984). *The Morass: United States Intervention in Central America*. New York: Harper & Row.

Wickstrom, James. (1983). "Memorial Day Sermon." Source unknown, taped by Posse Comitatus.

Wiggins, Michael E. (1985). "The Relationship of Extreme Right-Wing Ideologies and Geographical Distribution of Select Right-Wing Groups." Paper presented at the annual meeting of the Academy of Criminal Justice Sciences, Las Vegas, NV (March).

Wiggins, Michael E. (1986). "The Turner Diaries: Blueprint for Right-Wing Extremist Violence." Paper presented at the annual meeting of the Academy of Criminal Justice Sciences, Orlando, FL (March).

Wilkinson, Paul. (1974). *Political Terrorism*. New York: Wiley.

Wilkinson, Paul. (1986). "Trends in International Terrorism and the American Response." In Lawrence Freedman et al. (eds.), *Terrorism and International Order*. London: Routledge & Kegan Paul.

Willrich, Mason and Theodore Taylor. (1974). *Nuclear Theft: Risks and Safeguards*. Cambridge, MA: Ballinger.

Winchester, James H. (1974). "Kidnapping Unlimited." *Reader's Digest* (July): 70–74.

Winchester, Simon. (1974). *Northern Ireland in Crisis*. New York: Holmes and Meier.

Windsor, Phillip. (1986). "The Middle East and Terrorism." In Lawrence Freedman et al. (eds.), *Terrorism and International Order*. London: Routledge & Kegan Paul.

Wolf, John B. (1981). *Fear of Fear*. New York: Plenum.

Woodcock, George. (1962). *Anarchism: A History of Liberation Ideas and Movements*. Harmondsworth, England: Penguin.

Woodham-Smith, Cecil. (1962). *The Great Hunger*. New York: Harper & Row.

Wright, Jeffery W. (1984). "Terrorism: A Mode of Warfare." Fort Leavenworth, KS: U.S. Army Command and General Staff College, FC 100-37.

Wright, Robin. (1986). *Sacred Rage*. New York: Touchstone.

Wynia, Gary W. (1986). *Argentina*. New York: Holmes and Holmes.

Yodfat, Aryeh Y. and Yuval Aron-Ohanna. (1981). *PLO Strategy and Tactics*. London: Croom Helm.

Index